# THE WORKS OF JOHN DRYDEN

*General Editor*

ALAN ROPER

*Textual Editor*

VINTON A. DEARING

# VOLUME FIVE

### EDITOR

*William Frost*

### TEXTUAL EDITOR

*Vinton A. Dearing*

FRONTISPIECE OF *The Works of Virgil in English* (1697)
(MACDONALD 33A)

VOLUME V

# The Works
# of John Dryden

## Poems

THE WORKS OF VIRGIL IN ENGLISH
1697

*University of California Press*
*Berkeley   Los Angeles   London*
1987

UNIVERSITY OF CALIFORNIA PRESS
Berkeley and Los Angeles, California

UNIVERSITY OF CALIFORNIA PRESS, LTD.
London, England

The copy texts of this edition have been drawn in
the main from the Dryden Collection of the
William Andrews Clark Memorial Library

*In Gratitude*
*for Their Encouragement of the Editors*
*and for Their Support of the Edition*
*Volumes V and VI*
*of the California Dryden*
*Are Respectfully Dedicated to*
*Charles E. Young, Chancellor,*
*and to*
*William D. Schaefer, Vice-Chancellor,*
*U C L A*

# Preface

*The folio first edition of Dryden's Virgil, lavishly illustrated and sold by subscription as well as offered for regular sale, remains a fascinating piece of bookmaking, in part because some surviving manuscripts concerning contractual arrangements between Dryden and his publisher, Jacob Tonson, together with some of Dryden's letters, chiefly to Tonson, document the progress of Dryden's labor and the book's eventual production to a degree unusual for the period. The book was sold unbound, and con-stituted a sort of kit complete with assembly instructions, a set of* Directions to the Binders how to place the Several Parts of this Book. *These directions, bewildering in their seeming illogic, are placed, prophetically, at the bottom of a page otherwise devoted to errata, which were testily drawn up by Dryden himself. Un-surprisingly, not all copies are bound in accordance with the directions, perhaps because some first owner or his binder yearned for a better, or any, logic in the ordering of parts, or perhaps because the directions were not encountered until the end of the book's fourth part.*

*The illustrations caused further problems. All but two illus-trated the text of the translation and were taken from plates used for Ogilby's earlier translation of Virgil and retouched for Dry-den's. Retouching included the addition of the name and arms of each of the principal subscribers and the keying of each illustra-tion to the appropriate line of text. But the appropriate line could not always be fixed with assurance, in part because the original illustrations in Ogilby's Virgil do not always and obvi-ously illustrate the scenes supposedly illustrated. The original illustrations are keyed to Virgil's Latin rather than Ogilby's Eng-lish, and sometimes the key shows the beginning and ending of, say, a fifty-verse episode, with the accompanying illustration dis-playing, in effect, a split scene and reminding us again of Les-sing's distinction between the temporal medium of poetry and the spatial medium of painting. As if to simplify, but in fact to intensify the problem, someone decided that for Dryden's Virgil the Latin keys would be replaced by keys to a single line of Dryden's translation. Unsurprisingly, and much like the print-er—he who generated the errata—the engraver, or perhaps Ton-*

son's supervisor, made mistakes: the same illustration will be keyed to different parts of the text in different copies, in one copy correctly and evidently cancelling the key in another. In still other copies the binder erred, misplacing properly keyed illustrations. One cut, which we have tipped in as an illustrated half-title to Dryden's Aeneis, was so obviously anomalous, so difficult to place by owners of subscription copies and their binders, that it appears in widely different places or not at all.

Making the 1697 folio obviously posed problems for author, printer, bookseller, engraver, binder, and first owner. Variations between copies show that the problems were not always solved. The folio, nonetheless, or partly because of these things, retains its fascination as a book. The present edition accordingly attempts to convey the folio's charm and eccentricity by placing all material as in the folio, except for its frontispiece, which we have relocated to serve as frontispiece to our Volume V. Strictly, of course, the folio as such never existed: there were only individual copies, each of them unique. But the idea of the folio is discernible, if undeniably puzzling, and it is this idea which the present edition attempts to follow. Doing so has involved modifying the format adopted for other volumes of the California Dryden. Thus, material contributed by others, like Chetwood's life of Virgil or Addison's preface to the Georgics, is interspersed with Dryden's contributions, as in the folio, instead of removed to appendixes, which we have reserved, among other things, for documents concerning Dryden's arrangements with Tonson. We have included the original list of errata, incorporating as they do Dryden's own comments, although we have renumbered page and line numbers to accord with our text, in which we have also made the changes called for by the errata.

The illustrations posed as many problems for us as they did for the makers of the 1697 folio. We have had to reline some parts of the translation to correct the folio, thus invalidating the line-keys on some illustrations. Then, too, other illustrations are miskeyed in the folio by several lines. We have tried to place all illustrations appropriately and show in our list of illustrations what we take to be the first lines of scenes illustrated. As far as possible, we follow the folio in making illustrations face the text *they illustrate, but the engravings were tipped into the folio with blank versos, a method too costly, producing volumes too bulky, for us to follow. We have accordingly printed the illustrations on the recto or verso of a page of our text and as a result have sometimes had to make them precede or follow instead of face the text illustrated. Including all the illustrations in affordable books has also meant that these volumes have been printed from reproduction proof by offset lithography, although the text was first composed in Linotype Baskerville on hot-metal, linecasting equipment in order to preserve a uniformity of type-face with other volumes in the edition.*

*Rather than make each volume a discrete unit with its own text and apparatus, as is customary in this edition, we decided the folio's quality was best preserved by treating our volumes as a single unit with continuous pagination, starting the text in Volume V, completing it in Volume VI, and assigning all of our apparatus to the concluding pages of Volume VI. Had we followed our customary format, we would necessarily have interrupted a properly continuous text with part of our apparatus and added the remaining apparatus after the text was completed. To balance the volumes, we would also have been forced to divide the text of Dryden's* Aeneis *between them, breaking it, probably, after Book II. The method we have adopted still necessitates dividing the text of the* Aeneis *between the volumes, but we are now able to divide it at the most natural break in the* Aeneid, *after Book VI. As a further compensation for dividing the text in this way, we have been able to add one appropriate illustration to the 103 found in the folio and have used as frontispiece for our Volume VI a facsimile of Dryden's draft advertisement for second subscribers to his Virgil. By his contract with Tonson, Dryden could not advertise for second subscriptions until he had translated the* Eclogues, Georgics, *and first six books of the* Aeneid.

*We already know from an informal canvas that not everyone will endorse our departure from the format customary in this edition, although many will. We hope, though, that those who prefer uniformity will understand our reasons for wishing to accommodate our edition to the folio and the folio to our edition.*

## Volume VI

# Illustrations for Volume V

# THE WORKS OF VIRGIL IN ENGLISH

# THE
# WORKS

## OF
# VIRGIL:

### Containing His
# PASTORALS,

# GEORGICS,

## AND
# ÆNEIS.

Tranſlated into Engliſh Verſe; By
Mr. *DRYDEN.*

Adorn'd with a Hundred Sculptures.

*Sequiturque Patrem non paſſibus Æquis.* Virg. Æn. 2.

## LONDON,

Printed for *Jacob Tonſon,* at the *Judges-Head* in *Fleetſtreet,*
near the *Inner-Temple-Gate,* MDCXCVII.

TITLE PAGE OF THE FIRST EDITION (MACDONALD 33A)

## The Works of Virgil in English

### TO THE RIGHT HONOURABLE
Hugh Lord Clifford, BARON of *Chudleigh.*

*My Lord,*

I have found it not more difficult to Translate *Virgil,* than to find such Patrons as I desire for my Translation. For though *England* is not wanting in a Learned Nobility, yet such are my unhappy Circumstances, that they have confin'd me to a narrow choice. To the greater part, I have not the Honour to be known; and to some of them I cannot shew at present, by any publick Act, that grateful Respect which I shall ever bear them in my heart. Yet I have no reason to complain of Fortune, since
10 in the midst of that abundance I could not possibly have chosen better, than the Worthy Son of so Illustrious a Father. He was the Patron of my Manhood, when I Flourish'd in the opinion of the World; though with small advantage to my Fortune, 'till he awaken'd the remembrance of my Royal Master. He was that *Pollio,* or that *Varus,* who introduc'd me to *Augustus:* And tho' he soon dismiss'd himself from State-Affairs, yet in the short time of his Administration he shone so powerfully upon me, that like the heat of a *Russian*-Summer, he ripen'd the Fruits of Poetry in a cold Clymate; and gave me wherewithal to subsist at least,
20 in the long Winter which succeeded. What I now offer to your Lordship, is the wretched remainder of a sickly Age, worn out with Study, and oppress'd by Fortune: without other support than the Constancy and Patience of a Christian. You, my Lord, are yet in the flower of your Youth, and may live to enjoy the benefits of the Peace which is promis'd *Europe:* I can only hear of that Blessing: for Years, and, above all things, want of health, have shut me out from sharing in the happiness. The Poets, who condemn their *Tantalus* to Hell, had added to his Torments, if they had plac'd him in *Elysium,* which is the proper Emblem of
30 my Condition. The Fruit and the Water may reach my Lips, but cannot enter: And if they cou'd, yet I want a Palate as well

ments of *Virgil's* Poetry: Coursely Translated I confess, but
which yet retains some Beauties of the Author, which neither
the barbarity of our Language, nor my unskilfulness cou'd so
much sully, but that they appear sometimes in the dim mirrour
which I hold before you. The Subject is not unsuitable to your
Youth, which allows you yet to Love, and is proper to your
present Scene of Life. Rural Recreations abroad, and Books at
home, are the innocent Pleasures of a Man who is early Wise;
and gives Fortune no more hold of him, than of necessity he
10 must. 'Tis good, on some occasions to think beforehand as little
as we can; to enjoy as much of the present as will not endanger
our futurity; and to provide our selves of the Vertuoso's Saddle,
which will be sure to amble, when the World is upon the hard-
est trott. What I humbly offer to your Lordship, is of this nature.
I wish it pleasant, and am sure 'tis innocent. May you ever con-
tinue your esteem for *Virgil;* and not lessen it, for the faults of
his Translatour; who is with all manner of Respect, and sense
of Gratitude,

*My Lord,*

*Your Lordship's most Humble,*

*and most Obedient Servant,*

JOHN DRYDEN.

---

12   the Vertuoso's] *the* Vertuoso's F1–2.

# *The Life of Pub. Virgilius Maro*

## [By Knightly Chetwood]

VIRGIL was born at *Mantua*, which City was built no less than Three Hundred Years before *Rome;* and was the Capital of the New *Hetruria,* as himself, no less Antiquary, than Poet, assures us. His Birth is said to have happen'd in the first Consulship of *Pompey* the Great, and *Lic. Crassus;* but since the Relater of this presently after contradicts himself; and *Virgil*'s manner of Addressing to *Octavius,* implies a greater difference of Age than that of Seven Years, as appears by his First Pastoral, and other places; it is reasonable to set the Date of it 10 something backward: And the Writer of his Life having no certain Memorials to work upon, seems to have pitched upon the two most Illustrious Consuls he could find about that time, to signalize the Birth of so Eminent a Man. But it is beyond all Question, that he was Born on, or near the Fifteenth of *October:* Which Day was kept Festival in honour of his Memory, by the *Latin,* as the Birth-Day of *Homer* was by the *Greek* Poets. And so near a resemblance there is, betwixt the Lives of these two famous *Epic* Writers, that *Virgil* seems to have follow'd the *Fortune* of the other, as well as the Subject and manner of his 20 Writing. For *Homer* is said to have been of very mean Parents, such as got their Bread by Day-labour; so is *Virgil*. *Homer* is said to be *Base Born;* so is *Virgil:* The former to have been born in the open Air, in a Ditch, or by the Bank of a River; so is the latter. There was a Poplar Planted near the place of *Virgil*'s Birth, which suddenly grew up to an unusual heighth and bulk, and to which the Superstitious Neighbourhood attributed marvellous Vertue. *Homer* had his Poplar too, as *Herodotus* relates, which was visited with great Veneration. *Homer* is describ'd by one of the Ancients, to have been of a slovenly and neglected 30 Meen and Habit, so was *Virgil*. Both were of a very delicate and sickly Constitution: Both addicted to Travel, and the study of

14 *October:*] ~. F1–2.          22 *Virgil:*] ~. F1–2.

Astrology: Both had their Compositions usurp'd by others: Both
Envy'd and traduc'd during their Lives. We know not so much
as the true Names of either of them with any exactness: For the
Criticks are not yet agreed how the word [*Virgil*] should be Writ-
ten; and of *Homer's* Name there is no certainty at all. Whosoever
shall consider this Parallel in so many particulars; (and more
might be added) would be inclin'd to think, that either the same
Stars Rul'd strongly at the Nativities of them both, or what is a
great deal more probable; that the *Latin* Grammarians want-
10 ing Materials for the former part of *Virgil's* Life, after the *Leg-
endary Fashion,* supply'd it out of *Herodotus;* and like ill Face-
Painters, not being able to hit the true *Features,* endeavour'd to
make amends by a great deal of impertinent *Landscape* and
*Drapery.*

Without troubling the Reader with needless Quotations, now,
or afterwards; the most probable Opinion is, that *Virgil* was the
Son of a Servant, or Assistant to a wandring *Astrologer;* who
practis'd Physic. For *Medicus, Magus,* as *Juvenal* observes, usu-
ally went together; and this course of Life was follow'd by a
20 great many *Greeks* and *Syrians;* of one of which Nations it seems
not improbable, that *Virgil's* Father was. Nor could a Man of
that Profession have chosen a fitter place to settle in, than that
most Superstitious Tract of *Italy;* which by her ridiculous Rites
and Ceremonies as much enslav'd the *Romans,* as the *Romans*
did the *Hetrurians* by their Arms. This Man therefore having
got together some Money, which Stock he improv'd by his Skill
in Planting and Husbandry, had the good Fortune, at last, to
Marry his Masters Daughter, by whom he had *Virgil;* and this
Woman seems, by her Mothers side, to have been of good Ex-
30 traction; for she was nearly related to *Quintilius Varus,* whom
*Paterculus* assures us to have been of an Illustrious, tho' not
*Patrician* Family; and there is honourable mention made of it
in the History of the second *Carthaginian* War. It is certain, that
they gave him very good Education, to which they were inclin'd;
not so much by the Dreams of his Mother, and those presages
which *Donatus* relates, as by the early indications which he gave
of a sweet Disposition, and Excellent Wit. He passed the first

31  of an] F2; an F1.                    32  *Patrician*] Patrician F1–2.

Seven Years of his Life at *Mantua,* not Seventeen, as *Scaliger*
miscorrects his Author; for the *initia ætatis* can hardly be sup-
posed to extend so far. From thence he removed to *Cremona,* a
Noble *Roman* Colony, and afterwards to *Milan:* In all which
places he prosecuted his Studies with great application; he read
over, all the best *Latin,* and *Greek* Authors, for which he had
convenience by the no remote distance of *Marseils,* that famous
*Greek* Colony, which maintain'd its Politeness, and Purity of
Language, in the midst of all those Barbarous Nations amongst
10 which it was seated: And some Tincture of the latter seems to
have descended from them down to the Modern *French.* He fre-
quented the most Eminent Professors of the *Epicurean* Philoso-
phy, which was then much in vogue, and will be always in de-
clining and sickly States. But finding no satisfactory Account
from his Master *Syron,* he pass'd over to the *Academick School,*
to which he adher'd the rest of his Life, and deserv'd, from a great
Emperour, the Title of the *Plato* of *Poets.* He compos'd at leisure
hours a great number of Verses, on various Subjects; and desirous
rather of a *great,* than *early* Fame, he permitted his Kinsman,
20 and Fellow-student *Varus,* to derive the Honour of one of his
Tragedies to himself. Glory neglected in proper time and place,
returns often with large Increase, and so he found it: For *Varus*
afterwards prov'd a great Instrument of his Rise: In short, it was
here that he form'd the *Plan,* and collected the Materials of all
those excellent Pieces which he afterwards finish'd, or was forc'd
to leave less perfect by his Death. But whether it were the Un-
wholsomness of his Native Air, of which he somewhere com-
plains, or his too great abstinence, and Night-watchings at his
Study, to which he was always addicted, as *Augustus* observes;
30 or possibly the hopes of improving himself by Travel, he re-
solv'd to Remove to the more Southern Tract of *Italy;* and it was
hardly possible for him not to take *Rome* in his Way; as is evi-
dent to any one who shall cast an Eye on the Map of *Italy:* And
therefore the late *French* Editor of his Works is mistaken, when
he asserts that he never saw *Rome,* 'till he came to Petition for
his Estate: He gain'd the Acquaintance of the Master of the
Horse to *Octavius,* and Cur'd a great many Diseases of Horses,

4  *Milan:*] ∼. F1–2.                34  Editor] *Editor* F1–2.

by methods they had never heard of: It fell out, at the same time, that a very fine Colt, which promised great Strength and Speed, was presented to *Octavius: Virgil* assur'd them, that he came of a faulty Mare, and would prove a Jade; upon trial it was found as he had said; his Judgment prov'd right in several other instances, which was the more surprizing, because the *Romans* knew least of Natural Causes of any civiliz'd Nation in the World: And those Meteors, and Prodigies which cost them incredible Sums to expiate, might easily have been accounted for, by no very profound Naturalist. It is no wonder, therefore, that *Virgil* was in so great Reputation, as to be at last Introduced to *Octavius* himself. That Prince was then at variance with *Marc. Antony*, who vex'd him with a great many Libelling Letters, in which he reproaches him with the baseness of his Parentage, that he came of a *Scrivener*, a *Ropemaker*, and a *Baker*, as *Suetonius* tells us: *Octavius* finding that *Virgil* had passed so exact a judgment upon the Breed of Dogs, and Horses, thought that he possibly might be able to give him some Light concerning his *own*. He took him into his Closet, where they continu'd in private a considerable time. *Virgil* was a great Mathematician, which, in the Sense of those times, took in Astrology: And if there be any thing in that Art, which I can hardly believe; if that be true which the Ingenious *De le Chambre* asserts confidently, that from the Marks on the Body, the Configuration of the Planets at a Nativity may be gathered, and the Marks might be told by knowing the Nativity; never had one of those Artists a fairer Opportunity to shew his skill, than *Virgil* now had; for *Octavius* had Moles upon his Body, exactly resembling the Constellation call'd *Ursa Major*. But *Virgil* had other helps: The Predictions of *Cicero*, and *Catulus*, and that Vote of the Senate had gone abroad, that no Child Born at *Rome*, in the Year of his Nativity, should be bred up; because the Seers assur'd them that an Emperour was Born that Year. Besides this, *Virgil* had heard of the *Assyrian*, and *Egyptian* Prophecies, (which in truth, were no other but the *Jewish*,) that about that time a great King was to come into the World. Himself takes notice of them, *Æn. 6.* where he uses a very significant Word, (now in all Liturgies) *hujus in adventu,* so in another place, *adventu propiore Dei.*

> *At his foreseen approach already quake,*
> Assyrian *Kingdoms, and* Mœotis *Lake.*
> Nile *hears him knocking at his seven-fold Gates*———

Every one knows whence this was taken: It was rather a mistake, than impiety in *Virgil,* to apply these Prophesies which belonged to the Saviour of the World to the Person of *Octavius,* it being a usual piece of flattery for near a Hundred Years together, to attribute them to their Emperours, and other great Men. Upon the whole matter, it is very probable, that *Virgil* Predicted to him the Empire at this time. And it will appear yet the more, if we consider that he assures him of his being receiv'd into the Number of the Gods, in his First *Pastoral,* long before the thing came to pass; which Prediction seems grounded upon his former Mistake. This was a secret, not to be divulg'd at that time, and therefore it is no wonder that the slight Story in *Donatus* was given abroad to palliate the matter. But certain it is, that *Octavius* dismissed him with great Marks of esteem, and earnestly recommended the Protection of *Virgil's* Affairs to *Pollio,* then Lieutenant of the *Cis-Alpine Gaule,* where *Virgil's* Patrimony lay. This *Pollio* from a mean Original, became one of the most Considerable Persons of his time: A good General, Orator, States-man, Historian, Poet, and Favourer of Learned Men; above all, he was a Man of *Honour* in those critical times: He had join'd with *Octavius,* and *Antony,* in revenging the Barbarous Assassination of *Julius Cæsar:* When they two were at variance, he would neither follow *Antony,* whose courses he detested, nor join with *Octavius* against him, out of a grateful Sense of some former Obligations. *Augustus,* who thought it his interest to oblige Men of Principles, notwithstanding this, receiv'd him afterwards into Favour, and promoted him to the highest Honours. And thus much I thought fit to say of *Pollio,*

---

2-3 *adventu propiore Dei*] F2; *adventante Dea* F1.
8-9 Prophesies which belonged to the Saviour of the World] F2; Prophesies F1.

indebted, than to any other *Greek* Writer, excepting *Homer.* The Reader will be satisfied of this, if he consult that Author in his own Language, for the Translation is a great deal more obscure than the Original.

Whilst *Virgil* thus enjoy'd the sweets of a Learn'd Privacy, the Troubles of *Italy* cut off his little Subsistance; but by a strange turn of Human Affairs, which ought to keep good Men from ever despairing; the loss of his Estate prov'd the effectual way of making his Fortune. The occasion of it was this; *Octavius,* as himself relates, when he was but Nineteen Years of Age, by a Masterly stroke of Policy, had gain'd the *Veteran* Legions into his Service, (and by that step, out-witted all the Republican Senate:) They grew now very clamorous for their Pay: The Treasury being Exhausted, he was forc'd to make Assignments upon Land, and none but in *Italy* it self would content them. He pitch'd upon *Cremona* as the most distant from *Rome;* but that not suffising, he afterwards threw in part of the State of *Mantua. Cremona* was a Rich and noble Colony, setled a little before the Invasion of *Hannibal.* During that Tedious and Bloody War, they had done several important Services to the Common-Wealth. And when Eighteen other Colonies, pleading Poverty and Depopulation, refus'd to contribute Money, or to raise Recruits; they of *Cremona* voluntarily paid a double Quota of both: But past Services are a fruitless Plea; Civil Wars are one continued Act of Ingratitude: In vain did the Miserable Mothers, with their famishing Infants in their Arms, fill the Streets with their Numbers, and the Air with Lamentations; the Craving Legions were to be satisfi'd at any rate. *Virgil,* involv'd in the common Calamity, had recourse to his old Patron *Pollio,* but he was, at this time, under a Cloud; however, compassionating so worthy a Man, not of a make to struggle thro' the World, he did what he could, and recommended him to *Mæcenas,* with whom he still kept a private Correspondence. The Name of this great Man being much better known than one part of his Character, the Reader, I presume, will not be displeas'd if I supply it in this place.

---

32   *Mæcenas*] *Mecænas* F1–2 *(and similarly below, except as noted).*

Tho' he was of as deep Reach, and easie dispatch of Business as any in his time, yet he designedly liv'd beneath his true Character. Men had oftentimes medled in Publick Affairs, that they might have more ability to furnish for their Pleasures: *Mæcenas,* by the honestest Hypocrisie that ever was, pretended to a Life of Pleasure, that he might render more effectual Service to his Master. He seem'd wholly to amuse himself with the Diversions of the Town, but under that Mask he was the greatest Minister of his Age. He would be carried in a careless, effeminate posture
10 thro' the Streets in his Chair, even to the degree of a Proverb, and yet there was not a Cabal of ill dispos'd Persons which he had not early notice of; and that too in a City as large as *London* and *Paris,* and perhaps two or three more of the most populous put together. No Man better understood that Art so necessary to the *Great;* the Art of *declining Envy:* Being but of a Gentleman's Family, not *Patrician,* he would not provoke the Nobility by accepting invidious Honours; but wisely satisfi'd himself that he had the *Ear* of *Augustus,* and the *Secret* of the Empire. He seems to have committed but one great Fault, which was the
20 trusting a Secret of high Consequence to his Wife; but his Master, enough Uxorious himself, made his *own* Frailty more excusable, by generously forgiving that of his Favourite. He kept in all his Greatness exact measures with his Friends; and chusing them wisely, found, by Experience, that good *Sense and Gratitude* are almost inseparable. This appears in *Virgil* and *Horace;* the former, besides the Honour he did him to all Posterity, return'd his Liberalities at his Death: The other, whom *Mæcenas* recommended with his last Breath, was too generous to stay behind, and enjoy the Favour of *Augustus:* He only desir'd a place
30 in his Tomb, and to mingle his Ashes with those of his deceased Benefactor. But this was Seventeen Hundred Years ago. *Virgil,* thus powerfully supported, thought it mean to Petition for himself alone, but resolutely solicits the Cause of his whole Country, and seems, at first, to have met with some Encouragement: But the matter cooling, he was forc'd to sit down contented with the Grant of his own Estate. He goes therefore to *Mantua,* produces his Warrant to a Captain of Foot, whom he found in his House; *Arrius* who had eleven Points of the Law, and fierce of the Ser-

*esse* by the Shrine of the new God: And this became a Fashion
not to be dispens'd with amongst the Ladies: The Devotion was
wondrous great amongst the *Romans,* for it was their Interest,
and, which sometimes avails more, it was the *Mode. Virgil,* tho'
he despis'd the Heathen Superstitions, and is so bold as to call
*Saturn* and *Janus,* by no better a Name than that of *Old Men,*
and might deserve the Title of *Subverter* of Superstitions, as well
as *Varro,* thought fit to follow the *Maxim* of *Plato* his Master;
that every one should serve the Gods after the Usage of his own
10 Country, and therefore was not the last to present his Incense,
which was of too *Rich* a Composition for *such* an *Altar:* And by
his Address to *Cæsar* on this occasion, made an unhappy Prece-
dent to *Lucan* and other Poets which came after him, *Geor.* 1.
and 3. And this Poem being now in great forwardness, *Cæsar,*
who in imitation of his Predecessor *Julius,* never intermitted his
Studies in the Camp, and much less in other places, refreshing
himself by a short stay in a pleasant Village of *Campania,* would
needs be entertained with the rehearsal of some part of it. *Virgil*
recited with a marvellous *Grace,* and sweet Accent of Voice, but
20 his Lungs failing him, *Mæcenas* himself supplied his place for
what remained. Such a piece of condescension wou'd now be
very surprizing, but it was no more than customary amongst
Friends, when Learning pass'd for Quality. *Lelius,* the second
Man of *Rome* in his time, had done as much for that Poet, out
of whose Dross *Virgil* would sometimes pick Gold; as himself
said, when one found him reading *Ennius:* (the like he did by
some Verses of *Varro,* and *Pacuvius, Lucretius,* and *Cicero,* which
he inserted into his Works.) But Learned Men then liv'd easy
and familiarly with the great: *Augustus* himself would some-
30 times sit down betwixt *Virgil* and *Horace,* and say jeastingly,
that he sate betwixt Sighing and Tears, alluding to the Asthma
of one, and Rheumatick Eyes of the other; he would frequently
Correspond with them, and never leave a Letter of theirs un-
answered: Nor were they under the constraint of formal Super-
scriptions in the beginning, nor of violent Superlatives at the
close of their Letter: The invention of these is a Modern Re-

---

21   condescension] condecension F1–2.        25   *Virgil*] F2; he F1.
36–1   Refinement:] ~. F1–2.

finement: *In which this may be remarked, in passing, that (humble Servant) is respect, but (Friend) an affront, which notwithstanding implies the former, and a great deal more.* Nor does true Greatness lose by such Familiarity; and those who have it not, as *Mæcenas* and *Pollio* had, are not to be accounted Proud, but rather very Discreet, in their Reserves. Some Play-house Beauties do wisely to be seen at a distance, and to have the Lamps twinckle betwixt them and the Spectators.

But now *Cæsar,* who tho' he were none of the greatest Souldiers, was certainly the greatest Traveller, of a Prince, that had ever been, (for which *Virgil* so dexterously Complements him, *Æneid* 6.) takes a Voyage to *Ægypt,* and having happily finish'd the War, reduces that mighty Kingdom into the Form of a Province; over which he appointed *Gallus* his Lieutenant. This is the same Person to whom *Virgil* addresses his Tenth Pastoral; changing, in compliance to his Request, his purpose of limiting them to the number of the Muses. The Praises of this *Gallus* took up a considerable part of the Fourth Book of the *Georgics,* according to the general consent of Antiquity: But *Cæsar* would have it put out, and yet the Seam in the Poem is still to be discern'd; and the matter of *Aristæus's* recovering his Bees, might have been dispatched in less compass, without fetching the Causes so far, or interessing so many Gods and Goddesses in *that* Affair. Perhaps some Readers may be inclin'd to think this, tho' very much labour'd, not the most entertaining part of that Work; so hard it is for the greatest Masters to Paint against their Inclination. But *Cæsar* was contented that he shou'd be mention'd in the last Pastoral, because it might be taken for a Satyrical sort of Commendation; and the Character he there stands under, might help to excuse his Cruelty, in putting an Old Servant to death for no very great Crime.

And now having ended, as he begins his *Georgics,* with solemn mention of *Cæsar,* an Argument of his Devotion to him: He begins his *Æneis,* according to the common account, being now turn'd of Forty. But that Work had been, in truth, the Subject of much earlier Meditation. Whilst he was working upon the

12   *Æneid*] F2; ~. F1.             13   the War] F2; that War F1.
27   contented that] F2; pleas'd F1 (*uncorrected state*), content F1 (*corrected state*).
36   Whilst] F2; Whil'st F1.

first Book of it, this passage, so very remarkable in History, fell
out, in which *Virgil* had a great share.

 *Cæsar,* about this time, either cloy'd with Glory, or terrifi'd
by the Example of his Predecessor; or to gain the Credit of Mod-
eration with the People, or possibly to feel the Pulse of his
Friends, deliberated whether he should retain the Soveraign
Power, or restore the Commonwealth. *Agrippa,* who was a very
honest Man, but whose View was of no great extent, advis'd him
to the latter; but *Mæcenas,* who had throughly studied his Mas-
10 ter's Temper, in an Eloquent Oration, gave contrary Advice.
That Emperour was too Politick to commit the over-sight of
*Cromwell,* in a deliberation something resembling this. *Crom-
well* had never been more desirous of the *Power,* than he was
afterwards of the Title of King: And there was nothing, in which
the Heads of the Parties, who were all his Creatures, would not
comply with him: But by too vehement Allegation of Arguments
against it, he, who had out-witted every body besides, at last out-
witted himself, by too deep dissimulation: For his Council,
thinking to make their Court by assenting to his judgment,
20 voted unanimously *for him* against *his Inclination;* which sur-
priz'd and troubled him to such a degree, that as soon as he had
got into his Coach, he fell into a Swoon. But *Cæsar* knew his
People better, and his Council being thus divided, he ask'd *Vir-
gil's* Advice: Thus a Poet had the Honour of determining the
greatest Point that ever was in Debate, betwixt the Son-in-Law,
and Favourite of *Cæsar. Virgil* deliver'd his Opinion in Words
to this effect. *The change of a Popular into an Absolute Govern-
ment, has generally been of very ill Consequence: For betwixt
the Hatred of the People, and Injustice of the Prince, it of neces-*
30 *sity comes to pass that they live in distrust, and mutual Apprehen-
sions. But if the Commons knew a just Person, whom they en-
tirely confided in, it would be for the advantage of all Parties, that
such a one should be their Soveraign: Wherefore if you shall
continue to administer Justice impartially, as hitherto you have
done, your Power will prove safe to your self, and beneficial to
Mankind.* This excellent Sentence, which seems taken out of
*Plato,* (with whose Writings the Grammarians were not much ac-

37 Grammarians] *Grammarians* F1–2.

quainted, and therefore cannot reasonably be suspected of For-
gery in this matter,) contains the true state of Affairs at that
time: For the *Commonwealth Maxims* were now no longer prac-
ticable; the *Romans* had only the haughtiness of the Old Com-
monwealth left, without one of its *Virtues*. And this Sentence
we find, almost in the same words, in the first Book of the *Æneis,*
which at this time he was writing; and one might wonder that
none of his Commentators have taken notice of it. He compares
a Tempest to a Popular Insurrection, as *Cicero* had compar'd a
10 Sedition to a Storm, a little before.

> *Ac veluti magno in populo, cum sæpe coorta est*
> *Seditio, sævitque animis ignobile vulgus*
> *Jamque faces, ac saxa volant, furor arma ministrat.*
> *Tum pietate gravem, & meritis si forte virum quem*
> *Conspexere silent, arrectisque auribus adstant.*
> *Ille regit dictis animos, & pectora mulcet.*

*Piety* and *Merit* were the two great Virtues which *Virgil* every
where attributes to *Augustus,* and in which that Prince, at least
Politickly, if not so truly, fix'd his Character, as appears by the
20 *Marmor Ancyr.* and several of his Medals. *Franshemius,* the
Learn'd Supplementor of *Livy,* has inserted this Relation into
his History; nor is there any Reason, why *Ruæus* should account
it fabulous. The Title of a Poet in those days did not abate, but
heighten the Character of the gravest Senator. *Virgil* was one of
the best and wisest Men of his time, and in so popular esteem,
that one hundred Thousand *Romans* rose when he came into
the Theatre, and paid him the same Respect they us'd to *Cæsar*
himself, as *Tacitus* assures us. And if *Augustus* invited *Horace*
to assist him in Writing his Letters, and every body knows that
30 the *rescripta Imperatorum* were the Laws of the Empire; *Virgil*
might well deserve a place in the Cabinet-Council.

And now he prosecutes his *Æneis,* which had Anciently the
Title of the *Imperial Poem,* or *Roman History,* and deservedly;

---

8  He compares] F2; he Compares F1.
12  *sævitque*] F1 *(corrected state);* *sævit que* F1 *(uncorrected state),* F2.
22  any] F2; any good F1.          32  he] F2; *Virgil* F1.

for though he were too Artful a Writer to set down Events in
exact Historical order, for which *Lucan* is justly blam'd; yet are
all the most considerable Affairs and Persons of *Rome* compriz'd
in this Poem. He deduces the History of *Italy* from before *Saturn*
to the Reign of King *Latinus;* and reckons up the Successors of
*Æneas,* who Reign'd at *Alba,* for the space of three hundred
Years, down to the Birth of *Romulus;* describes the Persons and
principal Exploits of all the Kings, to their Expulsion, and the
settling of the Commonwealth. After this, he touches promiscu-
ously the most remarkable Occurrences at home and abroad,
but insists more particularly upon the Exploits of *Augustus;*
insomuch, that tho' this Assertion may appear, at first, a little
surprizing; he has in his Works deduc'd the History of a con-
siderable part of the World from its *Original,* thro' the *Fabulous*
and *Heroick* Ages, thro' the *Monarchy* and *Commonwealth* of
*Rome,* for the space of four Thousand Years, down to within
less than Forty of our Saviour's time, of whom he has preserv'd
a most Illustrious Prophecy. Besides this, he points at many re-
markable Passages of History under feign'd Names: the destruc-
tion of *Alba,* and *Veii,* under that of *Troy:* The Star *Venus,*
which, *Varro* says, guided *Æneas* in his Voyage to *Italy,* in that
Verse,

> *Matre deâ monstrante viam.*————

*Romulus* his Lance taking Root, and Budding, is describ'd in
that Passage concerning *Polydorus, lib. 3.*

> ————*Confixum ferrea texit*
> *Telorum seges, & jaculis increvit acutis.*

The Stratagem of the *Trojans* boring Holes in their Ships,
and sinking them, lest the *Latins* should Burn them, under that
Fable of their being transform'd into *Sea-Nymphs:* And there-
fore the Ancients had no such Reason to condemn that Fable as

---

23   *viam.*————] ∼·ₐ F1–2.
25   *lib.*] lib. F1–2.
29   sinking them,] *comma prints as period in some copies of F1.*

groundless and absurd. *Cocles* swimming the River *Tyber,* after the Bridge was broken down behind him, is exactly painted in the Four last Verses of the Ninth Book, under the Character of *Turnus. Marius* hiding himself in the Morass of *Minturnæ,* under the Person of *Sinon:*

> *Limosoque lacu per Noctem obscuras in ulvâ*
> *Delitui———*

Those Verses in the Second Book concerning *Priam;*

> *———Jacet ingens littore truncus,* &c.

seem originally made upon *Pompey* the *Great.* He seems to touch the Imperious, and Intriguing Humour of the Empress *Livia,* under the Character of *Juno.* The irresolute and weak *Lepidus* is well represented under the Person of King *Latinus; Augustus* with the Character of *Pont. Max.* under that of *Æneas;* and the *rash Courage* (always Unfortunate in *Virgil*) of *Marc. Anthony* in *Turnus;* the railing Eloquence of *Cicero* in his *Phillipics* is well imitated in the Oration of *Drances;* the dull faithful *Agrippa,* under the person of *Achates;* accordingly this Character is flat: *Achates* kills but one Man, and himself receives one slight Wound, but neither says nor does any thing very considerable in the whole Poem. *Curio,* who sold his Country for about Two hundred Thousand Pound, is stigmatiz'd in that Verse,

> *Vendidit hic auro patriam, dominumque potentem*
> *Imposuit.———*

*Livy* relates that presently after the death of the two *Scipio's* in *Spain,* when *Martius* took upon him the Command, a Blazing Meteor shone around his Head, to the astonishment of his Souldiers: *Virgil* transfers this to *Æneas.*

> *Lætasque vomunt duo tempora flammas.*

9 ———*Jacet*] ∧∼ F1–2.
22 stigmatiz'd] F2; touch'd F1.
23 *potentem*] ∼. F1–2.

15 *Marc.*] F2; ∼∧ F1.
22 Verse,] ∼. F1–2.
27 astonishment] F2; astonishmeut F1.

It is strange that the Commentators have not taken notice of this. Thus the ill Omen which happen'd a little before the Battel of *Thrasimen,* when some of the Centurions Lances took Fire miraculously, is hinted in the like accident which befel *Acestes,* before the Burning of the *Trojan* Fleet in *Sicily.* The Reader will easily find many more such Instances. In other Writers there is often well cover'd *Ignorance;* in *Virgil,* conceal'd *Learning.*

His silence of some Illustrious Persons is no less worth observation. He says nothing of *Scævola,* because he attempted to As-
10 sassinate a King, tho' a declar'd Enemy: Nor of the Younger *Brutus;* for he *effected* what the other *endeavour'd:* Nor of the Younger *Cato,* because he was an implacable Enemy of *Julius Cæsar;* nor could the mention of him be pleasing to *Augustus;* and that Passage

————*His Dantem jura Catonem,*

may relate to his Office, as he was a very severe Censor. Nor would he name *Cicero,* when the occasion of mentioning him came full in his way; when he speaks of *Catiline;* because he afterwards approv'd the Murder of *Cæsar,* tho' the Plotters were
20 too wary to trust the Orator with their Design. Some other Poets knew the Art of Speaking well; but *Virgil,* beyond this, knew the admirable Secret of being *eloquently silent.* Whatsoever was most curious in *Fabius Pictor, Cato* the Elder, *Varro,* in the *Ægyptian* Antiquities, in the Form of Sacrifice, in the Solemnities of making Peace and War, is preserv'd in this Poem. *Rome* is still above ground, and flourishing in *Virgil.* And all this he performs with admirable brevity. The *Æneis* was once near twenty times bigger than he left it; so that he spent as much time in blotting out, as some Moderns have done in Writing whole
30 Volumes. But not one Book has his finishing Strokes: The sixth seems one of the most perfect, the which, after long entreaty, and sometimes threats of *Augustus,* he was at last prevail'd upon to recite: This fell out about four Years before his own Death: That of *Marcellus,* whom *Cæsar* design'd for his Successor, hap-

---

10  Enemy:] ～. F1–2.                    11  *endeavour'd:*] ～. F1–2.
15  ————*His*] ∧～ F1–2.              27  performs] F2; does F1.

pen'd a little before this Recital: *Virgil* therefore with his usual
dexterity, inserted his Funeral Panegyrick in those admirable
Lines, beginning,

*O nate, ingentem luctum ne quære tuorum,* &c.

His Mother, the Excellent *Octavia,* the *best Wife of the worst
Husband that ever was,* to divert her Grief, would be of the
Auditory. The Poet artificially deferr'd the naming *Marcellus,*
'till their Passions were rais'd to the highest; but the mention of
it put both Her and *Augustus* into such a Passion of weeping,
10 that they commanded him to proceed no further; *Virgil* answer'd,
that he had already ended that Passage. Some relate, that *Oc-
tavia* fainted away; but afterwards she presented the Poet with
two Thousand one Hundred Pounds, odd Money; a round Sum
for Twenty Seven Verses. But they were *Virgil*'s. Another Writer
says, that with a Royal Magnificence, she order'd him Massy
Plate, unweigh'd, to a great value.

And now he took up a Resolution of Travelling into *Greece,*
there to set the last Hand to this Work; purposing to devote the
rest of his Life to Philosophy, which had been always his prin-
20 cipal Passion. He justly thought it a foolish Figure for a grave
Man to be over-taken by Death, whilst he was weighing the Ca-
dence of Words, and measuring Verses; unless Necessity should
constrain it, from which he was well secur'd by the liberality of
that Learned Age. But he was not aware, that whilst he allotted
three Years for the Revising of his Poem, he drew Bills upon a
*failing Bank:* For unhappily meeting *Augustus* at *Athens,* he
thought himself oblig'd to wait upon him into *Italy,* but being
desirous to see all he could of the *Greek* Antiquities, he fell into
a languishing Distemper at *Megara;* this, neglected at first,
30 prov'd Mortal. The agitation of the Vessel, for it was now Au-
tumn, near the time of his Birth, brought him so low, that he
could hardly reach *Brindisi.* In his Sickness he frequently, and
with great importunity, call'd for his Scrutore, that he might
Burn his *Æneis,* but *Augustus* interposing by his Royal Au-

---

14  Verses. But they were *Virgil*'s.] F2; Verses. F1.
30-31  Autumn] *Autumn* F1-2.

thority, he made his last Will, of which something shall be said afterwards: And considering probably how much *Homer* had been disfigur'd by the Arbitrary Compilers of his Works, oblig'd *Tucca* and *Varius* to add nothing, nor so much as fill up the Breaks he left in his Poem. He order'd that his Bones should be carried to *Naples,* in which place he had pass'd the most agreeable part of his Life. *Augustus,* not only as Executor, and Friend, but according to the Duty of the *Pont. Max.* when a Funeral happen'd in his Family, took care himself to see the Will punc-
10 tually executed. He went out of the World with all that calmness of Mind with which the Ancient Writer of his Life says he came into it, making the Inscription of his Monument himself; for he *began* and *ended* his Poetical Compositions with an *Epitaph.* And this he made exactly according to the Law of his Master *Plato* on such occasions, without the least ostentation.

> *I sung Flocks, Tillage, Heroes;* Mantua *gave*
> *Me Life,* Brundusium *Death,* Naples *a Grave.*

*A short Account of his Person, Manners and Fortune.*

He was of a very swarthy Complexion, which might proceed
20 from the Southern Extraction of his Father, tall and wide-shoulder'd, so that he may be thought to have describ'd himself under the Character of *Musæus,* whom he calls the best of Poets,

> ————*Medium nam plurima turba*
> *Hunc habet, atque humeris extantem suspicit altis.*

His Sickliness, Studies, and the Troubles he met with, turn'd his Hair gray before the usual time; he had an hesitation in his Speech, as many other great Men: It being rarely found that

---

2  afterwards:] ∼. F1–2.                    12  it, making] ∼. Making F1–2.
16  Mantua] *Mantua* F1–2.
17  Brundusium] *Brundusium* F2; *Brandusium* F1.
17  Naples] *Naples* F1–2.                   22  Poets,] ∼. F1–2.
24  *extantem*] *ex tantem* F1–2.            25  turn'd] F2; made F1.

a very fluent Elocution, and depth of judgment meet in the same
Person. His Aspect and Behaviour rustick, and ungraceful: And
this defect was not likely to be rectify'd in the place where he
first liv'd, nor afterwards, because the weakness of his Stomach
would not permit him to use his Exercises; he was frequently
troubled with the Head-ach, and spitting of Blood; spare of
Dyet, and hardly drank any Wine. Bashful to a fault; and when
People crouded to see him, he would slip into the next Shop,
or by-passage, to avoid them. As this Character could not recom-
10 mend him to the fair Sex; he seems to have as little considera-
tion for them as *Euripides* himself. There is hardly the Char-
acter of one good Woman to be found in his Poems: He uses the
Word [*Mulier*] but once in the whole *Æneis,* then too by way
of Contempt, rendring literally a piece of a Verse out of *Homer.*
In his Pastorals he is full of invectives against Love: In the
*Georgics* he appropriates all the *rage* of *it* to the Females. He
makes *Dido,* who never deserv'd that Character, Lustful and Re-
vengeful to the utmost degree; so as to dye devoting her Lover
to destruction; so *changeable,* that the *Destinies* themselves could
20 not fix the time of her Death; but *Iris,* the Emblem of *Incon-
stancy,* must determine it. Her Sister is something worse. He is
so far from passing such a Complement upon *Helen,* as the
grave Old Councellour in *Homer* does, after nine Years War,
when upon the sight of her he breaks out into this Rapture in
the presence of King *Priam,*

> *None can the cause of these long Wars despise;*
> *The* Cost *bears no proportion to the* Prize:
> Majestick Charms *in every Feature shine;*
> *Her* Air, *her* Port, *her* accent *is* Divine.
> 30 *However let the* fatal *Beauty go,* &c.

*Virgil* is so far from this complaisant Humour, that his Heroe
falls into an unmanly and ill-tim'd deliberation, whether he
should not kill her in a Church; which directly contradicts what
*Deiphobus* says of her, *Æneid* 6. in that place where every body
tells the truth. He transfers the dogged Silence of *Ajax* his Ghost,

---

20 Death; but] F2; ∼. But F1.      31 Heroe] *Heroe* F1–2.

to that of *Dido;* tho' that be no very natural Character to an
injur'd Lover, or a Woman. He brings in the *Trojan* Matrons
setting their own Fleet on Fire; and running afterwards, like
Witches on their *Sabbat,* into the Woods. He bestows indeed
some Ornaments upon the Character of *Camilla;* but soon abates
his Favour, by calling her *aspera & horrenda Virgo:* He places
her in the Front of the line for an ill Omen of the Battel, as one
of the Ancients has observ'd. We may observe, on this occasion,
it is an Art peculiar to *Virgil,* to intimate the Event by some
10 preceding Accident. He hardly ever describes the rising of the
Sun, but with some circumstance which fore-signifies the For-
tune of the Day. For instance, when *Æneas* leaves *Africa* and
Queen *Dido,* he thus describes the fatal Morning:

> *Tithoni croceum linquens Aurora cubile.*

[And for the Remark, we stand indebted to the curious Pencil
of *Pollio.*] The *Mourning Fields* (*Æneid* 6.) are crowded with
Ladies of a lost Reputation: Hardly one Man gets admittance,
and that is *Cæneus,* for a very good Reason. *Latinus* his Queen
is turbulent, and ungovernable, and at last hangs her self: And
20 the fair *Lavinia* is disobedient to the Oracle, and to the King,
and looks a little flickering after *Turnus.* I wonder at this the
more, because *Livy* represents her as an excellent Person, and
who behav'd her self with great Wisdom in her Regency during
the minority of her Son: So that the Poet has done her Wrong,
and it reflects on her Posterity. His Goddesses make as ill a
Figure; *Juno* is always in a rage, and the Fury of Heaven: *Venus*
grows so unreasonably confident, as to ask her Husband to forge
Arms for her Bastard Son; which were enough to provoke one
of a more Phlegmatick Temper than *Vulcan* was. Notwithstand-
30 ing all this raillery of *Virgil's,* he was certainly of a very Amor-
ous disposition, and has describ'd all that is most delicate in the
Passion of Love; but he Conquer'd his natural Inclinations by
the help of Philosophy; and refin'd it into Friendship, to which
he was extreamly sensible. The Reader will admit of or reject

---

8–10  observ'd. We ... Accident.] F2; ~; (we ... ~.) F1.
14  *linquens*] *linguens* F1–2.          16  *Æneid*] ~. F1–2.

the following Conjecture, with the free leave of the Writer, who will be equally pleas'd either way. *Virgil* had too great an Opinion of the Influence of the Heavenly Bodies: And, as an Ancient Writer says, he was born under the Sign of *Virgo,* with which Nativity he much pleas'd himself, and would exemplifie her *Vertues* in his Life. Perhaps it was thence that he took his Name of *Virgil* and *Parthenias,* which does not necessarily signifie *Baseborn. Donatus,* and *Servius,* very good Grammarians, give a quite contrary sense of it. He seems to make allusion to this Original

10 of his Name in that Passage,

> *Illo Virgilium me tempore dulcis alebat,*
> *Parthenope.*————

And this may serve to illustrate his Complement to *Cæsar,* in which he invites him into his own Constellation,

> *Where, in the void of Heaven, a place is free,*
> *Betwixt the* Scorpion, *and the* Maid *for thee:*

Thus placing him betwixt Justice and Power, and in a Neighbour Mansion to his own; for *Virgil* suppos'd Souls to ascend again to their *proper,* and *congenial Stars.* Being therefore of

20 this Humour, it is no wonder that he refus'd the Embraces of the Beautiful *Plotia,* when his indiscreet Friend almost threw her into his Arms.

But however he stood affected to the Ladies, there is a dreadful Accusation brought against him for the most unnatural of all Vices, which by the Malignity of Humane nature has found more Credit in latter times than it did near his own. This took not its rise so much from the *Alexis,* in which Pastoral there is not one immodest Word; as from a sort of ill-nature, that will not let any one be without the imputation of some Vice; and

30 principally because he was so strict a follower of *Socrates* and

3–4  And, as an . . . he] F2; An . . . that he F1.
5  he much] F2; perhaps he F1.
12  *Parthenope.*————] ∼ . ∧ F1–2.
16  *thee:*] ∼. F1–2.
19  *proper,* and *congenial*] F2 (*congeneal*); *proper* F1.

*Plato.* In order therefore to his Vindication, I shall take the matter a little higher.

The *Cretans* were Anciently much addicted to Navigation, insomuch that it became a *Greek* Proverb, (tho' omitted, I think, by the Industrious *Erasmus,*) *A Cretan that does not know the Sea.* Their Neighbourhood gave them occasion of frequent Commerce with the *Phœnicians,* that accursed People, who infected the *Western* World with endless Superstitions, and gross immoralities. From them it is probable, that the *Cretans* learn'd this
10 infamous Passion, to which they were so much addicted, that *Cicero* remarks, in his Book *de Rep.* that it was *a disgrace for a young Gentleman to be without Lovers.* Socrates, who was a great Admirer of the *Cretan* Constitutions, set his excellent Wit to find out some good Cause, and Use of this Evil Inclination, and therefore gives an Account, wherefore Beauty is to be lov'd, in the following Passage; for I will not trouble the Reader, weary perhaps already, with a long *Greek* Quotation. *There is but one Eternal, Immutable, Uniform Beauty; in contemplation of which, our Soveraign Happiness does consist: And therefore a*
20 *true Lover considers Beauty and Proportion as so many Steps and Degrees, by which he may ascend from the particular to the general, from all that is lovely of Feature, or regular in Proportion, or charming in Sound, to the general Fountain of all Perfection. And if you are so much transported with the sight of Beautiful Persons, as to wish neither to Eat or drink, but pass your whole Life in their Conversation; to what extasie would it raise you to behold the Original Beauty, not fill'd up with Flesh and Blood, or varnish'd with a fading mixture of Colours, and the rest of Mortal Trifles and Fooleries, but separate, unmix'd,*
30 *uniform, and divine,* &c. Thus far *Socrates,* in a strain, much beyond the *Socrate Crétien* of Mr. *Balsac:* And thus that admirable Man lov'd his *Phædon,* his *Charmides,* and *Theætetus;* and thus *Virgil* lov'd his *Alexander,* and *Cebes,* under the feign'd Name of *Alexis:* He receiv'd them illiterate, but return'd them

---

4   a] F2; A F1.                          5   *A*] A F1–2.
7   *Phœnicians*] *Phænicians* F1–2      17   already,] ~ₐ F1–2.
23  *all*] F2; *all Beauty and* F1.
26  *their Conversation*] F2; *looking on them* F1.
32  *Phædon*] *Phædon* F1–2.

to their Masters, the one a good Poet, and the other an excellent
Grammarian: And to prevent all possible Misinterpretations, he
warily inserted into the liveliest Episode in the whole *Æneis,*
these words,

*Nisus amore pio pueri*————

and in the Sixth, *Quique pii vates.* He seems fond of the Words,
*castus, pius, Virgo,* and the Compounds of it; and sometimes
stretches the Use of that word further than one would think he
reasonably should have done, as when he attributes it to *Pasiphaè*
10 her self.

Another Vice he is Tax'd with, is Avarice; because he dy'd
Rich, and so indeed he did in comparison of modern Wealth;
his Estate amounts to near Seventy Five Thousand Pounds of our
Money: But *Donatus* does not take notice of this as a thing
extraordinary; nor was it esteem'd so great a Matter, when the
Cash of a great part of the World lay at *Rome; Antony* himself
bestow'd at once Two Thousand Acres of Land in one of the
best Provinces of *Italy,* upon a ridiculous Scribler, who is nam'd
by *Cicero* and *Virgil.* A late Cardinal us'd to purchase ill flattery
20 at the Expence of 100000 Crowns a Year. But besides *Virgil*'s
other Benefactors, he was much in favour with *Augustus,* whose
Bounty to him had no limits, but such as the Modesty of *Virgil*
prescrib'd to it. Before he had made his own Fortune, he setled
his Estate upon his Parents and Brothers; sent them Yearly large
Sums, so that they liv'd in great Plenty and Respect; and at his
Death, divided his Estate betwixt *Duty* and *Gratitude,* leaving
one half to his Relations, and the other to *Mæcenas,* to *Tucca*
and *Varius,* and a considerable Legacy to *Augustus,* who had
introduc'd a politick Fashion of being in every bodies Will;
30 which alone was a fair Revenue for a Prince. *Virgil* shews his
detestation of this Vice, by placing in the front of the Damn'd
those who did not relieve their Relations and Friends; for the
*Romans* hardly ever extended their Liberality further; and there-

---

1   Masters] *Masters* F1–2.      3   Episode] *Episode* F1–2.
5–6   *pueri*————/and] ~./And F1–2.      9   *Pasiphaè*] *Pasiphaé* F1–2.
18   Scribler] F2; Poet F1.      27   *Mæcenas*] *Mecenas* F1–2.

fore I do not remember to have met in all the *Latin* Poets, one
Character so noble as that short one in *Homer,*

$$\text{———}\Phi\text{ί}\lambda o\varsigma\ \delta'\ \mathring{\eta}\nu\ \mathring{\alpha}\nu\theta\rho\acute{\omega}\pi o\iota\sigma\iota,$$
$$\pi\acute{\alpha}\nu\tau\alpha\varsigma\ \gamma\grave{\alpha}\rho\ \phi\iota\lambda\acute{\epsilon}\epsilon\sigma\kappa\epsilon\text{———}$$

On the other hand, he gives a very advanc'd place in *Elysium*
to good Patriots, &c. Observing in all his Poem, that Rule so
Sacred amongst the *Romans, That there shou'd be no Art al-
low'd, which did not tend to the improvement of the People in
Virtue.* And this was the Principle too of our Excellent Mr.
10 *Waller,* who us'd to say that he wou'd raze any Line out of his
Poems, which did not imply some Motive to Virtue; but he was
unhappy in the choice of the Subject of his admirable vein in
Poetry. The Countess of *C.* was the *Helen of her Country.* There
is nothing in Pagan Philosophy more true, more just, and regu-
lar than *Virgil's* Ethics; and it is hardly possible to sit down to
the serious perusual of his Works, but a Man shall rise more
dispos'd to virtue and goodness, as well as most agreeably enter-
tain'd: The contrary to which disposition, may happen some-
times upon the reading of *Ovid,* of *Martial,* and several other
20 second rate Poets. But of the *Craft* and *Tricking* part of Life,
with which *Homer* abounds, there is nothing to be found in
*Virgil;* and therefore *Plato,* who gives the former so many good
words, perfumes, Crowns, but at last *Complementally Banishes*
him his Commonwealth, wou'd have intreated *Virgil* to stay with
him, (if they had liv'd in the same Age,) and intrusted him with
some important Charge in his Government. Thus was his *Life*
as chast as his *Stile,* and those who can Critick his *Poetry,* can
never find a blemish in his *Manners;* and one would rather wish
to have that *purity* of *Mind,* which the Satyrist himself attributes
30 to him; that friendly disposition, and evenness of temper, and
patience, which he was Master of in so eminent a degree, than to
have the honour of being Author of the *Æneis,* or even of the
*Georgics* themselves.

2   *Homer,*] ∼. F1–2.                    4   πάντας] F2; πάνται F1.
15   Ethics] *Ethics* F1–2.               17–18   entertain'd:] ∼. F1–2.

Having therefore so little relish for the usual amusements of the world, he prosecuted his Studies without any considerable interruption, during the whole course of his Life, which one may reasonably conjecture to have been something longer than 52 years; and therefore it is no wonder that he became the most general Scholar that *Rome* ever bred, unless some one should except *Varro*. Besides the exact knowledge of Rural Affairs, he understood Medicine, to which Profession he was design'd by his Parents. A Curious *Florist,* on which Subject one wou'd wish
10 he had writ, as he once intended: So profound a Naturalist, that he has solv'd more *Phænomena* of Nature upon sound Principles, than *Aristotle* in his *Physics.* He studied Geometry, the most opposite of all Sciences to a Poetick Genius, and Beauties of a lively imagination; but this promoted the order of his Narrations, his propriety of Language, and clearness of Expression, for which he was justly call'd the *Pillar of the Latin Tongue.* This Geometrical Spirit was the cause, that to fill up a Verse he would not insert one superfluous word; and therefore deserves that Character which a Noble and Judicious Writer has given him,
20 \**That he never says too little nor too much.* Nor cou'd any one ever fill up the Verses he left imperfect. There is one supply'd near the beginning of the First Book; *Virgil* left the Verse thus,

————*Hic illius arma,*
*Hic currus fuit*————

The rest is none of his.

He was so good a Geographer, that he has not only left us the finest description of *Italy* that ever was; but besides, was one of the few Ancients who knew the true System of the Earth, its being Inhabited round about under the *Torrid Zone,* and near

---

\* *Essay of Poetry* by the Marquess of *Normanby.*

---

19 Writer] F2; Critick F1.
20 *That* . . . [*to*] . . . *much.*] F2; *in romans in F1.*
22–23 thus,/————*Hic*] ~. ———— ~ F1; ~, ———— ~ F2.
24–25 *fuit*————/The] ~————the F1–2.
25 his] F2; *Virgil's* F1.
footnote *Poetry* by the Marquess of *Normanby.*] F2; *Poetry.* F1.

the Poles. *Metrodorus,* in his five Books of the *Zones,* justifies him from some Exceptions made against him by *Astronomers.* His Rhetorick was in such general esteem, that Lectures were read upon it in the Reign of *Tiberius,* and the Subject of Declamations taken out of him. *Pollio* himself, and many other Ancients Commented him. His Esteem degenerated into a kind of Superstition. The known Story of Mr. *Cowley* is an instance of it. But the *sortes Virgilianæ* were condemn'd by St. *Augustin,* and other Casuists. *Abienus,* by an odd Design, put all *Virgil* and
10   *Livy* into *Iambick* Verse; and the Pictures of those two were hung in the most Honourable place of Publick Libraries, and the Design of taking them down, and destroying *Virgil*'s Works, was look'd upon as one of the most Extravagant amongst the many *Brutish* Frenzies of *Caligula.*

*Preface to the Pastorals,*
*With a short Defence of Virgil,*
*Against some of the Reflections*
*of Monsieur Fontanelle.*

[By Knightly Chetwood]

As the Writings of greatest Antiquity are in Verse, so of all sorts of Poetry, *Pastorals* seem the most Ancient; being form'd upon the Model of the First *Innocence,* and *Simplicity,* which the Moderns, better to dispence themselves from imitating, have wisely thought fit to treat as *Fabulous,* and *impracticable;* and yet they, by obeying the *unsophisticated* Dictates of Nature, enjoy'd the most valuable Blessings of Life; a vigorous Health of Body, with a constant serenity, and freedom of Mind, whilst we, with all our fanciful Refinements, can
10 scarcely pass an Autumn without some access of a Feaver, or a whole Day, not ruffled by some unquiet Passion. He was not then look'd upon as a very Old Man; who reach'd to a greater Number of Years, than in these times an ancient Family can reasonably pretend to; and we know the Names of several, who saw, and practis'd the World for a longer space of time, than we can read the Account of in any one entire Body of History. In short, they invented the most useful Arts, *Pastorage, Tillage, Geometry, Writing, Musick, Astronomy,* &c. Whilst the Moderns, like Extravagant Heirs, made rich by their Industry, ingratefully de-
20 ride the good Old *Gentlemen,* who left them the *Estate.* It is not therefore to be wonder'd at, that *Pastorals* are fallen into Disesteem, together with that Fashion of Life, upon which they were grounded. And methinks, I see the Reader already uneasie at this Part of *Virgil,* counting the Pages, and posting to the *Æneis;* so delightful an entertainment is the very Relation of publick Mischief, and slaughter, now become to Mankind: and yet *Virgil* pass'd a much different judgment on his own Works: He valu'd most this part, and his *Georgics,* and depended upon them

Monarchies in the World, were Shepherds: And the Subject of
Husbandry has been adorn'd by the *Writings* and *Labour* of
more than twenty *Kings*. It ought not therefore to be matter of
surprize to a Modern Writer, that Kings, the *Shepherds* of the
*People* in *Homer,* laid down their first *Rudiments* in tending
their *mute Subjects;* nor that the Wealth of *Ulysses* consisted
in Flocks and Herds, the Intendants over which, were then in
equal esteem with Officers of State in latter times. And therefore
*Eumæus* is call'd Δῖος ὑφορβός in *Homer;* not so much because
10 *Homer* was a lover of a Countrey Life, to which he rather seems
averse, but by reason of the Dignity and Greatness of his Trust,
and because he was the Son of a *King,* stollen away, and Sold by
the *Phœnician* Pyrates, which the Ingenious Mr. *Cowley* seems
not to have taken notice of. Nor will it seem strange, that the
Master of the Horse to King *Latinus,* in the Ninth *Æneid,* was
found in the homely Employment of cleaving Blocks, when
news of the first Skirmish betwixt the *Trojans* and *Latins* was
brought to him.

   Being therefore of such Quality, they cannot be suppos'd so
20 very *ignorant* and *unpolish'd;* the Learning and good breeding
of the World was then in the hands of such People. He who was
chosen by the consent of all Parties to *arbitrate* so delicate an
affair, as which was the *fairest* of the three *Celebrated Beauties*
of *Heaven;* he who had the address to debauch away *Helen*
from her *Husband,* her Native *Country,* and from a *Crown,*
understood what the *French* call by the too soft name of *Gal-
lanterie;* he had Accomplishments enough, how ill use soever
he made of them. It seems therefore that Mr. *F.* had not duly
consider'd the matter, when he reflected so severely upon *Virgil,*
30 as if he had not observ'd the Laws of *decency* in his *Pastorals,*
in making Shepherds speak to things *beside* their *Character,*
and *above* their *Capacity.* He *stands amaz'd that Shepherds
should thunder out,* as he expresses himself, *the formation of
the World, and that too according to the System of* Epicurus.

---

6   *Ulysses*] F1 (*corrected state*); Ulisses F1 (*uncorrected state*), F2.
9   ὑφορβός] ὕφορβος F1–2.                    13   *Phœnician*] Phænician F1–2.
26–27   *Gallanterie*] F2; Gallantry F1.
32   their *Capacity.*] their *Capacity* F1–2.
33   *out,* as he expresses himself] out, as he expresses himself F1–2.

*In truth,* says he, page 176, *I cannot tell what to make of this whole piece;* (*the Sixth* Past.) *I can neither comprehend the Design of the Author, nor the Connexion of the parts; first come the Ideas of Philosophy, and presently after those incoherent Fables,* &c. To expose him yet more, he subjoyns, *it is* Silenus *himself who makes all this absurd Discourse.* Virgil *says indeed that he had drank too much the day before; perhaps the Debauch hung in his head when he compos'd this Poem,* &c. Thus far Mr. *F.* who, to the disgrace of Reason, as himself ingenuously

10 owns, first built his House, and then studied *Architecture;* I mean first Compos'd his *Eclogues,* and then studied the Rules. In answer to this, we may observe, first, that this very *Pastoral* which he singles out to triumph over, was recited by a Famous Player on the *Roman* Theatre, with marvellous applause; insomuch that *Cicero* who had heard part of it only, order'd the whole to be rehears'd, and struck with admiration of it, conferr'd then upon *Virgil* the Glorious Title of

*Magnæ spes alteræ Romæ.*

Nor is it Old *Donatus* only who relates this, we have the same
20 account from another very Credible and Ancient Author; so that here we have the judgment of *Cicero,* and the People of *Rome,* to confront the single Opinion of this adventrous Critick. A Man ought to be well assur'd of his own Abilities, before he attack an Author of *establish'd* Reputation. If Mr. *F.* had perus'd the fragments of the *Phœnician* Antiquity, trac'd the progress of Learning thro' the Ancient *Greek* Writers, or so much as Consulted his Learned Countrey-Man *Huetius,* he would have found, (which falls out unluckily for him) that a *Chaldæan* Shepherd discover'd to the *Ægyptians* and *Greeks* the *Creation of the*
30 *World.* And what Subject more fit for such a *Pastoral,* than that Great Affair which was first notified to the World by one of that *Profession?* Nor does it appear, (what he takes for granted) that *Virgil* describes the Original of the World according to the Hypothesis of *Epicurus;* he was too well seen in Antiquity to commit such a gross Mistake; there is not the least mention of *Chance*

---

1    *In truth,* says he, page 176, *I*] *In truth,* says he, page 176. I F1–2.
25    *Phœnician*] Phænician F1–2.          33–34    the Hypothesis] *the* Hypothesis F1–2.

awe, than the Omnipotent Power of *transforming* the Species
of Creatures at their pleasure? Their Families liv'd in Groves,
near the clear Springs; and what better warning could be given
to the hopeful young Shepherds, than that they should not gaze
too much into the Liquid dangerous Looking-glass, for fear of
being *stoln* by the *Water-Nymphs,* that is, falling and being
drown'd, as *Hylas* was? *Pasiphaè's* monstrous passion for a *Bull,*
is certainly a Subject enough fitted for *Bucolics:* Can Mr. *F.* Tax
*Silenus* for fetching *too* far the Transformation of the Sisters of
10 *Phaeton* into *Trees,* when perhaps they sat at that very time un-
der the hospitable shade of those Alders and Poplars? Or the
Metamorphosis of *Philomela* into that ravishing Bird, which
makes the sweetest musick of the *Groves?* If he had look'd into
the Ancient *Greek* Writers, or so much as Consulted honest
*Servius,* he would have discover'd that under the Allegory of
this *drunkenness* of *Silenus,* the refinement and *exaltation* of
Mens *Minds* by *Philosophy* was intended. But if the Author of
these Reflections can take such flights in his Wine, it is almost
pity that drunkenness shou'd be a Sin, or that he shou'd ever
20 want good store of *Burgundy,* and *Champaign.* But indeed he
seems not to have ever drank out of *Silenus* his Tankard, when
he compos'd either his *Critique,* or *Pastorals.*

His Censure on the Fourth seems worse grounded than the
other; it is Entituled in some ancient Manuscripts, *The History
of the Renovation of the World;* he complains *that he cannot
understand what is meant by those many Figurative Expressions:*
But if he had consulted the younger *Vossius* his Dissertation on
this *Pastoral,* or read the Excellent Oration of the Emperour
*Constantine,* made *French* by a good Pen of their own, he would
30 have found there the plain interpretation of all those Figurative
Expressions; and withall, very strong proofs of the truth of the
Christian Religion; such as Converted Heathens, as *Valerianus,*

---

3    near the] F2; *near* F1.
7    *Pasiphaè's*] Pasiphea's F1; Pasiphae's F2.
8    *Bucolics:*] F2; Bucolic's? F1.
9    *too* far] F2; too far F1.
11–12  and ... Metamorphosis] F2; *or ... Metamorphoses* F1.
22   compos'd] F2; *made* F1.
24–25  *The History of the Renovation*] *The History of the* Renovation F1–2.
30   interpretation] F2; *inerpretation* F1.

and others: And upon account of this Piece, the most Learn'd of all the *Latin* Fathers calls *Virgil* a *Christian*, even before *Christianity*. *Cicero* takes notice of it in his Books of Divination, and *Virgil* probably had put it in Verse a considerable time before the Edition of his *Pastorals*. Nor does he appropriate it to *Pollio*, or *his Son*, but *Complementally* dates it from his Consulship. And therefore some one who had not so kind thoughts of Mr. *F.* as I, would be inclin'd to think him as bad a *Catholick* as *Critick* in this place.

10 But, in respect to some Books he has wrote since, I pass by a great part of this, and shall only touch briefly some of the Rules of this sort of Poem.

The First is, that an air of Piety upon all occasions should be maintain'd in the whole Poem: This appears in all the Ancient *Greek* Writers; as *Homer, Hesiod, Aratus,* &c. And *Virgil* is so exact in the observation of it, not only in this Work, but in his *Æneis* too, that a Celebrated *French* Writer taxes him for permitting *Æneas* to do nothing without the assistance of some God. But by this it appears, at least, that Mr. St. *Eur.* is no *Jansenist.*

Mr. *F.* seems a little defective in this point; he brings in a pair of Shepherdesses disputing very warmly, whether *Victoria* be a *Goddess,* or a *Woman.* Her great condescension and compassion, her affability and goodness, none of the meanest Attributes of the Divinity, pass for convincing Arguments that she *could not* possibly be a Goddess.

> *Les Déesses toujours fières & méprisantes*
> *Ne rassureroient point les Bergères tremblantes*
> *Par d'obligeans discours, des souris gracieux;*
> 30 *Mais tu l'as veu; cette Auguste Personne*
> *Qui vient de paroistre en ces lieux*
> *Prend soin de rassurer au moment qu'elle étonne.*
> *Sa bonté descendant sans peine jusqu'à nous.*

2  of all] F2; *of* F1.                    2  the *Latin*] the Latin F1–2.
10  But, ... to ... since, I pass by] F2; *I pass by, ... therefore to ... since,* F1.
15  *Homer, Hesiod, Aratus,*] F2; Homer, F1.
22  *Victoria*] F2; Victoria, *(none of the fittest Names for a Shepherdess)* F1.
27  *toujours fières*] toûjours fieres F1–2.
28  *rassureroient ... Bergères*] rassureroiént ... Bergeres F1–2.

In short, she has too many *Divine Perfections* to be a *Deity*, and therefore she is a Mortal [which was the thing to be prov'd.] It is directly contrary to the practice of all ancient Poets, as well as to the Rules of decency and Religion, to make such odious Preferences. I am much surpriz'd therefore that he should use such an argument as this.

> Cloris, *as-tu veu des Déesses*
> *Avoir un air si facile & si doux?*

Was not *Aurora*, and *Venus*, and *Luna*, and I know not how
10 many more of the Heathen Deities too easie of access to *Tithonus*, to *Anchises*, and to *Endimion?* Is there any thing more Sparkish and better humour'd than *Venus* her accosting her Son in the Desarts of *Lybia?* or than the behaviour of *Pallas* to *Diomedes*, one of the most perfect and admirable Pieces of all the *Iliads;* where she condescends to *raillé* him so agreeably; and notwithstanding her *severe Vertue,* and all the Ensigns of *Majesty,* with which she so *terribly adorns* her self, condescends to ride with him in his Chariot? But the *Odysses* are full of greater instances of condescension than this.
20     This brings to mind that Famous passage of *Lucan,* in which he prefers *Cato* to all the Gods at once,

> *Victrix causa deis placuit sed victa Catoni.*

Which *Brébœuf* has render'd so flatly, and which may be thus Paraphras'd,

> *Heaven meanly with the Conquerour did comply,*
> *But* Cato *rather than submit would die.*

It is an unpardonable presumption in any sort of Religion to complement their *Princes* at the expence of their *Deities.*

4–5   Preferences] F2; *Comparisons* F1.          7   Cloris, *as-tu*] Cloris, as-tu F1–2.
15   to *raillé*] F2; *to rally* F1.                       23   *Brébœuf*] Brelæuf F1–2.
24   Paraphras'd,] ~. F1–2.                             28   of their] *of* their F1–2.

But letting that pass, this whole *Eclogue* is but a long Para-
phrase of a trite Verse in *Virgil,* and *Homer,*

Nec vox Hominem sonat, O Dea certe.

So true is that Remark of the Admirable *E.* of *Roscomon,* if
apply'd to the *Romans,* rather I fear than to the *English,* since his
own Death,

————*one* sterling *Line,*
*Drawn to* French *Wire, would thro' whole pages shine.*

Another Rule is, that the Characters should represent that
10 Ancient Innocence, and unpractis'd Plainness, which was then
in the World. *P. Rapine* has gather'd many Instances of this out
of *Theocritus,* and *Virgil;* and the Reader can do it as well him-
self. But Mr. *F.* transgress'd this Rule, when he hid himself in
the Thicket, to listen to the private Discourse of the two Shep-
herdesses. This is not only ill Breeding at *Versailles;* the *Arca-
dian Shepherdesses* themselves would have set their Dogs upon
one for such an unpardonable piece of Rudeness.
A Third Rule is, That there should be some Ordonnance,
some Design, or little Plot, which may deserve the Title of a
20 Pastoral *Scene.* This is everywhere observ'd by *Virgil,* and par-
ticularly remarkable in the first *Eclogue;* the standard of all *Pas-
torals;* a Beautiful *Landscape* presents it self to your view, a
Shepherd with his Flock around him, resting securely under a
spreading Beech, which furnish'd the first Food to our Ancestors.
Another in quite different Situation of Mind and Circumstances,
the Sun setting, the Hospitality of the more fortunate Shepherd,
*&c.* And here Mr. *F.* seems not a little wanting.
A Fourth Rule, and of great importance in this delicate sort
of Writing, is, that there be choice diversity of Subjects; that the
30 *Eclogues,* like a Beautiful Prospect, should Charm by its Variety.
*Virgil* is admirable in this Point, and far surpasses *Theocritus,*
as he does every where, when Judgment and Contrivance have

---

6  Death,] ∼. F1–2.                    20  everywhere] *every where* F1–2.
21–22  all *Pastorals*] all Pastorals F1–2.

the principal part. The Subject of the first *Pastoral* is hinted above.

The Second contains the Love of *Coridon* for *Alexis,* and the seasonable reproach he gives himself, that he left his Vines half prun'd, (which according to the *Roman Rituals,* deriv'd a Curse upon the Fruit that grew upon it) whilst he pursu'd an Object undeserving his Passion.

The Third, a sharp Contention of two Shepherds for the Prize of Poetry.

10    The Fourth contains the Discourse of a Shepherd Comforting himself in a declining Age, that a better was ensuing.

The Fifth a Lamentation for a Dead Friend, the first draught of which is probably more Ancient than any of the *Pastorals* now extant; his Brother being at first intended; but he afterwards makes his Court to *Augustus,* by turning it into an Apotheosis of *Julius Cæsar.*

The Sixth is the *Silenus.*

The Seventh, another Poetical Dispute, first Compos'd at *Mantua.*

20    The Eighth is the Description of a despairing Lover, and a Magical Charm.

He sets the Ninth after all these, very modestly, because it was particular to himself; and here he would have ended that Work, if *Gallus* had not prevail'd upon him to add one more in his Favour.

Thus Curious was *Virgil* in *diversifying* his Subjects. But Mr. *F.* is a great deal too Uniform; begin where you please, the Subject is still the same. We find it true what he says of himself,

*Toujours, toujours de l'Amour.*

30    He seems to take *Pastorals* and *Love-Verses* for the same thing. Has Human Nature no other Passion? Does not *Fear, Ambition, Avarice, Pride,* a Capricio of Honour, and *Laziness* it self often Triumph over *Love?* But this Passion does all, not only in *Pas-*

---

13    the *Pastorals*] the Pastorals F1–2.
15    Apotheosis] *Apothesis* F1–2.
29    *Toujours, toujours*] Toûjours, toûjours F1–2.

*torals,* but in *Modern Tragedies* too. A Heroe can no more *Fight,* or be *Sick,* or *Dye,* than he can be *Born* without a *Woman.* But *Dramatic's* have been compos'd in compliance to the Humour of the Age, and the prevailing Inclination of the great, whose *Example* has a more powerful Influence, not only in the little Court behind the Scenes, but on the great Theatre of the World. However this inundation of *Love-Verses* is not so much an effect of their Amorousness, as of immoderate *Self-love:* This being the only sort of Poetry, in which the Writer can, not only with-
10 out Censure, but even with *Commendation,* talk of *himself.* There is generally more of the Passion of *Narcissus,* than concern for *Chloris* and *Corinna* in this whole Affair. Be pleas'd to look into almost any of those Writers, and you shall meet every where that *eternal Moy,* which the admirable *Paschal* so judiciously condemns. *Homer* can never be enough admir'd for this one so particular Quality, that he never speaks of himself, either in the *Iliad,* or the *Odysses;* and if *Horace* had never told us his Gene-alogy, but left it to the Writer of his Life, perhaps he had not been a loser by it. This Consideration might induce those great
20 Criticks, *Varius* and *Tucca,* to raze out the four first Verses of the *Æneis,* in great measure, for the sake of that unlucky *Ille ego.* But extraordinary *Genius's* have a sort of Prerogative, which may dispence them from Laws, binding to *Subject-Wits.* How-ever, the Ladies have the less Reason to be pleas'd with those Addresses, of which the Poet takes the greater share to himself. Thus the *Beau* presses into their *Dressing-Room,* but it is not so much to adore their fair Eyes, as to adjust his own Steenkirk and Peruke, and set his Countenance in their Glass.

A fifth Rule, (which one may hope will not be contested) is
30 that the Writer should shew in his Compositions, some competent skill of the Subject matter, that which makes the Character of the Persons introduc'd. In this, as in all other Points of Learning, Decency, and Oeconomy of a Poem, *Virgil* much excells his Mas-ter *Theocritus.* The *Poet* is better skill'd in *Husbandry* than those that get their Bread by *it.* He describes the Nature, the

1  but in] F2; *but on* F1.  
5  more] F2; *very* F1.  
7  is] F2; *'tis* F1.  
17  if *Horace*] F2; *if Horace* F1.  
2  or be] or *be* F1–2.  
7  However this] F2; *This* F1.  
8  *Self-love:*] ~. F1–2.  
27–28  Steenkirk] F2; *Steenzkirk* F1.

*Greeks* in this sort of Poem, as very Ancient and Natural: *Lyrics,
Iambics, &c.* being Invented afterwards: but there is so great a
difference in the Numbers, of which it may be compounded,
that it may pass rather for a *Genus,* than *Species,* of Verse. Who-
soever shall compare the *numbers* of the three following Verses,
will quickly be sensible of the truth of this Observation.

> *Tityre, tu patulæ recubans sub tegmine fagi.*

The first of the *Georgics,*

> *Quid faciat lætas segetes, quo sydere terram.*

10 And of the *Æneis,*

> *Arma, virumque cano, Trojæ qui Primus ab oris.*

The *Sound* of the Verses, is almost as different as the *Subjects.*
But the *Greek* Writers of *Pastoral,* usually limited themselves
to the Example of the first; which *Virgil* found so exceedingly
difficult, that he quitted it, and left the Honour of that part to
*Theocritus.* It is indeed probable, that what we improperly call
*rhyme,* is the most Ancient sort of Poetry; and Learned Men have
given good Arguments for it; and therefore a *French* Historian
commits a gross mistake, when he attributes that Invention to a
20 King of *Gaul,* as an *English* Gentleman does, when he makes a
*Roman* Emperour the Inventor of it. But the *Greeks* who under-
stood fully the force and power of *Numbers,* soon grew weary
of this Childish sort of Verse, as the Younger *Vossius* justly calls
it, and therefore those rhyming Hexameters, which *Plutarch* ob-
serves in *Homer himself,* seem to be the Remains of a barbarous
Age. *Virgil* had them in such abhorrence, that he would rather
make a false *Syntax,* than what we call a Rhime. Such a Verse
as this,

> *Vir precor Uxori, frater succurre Sorori,*

---

1   *Greeks*] F2; Latins F1.                1   Natural:] ∼. F1–2.
8   The] *indented in F1–2.*                10   And ... *Æneis,*] and ... ∼. F1–2.
27–28   Rhime. Such ... this,] ∼, *such* ... ∼ʌ F1–2.
29   Sorori,] ∼. F1–2.

was passable in *Ovid,* but the nice Ears in *Augustus* his Court could not pardon *Virgil* for

> At Regina Pyra.————

So that the principal Ornament of Modern Poetry, was accounted *deformity* by the *Latins,* and *Greeks;* it was they who invented the different terminations of words, those happy compositions, those short monosyllables, those transpositions for the elegance of the sound and sense, which are wanting so much in modern Languages. The *French* sometimes crowd together ten, or twelve Monosyllables, into one disjoynted Verse; they may understand the nature of, but cannot imitate, those wonderful *Spondees* of *Pythagoras,* by which he could suddenly pacifie a Man that was in a violent transport of anger; nor those *swift numbers* of the Priests of *Cybele,* which had the force to enrage the most *sedate* and *Phlegmatick* Tempers. Nor can any Modern put into his own Language the *Energy* of that single Poem of *Catullus,*

> Super alta vectus, Atys, &c.

*Latin* is but a corrupt dialect of *Greek;* and the *French, Spanish,* and *Italian,* a corruption of *Latine;* and therefore a Man might as well go about to persuade me that *Vinegar* is a *Nobler* Liquor than *Wine,* as that the modern Compositions can be as graceful and harmonious as the *Latine* it self. The *Greek* Tongue very naturally falls into *Iambicks,* and therefore the diligent Reader may find six or seven and twenty of them in those accurate Orations of *Isocrates.* The *Latin* as naturally falls into *Heroic;* and therefore the beginning of *Livy*'s History is half an Hexameter, and that of *Tacitus* an entire one. *The *Roman* Historian de-

---

* Livy.

---

1   was] *Was* F1–2.
2   Virgil] F2; ~, F1.
3   Pyra.————] ~·.ᴧ F1–2.
18   *Latin* is] *Latin is* F1–2.
27   *The [*and footnote*]] F2; ᴧ*The* [*and no footnote*] F1.

scribing the glorious effort of a Colonel to break thro' a *Brigade* of the Enemies, just after the defeat at *Cannæ,* falls, unknowingly, into a Verse not unworthy *Virgil* himself,

> *Hæc ubi dicta dedit, stringit gladium, cuneoq;*
> *Facto per medios,* &c.

Ours and the *French* can at best but fall into Blank Verse, which is a fault in Prose. The misfortune indeed is common to us both, but we deserve more compassion, because we are not vain of our Barbarities. As Age brings Men back into the state
10 and infirmities of Childhood, upon the fall of their Empire, the *Romans doted* into *Rhime,* as appears sufficiently by the *Hymns* of the *Latin Church;* and yet a great deal of the *French* Poetry does hardly deserve that poor title. I shall give an instance out of a Poem which had the good luck to gain the Prize in 1685, for the Subject deserv'd a Nobler Pen.

> *Tous les jours ce grand Roy des autres Roys l'exemple,*
> *S'ouvre un nouveau chemin au faiste de ton temple, &c.*

The Judicious *Malherbe* exploded this sort of Verse near Eighty Years ago. Nor can I forbear wondering at that passage
20 of a Famous Academician, in which he, most compassionately, excuses the Ancients for their not being so exact in their Compositions, as the Modern *French,* because they wanted a *Dictionary,* of which the *French* are at last happily provided. If *Demosthenes* and *Cicero* had been so lucky as to have had a *Dictionary,* and such a Patron as Cardinal *Richelieu,* perhaps they might have aspir'd to the honour of *Balzac*'s Legacy of *Ten Pounds, Le prix de l' Eloquence.*

On the contrary, I dare assert that there are hardly ten Lines in either of those great Orators, or even in the Catalogue of
30 *Homer*'s Ships, which is not more harmonious, more truly *Rythmical,* than most of the *French,* or *English* Sonnets; and therefore they lose, at least, one half of their native Beauty by Translation.

---

3    himself,] ∼. F1–2.
24   *Demosthenes* and *Cicero*] F2; Cicero *and* Demosthenes F1.

I cannot but add one Remark on this occasion, that the *French* Verse is oftentimes not so much as Rhime, in the lowest Sense; for the Childish repetition of the same Note cannot be call'd *Musick;* such Instances are infinite, as in the forecited Poem.

| | | |
|---|---|---|
| *Épris* | *Trophée* | *caché;* |
| *Mépris* | *Orphée* | *cherché.* |

Mr. *Boileau* himself has a great deal of this μονοτονία, not by his own neglect, but purely by the faultiness and poverty of the *French* Tongue. Mr. *F.* at last goes into the *excessive Paradoxes*
10 of Mr. *Perrault,* and boasts of the vast number of their Excellent Songs, preferring them to the *Greek* and *Latin.* But an ancient Writer of as good Credit, has assur'd us, that Seven Lives would hardly suffice to read over the *Greek Odes;* but a few Weeks would be sufficient, if a Man were so very idle as to read over all the *French.* In the mean time I should be very glad to see a Catalogue of but fifty of theirs with

*Exact propriety of word and thought.

Notwithstanding all the high Encomiums, and mutual Gratulations which they give one another; (for I am far from censuring
20 the whole of that Illustrious Society, to which the Learned World is much oblig'd) after all those Golden Dreams at the *Louvre,* that their Pieces will be as much valu'd ten, or twelve Ages hence, as the ancient *Greek,* or *Roman,* I can no more get it into my head that they will last so long, than I could believe the Learned Dr. *H——k* [of the *Royal Society,*] if he should pretend to shew me a *Butterflye* that had liv'd a *thousand Winters.*

---

* Essay of Poetry.

---

5   *Épris Trophée*] 'Epris Trophee F1–2.
6   *Mépris Orphée*] Mepris Orphee F1–2.
10   Excellent] F2; *Excelleut* F1.
21   *Louvre*] L'Ouvre F1–2.
22   their] F2; *Modern* F1.
25   *H——k*] H——K. F1–2.

When Mr. *F.* wrote his *Eclogues,* he was so far from equalling *Virgil,* or *Theocritus,* that he had some pains to take before he could understand in what the principal *Beauty,* and *Graces* of their Writings do consist.

---

4   consist.] *F1 appends a quotation*: Cum mortuis non nisi larvæ luctantur.

## Commendatory Poems

### To Mr. Dryden, *on his Excellent Translation*
### *of* VIRGIL.

WHEN e're Great *VIRGIL*'s lofty Verse I see,
    The Pompous Scene Charms my admiring Eye:
    There different Beauties in perfection meet;
The Thoughts as proper, as the Numbers sweet:
And When wild Fancy mounts a daring height,
Judgment steps in, and moderates her flight.
Wisely he manages his Wealthy Store,
Still says enough, and yet implies still more:
For tho' the weighty Sense be closely wrought,
10 The Reader's left t'improve the pleasing thought.

    Hence we despair'd to see an *English* dress
Should e're his Nervous Energy express;
For who could that in fetter'd Rhyme inclose,
Which without loss can scarce be told in Prose?

    But you, Great Sir, his Manly Genius raise;
And make your Copy share an equal praise.
O how I see thee in soft Scenes of Love,
Renew those Passions he alone could move!
Here *Cupid*'s Charms are with new Art exprest,
20 And pale *Eliza* leaves her peaceful rest:
Leaves her *Elysium,* as if glad to live,  ⎫
To Love, and Wish, to Sigh, Despair and Grieve, ⎬
And Die again for him that would again deceive. ⎭
Nor does the Mighty *Trojan* less appear
Than *Mars* himself amidst the storms of War.
Now his fierce Eyes with double fury glow,
And a new dread attends th' impending blow:

11    *English*] English F1–2.
21    *Elysium*] *Elisium* F1; *Elizium* F2.

*Page numbers adjusted to our text. Also:* 54 Mrs. Dorothy Brownlow] ~. Ann ~
F1–2.    68 Christopher Knight] John ~ F1–2.

## The Names of the second SUBSCRIBERS.

A.
*Lord* Ashley.
*Sir* James Ash, *Bar.*
*Sir* Francis Andrew, *Bar.*
Charles Adderley, *Esq;*
*Mrs.* Ann Ash.
Edw. Ash *Esq;*
*Mr.* Francis Atterbury.
Sam. Atkins, *Esq;*
Tho. Austen *Esq;*
Ro. Austen, *Esq;*

B.
*Earl of* Bullingbrook.
*Sir* Ed. Bettenson, *Bar.*
*Sir* Tho. Pope Blount, *Bar.*
*Sir* John Bolles.
*Sir* Will. Bowes.
Will. Blathwayt, *Esq; Secretary of War.*
Will. Barlow, *Esq;*
Peregrine Bertye, *Esq;*
Will. Bridgman, *Esq;*
Orlando Bridgman, *Esq;*
Will. Bridges, *Esq;*
Char. Bloodworth, *Esq;*
*The Hon.* Henry Boyl, *Esq;*
Rich. Boyl, *Esq;*
Chidley Brook, *Esq;*
Will. Bromley, *Esq; of Warwickshire.*
Mich. Bruneau, *Esq;*
Tho. Bulkley, *Esq;*
Theoph. Butler, *Esq;*
*Capt.* John Berkeley.
*Mr.* Jo. Bowes, *Prebend of Durham.*
*Mr.* Jeremiah Ball.
*Mr.* John Ball.
*Mr.* Richard Banks.
*Mrs.* Elizabeth Barry.

*Mr.* Beckford.
*Mr.* Tho. Betterton.
*Mrs.* Catharine Blount.
*Mr.* Bond.
*Mr.* Bond.
*Mrs.* Ann Bracegirdle.
*Mr.* Samuel Brockenborough.
*Mrs.* Elizabeth Brown.
*Mr.* Moses Bruche.
*Mr.* Lancelton Burton.

C.
*Earl of* Clarendon.
*Lord* Hen. Cavendish.
*Lord* Clifford.
*Lord* Coningsby.
*Lord* Cutts.
*Lady* Chudleigh *of the West.*
*The Hon.* Char. Cornwallis, *Son to the Lord* Cornwallis.
*Sir* Walt. Clarges, *Bar.*
*Sir* Ro. Cotton.
*Sir* Will. Cooper.
*The Ho.* Will. Cheyney.
James Calthorp, *Esq;*
Charles Chamberlayn, *Esq;*
Edmond Clifford, *Esq;*
Charles Cocks, *Esq;*
Tho. Coel, *Esq;*
Tho. Coke, *Esq;*
Hugh Colville, *Esq;*
Jo. Crawley, *Esq;*
Courtney Crocker, *Esq;*
Henry Curwyn, *Esq;*
*Capt.* James Conoway.
*Mr.* Will. Claret.
*Mr.* John Clancy.
*Mr.* Will. Congreve.
*Mr.* Henry Cook.
*Mr.* Will. Cooper.
*Mrs.* Elizabeth Creed.

D.
*Dutchess of* Devonshire.
Paul Docmenique, *Esq;*
Mountague Drake, *Esq;*
Will. Draper, *Esq;*
*Mr.* Mich. Dahl.
*Mr.* Davenport.
*Mr.* Will. Delawn.
*Mrs.* Dorothy Draycot.
*Mr.* Edward Dryden.

E.
*Earl of* Essex.
*Sir* Edw. Ernle.
Will. Elson, *Esq;*
Tho. Elyot, *Esq;*
Thomas Earl, *Major General.*

F.
*Sir* Edm. Fettiplace, *Bar.*
*Sir* Will. Forester.
*Sir* James Forbys.
*Lady* Mary Fenwick.
*The Ho.* Colon. Finch.
*The Ho. Doctour* Finch.
*The Ho.* Will. Fielding.
Rich. Francklin, *Postmaster, Esq;*
Charles Fergesen, *Esq; Com. of the Navy.*
*Doctor* Fuller, *D. of Lincoln.*
Henry Farmer, *Esq;*
Tho. Finch, *Esq;*
Tho. Frewin, *Esq;*
*Mr.* George Finch.

G.
*Sir* Bevill Granville, *Bar.*
Oliver St. George, *Esq;*
Tho. Gifford, *Esq;*
Rich. Goulston, *Esq;*
Richard Graham, *Esq;*
Fergus Grahme, *Esq;*
Will. Grove, *Esq;*

Dr. Garth, *M. D.*
*Mr.* George Goulding.
*Mr.* Grinlin Guibbons.

H.

*Lord* Archibald Hamilton.
*Lord* Hide.
*Sir* Richard Haddock.
*Sir* Christop. Hales, *Bar.*
*Sir* Tho. Hussey.
Rob. Harley, *Esq;*
Rob. Henley, *Esq;*
   *Memb. of Parl.*
Will. Hewer, *Esq;*
Roger Hewett, *Esq;*
He. Heveningham, *Esq;*
John Holdworthy, *Esq;*
Matt. Holdworthy, *Esq;*
Nath. Hornby, *Esq;*
*The Ho.* Bern. Howard.
Craven Howard *Esq;*
Mansel Howe, *Esq;*
Sam. Hunter, *Esq;*
*Mr.* Edward Hastwell.
*Mr.* Nich. Hawksmore.
*Mr.* Whitfeild Hayter.
*Mr.* Peter Henriques.
*Mr.* Ro. Huckwell.

J.

John James, *Esq;*
William Jenkins, *Esq;*
Sam. Jones, *Esq;*
*Mr.* Edw. Jefferyes.

K.

Jos. Keally, *Esq;*
*Coll.* James Kendall.
*Dr.* Knipe.
*Mr.* Mich. Kinkead.

L.

*Sir* Berkeley Lucy. *Ba.*
*Lady* Jane Leveson-Gower.
Tho. Langley, *Esq;*
Patrick Lamb, *Esq;*
Will. Latton, *Esq;*
James Long *of Draycot, Esq;*
Will. Lownds, *Esq;*
Dennis Lydal, *Esq;*

*Mr.* Char. Longueville.

M.

Char. Mannours, *Esq;*
Tho. Mansell, *Esq;*
Bussy Mansel, *Esq;*
Will. Martyn, *Esq;*
Henry Maxwell, *Esq;*
Charles Mein, *Esq;*
Rich. Minshul, *Esq;*
Ro. Molesworth, *Esq;*
*The Ho.* Henry Mordaunt, *Esq;*
George Moult, *Esq;*
Christoph. Mountague. *Esq;*
Walter Moyl, *Esq;*
*Mr.* Charles Marbury.
*Mr.* Christoph. Metcalf.
*Mrs.* Monneux.

N.

*Lord* Norris.
Henry Nevile, *Esq;*
William Norris, *Esq;*
*Mr.* William Nicoll.

O.

Ro. Orme, *Esq;*
*Dr.* Oliver, *M. D.*
*Mr.* Mich. Owen.

P.

*The Right Hon.* Charles *Earl of Peterborough.*
*Sir* Henry Peachy, *Bar.*
*Sir* John Phillips, *Bar.*
*Sir* John Pykering *Bar.*
*Sir* John Parsons,
Ro. Palmer, *Esq;*
Guy Palmes, *Esq;*
Ben. Parry, *Esq;*
Sam. Pepys, *Esq;*
James Petre, *Esq;*
Will. Peysley, *Esq;*
Craven Peyton, *Esq;*
John Pitts, *Esq;*
Will. Plowden *of Plowden, Esq;*
*Mr.* Theoph. Pykering, *Prebend. of Durham.*
*Coll.* Will. Parsons.
*Captain* Phillips.

*Captain* Pitts.
*Mr.* Daniel Peck.

R.

*Dutchess of* Richmond.
*Earl of* Radnor.
*Lord* Ranelagh.
Tho. Rawlins, *Esq;*
Will. Rider, *Esq;*
Francis Roberts, *Esq;*
*Mr.* Rose.

S.

*Lord* Spencer.
*Sir* Tho. Skipwith, *Bar.*
*Sir* John Seymour.
*Sir* Char. Skrimpshire.
J. Scroop *of Danby, Esq;*
Ralph. Sheldon, *Com. Warw. Esq;*
Edw. Sheldon, *Esq;*
John Smith, *Esq;*
James Sothern, *Esq;*
*The Ho.* James Stanley, *Esq;*
Ro. Stopford, *Esq;*
*The Hon. Major Gen.* Edw. Sackville.
*Col.* J. Stanhope.
*Col.* Strangways.
*Mr.* James Seamer.
*Mr.* William Seeks.
*Mr.* Joseph Sherwood.
*Mr.* Laurence Smith.
*Mr.* Tho. Southern.
*Mr.* Paris Slaughter.
*Mr.* Lancelot Stepney.

T.

*Sir* John Trevillion, *Bar.*
*Sir* Edm. Turner.
Henry Temple, *Esq;*
Ashburnam Toll, *Esq;*
Sam. Travers, *Esq;*
John Tucker, *Esq;*
*Maj. Gen.* Charles Trelawney.
*Maj. Gen.* Trelawney.
*Col.* John Tidcomb.
*Col.* Trelawney.
*Mr.* George Townsend.
*Mr.* Tho. Tyldesley.

*Mr.* Tyndall.

V.

John Verney, *Esq;*
Henry Vernon, *Esq;*
James Vernon, *Esq;*

W.

*Ld. Marquiss of* Win-
chester.

*Earl of* Weymouth.
*Lady* Windham.
*Sir* John Walter, *Bar.*
*Sir* John Woodhouse, *B.*
*Sir* Francis Windham.
James Ward, *Esq;*
William Wardour, *Jun.*
*Esq;*

Will. Welby, *Esq;*
Will. Weld, *Esq;*
Th. Brome Whorwood,
*Esq;*
Salw. Winnington, *Esq;*
*Col.* Cornelius Wood.
*Mrs.* Mary Walter.
*Mr.* Leonard Wessel.

---

*Sir* James Ash, *Bar.*] *twice in F1–2.*     *Dr.* Garth] ∼. Gath F1–2.

To the Right Hon.ble John Lord Sommers
Baron of Evesham L.d High Chancell.r
of England &c.

# *VIRGIL'S PASTORALS*

## *The First Pastoral*
## *or, Tityrus and Meliboeus*

### THE ARGUMENT.

*The Occasion of the First Pastoral was this.* When Augustus *had setled himself in the* Roman *Empire, that he might reward his* Veteran *Troops for their past Service, he distributed among 'em all the Lands that lay about* Cremona *and* Mantua: *turning out the right Owners for having sided with his Enemies.* Virgil *was a Sufferer among the rest; who afterwards recover'd his Estate by* Mæcenas's *Intercession, and as an Instance of his Gratitude compos'd the following Pastoral, where he sets out his own Good Fortune in the Person of* Tityrus, *and the Calamities of his* Mantuan *Neighbours in the Character of* Meliboeus.

### *MELIBŒUS.*

BENEATH the Shade which Beechen Boughs diffuse,
You *Tity'rus* entertain your Silvan Muse:
Round the wide World in Banishment we rome,
Forc'd from our pleasing Fields and Native Home:
While stretch'd at Ease you sing your happy loves:
And *Amarillis* fills the shady Groves.

### *TITYRUS.*

These Blessings, Friend, a Deity bestow'd:
For never can I deem him less than God.
The tender Firstlings of my Woolly breed
10 Shall on his holy Altar often bleed.
He gave my Kine to graze the Flowry Plain:
And to my Pipe renew'd the Rural Strain.

---

7   Mæcenas's] Mecænas's F1a–b, F2.
10   Meliboeus] F1b, F2; Melibæus F1a.

### MELIBŒUS.

I envy not your Fortune, but admire,
That while the raging Sword and wastful Fire
Destroy the wretched Neighbourhood around,
No Hostile Arms approach your happy ground.
Far diff'rent is my Fate: my feeble Goats
With pains I drive from their forsaken Cotes.
And this you see I scarcely drag along,
20 Who yeaning on the Rocks has left her Young;
(The Hope and Promise of my failing Fold:)
My Loss by dire Portents the Gods foretold:
For had I not been blind I might have seen
Yon riven Oak, the fairest of the Green,
And the hoarse Raven, on the blasted Bough,
By croaking from the left presag'd the coming Blow.
But tell me, *Tityrus,* what Heav'nly Power
Preserv'd your Fortunes in that fatal Hour?

### TITYRUS.

Fool that I was, I thought Imperial *Rome*　﹀
30 Like *Mantua,* where on Market-days we come,　﹜
And thether drive our tender Lambs from home.﹀
So Kids and Whelps their Syres and Dams express:
And so the Great I measur'd by the Less.
But Country Towns, compar'd with her, appear
Like Shrubs, when lofty Cypresses are near.

### MELIBŒUS.

What Great Occasion call'd you hence to *Rome?*

---

22　Loss] F1a, F2; loss F1b.
26　By croaking from the left] F2; With frequent Crokes F1a–b.
36　Great] F1a, F2; great F1b.

*TITYRUS.*

Freedom, which came at length, tho' slow to come:
Nor did my Search of Liberty begin,
Till my black Hairs were chang'd upon my Chin.
40 Nor *Amarillis* wou'd vouchsafe a look,
Till *Galatea*'s meaner bonds I broke.
Till then a helpless, hopeless, homely Swain,
I sought not Freedom, nor aspir'd to Gain:
Tho' many a Victim from my Folds was bought,
And many a Cheese to Country Markets brought,
Yet all the little that I got, I spent,
And still return'd as empty as I went.

*MELIBŒUS.*

We stood amaz'd to see your Mistress mourn;
Unknowing that she pin'd for your return:
50 We wonder'd why she kept her Fruit so long,
For whom so late th' ungather'd Apples hung.
But now the Wonder ceases, since I see
She kept them only, *Tityrus,* for thee.
For thee the bubling Springs appear'd to mourn,
And whisp'ring Pines made vows for thy return.

*TITYRUS.*

What shou'd I do? while here I was enchain'd,
No glimpse of Godlike Liberty remain'd:
Nor cou'd I hope in any place, but there,
To find a God so present to my Pray'r.
60 There first the Youth of Heav'nly Birth I view'd;
For whom our Monthly Victims are renew'd.
He heard my Vows, and graciously decreed
My Grounds to be restor'd, my former Flocks to feed.

41  *Galatea's*] F1a, F2; *Galeatea's* F1b.   43  Freedom] F1a; freedom F1b, F2.
50  Fruit] F1a, F2; ~, F1b.   56  do?] ~! F1a–b, F2.
57  remain'd:] ~? F1a–b, F2.

*MELIBŒUS.*

O Fortunate Old Man! whose Farm remains ⎫
For you sufficient, and requites your pains, ⎬
Tho' Rushes overspread the Neighb'ring Plains: ⎭
Tho' here the Marshy Grounds approach your Fields,
And there the Soyl a Stony Harvest yields.
Your teeming Ewes shall no strange Meadows try,
70 Nor fear a Rott from tainted Company.
Behold yon bord'ring Fence of Sallow Trees
Is fraught with Flow'rs, the Flow'rs are fraught with Bees:
The buisie Bees with a soft murm'ring Strain
Invite to gentle sleep the lab'ring Swain.
While from the Neighb'ring Rock, with rural Songs,
The Pruner's Voice the pleasing Dream prolongs;
Stock-Doves and Turtles tell their Am'rous pain,
And from the lofty Elms of Love complain.

*TITYRUS.*

Th' Inhabitants of Seas and Skies shall change,
80 And Fish on shoar and Stags in Air shall range,
The banish'd *Parthian* dwell on *Arar's* brink,
And the blue *German* shall the *Tigris* drink:
E're I, forsaking Gratitude and Truth,
Forget the Figure of that Godlike Youth.

*MELIBŒUS.*

But we must beg our Bread in Climes unknown,
Beneath the scorching or the freezing Zone.
And some to far *Oaxis* shall be sold;
Or try the *Lybian* Heat, or *Scythian* Cold:
The rest among the *Britains* be confin'd;

---

66  Plains:] ~. F1a–b, F2.          68  Stony] F1a, F2; stony F1b.
75  rural] F1a, F2; Rural F1b.      88  Cold:] ~. F1a–b, F2.
89  *Britains*] F1a, F2; *Britans* F1b.

90 A Race of Men from all the World dis-join'd.
O must the wretched Exiles ever mourn,
Nor after length of rowling Years return?
Are we condemn'd by Fates unjust Decree,
No more our Houses and our Homes to see?
Or shall we mount again the Rural Throne,
And rule the Country Kingdoms, once our own?
Did we for these Barbarians plant and sow,
On these, on these, our happy Fields bestow?
Good Heav'n what dire Effects from Civil Discord flow!
100 Now let me graff my Pears, and prune the Vine;
The Fruit is theirs, the Labour only mine.
Farewel my Pastures, my Paternal Stock,
My fruitful Fields, and my more fruitful Flock!
No more, my Goats, shall I behold you climb
The steepy Cliffs, or crop the flowry Thyme!
No more, extended in the Grot below,
Shall see you browzing on the Mountain's brow
The prickly Shrubs; and after on the bare,
Lean down the deep Abyss, and hang in Air.
110 No more my Sheep shall sip the Morning Dew;
No more my Song shall please the Rural Crue:
Adieu, my tuneful Pipe! and all the World adieu!


*TITYRUS.*

This Night, at least, with me forget your Care;
Chesnuts and Curds and Cream shall be your fare:
The Carpet-ground shall be with Leaves o'respread;
And Boughs shall weave a Cov'ring for your Head.
For see yon sunny Hill the Shade extends;
And curling Smoke from Cottages ascends.

---

92  rowling] F1a, F2; rowl'ing F1b.          93  condemn'd] F1a, F2; condem'd F1b.
96  own?] ~! F1a–b, F2.                      99  Heav'n] F1a, F2; ~, F1b.
105  flowry] F1a, F2; flow'ry F1b.           109  deep] F1a, F2; Deep F1b.

Sculp: Ven: W: Hollar fecit 1668

To the Right Hon:ble                    Thomas Earle
of Pembroke                           and Montgomery,
     Lord                              Privy Seale &c:

Past: 2.

# The Second Pastoral
## or, Alexis

THE ARGUMENT.

*The Commentators can by no means agree on the Person of
Alexis, but are all of opinion that some Beautiful Youth is meant
by him, to whom* Virgil *here makes Love; in* Corydon's *Language
and Simplicity. His way of Courtship is wholly Pastoral: He com-
plains of the Boys Coyness, recommends himself for his Beauty
and Skill in Piping; invites the Youth into the Country, where
he promises him the Diversions of the Place; with a suitable
Present of Nuts and Apples: But when he finds nothing will pre-
vail, he resolves to quit his troublesome Amour, and betake him-
self again to his former Business.*

YOUNG *Corydon,* th' unhappy Shepherd Swain,
    The fair *Alexis* lov'd, but lov'd in vain:
    And underneath the Beechen Shade, alone,
Thus to the Woods and Mountains made his moan.
Is this, unkind *Alexis,* my reward,
And must I die unpitied, and unheard?
Now the green Lizard in the Grove is laid,
The Sheep enjoy the coolness of the Shade;
And *Thestilis* wild Thime and Garlick beats
10 For Harvest Hinds, o'respent with Toyl and Heats:
While in the scorching Sun I trace in vain
Thy flying footsteps o're the burning plain.
The creaking Locusts with my Voice conspire,
They fry'd with Heat, and I with fierce Desire.
How much more easie was it to sustain
Proud *Amarillis,* and her haughty Reign,
The Scorns of Young *Menalcas,* once my care,
Tho' he was black, and thou art Heav'nly fair.
Trust not too much to that enchanting Face;

---

6  unpityed] F1a, F2; unpitied F1b.     9  Garlick] F1a, F2; Garlike F1b.
12  plain] F1a, F2; Plain F1b.

20 Beauty's a Charm, but soon the Charm will pass:
   White Lillies lie neglected on the Plain,
   While dusky Hyacinths for use remain.
   My Passion is thy Scorn; nor wilt thou know
   What Wealth I have, what Gifts I can bestow:
   What Stores my Dairies and my Folds contain;
   A thousand Lambs that wander on the Plain:
   New Milk that all the Winter never fails,
   And all the Summer overflows the Pails:
   *Amphion* sung not sweeter to his Herd,
30 When summon'd Stones the *Theban* Turrets rear'd.
   Nor am I so deform'd; for late I stood
   Upon the Margin of the briny Flood:
   The Winds were still, and if the Glass be true,
   With *Daphnis* I may vie, tho' judg'd by you.
   O leave the noisie Town, O come and see
   Our Country Cotts, and live content with me!
   To wound the Flying Deer, and from their Cotes
   With me to drive a-field, the browzing Goats:
   To pipe and sing, and in our Country Strain
40 To Copy, or perhaps contend with *Pan*.
   *Pan* taught to joyn with Wax unequal Reeds,
   *Pan* loves the Shepherds, and their Flocks he feeds:
   Nor scorn the Pipe; *Amyntas,* to be taught,
   With all his Kisses would my Skill have bought.
   Of seven smooth Joynts a mellow Pipe I have,
   Which with his dying Breath *Damœtas* gave:
   And said, This, *Corydon,* I leave to thee;
   For only thou deserv'st it after me.
   His Eyes *Amyntas* durst not upward lift,
50 For much he grudg'd the Praise, but more the Gift.
   Besides two Kids that in the Valley stray'd,
   I found by chance, and to my fold convey'd:
   They drein two bagging Udders every day;
   And these shall be Companions of thy Play:

38  a-field] F1a, F2; a-Field F1b.          43  scorn] F1 *errata,* F2; scorns F1a–b.
45  Joynts] F1a, F2; joints F1b.            53  two] F1a, F2; to F1b.
54  Play:] ∼. F1a–b, F2.

Both fleck'd with white, the true *Arcadian* Strain,
Which *Thestilis* had often beg'd in vain:
And she shall have them, if again she sues,
Since you the Giver and the Gift refuse.
Come to my longing Arms, my lovely care,
60 And take the Presents which the Nymphs prepare.
White Lillies in full Canisters they bring,
With all the Glories of the Purple Spring:
The Daughters of the Flood have search'd the Mead
For Violets pale, and cropt the Poppy's Head:
The Short *Narcissus* and fair Daffodil,
Pancies to please the Sight, and Cassia sweet to smell:
And sct soft Hyacinths with Iron blue,
To shade marsh Marigolds of shining Hue:
Some bound in Order, others loosely strow'd,
70 To dress thy Bow'r, and trim thy new Abode.
My self will search our planted Grounds at home,
For downy Peaches and the glossie Plum:
And thrash the Chesnuts in the Neighb'ring Grove,
Such as my *Amarillis* us'd to love.
The Laurel and the Myrtle sweets agree;
And both in Nosegays shall be bound for thee.
Ah, *Corydon,* ah poor unhappy Swain,
*Alexis* will thy homely Gifts disdain:
Nor, shouldst thou offer all thy little Store,
80 Will rich *Iolas* yield, but offer more.
What have I done, to name that wealthy Swain?
So powerful are his Presents, mine so mean!
The Boar amidst my Crystal Streams I bring;
And Southern Winds to blast my flowry Spring.
Ah cruel Creature, whom dost thou despise?
The Gods to live in Woods have left the Skies.
And Godlike *Paris* in th' *Idean* Grove,
To *Priam's* Wealth prefer'd *Oenone's* Love.
In Cities which she built, let *Pallas* Reign;

62  Spring:] $\sim$, F1a–b, F2.
79  shouldst] F1a, F2; should'st F1b.
84  flowry] F1a, F2; flow'ry F1b.

68  Hue:] $\sim$. F1a–b, F2.
81  Swain?] $\sim$, F1a–b, F2.
85  Ah] F1a, F2; $\sim$, F1b.

90  Tow'rs are for Gods, but Forrests for the Swain.
The greedy Lyoness the Wolf pursues,
The Wolf the Kid, the wanton Kid the Browze:
*Alexis* thou art chas'd by *Corydon;*
All follow sev'ral Games, and each his own.
See from afar the Fields no longer smoke,
The sweating Steers unharnass'd from the Yoke,
Bring, as in Triumph, back the crooked Plough;
The Shadows lengthen as the Sun goes Low.
Cool Breezes now the raging Heats remove;
100  Ah, cruel Heaven! that made no Cure for Love!
I wish for balmy Sleep, but wish in vain:
Love has no bounds in Pleasure, or in Pain.
What frenzy, Shepherd, has thy Soul possess'd?
Thy Vinyard lies half prun'd, and half undress'd.
Quench, *Corydon,* thy long unanswer'd fire:
Mind what the common wants of Life require.
On willow Twigs employ thy weaving care:
And find an easier Love, tho' not so fair.

---

103  possess'd?] ∼, F1a–b, F2.

E. Clern. in.    P. mbart sculpsit. londi.

To the Right Hon:ble Charles Sackvill
Earle of Dorsett & Midlesex Lord
Chamberlain of his Maj:ts houshould &c

Past: 3.

# The Third Pastoral
## or, Palæmon

Menalcas, Damætas, Palæmon.

### THE ARGUMENT.

Damætas *and* Menalcas, *after some smart strokes of Country Railery, resolve to try who has the most Skill at a Song; and accordingly make their Neighbour* Palæmon *Judge of their Performances: Who, after a full hearing of both Parties, declares himself unfit for the Decision of so weighty a Controversie, and leaves the Victory undetermin'd.*

### MENALCAS.

Ho, Swain, what Shepherd owns those ragged Sheep?

### DAMÆTAS.

*Ægon*'s they are, he gave 'em me to keep.

### MENALCAS.

Unhappy Sheep of an Unhappy Swain,   ⎫
While he *Neæra* courts, but courts in vain,   ⎬
And fears that I the Damsel shall obtain;   ⎭
Thou, Varlet, dost thy Master's gains devour:
Thou milk'st his Ewes, and often twice an hour;
Of Grass and Fodder thou defraud'st the Dams:
And of their Mothers Duggs the starving Lambs.

### DAMÆTAS.

10    Good words, young Catamite, at least to Men:
We know who did your Business, how, and when:

---

1   Swain] F2; Groom F1.      11   when:] ~. F1–2.

Instructed in his Trade the Lab'ring Swain,
And when to reap, and when to sowe the Grain?

### DAMÆTAS.

And I have two, to match your pair, at home;
The Wood the same, from the same Hand they come:
The kimbo Handles seem with Bears-foot carv'd;
And never yet to Table have been serv'd:
Where *Orpheus* on his Lyre laments his Love,
70 With Beasts encompass'd, and a dancing Grove:
But these, nor all the Proffers you can make,
Are worth the Heifar which I set to stake.

### MENALCAS.

No more delays, vain Boaster, but begin:
I prophecy before-hand I shall win.
*Palæmon* shall be Judge how ill you rhime,
I'll teach you how to brag another time.

### DAMÆTAS.

Rhymer come on, and do the worst you can:
I fear not you, nor yet a better Man.
With Silence, Neighbour, and Attention wait:
80 For 'tis a business of a high Debate.

### PALÆMON.

Sing then; the Shade affords a proper place;
The Trees are cloath'd with Leaves, the Fields with Grass;
The Blossoms blow; the Birds on bushes sing;
And Nature has accomplish'd all the Spring.
The Challenge to *Damætas* shall belong,
*Menalcas* shall sustain his under Song:
Each in his turn your tuneful numbers bring;
By turns the tuneful Muses love to sing.

88   By] F2; In F1.

### DAMÆTAS.

From the great Father of the Gods above
90 My Muse begins; for all is full of *Jove;*
To *Jove* the care of Heav'n and Earth belongs;
My Flocks he blesses, and he loves my Songs.

### MENALCAS.

Me *Phœbus* loves; for He my Muse inspires;
And in her Songs, the warmth he gave, requires.
For him, the God of Shepherds and their Sheep,
My blushing Hyacinths, and my Bays I keep.

### DAMÆTAS.

My *Phillis* me with pelted Apples plyes; )
Then tripping to the Woods the Wanton hies: }
And wishes to be seen, before she flies. )

### MENALCAS.

100 But fair *Amyntas* comes unask'd to me; )
And offers Love; and sits upon my knee: }
Not *Delia* to my Dogs is known so well as he. )

### DAMÆTAS.

To the dear Mistress of my Love-sick Mind,
Her Swain a pretty Present has design'd:
I saw two Stock-doves billing, and e're long
Will take the Nest, and Hers shall be the Young.

### MENALCAS.

Ten ruddy Wildings in the Wood I found,
And stood on tip-toes, reaching from the ground;

---

97 My *Phillis* me with pelted Apples] F2 (*Phyllis* Me); With pelted Fruit, me *Galatea* F1.

### DAMÆTAS.

150    From Rivers drive the Kids, and sling your Hook;
Anon I'll wash 'em in the shallow Brook.


### MENALCAS.

To fold, my Flock; when Milk is dry'd with heat,
In vain the Milk-maid tugs an empty Teat.


### DAMÆTAS.

How lank my Bulls from plenteous pasture come!
But Love that drains the Herd, destroys the Groom.


### MENALCAS.

My Flocks are free from Love; yet look so thin,
Their bones are barely cover'd with their Skin.
What magick has bewitch'd the woolly Dams,
And what ill Eyes beheld the tender Lambs?


### DAMÆTAS.

160    Say, where the round of Heav'n, which all contains, ⎫
To three short Ells on Earth our sight restrains: ⎬
Tell that, and rise a *Phœbus* for thy pains. ⎭


### MENALCAS.

Nay tell me first, in what new Region springs
A Flow'r, that bears inscrib'd the names of Kings:
And thou shalt gain a Present as Divine
As *Phœbus* self; for *Phillis* shall be thine.

*PALÆMON.*

So nice a diff'rence in your Singing lyes,
That both have won, or both deserv'd the Prize.
Rest equal happy both; and all who prove
170 The bitter Sweets, and pleasing Pains of Love.
Now dam the Ditches, and the Floods restrain:
Their moisture has already drench'd the Plain.

F. Clein inv: Lombart Sculpsit London:

To the Right Hon.<sup>ble</sup>                    Lionel Cranfeild
Sackvill Lord Buck-                    hurst, eldest son of
Charles Earle of                    Dorsett & Midlesex.

Pag: 4

## *The Fourth Pastoral*
## *or, Pollio*

THE ARGUMENT.

*The Poet celebrates the Birth-day of* Saloninus, *the Son of* Pollio, *born in the Consulship of his Father, after the taking of* Salonæ, *a City in* Dalmatia. *Many of the Verses are translated from one of the Sybils, who prophesie of our Saviour's Birth.*

S ICILIAN Muse begin a loftier strain!
    Though lowly Shrubs and Trees that shade the Plain,
    Delight not all; *Sicilian* Muse, prepare
To make the vocal Woods deserve a Consul's care.
The last great Age, foretold by sacred Rhymes,
Renews its finish'd Course, *Saturnian* times
Rowl round again, and mighty years, begun
From their first Orb, in radiant Circles run.
The base degenerate Iron-off-spring ends;
10 A golden Progeny from Heav'n descends;
O chast *Lucina* speed the Mother's pains,
And haste the glorious Birth; thy own *Apollo* reigns!
The lovely Boy, with his auspicious Face,
Shall *Pollio*'s Consulship and Triumph grace;
Majestick Months set out with him to their appointed Race.
The Father banish'd Virtue shall restore,
And Crimes shall threat the guilty world no more.
The Son shall lead the life of Gods, and be
By Gods and Heroes seen, and Gods and Heroes see.
20 The jarring Nations he in peace shall bind,
And with paternal Virtues rule Mankind.
Unbidden Earth shall wreathing Ivy bring,
And fragrant Herbs (the promises of Spring)
As her first Off'rings to her Infant King.

---

3 prepare] F2; pepare F1; *(see collation for different text in* O1–2*).*

The Goats with strutting Dugs shall homeward speed,
And lowing Herds, secure from Lyons feed.
His Cradle shall with rising Flow'rs be crown'd;
The Serpents Brood shall die: the sacred ground
Shall Weeds and pois'nous Plants refuse to bear,
30  Each common Bush shall *Syrian* Roses wear.
But when Heroick Verse his Youth shall raise,
And form it to Hereditary Praise;
Unlabour'd Harvests shall the Fields adorn,
And cluster'd Grapes shall blush on every Thorn.
The knotted Oaks shall show'rs of Honey weep,
And through the Matted Grass the liquid Gold shall creep.
Yet, of old Fraud some footsteps shall remain,
The Merchant still shall plough the deep for gain:
Great Cities shall with Walls be compass'd round;
40  And sharpen'd Shares shall vex the fruitful ground.
Another *Tiphys* shall new Seas explore,
Another *Argos* land the Chiefs, upon th' *Iberian* Shore:
Another *Helen* other Wars create,
And great *Achilles* urge the *Trojan* Fate:
But when to ripen'd Man-hood he shall grow,
The greedy Sailer shall the Seas forego;
No Keel shall cut the Waves for foreign Ware;
For every Soil shall every Product bear.
The labouring Hind his Oxen shall disjoyn,
50  No Plow shall hurt the Glebe, no Pruning-hook the Vine:
Nor Wooll shall in dissembled Colours shine.
But the luxurious Father of the Fold,
With native Purple, or unborrow'd Gold,
Beneath his pompous Fleece shall proudly sweat:
And under *Tyrian* Robes the Lamb shall bleat.
The Fates, when they this happy Web have spun,
Shall bless the sacred Clue, and bid it smoothly run.
Mature in years, to ready Honours move,
O of Cœlestial Seed! O foster Son of *Jove!*

---

36  Gold] O1–2, F1 *errata*, F2; Cold F1.    41  *Tiphys*] *Typhis* O1–2, F1–2.
42  Shore:] ~. F1–2; *different text in O1–2.*
57  Shall] O1–2, F2; shall F1.

60 See, lab'ring Nature calls thee to sustain
The nodding Frame of Heav'n, and Earth, and Main;
See to their Base restor'd, Earth, Seas, and Air,
And joyful Ages from behind, in crowding Ranks appear.
To sing thy Praise, wou'd Heav'n my breath prolong,
Infusing Spirits worthy such a Song;
Not *Thracian Orpheus* should transcend my Layes,
Nor *Linus* crown'd with never-fading Bayes:
Though each his Heav'nly Parent shou'd inspire;
The Muse instruct the Voice, and *Phœbus* tune the Lyre.
70 Shou'd *Pan* contend in Verse, and thou my Theme,
*Arcadian* Judges shou'd their God condemn.
Begin, auspicious Boy, to cast about
Thy Infant Eyes, and with a smile, thy Mother single out;
Thy Mother well deserves that short delight,
The nauseous Qualms of ten long Months and Travel to requite.
Then smile; the frowning Infant's Doom is read,
No God shall crown the Board, nor Goddess bless the Bed.

*MENALCAS.*

Begin you first; if either *Alcon*'s Praise,
Or dying *Phillis* have inspir'd your Lays:
If her you mourn, or *Codrus* you commend,
Begin, and *Tityrus* your Flock shall tend.

*MOPSUS.*

Or shall I rather the sad Verse repeat,
Which on the Beeches bark I lately writ?
I writ, and sung betwixt; now bring the Swain
20 Whose Voice you boast, and let him try the Strain.

*MENALCAS.*

Such as the Shrub to the tall Olive shows,
Or the pale Sallow to the blushing Rose;
Such is his Voice, if I can judge aright,
Compar'd to thine, in sweetness and in height.

*MOPSUS.*

No more, but sit and hear the promis'd Lay,
The gloomy Grotto makes a doubtful day.
The Nymphs about the breathless Body wait
Of *Daphnis,* and lament his cruel Fate.
The Trees and Floods were witness to their Tears:
30 At length the rumour reach'd his Mother's Ears.
The wretched Parent, with a pious haste,
Came running, and his lifeless Limbs embrac'd.
She sigh'd, she sob'd, and, furious with despair, ⎫
She rent her Garments, and she tore her Hair: ⎬
Accusing all the Gods and every Star. ⎭
The Swains forgot their Sheep, nor near the brink
Of running Waters brought their Herds to drink.

---

18  writ?] ∼: F1–2.

The thirsty Cattle, of themselves, abstain'd
From Water, and their grassy Fare disdain'd.
40 The death of *Daphnis* Woods and Hills deplore,⎫
They cast the sound to *Lybia*'s desart Shore;⎬
The *Lybian* Lyons hear, and hearing roar.⎭
Fierce Tygers *Daphnis* taught the Yoke to bear;
And first with curling Ivy dress'd the Spear:
*Daphnis* did Rites to *Bacchus* first ordain;
And holy Revels for his reeling Train.
As Vines the Trees, as Grapes the Vines adorn,
As Bulls the Herds, and Fields the Yellow Corn;
So bright a Splendor, so divine a Grace,
50 The glorious *Daphnis* cast on his illustrious Race.
When envious Fate the Godlike *Daphnis* took,
Our guardian Gods the Fields and Plains forsook:
*Pales* no longer swell'd the teeming Grain,
Nor *Phœbus* fed his Oxen on the Plain:
No fruitful Crop the sickly Fields return;
But Oats and Darnel choak the rising Corn.
And where the Vales with Violets once were crown'd,
Now knotty Burrs and Thorns disgrace the Ground.
Come, Shepherds, come, and strow with Leaves the Plain;
60 Such Funeral Rites your *Daphnis* did ordain.
With Cypress Boughs the Crystal Fountains hide,
And softly let the running Waters glide;
A lasting Monument to *Daphnis* raise;
With this Inscription to record his Praise,
*Daphnis,* the Fields Delight, the Shepherd's Love,
Renown'd on Earth, and deify'd above:
Whose Flock excell'd the fairest on the Plains,
But less than he himself surpass'd the Swains.


MENALCAS.

Oh Heavenly Poet! such thy Verse appears,
70 So sweet, so charming to my ravish'd Ears,

---

66   above:]  ∼. F1–2.

As to the weary Swain, with cares opprest,
Beneath the Silvan Shade, refreshing Rest:
As to the feavorish Travellor, when first
He finds a Crystal Stream to quench his thirst.
In singing, as in piping, you excell;
And scarce your Master could perform so well.
O fortunate young Man, at least your Lays
Are next to his, and claim the second Praise.
Such as they are my rural Songs I join,
80 To raise our *Daphnis* to the Pow'rs Divine;
For *Daphnis* was so good, to love what-e're was mine.

### MOPSUS.

How is my Soul with such a Promise rais'd!
For both the Boy was worthy to be prais'd,
And *Stimichon* has often made me long,
To hear, like him, so soft so sweet a Song.

### MENALCAS.

*Daphnis,* the Guest of Heav'n, with wondring Eyes,
Views in the Milky Way, the starry Skyes:
And far beneath him, from the shining Sphere,
Beholds the moving Clouds, and rolling Year.
90 For this, with chearful Cries the Woods resound;
The Purple Spring arrays the various ground:
The Nymphs and Shepherds dance; and *Pan* himself is Crown'd.
The Wolf no longer prowls for nightly Spoils,
Nor Birds the Sprindges fear, nor Stags the Toils:
For *Daphnis* reigns above; and deals from thence
His Mothers milder Beams, and peaceful Influence.
The Mountain tops unshorn, the Rocks rejoice;
The lowly Shrubs partake of Humane Voice.
Assenting Nature, with a gracious nod,
100 Proclaims him, and salutes the new-admitted God.

Be still propitious, ever good to thine:
Behold four hallow'd Altars we design;
And two to thee, and two to *Phœbus* rise;
On both are offer'd Annual Sacrifice.
The holy Priests, at each returning year,
Two Bowls of Milk, and two of Oil shall bear;
And I my self the Guests with friendly Bowls will chear.
Two Goblets will I crown with sparkling Wine,
The gen'rous Vintage of the *Chian* Vine;
110 These will I pour to thee, and make the Nectar thine.
In Winter shall the Genial Feast be made
Before the fire; by Summer in the shade.
*Damœtas* shall perform the Rites Divine;
And *Lictian Ægon* in the Song shall join.
*Alphesibœus,* tripping, shall advance;
And mimick Satyrs in his antick Dance.
When to the Nymphs our annual Rites we pay,
And when our Fields with Victims we survey:
While savage Boars delight in shady Woods,
120 And finny Fish inhabit in the Floods;
While Bees on Thime, and Locusts feed on Dew,
Thy gratful Swains these Honours shall renew.
Such Honours as we pay to Pow'rs Divine,
To *Bacchus* and to *Ceres,* shall be thine.
Such annual Honours shall be giv'n, and thou
Shalt hear, and shalt condemn thy Suppliants to their Vow.


    *MOPSUS.*

    What Present worth thy Verse can *Mopsus* find?
Not the soft Whispers of the Southern Wind,
That play through trembling Trees, delight me more;
130 Nor murm'ring Billows on the sounding Shore;
Nor winding Streams that through the Valley glide;
And the scarce cover'd Pebbles gently chide.

---

104  both are] F2; each is F1.      115  *Alphesibœus*] *Alphesibœus* F1–2.
127  find?] ~! F1–2.

*MENALCAS.*

Receive you first this tuneful Pipe; the same
That play'd my *Coridon*'s unhappy Flame.
The same that sung *Neæra*'s conqu'ring Eyes;
And, had the Judge been just, had won the Prize.

*MOPSUS.*

Accept from me this Sheephook in exchange,
The Handle Brass; the Knobs in equal range.
*Antigenes,* with Kisses, often try'd          )
140 To beg this Present, in his Beauty's Pride;  }
When Youth and Love are hard to be deny'd. )
But what I cou'd refuse, to his Request,
Is yours unask'd, for you deserve it best.

And now the setting Sun had warn'd the Swain
To call his counted Cattle from the Plain:
Yet still th' unweary'd Syre pursues the tuneful Strain:
Till unperceiv'd the Heav'ns with Stars were hung:
And sudden Night surpriz'd the yet unfinish'd Song.

123  Strain:] ∼. F1–2.

And a new Sun to the new World arose.
And Mists condens'd to Clouds obscure the Skie;
And Clouds dissolv'd, the thirsty Ground supply.
The rising Trees the lofty Mountains grace:
60  The lofty Mountains feed the Savage Race,
Yet few, and strangers, in th' unpeopl'd Place.
From thence the birth of Man the Song pursu'd,
And how the World was lost, and how renew'd:
The Reign of *Saturn,* and the Golden Age;
*Prometheus* Theft, and *Jove*'s avenging Rage:
The Cries of *Argonauts* for *Hylas* drown'd;
With whose repeated Name the Shoars resound:
Then mourns the madness of the *Cretan* Queen;
Happy for her if Herds had never been.
70  What fury, wretched Woman, seiz'd thy Breast?
The Maids of *Argos* (tho with rage possess'd,
Their imitated lowings fill'd the Grove)
Yet shun'd the guilt of thy prepost'rous Love:
Nor sought the Youthful Husband of the Herd,
Though lab'ring Yokes on their own Necks they fear'd;
And felt for budding Horns on their smooth forheads rear'd.
Ah, wretched Queen! you range the pathless Wood;
While on a flowry Bank he chaws the Cud:
Or sleeps in Shades, or thro' the Forest roves;
80  And roars with anguish for his absent Loves.
Ye Nymphs, with toils, his Forest-walk surround;
And trace his wandring Footsteps on the ground.
But, ah! perhaps my Passion he disdains;
And courts the milky Mothers of the Plains.
We search th' ungrateful Fugitive abroad;
While they at home sustain his happy load.

60  Race,] F2; ∼. F1.                    61  *added in* F2.
63  renew'd:] ∼. F1–2.                 65  Rage:] ∼. F1–2.
67  resound:] ∼. F1–2.                70  Breast?] ∼! F1–2.
73  thy] F1 *errata,* F2; this F1.    73  Love:] ∼. F1–2.
74  Herd,] F2; ∼; F1.
75–76  *in F1 as follows:*
         Tho tender and untry'd the Yoke he fear'd.
         Tho soft and white as flakes of falling Snow;
         And scarce his budding Horns had arm'd his brow.

Proceed, my Muse: Two Satyrs, on the ground,
20 Stretch'd at his Ease, their Syre *Silenus* found.
Dos'd with his fumes, and heavy with his Load,
They found him snoring in his dark abode;
And seis'd with Youthful Arms the drunken God.
His rosie Wreath was dropt not long before,
Born by the tide of Wine, and floating on the floor.
His empty Can, with Ears half worn away,
Was hung on high, to boast the triumph of the day.
Invaded thus, for want of better bands,
His Garland they unstring, and bind his hands:
30 For by the fraudful God deluded long,
They now resolve to have their promis'd Song.
*Ægle* came in, to make their Party good;
The fairest Naïs of the neighbouring Flood,
And, while he stares around, with stupid Eyes,
His Brows with Berries, and his Temples dyes.
He finds the Fraud, and, with a Smile, demands
On what design the Boys had bound his hands.
Loose me, he cry'd; 'twas Impudence to find
A sleeping God, 'tis Sacriledge to bind.
40 To you the promis'd Poem I will pay;
The Nymph shall be rewarded in her way.
He rais'd his voice; and soon a num'rous throng
Of tripping Satyrs crowded to the Song.
And Sylvan Fauns, and Savage Beasts advanc'd,
And nodding Forests to the Numbers danc'd.
Not by *Hæmonian* Hills the *Thracian* Bard,
Nor awful *Phœbus* was on *Pindus* heard,
With deeper silence, or with more regard.
He sung the secret Seeds of Nature's Frame;
50 How Seas, and Earth, and Air, and active Flame,
Fell through the mighty Void; and in their fall
Were blindly gather'd in this goodly Ball.
The tender Soil then stiffning by degrees,
Shut from the bounded Earth, the bounding Seas.
Then Earth and Ocean various Forms disclose;

20 *Silenus*] F2; *Sylenus* F1.     33 Naïs] *Nais* F1-2.

He sung the Lover's fraud; the longing Maid,
With golden Fruit, like all the Sex, betray'd:
The Sisters mourning for their Brother's loss;
90 Their Bodies hid in Barks, and furr'd with Moss:
How each a rising Alder now appears;
And o're the *Po* distils her Gummy Tears:
Then sung, how *Gallus* by a Muses hand,
Was led and welcom'd to the sacred Strand:
The Senate rising to salute their Guest;
And *Linus* thus their gratitude express'd.
Receive this Present, by the Muses made;
The Pipe on which th' *Ascræan* Pastor play'd:
With which of old he charm'd the Savage Train:
100 And call'd the Mountain Ashes to the Plain.
Sing thou on this, thy *Phœbus*; and the Wood
Where once his Fane of *Parian* Marble stood.
On this his ancient Oracles rehearse;
And with new Numbers grace the God of Verse.
Why shou'd I sing the double *Scylla's* Fate,
The first by Love transform'd, the last by Hate?
A beauteous Maid above, but Magick Arts,
With barking Dogs deform'd her neather parts.
What Vengeance on the passing Fleet she pour'd,
110 The Master frighted, and the Mates devour'd.
Then ravish'd *Philomel* the Song exprest;
The Crime reveal'd; the Sisters cruel Feast;
And how in Fields the Lapwing *Tereus* reigns;
The warbling Nightingale in Woods complains:
While *Progne* makes on Chymney tops her moan;
And hovers o're the Palace once her own.
Whatever Songs besides, the *Delphian* God
Had taught the Laurels, and the *Spartan* Flood,
*Silenus* sung: the Vales his Voice rebound;
120 And carry to the Skies the sacred Sound.

88  betray'd:] ~. F1-2.          90  Moss:] ~. F1-2.
92  Tears:] ~. F1-2.            94  Strand:] ~. F1-2
106  Hate?] ~. F1-2.           114  complains:] ~.

To the Right Hon.ble Henry Lord
Herbert Baron of Chirbury. &c.
FORTITUDINE ET PRUDENTIA
Paſt: 7.

# *The Seventh Pastoral*
## *or, Melibœus*

### THE ARGUMENT.

*Melibœus here gives us the Relation of a sharp Poetical Contest between* Thyrsis *and* Corydon; *at which he himself and* Daphnis *were present; who both declar'd for* Corydon.

BENEATH a Holm, repair'd two jolly Swains;
    Their Sheep and Goats together graz'd the Plains:
    Both young *Arcadians,* both alike inspir'd
To sing, and answer as the Song requir'd.
*Daphnis,* as Umpire, took the middle Seat;
And Fortune thether led my weary Feet.
For while I fenc'd my Myrtles from the Cold,
The Father of my Flock had wander'd from the Fold.
Of *Daphnis* I enquir'd; he, smiling, said,
10 Dismiss your Fear, and pointed where he fed.
And, if no greater Cares disturb your Mind,
Sit here with us, in covert of the Wind.
Your lowing Heyfars, of their own accord,
At wat'ring time will seek the neighb'ring Ford.
Here wanton *Mincius* windes along the Meads,
And shades his happy Banks with bending Reeds:
And see from yon old Oak, that mates the Skies,
How black the Clouds of swarming Bees arise.
What shou'd I do? nor was *Alcippe* nigh,
20 Nor absent *Phillis* cou'd my care supply,
To house, and feed by hand my weaning Lambs,
And drain the strutting Udders of their Dams.
Great was the strife betwixt the Singing Swains:
And I preferr'd my Pleasure to my Gains.
Alternate Rhime the ready Champions chose:
These *Corydon* rehears'd, and *Thyrsis* those.

---

2  Plains:] ∼. F1–2.         19  do?] ∼! F1–2.
22  Dams.] ∼? F1–2.

### CORYDON.

Yee Muses, ever fair, and ever young,
Assist my Numbers, and inspire my Song.
With all my *Codrus* O inspire my Breast,
30 For *Codrus* after *Phœbus* sings the best.
Or if my Wishes have presum'd too high,
And stretch'd their bounds beyond Mortality,
The praise of artful Numbers I resign:
And hang my Pipe upon the Sacred Pine.

### THYRSIS.

*Arcadian* Swains, your Youthful Poet crown
With Ivy Wreaths; tho surly *Codrus,* frown.
Or if he blast my Muse with envious Praise,
Then fence my Brows with Amuletts of Bays:
Lest his ill Arts or his malicious Tongue
40 Shou'd poyson, or bewitch my growing Song.

### CORYDON.

These Branches of a Stag, this tusky Boar
(The first essay of Arms untry'd before)
Young *Mycon* offers, *Delia,* to thy Shrine;
But speed his hunting with thy Pow'r divine,
Thy Statue then of *Parian* Stone shall stand;
Thy Legs in Buskins with a Purple Band.

### THYRSIS.

This Bowl of Milk, these Cakes, (our Country Fare,) )
For thee, *Priapus,* yearly we prepare: }
Because a little Garden is thy care. )
50 But if the falling Lambs increase my Fold,
Thy Marble Statue shall be turn'd to Gold.

---

38   Amuletts of Bays:] *Amuletts* ~ ~. F1–2.
48   prepare:] ~. F1–2.

*CORYDON.*

Fair *Galathea,* with thy silver Feet,
O, whiter than the Swan, and more than *Hybla* sweet;
Tall as a Poplar, taper as the Bole,
Come charm thy Shepherd, and restore my Soul.
Come when my lated Sheep, at night return;
And crown the silent Hours, and stop the rosy Morn.

*THYRSIS.*

May I become as abject in thy sight,
As Sea-weed on the Shore, and black as Night:
60 Rough as a Bur, deform'd like him who chaws
*Sardinian* Herbage to contract his Jaws;
Such and so monstrous let thy Swain appear,
If one day's Absence looks not like a Year.
Hence from the Field, for Shame: the Flock deserves
No better Feeding, while the Shepherd starves.

*CORYDON.*

Ye mossy Springs, inviting easie Sleep,
Ye Trees, whose leafy Shades those mossy Fountains keep,
Defend my Flock, the Summer heats are near,
And Blossoms on the swelling Vines appear.

*THYRSIS.*

70 With heapy Fires our chearful Hearth is crown'd;
And Firs for Torches in the Woods abound:
We fear not more the Winds, and wintry Cold,
Than Streams the Banks, or Wolves the bleating Fold.

*CORYDON.*

Our Woods, with Juniper and Chesnuts crown'd, ⎫
With falling Fruits and Berries paint the Ground; ⎬
And lavish Nature laughs, and strows her Stores around. ⎭

But if *Alexis* from our Mountains fly,
Ev'n running Rivers leave their Channels dry.

### THYRSIS.

    Parch'd are the Plains, and frying is the Field,
80 Nor with'ring Vines their juicy Vintage yield.
But if returning *Phillis* bless the Plain,    ⎫
The Grass revives; the Woods are green again; ⎬
And *Jove* descends in Show'rs of kindly Rain.  ⎭

### CORYDON.

    The Poplar is by great *Alcides* worn:
The Brows of *Phœbus* his own Bays adorn.
The branching Vine the jolly *Bacchus* loves;
The *Cyprian* Queen delights in Mirtle Groves.
With Hazle, *Phillis* crowns her flowing Hair,    ⎫
And while she loves that common Wreath to wear, ⎬
90 Nor Bays, nor Myrtle Bows, with Hazle shall compare. ⎭

### THYRSIS.

    The towring Ash is fairest in the Woods;
In Gardens Pines, and Poplars by the Floods:
But if my *Lycidas* will ease my Pains,
And often visit our forsaken Plains;
To him the tow'ring Ash shall yield in Woods;
In Gardens Pines, and Poplars by the Floods.

### MELIBŒUS.

    These Rhymes I did to Memory commend,
When Vanquish'd *Thyrsis* did in vain contend;
Since when, tis *Corydon* among the Swains,
100 Young *Corydon* without a Rival Reigns.

---

89  wear,] ∼; F1–2.
97–100  *in F1 as follows:*
        I've heard: and, *Thyrsis*, you contend in vain: ⎫
        For *Corydon*, young *Corydon* shall reign, ⎬
        The Prince of Poets, on the *Mantuan* Plain. ⎭

To the Rig.t Hon.ble      Charles L.d Clifford.
Baron of            Lounsbrough
in the County      of York

past.8.

## The Eighth Pastoral
## or, Pharmaceutria

### THE ARGUMENT.

*This Pastoral contains the Songs of* Damon *and* Alphesibœus.
*The first of 'em bewails the loss of his Mistress, and repines at the
Success of his Rival* Mopsus. *The other repeats the Charms of
some Enchantress, who endeavour'd by her Spells and Magic to
make* Daphnis *in Love with her.*

THE mournful Muse of two despairing Swains,
    The Love rejected, and the Lovers' pains;
    To which the salvage Lynxes listning stood,
The Rivers stood on heaps, and stop'd the running Flood,
The hungry Herd their needful Food refuse;
Of two despairing Swains, I sing the mournful Muse.

    Great *Pollio,* thou for whom thy *Rome* prepares
The ready Triumph of thy finish'd Wars,
Whither *Timavus* or th' *Illirian* Coast,
10 Whatever Land or Sea thy presence boast;
Is there an hour in Fate rescrv'd for me,
To Sing thy Deeds in Numbers worthy thee?
In numbers like to thine, cou'd I rehearse
Thy lofty Tragick Scenes, thy labour'd Verse;
The World another *Sophocles* in thee,
Another *Homer* shou'd behold in me:
Amidst thy Laurels let this Ivy twine,
Thine was my earliest Muse; my latest shall be thine.
    Scarce from the World the Shades of Night withdrew;
20 Scarce were the Flocks refresh'd with Morning Dew,
When *Damon* stretch'd beneath an Olive Shade,
And wildly staring upwards, thus inveigh'd
Against the conscious Gods, and curs'd the cruel Maid.

3  Lynxes] *Linxes* F1–2.
19  the World the Shades of Night] F2; our upper World the Shades F1.

Star of the Morning, why dost thou delay?
Come, *Lucifer,* drive on the lagging Day.
While I my *Nisa*'s perjur'd Faith deplore;
Witness ye Pow'rs, by whom she falsely swore!
The Gods, alas, are Witnesses in vain;
Yet shall my dying Breath to Heav'n complain.
30 Begin with me, my Flute, the sweet *Mænalian* Strain.

   The Pines of *Mænalus,* the vocal Grove,
Are ever full of Verse, and full of Love:
They hear the Hinds, they hear their God complain;
Who suffer'd not the Reeds to rise in vain:
Begin with me, my Flute, the sweet *Mænalian* Strain.

   *Mopsus* triumphs; he weds the willing Fair:
When such is *Nisa*'s choice, what Lover can despair?
Now Griffons join with Mares; another Age
Shall see the Hound and Hind their Thirst asswage,
40 Promiscuous at the Spring: Prepare the Lights,
O *Mopsus!* and perform the bridal Rites.
Scatter thy Nuts among the scrambling Boys:
Thine is the Night; and thine the Nuptial Joys.
For thee the Sun declines: O happy Swain!
Begin with me, my Flute, the sweet *Mænalian* Strain.

   O, *Nisa!* Justly to thy Choice condemn'd,
Whom hast thou taken, whom hast thou contemn'd?
For him, thou hast refus'd my browzing Herd,
Scorn'd my thick Eye-brows, and my shaggy Beard.
50 Unhappy *Damon* sighs, and sings in vain:
While *Nisa* thinks no God regards a Lover's pain.
Begin with me, my Flute, the sweet *Mænalian* Strain.

   I view'd thee first; how fatal was the View!
And led thee where the ruddy Wildings grew,
High on the planted hedge, and wet with Morning Dew.

---

37  despair?] ∼! F1–2.                    47  contemn'd?] ∼! F1–2.
53  *not indented in F1–2.*

Then scarce the bending Branches I cou'd win;
The callow Down began to cloath my Chin;
I saw, I perish'd; yet indulg'd my Pain:
Begin with me, my Flute, the sweet *Mænalian* Strain.

60    I know thee, Love; in Desarts thou wert bred;
And at the Dugs of Salvage Tygers fed:
Alien of Birth, Usurper of the Plains:
Begin with me, my Flute, the sweet *Mænalian* Strains.

Relentless Love the cruel Mother led,
The Blood of her unhappy Babes to shed:
Love lent the Sword; the Mother struck the blow;
Inhuman she; but more inhuman thou:
Alien of Birth, Usurper of the Plains:
Begin with me, my Flute, the sweet *Mænalian* Strains.

70    Old doting Nature change thy Course anew:
And let the trembling Lamb the Wolf pursue:
Let Oaks now glitter with *Hesperian* Fruit,
And purple Daffodils from Alder shoot.
Fat Amber let the Tamarisk distil:
And hooting Owls contend with Swans in Skill:
Hoarse *Tity'rus* strive with *Orpheus* in the Woods:
And challenge fam'd *Arion* on the Floods.
Or, oh! let Nature cease; and *Chaos* reign:
Begin with me, my Flute, the sweet *Mænalian* Strain.

80    Let Earth be Sea; and let the whelming Tide,
The lifeless Limbs of luckless *Damon* hide:
Farewel, ye secret Woods, and shady Groves,
Haunts of my Youth, and conscious of my Loves!
From yon high Cliff I plunge into the Main;
Take the last Present of thy dying Swain:
And cease, my silent Flute, the sweet *Mænalian* Strain.

---

67    thou:] ~. F1–2.                    75    Skill:] ~. F1–2.

See, while my last endeavours I delay,
The waking Ashes rise, and round our Altars play!
Run to the Threshold, *Amaryllis,* hark,
Our *Hylax* opens, and begins to bark.
Good Heav'n! may Lovers what they wish believe;
Or dream their wishes, and those dreams deceive?
No more, my *Daphnis* comes; no more, my Charms;
160 He comes, he runs, he leaps to my desiring Arms.

---

156   *Hylax*] *Hylas* F1-2.              158   deceive?] ~! F1-2.

F.Cleyn.in.ͭ Lombart.sculpsit.londin.

To the Right Hon.ᵇˡᵉ      William Lord
Marquiſs of Hartington    Eldest Son to His Grace
      the Duke of          Devonſhire.

CAVENDO     TUTUS

Paſt.e.l.1.

# The Ninth Pastoral
## or, Lycidas, and Mœris

### THE ARGUMENT.

*When* Virgil, *by the Favour of* Augustus, *had recover'd his Patrimony near* Mantua, *and went in hope to take Possession, he was in danger to be slain by* Arius *the Centurion, to whom those Lands were assign'd by the Emperour, in reward of his Service against* Brutus *and* Cassius. *This Pastoral therefore is fill'd with complaints of his hard Usage; and the Persons introduc'd, are the Bayliff of* Virgil, Mœris, *and his Friend* Lycidas.

### LYCIDAS.

Ho *Mœris!* whether on thy way so fast?
This leads to Town.

### MŒRIS.

O *Lycidas,* at last
The Time is come I never thought to see,
(Strange Revolution for my Farm and me)
When the grim Captain in a surly Tone
Cries out, Pack up ye Rascals, and be gone.
Kick'd out, we set the best Face on't we cou'd, ⎫
And these two Kids, t' appease his angry Mood, ⎬
I bear, of which the Furies give him good. ⎭

### LYCIDAS.

10    Your Country Friends were told another Tale;
That from the sloaping Mountain to the Vale,

---

*Title Mœris*] MOERIS F1–2 *(and similarly throughout, except in the last line of the Argument and the heading above l. 31).*
3    *Centurion*] Centurion O1–2, F1–2.
6    *Pack*] pack O1–2, F1–2.

And dodder'd Oak, and all the Banks along,
*Menalcas* sav'd his Fortune with a Song.

### MŒRIS.

Such was the News, indeed, but Songs and Rhymes
Prevail as much in these hard Iron Times,
As would a plump of trembling Fowl, that rise
Against an Eagle sousing from the Skies.
And had not *Phœbus* warn'd me by the croak
Of an old Raven, from a hollow Oak,
20 To shun debate, *Menalcas* had been slain,
And *Mœris* not surviv'd him, to complain.

### LYCIDAS.

Now Heav'n defend! cou'd barb'rous Rage induce
The Brutal Son of *Mars,* t' insult the sacred Muse?
Who then shou'd sing the Nymphs, or who rehearse
The Waters gliding in a smoother Verse:
Or *Amaryllis* praise?————that Heav'nly Lay,
That shorten'd as we went, our tedious Way;
"O *Tity'rus,* tend my Herd, and see them fed; ⎫
To Morning Pastures, Evening Waters led: ⎬
30 And 'ware the *Lybian* Ridgils butting Head." ⎭

### MŒRIS.

Or what unfinish'd He to *Varus* read;
"Thy Name, O *Varus* (if the kinder Pow'rs
Preserve our Plains, and shield the *Mantuan* Tow'rs,
Obnoxious by *Cremona*'s neighb'ring Crime,)
The Wings of Swans, and stronger pinion'd Rhyme,

---

23    Muse?] ∼! F1–2; *see collation for different text in* O1–2.
25    Verse:] ∼! O1–2, F1–2.
26    praise?————] ∼ₐₐ O1–2; ∼,ₐ F1–2.
27    Way;] O1–2; ∼. F1–2.
28–30    "O . . . Head."] ₐ∼ . . . ∼·ₐ O1–2, F1–2.
32–37    "Thy . . . *Jove.*"] ₐ∼ . . . ∼·ₐ O1–2, F1–2.

Shall raise aloft, and soaring bear above
Th' immortal Gift of Gratitude to *Jove.*"

### LYCIDAS.

Sing on, sing on, for I can ne're be cloy'd,
So may thy Swarms the baleful Eugh avoid:
40 So may thy Cows their burden'd Bags distend,
And Trees to Goats their willing Branches bend.
Mean as I am, yet have the Muses made
Me free, a Member of the tuneful trade:
At least the Shepherds seem to like my Lays,
But I discern their Flatt'ry from their Praise:
I nor to *Cinna*'s Ears, nor *Varus* dare aspire;
But gabble like a Goose, amidst the Swan-like Quire.

### MŒRIS.

'Tis what I have been conning in my Mind:
Nor are they Verses of a Vulgar Kind.
50 "Come, *Galatea,* come, the Seas forsake;
What Pleasures can the Tides with their hoarse Murmurs make?
See, on the Shore inhabits purple Spring;
Where Nightingales their Love-sick Ditty sing;
See, Meads with purling Streams, with Flow'rs the Ground, )
The Grottoes cool with shady Poplars crown'd,       }
And creeping Vines on Arbours weav'd around.         )
Come then, and leave the Waves tumultuous roar,
Let the wild Surges vainly beat the Shore."

### LYCIDAS.

Or that sweet Song I heard with such delight;
60 The same you sung alone one starry Night;
The Tune I still retain, but not the Words.

---

47   Swan-like] *the hyphen failed to print in some copies of F1.*
50–58   "Come . . . Shore."] ʌ~ . . . ~·ʌ O1–2, F1–2.
55   cool] ~, O1–2, F1–2.

*MŒRIS.*

"Why, *Daphnis,* dost thou search in old Records,
To know the Seasons when the Stars arise?
See *Cæsar*'s Lamp is lighted in the Skies:
The Star, whose Rays the blushing Grapes adorn,
And swell the kindly ripening Ears of Corn.
Under this influence, graft the tender Shoot;
Thy Childrens Children shall enjoy the Fruit."
The rest I have forgot, for Cares and Time
70 Change all things, and untune my Soul to Rhime:
I cou'd have once sung down a Summer's Sun,
But now the Chime of Poetry is done.
My Voice grows hoarse; I feel the Notes decay,
As if the Wolves had seen me first to Day.
But these, and more than I to mind can bring,
*Menalcas* has not yet forgott to sing.

*LYCIDAS.*

Thy faint Excuses but inflame me more;
And now the Waves rowl silent to the Shore.
Husht Winds the topmost Branches scarcely bend,
80 As if thy tuneful Song they did attend:
Already we have half our way o'recome;
Far off I can discern *Bianor*'s Tomb;
Here, where the Labourer's hands have form'd a Bow'r
Of wreathing Trees, in Singing waste an Hour.
Rest here thy weary Limbs, thy Kids lay down,
We've Day before us yet, to reach the Town:
Or if e're Night the gath'ring Clouds we fear,
A Song will help the beating Storm to bear.
And that thou may'st not be too late abroad,
90 Sing, and I'll ease thy Shoulders of thy Load.

---

62–68 "Why . . . Fruit."] ‸~ . . . ~·‸ O1–2, F1–2.

*MŒRIS.*

Cease to request me, let us mind our way;
Another Song requires another Day.
When good *Menalcas* comes, if he rejoyce,
And find a Friend at Court, I'll find a Voice.

# The Tenth Pastoral
## or, Gallus

### THE ARGUMENT.

Gallus *a great Patron of* Virgil, *and an excellent Poet, was very deeply in Love with one* Citheris, *whom he calls* Lycoris; *and who had forsaken him for the Company of a Souldier. The Poet therefore supposes his Friend* Gallus *retir'd in his heighth of Melancholy into the Solitudes of* Arcadia, *(the celebrated Scene of Pastorals;) where he represents him in a very languishing Condition, with all the Rural Deities about him, pitying his hard Usage, and condoling his Misfortune.*

THY sacred Succour, *Arethusa,* bring,
　　To crown my Labour: 'tis the last I sing:
　　Which proud *Lycoris* may with Pity view; ⎞
The Muse is mournful, tho' the Numbers few.　　⎟
Refuse me not a Verse, to Grief and *Gallus* due.　⎠
So may thy Silver Streams beneath the Tide,
Unmix'd with briny Seas, securely glide.
Sing then, my *Gallus,* and his hopeless Vows;
Sing, while my Cattle crop the tender Browze.
10　The vocal Grove shall answer to the Sound,
And Echo, from the Vales, the tuneful Voice rebound.
What Lawns or Woods withheld you from his Aid, ⎞
Ye Nymphs, when *Gallus* was to Love betray'd;　⎟
To Love, unpity'd by the cruel Maid?　　　　⎠
Not steepy *Pindus* cou'd retard your Course,
Nor cleft *Parnassus,* nor th' *Aonian* Source:
Nothing that owns the Muses cou'd suspend
Your Aid to *Gallus, Gallus* is their Friend.
For him the lofty Laurel stands in Tears;

---

6–7　*Condition,] the comma failed to print in some copies of F1.*
2　sing:] ~. F1–2.

20 And hung with humid Pearls the lowly Shrub appears.
*Mænalian* Pines the Godlike Swain bemoan; ⎫
When spread beneath a Rock he sigh'd alone; ⎬
And cold *Lycæus* wept from every dropping Stone. ⎭
The Sheep surround their Shepherd, as he lyes:
Blush not, sweet Poet, nor the name despise:
Along the Streams his Flock *Adonis* fed;
And yet the Queen of Beauty blest his Bed.
The Swains and tardy Neat-herds came, and last
*Menalcas*, wet with beating Winter Mast.
30 Wond'ring, they ask'd from whence arose thy Flame;
Yet, more amaz'd, thy own *Apollo* came.
Flush'd were his Cheeks, and glowing were his Eyes:
Is she thy Care, is she thy Care? he cries.
Thy false *Lycoris* flies thy Love and thee; ⎫
And for thy Rival tempts the raging Sea, ⎬
The Forms of horrid War, and Heav'ns Inclemency. ⎭
*Sylvanus* came: his Brows a Country Crown
Of Fennel, and of nodding Lillies, drown.
Great *Pan* arriv'd; and we beheld him too,
40 His Cheeks and Temples of Vermilion Hue.
Why, *Gallus*, this immod'rate Grief, he cry'd:
Think'st thou that Love with Tears is satisfi'd?
The Meads are sooner drunk with Morning Dews;
The Bees with flow'ry Shrubs, the Goats with Brouze.
Unmov'd, and with dejected Eyes, he mourn'd:
He paus'd, and then these broken Words return'd.
'Tis past; and Pity gives me no Relief:
But you, *Arcadian* Swains, shall sing my Grief:
And on your Hills, my last Complaints renew;
50 So sad a Song is onely worthy you.
How light wou'd lye the Turf upon my Breast,
If you my Suff'rings in your Songs exprest!
Ah! that your Birth and Bus'ness had been mine;
To penn the Sheep, and press the swelling Vine!
Had *Phyllis* or *Amyntas* caus'd my Pain,

---

33  Care? he cries.] ∼, ∼∼? F1–2.        52  exprest!] ∼? F1–2.

Or any Nymph, or Shepherd on the Plain,
Tho *Phyllis* brown, tho black *Amyntas* were,
Are Violets not sweet, because not fair?
Beneath the Sallows, and the shady Vine,
60 My Loves had mix'd their pliant Limbs with mine;
*Phyllis* with Myrtle Wreaths had crown'd my Hair,
And soft *Amyntas* sung away my Care.
Come, see what Pleasures in our Plains abound;
The Woods, the Fountains, and the flow'ry ground.
As you are beauteous, were you half so true,
Here cou'd I live, and love, and dye with only you.
Now I to fighting Fields am sent afar,
And strive in Winter Camps with toils of War;
While you, (alas, that I shou'd find it so!)
70 To shun my sight, your Native Soil forgo,
And climb the frozen *Alps,* and tread th' eternal Snow.
Ye Frosts and Snows her tender Body spare,
Those are not Limbs for Ysicles to tear.
For me, the Wilds and Desarts are my Choice;
The Muses, once my Care; my once harmonious Voice.
There will I sing, forsaken and alone,
The Rocks and hollow Caves shall echo to my Moan.
The Rind of ev'ry Plant her Name shall know;
And as the Rind extends, the Love shall grow.
80 Then on *Arcadian* Mountains will I chase
(Mix'd with the Woodland Nymphs) the Salvage Race.
Nor Cold shall hinder me, with Horns and Hounds,
To thrid the Thickets, or to leap the Mounds.
And now methinks o're steepy Rocks I go;
And rush through sounding Woods, and bend the *Parthian* Bow:
As if with Sports my Sufferings I could ease,
Or by my Pains the God of Love appease.
My Frenzy changes, I delight no more
On Mountain tops, to chace the tusky Boar;
90 No Game but hopeless Love my thoughts pursue:
Once more ye Nymphs, and Songs, and sounding Woods adieu.
Love alters not for us, his hard Decrees,
Not tho beneath the *Thracian* Clime we freeze;

Or *Italy*'s indulgent Heav'n forgo;
And in mid-Winter tread *Sithonian* Snow:
Or when the Barks of Elms are scorch'd, we keep
On *Meroe*'s burning Plains the *Lybian* Sheep.
In Hell, and Earth, and Seas, and Heav'n above,
Love conquers all; and we must yield to Love.
100 My Muses, here your sacred Raptures end:
The Verse was what I ow'd my suff'ring Friend.
This while I sung, my Sorrows I deceiv'd,
And bending Osiers into Baskets weav'd.
The Song, because inspir'd by you, shall shine:
And *Gallus* will approve, because 'tis mine:
*Gallus,* for whom my holy Flames renew,
Each hour, and ev'ry moment rise in view:
As Alders, in the Spring, their Boles extend;
And heave so fiercely, that the Bark they rend.
110 Now let us rise, for hoarseness oft invades
The Singer's Voice, who sings beneath the Shades.
From Juniper, unwholsom Dews distill,
That blast the sooty Corn; the with'ring Herbage kill;
Away, my Goats, away: for you have browz'd your fill.

---

95  *Sithonian*] F2; *Scythonian* F1.          95  Snow:] ~. F1–2.
97  *Meroe's*] *Meroes* F1–2.                  105  mine:] ~. F1–2.

TO THE RIGHT HONOURABLE
*PHILIP* Earl of *Chesterfield*, &c.

*My Lord,*

I Cannot begin my Address to your Lordship, better than in the words of *Virgil,*

————*Quod optanti, Divum promittere Nemo
Auderet, volvenda Dies, en, attulit ultrò.*

Seven Years together I have conceal'd the longing which I had to appear before you: A time as tedious as *Æneas* pass'd in his wandring Voyage, before he reach'd the promis'd *Italy.* But I consider'd, that nothing which my meanness cou'd produce, was worthy of your Patronage. At last this happy Occasion of-fer'd, of Presenting to you the best Poem of the best Poet. If I balk'd this opportunity, I was in despair of finding such another; and if I took it, I was still uncertain whether you wou'd vouchsafe to accept it from my hands. 'Twas a bold venture which I made, in desiring your permission to lay my unworthy Labours at your feet. But my rashness has succeeded beyond my hopes: And you have been pleas'd not to suffer an Old Man to go discontented out of the World, for want of that protection, of which he had been so long Ambitious. I have known a Gentleman in disgrace, and not daring to appear before King *Charles* the Second, though he much desir'd it: At length he took the confidence to attend a fair Lady to the Court, and told His Majesty, that under her protection he had presum'd to wait on him. With the same hum-ble confidence I present my self before your Lordship, and at-tending on *Virgil* hope a gracious reception. The Gentleman succeeded, because the powerful Lady was his Friend; but I have too much injur'd my great Author, to expect he should inter-cede for me. I wou'd have Translated him, but according to the litteral *French* and *Italian* Phrases, I fear I have traduc'd him. 'Tis the fault of many a well-meaning Man, to be officious in a wrong place, and do a prejudice, where he had endeavour'd

*Eden* was not made for Beasts, though they were suffer'd to live in it, but for their Master, who studied God in the Works of his Creation. Neither cou'd the Devil have been happy there with all his Knowledge, for he wanted Innocence to make him so. He brought Envy, Malice, and Ambition into Paradise, which sour'd to him the sweetness of the Place. Wherever inordinate Affections are, 'tis Hell. Such only can enjoy the Country, who are capable of thinking when they are there, and have left their Passions behind them in the Town. Then they are prepar'd for Solitude; and in that Solitude is prepar'd for them

> *Et secura quies, & nescia fallere vita.*

As I began this Dedication with a Verse of *Virgil*, so I conclude it with another. The continuance of your Health, to enjoy that Happiness which you so well deserve, and which you have provided for your self, is the sincere and earnest Wish of

*Your Lordship's most Devoted,*

*and most Obedient Servant,*

JOHN DRYDEN.

# An Essay on the Georgics

## [By Joseph Addison]

VIRGIL may be reckon'd the first who introduc'd three new kinds of Poetry among the *Romans,* which he Copied after three the Greatest Masters of *Greece. Theocritus* and *Homer* have still disputed for the advantage over him in *Pastoral* and *Heroicks,* but I think all are Unanimous in giving him the precedence to *Hesiod* in his *Georgics.* The truth of it is, the Sweetness and Rusticity of a *Pastoral* cannot be so well exprest in any other Tongue as in the *Greek,* when rightly mixt and qualified with the *Doric* Dialect; nor can the Majesty of an
10 *Heroick* Poem any where appear so well as in this Language, which has a Natural greatness in it, and can be often render'd more deep and sonorous by the Pronunciation of the *Ionians.* But in the middle Stile, where the Writers in both Tongues are on a Level: we see how far *Virgil* has excell'd all who have written in the same way with him.

There has been abundance of Criticism spent on *Virgil's Pastorals* and *Æneids,* but the *Georgics* are a Subject which none of the *Criticks* have sufficiently taken into their Consideration; most of 'em passing it over in silence, or casting it under the same
20 head with *Pastoral;* a division by no means proper, unless we suppose the Stile of a Husbandman ought to be imitated in a *Georgic* as that of a Shepherd is in *Pastoral.* But tho' the Scene of both these Poems lies in the same place; the Speakers in them are of a quite different Character, since the Precepts of Husbandry are not to be deliver'd with the simplicity of a Plow-Man, but with the Address of a Poet. No Rules therefore that relate to *Pastoral,* can any way affect the *Georgics,* which fall under that Class of Poetry which consists in giving plain and direct Instructions to the Reader; whether they be Moral Duties, as
30 those of *Theognis* and *Pythagoras;* or Philosophical Specula-

10  *Heroick*] Heroick F1–2.

tions, as those of *Aratus* and *Lucretius;* or Rules of Practice, as those of *Hesiod* and *Virgil.* Among these different kinds of Subjects, that which the *Georgics* goes upon, is I think the meanest and the least improving, but the most pleasing and delightful. Precepts of Morality, besides the Natural Corruption of our Tempers, which makes us averse to them, are so abstracted from Ideas of Sense, that they seldom give an opportunity for those Beautiful Descriptions and Images which are the Spirit and Life of Poetry. Natural Philosophy has indeed sensible Objects to
10 work upon, but then it often puzzles the Reader with the Intricacy of its Notions, and perplexes him with the multitude of its Disputes. But this kind of Poetry I am now speaking of, addresses it self wholly to the Imagination: It is altogether Conversant among the Fields and Woods, and has the most delightful part of Nature for its Province. It raises in our Minds a pleasing variety of Scenes and Landskips, whilst it teaches us: and makes the dryest of its Precepts look like a Description. *A Georgic therefore is some part of the Science of Husbandry put into a pleasing Dress, and set off with all the Beauties and Embellish-*
20 *ments of Poetry.* Now since this Science of Husbandry is of a very large extent, the Poet shews his Skill in singling out such Precepts to proceed on, as are useful, and at the same time most capable of Ornament. *Virgil* was so well acquainted with this Secret, that to set off his first *Georgic,* he has run into a set of Precepts, which are almost foreign to his Subject, in that Beautiful account he gives us of the Signs in Nature, which precede the Changes of the Weather.

And if there be so much Art in the choice of fit Precepts, there is much more requir'd in the Treating of 'em; that they may
30 fall in after each other by a Natural unforc'd Method, and shew themselves in the best and most advantagious Light. They shou'd all be so finely wrought together into the same Piece, that no course Seam may discover where they joyn; as in a Curious Brede of Needle-Work, one Colour falls away by such just degrees, and another rises so insensibly, that we see the variety, without being able to distinguish the total vanishing of the one from the first appearance of the other. Nor is it sufficient to range and

22   proceed] F2; preceed F1.

dispose this Body of Precepts into a clear and easie Method, un-
less they are deliver'd to us in the most pleasing and agreeable
manner: For there are several ways of conveying the same Truth
to the Mind of Man, and to chuse the pleasantest of these ways, is
that which chiefly distinguishes Poetry from Prose, and makes
*Virgil*'s Rules of Husbandry pleasanter to read than *Varro*'s.
Where the Prose-writer tells us plainly what ought to be done,
the Poet often conceals the Precept in a description, and repre-
sents his Country-Man performing the Action in which he wou'd
10  instruct his Reader. Where the one sets out as fully and dis-
tinctly as he can, all the parts of the Truth, which he wou'd
communicate to us; the other singles out the most pleasing Cir-
cumstance of this Truth, and so conveys the whole in a more
diverting manner to the Understanding. I shall give one Instance
out of a multitude of this nature, that might be found in the
*Georgics,* where the Reader may see the different ways *Virgil* has
taken to express the same thing, and how much pleasanter every
manner of Expression is, than the plain and direct mention of
it wou'd have been. It is in the Second *Georgic* where he tells us
20  what Trees will bear Grafting on each other.

> *Et sæpe alterius ramos impune videmus,*
> *Vertere in alterius, mutatamq; insita mala*
> *Ferre pyrum, & prunis lapidosa rubescere corna.*
> ————*Steriles Platani malos gessere valentes,*
> *Castaneæ fagos, ornusq; incanuit albo*
> *Flore pyri:* Glandemq; sues fregere sub ulmis.
> ————*Nec longum tempus: & ingens*
> *Exijt ad Cælum ramis felicibus arbos;*
> *Miraturq; novas frondes, & non sua poma.*

30  Here we see the Poet consider'd all the Effects of this Union
between Trees of different kinds, and took notice of that Effect
which had the most surprize, and by consequence the most de-
light in it, to express the capacity that was in them of being thus
united. This way of Writing is every where much in use among
the Poets, and is particularly practis'd by *Virgil,* who loves to
suggest a Truth indirectly, and without giving us a full and open
view of it: To let us see just so much as will naturally lead the

Imagination into all the parts that lie conceal'd. This is wonderfully diverting to the Understanding, thus to receive a Precept, that enters as it were through a By-way, and to apprehend an Idea that draws a whole train after it: For here the Mind, which is always delighted with its own Discoveries, only takes the hint from the Poet, and seems to work out the rest by the strength of her own faculties.

But since the inculcating Precept upon Precept, will at length prove tiresom to the Reader, if he meets with no other Enter-
10 tainment, the Poet must take care not to encumber his Poem with too much Business; but sometimes to relieve the Subject with a Moral Reflection, or let it rest a while for the sake of a pleasant and pertinent digression. Nor is it sufficient to run out into beautiful and diverting digressions (as it is generally thought) unless they are brought in aptly, and are something of a piece with the main design of the *Georgic:* for they ought to have a remote alliance at least to the Subject, that so the whole Poem may be more uniform and agreeable in all its parts. We shou'd never quite lose sight of the Country, tho' we are some-
20 times entertain'd with a distant prospect of it. Of this nature are *Virgil*'s Descriptions of the Original of *Agriculture,* of the Fruitfulness of *Italy,* of a Country Life, and the like, which are not brought in by force, but naturally rise out of the principal Argument and Design of the Poem. I know no one digression in the *Georgics* that may seem to contradict this Observation, besides that in the latter end of the First Book, where the Poet launches out into a discourse of the Battel of *Pharsalia,* and the Actions of *Augustus:* But it's worth while to consider how admirably he has turn'd the course of his narration into its proper Channel, and
30 made his Husbandman concern'd even in what relates to the Battel, in those inimitable Lines,

> *Scilicet & tempus veniet, cum finibus illis*
> *Agricola incurvo terram molitus aratro,*
> *Exesa inveniet scabra rubigine pila:*
> *Aut gravibus rastris galeas pulsabit inanes,*
> *Grandiaq; effossis mirabitur ossa sepulchris.*

33   *incurvo*] *in curvo* F1–2.

And afterwards speaking of *Augustus*'s Actions, he still remembers that *Agriculture* ought to be some way hinted at throughout the whole Poem.

> ————*Non ullus Aratro*
> *Dignus honos: squalent abductis arva colonis:*
> *Et curvæ rigidum falces conflantur in Ensem.*

We now come to the Stile which is proper to a *Georgic;* and indeed this is the part on which the Poet must lay out all his strength, that his words may be warm and glowing, and that
10 every thing he describes may immediately present it self, and rise up to the Reader's view. He ought in particular to be careful of not letting his Subject debase his Stile, and betray him into a meanness of Expression, but every where to keep up his Verse in all the Pomp of Numbers, and Dignity of words.

I think nothing which is a Phrase or Saying in common talk, shou'd be admitted into a serious Poem: because it takes off from the Solemnity of the expression, and gives it too great a turn of Familiarity: much less ought the low Phrases and Terms of Art, that are adapted to Husbandry, have any place in such a
20 Work as the *Georgic,* which is not to appear in the natural simplicity and nakedness of its Subject, but in the pleasantest Dress that Poetry can bestow on it. Thus *Virgil,* to deviate from the common form of words, wou'd not make use of *Tempore* but *Sidere* in his first Verse, and every where else abounds with Metaphors, *Grecisms,* and Circumlocutions, to give his Verse the greater Pomp, and preserve it from sinking into a *Plebeian* Stile. And herein consists *Virgil*'s Master-piece, who has not only excell'd all other Poets, but even himself in the Language of his *Georgics;* where we receive more strong and lively *Ideas* of things
30 from his words, than we cou'd have done from the Objects themselves: and find our Imaginations more affected by his Descriptions, than they wou'd have been by the very sight of what he describes.

I shall now, after this short Scheme of Rules, consider the different success that *Hesiod* and *Virgil* have met with in this kind of Poetry, which may give us some further Notion of the Excel-

---

24–25 Metaphors ... Circumlocutions] *Metaphors ... Circumlocutions* F1–2.

Noble Instances, and very Sublime Expressions. The *Scythian* Winter-piece appears so very cold and bleak to the Eye, that a Man can scarce look on it without shivering. The Murrain at the end has all the expressiveness that words can give. It was here that the Poet strain'd hard to outdo *Lucretius* in the description of his Plague; and if the Reader wou'd see what success he had, he may find it at large in *Scaliger*.

But *Virgil* seems no where so well pleas'd, as when he is got among his Bees in the Fourth *Georgic:* And Ennobles the Actions of so trivial a Creature, with Metaphors drawn from the most important Concerns of Mankind. His Verses are not in a greater noise and hurry in the Battels of *Æneas* and *Turnus*, than in the Engagement of two Swarms. And as in his *Æneis* he compares the Labours of his *Trojans* to those of Bees and Pismires, here he compares the Labours of the Bees to those of the *Cyclops*. In short, the last *Georgic* was a good Prelude to the *Æneis;* and very well shew'd what the Poet could do in the description of what was really great, by his describing the Mockgrandeur of an Insect with so good a grace. There is more pleasantness in the little Platform of a Garden, which he gives us about the middle of this Book, than in all the spacious Walks and Water-works of *Rapin*'s. The Speech of *Proteus* at the end can never be enough admir'd, and was indeed very fit to conclude so Divine a Work.

After this particular account of the Beauties in the *Georgics,* I shou'd in the next place endeavour to point out its imperfections, if it has any. But tho' I think there are some few parts in it that are not so Beautiful as the rest, I shall not presume to name them, as rather suspecting my own Judgment, than I can believe a fault to be in that Poem, which lay so long under *Virgil*'s Correction, and had his last hand put to it. The first *Georgic* was probably Burlesqu'd in the Author's Lifetime; for we still find in the Scholiasts a Verse that ridicules part of a Line Translated from *Hesiod*.

> *Nudus Ara, sere Nudus*————

35   *not a separate line in F1–2.*

And we may easily guess at the Judgment of this extraordinary Critick, whoever he was, from his Censuring this particular Precept. We may be sure *Virgil* wou'd not have Translated it from *Hesiod,* had he not discover'd some Beauty in it; and indeed the Beauty of it is what I have before observ'd to be frequently met with in *Virgil,* the delivering the Precept so indirectly, and singling out the particular circumstance of Sowing and Plowing naked, to suggest to us that these Employments are proper only in the hot Season of the Year.

10     I shall not here compare the Stile of the *Georgics* with that of *Lucretius,* which the Reader may see already done in the Preface to the Second Volume of *Miscellany Poems;* but shall conclude this Poem to be the most Compleat, Elaborate, and finisht Piece of all Antiquity. The *Æneis* indeed is of a Nobler kind, but the *Georgic* is more perfect in its kind. The *Æneis* has a greater variety of Beauties in it, but those of the *Georgic* are more exquisite. In short, the *Georgic* has all the perfection that can be expected in a Poem written by the greatest Poet in the Flower of his Age, when his Invention was ready, his Imagination warm,
20 his Judgment settled, and all his Faculties in their full Vigour and Maturity.

---

15  *Æneis*] F2; *Æneid* F1.

To Sr Thomas Trevor — of the Inner Temple Knight
His Majestys — Attorny Generall.

Geor: 1 L. 1.

## VIRGIL'S GEORGICS

### The First Book of the Georgics

THE ARGUMENT.

*The Poet, in the beginning of this Book, propounds the general Design of each Georgic: And after a solemn Invocation of all the Gods who are any way related to his Subject, he addresses himself in particular to* Augustus, *whom he complements with Divinity; and after strikes into his Business. He shews the different kinds of Tillage proper to different Soils, traces out the Original of Agriculture, gives a Catalogue of the Husbandman's Tools, specifies the Employments peculiar to each Season, describes the changes of the Weather, with the Signs in Heaven and Earth that fore-bode them, instances many of the Prodigies that happen'd near the time of* Julius Cæsar's *Death, and shuts up all with a Supplication to the Gods for the Safety of* Augustus, *and the Preservation of* Rome.

WHAT makes a plenteous Harvest, when to turn
The fruitful Soil, and when to sowe the Corn;
The Care of Sheep, of Oxen, and of Kine;
And how to raise on Elms the teeming Vine:
The Birth and Genius of the frugal Bee,
I sing, *Mæcenas,* and I sing to thee.

Ye Deities! who Fields and Plains protect,
Who rule the Seasons, and the Year direct;
*Bacchus* and fost'ring *Ceres,* Pow'rs Divine,
10  Who gave us Corn for Mast, for Water Wine:
Ye Fawns, propitious to the Rural Swains,
Ye Nymphs that haunt the Mountains and the Plains,

---

10   *them, instances]* ∼. *Instances* F1–2.      11   *Death, and]* ∼. *And* F1–2.
6   *Mæcenas]* Mecænas F1–2.      10   Wine:] F2; ∼. F1.

Join in my Work, and to my Numbers bring
Your needful Succour, for your Gifts I sing:
And thou, whose Trident struck the teeming Earth,
And made a Passage for the Coursers Birth:
And thou, for whom the *Cæan* Shore sustains
Thy Milky Herds, that graze the Flow'ry Plains.
And thou, the Shepherds tutelary God,
20   Leave, for a while, O *Pan!* thy lov'd Abode:
And, if *Arcadian* Fleeces be thy Care,
From Fields and Mountains to my Song repair.
Inventor, *Pallas,* of the fat'ning Oyl;
Thou Founder of the Plough and Plough-man's Toyl;
And thou, whose Hands the Shrowd-like Cypress rear; ⎫
Come all ye Gods and Goddesses, that wear            ⎬
The rural Honours, and increase the Year:           ⎭
You, who supply the Ground with Seeds of Grain;
And you, who swell those Seeds with kindly Rain:
30   And chiefly thou, whose undetermin'd State
Is yet the Business of the Gods Debate:
Whether in after Times to be declar'd
The Patron of the World, and *Rome*'s peculiar Guard,
Or o're the Fruits and Seasons to preside,
And the round Circuit of the Year to guide:
Pow'rful of Blessings, which thou strew'st around,
And with thy Goddess Mother's Myrtle crown'd.
Or wilt thou, *Cæsar,* chuse the watry Reign,
To smooth the Surges, and correct the Main?
40   Then Mariners, in Storms, to thee shall pray,   ⎫
Ev'n utmost *Thule* shall thy Pow'r obey;           ⎬
And *Neptune* shall resign the Fasces of the Sea.   ⎭
The wat'ry Virgins for thy Bed shall strive,
And *Tethys* all her Waves in Dowry give.
Or wilt thou bless our Summers with thy Rays,
And seated near the Ballance, poise the Days:
Where in the Void of Heav'n a Space is free,

---

14   sing:] ~. F1–2.                    16   Birth:] ~. F1–2.
23   Oyl;] ~, F1–2.                     27   Year:] ~. F1–2.
35   guide:] ~. F1–2.

Betwixt the Scorpion and the Maid for thee?
The Scorpion ready to receive thy Laws,
50 Yields half his Region, and contracts his Claws.
Whatever part of Heav'n thou shalt obtain,
For let not Hell presume of such a Reign;
Nor let so dire a Thirst of Empire move
Thy Mind, to leave thy Kindred Gods above:
Tho' *Greece* admires *Elysium*'s blest Retreat,
Tho' *Proserpine* affects her silent Seat,
And importun'd by *Ceres* to remove,
Prefers the Fields below to those above.
But thou, propitious *Cæsar,* guide my Course,
60 And to my bold Endeavours add thy Force.
Pity the Poet's and the Ploughman's Cares,
Int'rest thy Greatness in our mean Affairs,
And use thy self betimes to hear and grant our Pray'rs.

    While yet the Spring is young, while Earth unbinds
Her frozen Bosom to the Western Winds;
While Mountain Snows dissolve against the Sun,
And Streams, yet new, from Precipices run:
Ev'n in this early Dawning of the Year,
Produce the Plough, and yoke the sturdy Steer,
70 And goad him till he groans beneath his Toil,
'Till the bright Share is bury'd in the Soil.
That Crop rewards the greedy Peasant's Pains,
Which twice the Sun, and twice the Cold sustains,
And bursts the crowded Barns, with more than promis'd Gains.
But e're we stir the yet unbroken Ground,
The various Course of Seasons must be found;
The Weather, and the setting of the Winds,
The Culture suiting to the sev'ral Kinds
Of Seeds and Plants; and what will thrive and rise,
80 And what the Genius of the Soil denies.
This Ground with *Bacchus,* that with *Ceres* suits:

---

48  Scorpion . . . Maid] *Scorpion . . . Maid* F1–2.
48  thee?] ~. F1–2.         49  Scorpion] *Scorpion* F1–2.
54  above:] ~. F1–2.        63  hear and grant] F2; hear F1.
67  run:] ~. F1–2.

That other loads the Trees with happy Fruits:
A fourth with Grass, unbidden, decks the Ground:
Thus *Tmolus* is with yellow Saffron crown'd:
*India,* black Ebon and white Ivory bears:
And soft *Idume* weeps her od'rous Tears.
Thus *Pontus* sends her Beaver Stones from far;
And naked *Spanyards* temper Steel for War.
*Epirus* for th' *Elean* Chariot breeds,
90 (In hopes of Palms,) a Race of running Steeds.
This is the Orig'nal Contract; these the Laws
Impos'd by Nature, and by Nature's Cause,
On sundry Places, when *Deucalion* hurl'd
His Mother's Entrails on the desart World:
Whence Men, a hard laborious Kind, were born.
Then borrow part of Winter for thy Corn;
And early with thy Team the Gleeb in Furrows turn:
That while the Turf lies open, and unbound,
Succeeding Suns may bake the Mellow Ground.
100 But if the Soil be barren, only scar
The Surface, and but lightly print the Share,
When cold *Arcturus* rises with the Sun:
Lest wicked Weeds the Corn shou'd over-run
In watry Soils; or lest the barren Sand
Shou'd suck the Moisture from the thirsty Land.
Both these unhappy Soils the Swain forbears,
And keeps a Sabbath of alternate Years:
That the spent Earth may gather heart again;
And, better'd by Cessation, bear the Grain.
110 At least where Vetches, Pulse, and Tares have stood,
And Stalks of Lupines grew (a stubborn Wood:)
Th' ensuing Season, in return, may bear
The bearded product of the Golden Year.
For Flax and Oats will burn the tender Field,
And sleepy Poppies harmful Harvests yield.
But sweet Vicissitudes of Rest and Toyl
Make easy Labour, and renew the Soil.

---

82 Fruits:] ~. F1–2.          94 His] his F1–2.
97 turn:] ~. F1–2.

Yet sprinkle sordid Ashes all around,
And load with fat'ning Dung thy fallow Ground.
120 Thus change of Seeds for meagre Soils is best;
And Earth manur'd, not idle, though at rest.
  Long Practice has a sure Improvement found,
With kindled Fires to burn the barren Ground;
When the light Stubble, to the Flames resign'd,
Is driv'n along, and crackles in the Wind:
Whether from hence the hollow Womb of Earth
Is warm'd with secret Strength for better Birth,
Or when the latent Vice is cur'd by Fire,
Redundant Humours thro' the Pores expire;
130 Or that the Warmth distends the Chinks, and makes
New Breathings, whence new Nourishment she takes;
Or that the Heat the gaping Ground constrains,
New Knits the Surface, and new Strings the Veins;
Lest soaking Show'rs shou'd pierce her secret Seat, ⎫
Or freezing *Boreas* chill her genial Heat;      ⎬
Or scorching Suns too violently beat.            ⎭
  Nor is the Profit small, the Peasant makes;
Who smooths with Harrows, or who pounds with Rakes
The crumbling Clods: Nor *Ceres* from on high
140 Regards his Labours with a grudging Eye;
Nor his, who plows across the furrow'd Grounds,
And on the Back of Earth inflicts new Wounds:
For he with frequent Exercise Commands
Th' unwilling Soil, and tames the stubborn Lands.
  Ye Swains, invoke the Pow'rs who rule the Sky,
For a moist Summer, and a Winter dry:
For Winter drout rewards the Peasant's Pain,
And broods indulgent on the bury'd Grain.
Hence *Mysia* boasts her Harvests, and the tops
150 Of *Gargarus* admire their happy Crops.
When first the Soil receives the fruitful Seed,
Make no delay, but cover it with speed:
So fenc'd from Cold; the plyant Furrows break,

---

125  Wind:] ⏑. F1–2.
132  constrains,] *the comma prints as a period in some copies of F1.*

Before the surly Clod resists the Rake.
And call the Floods from high, to rush amain
With pregnant Streams, to swell the teeming Grain.
Then when the fiery Suns too fiercely play,
And shrivell'd Herbs on with'ring Stems decay,
The wary Ploughman, on the Mountain's Brow,
160 Undams his watry Stores, huge Torrents flow;
And, ratling down the Rocks, large moisture yield,
Temp'ring the thirsty Fever of the Field:
And lest the Stem, too feeble for the freight,
Shou'd scarce sustain the head's unweildy weight,
Sends in his feeding Flocks betimes t' invade
The rising bulk of the luxuriant Blade;
E're yet th' aspiring Off-spring of the Grain
O'retops the ridges of the furrow'd Plain:
And drains the standing Waters, when they yield
170 Too large a Bev'rage to the drunken Field:
But most in Autumn, and the show'ry Spring,
When dubious Months uncertain weather bring;
When Fountains open, when impetuous Rain
Swells hasty Brooks, and pours upon the Plain;
When Earth with Slime and Mud is cover'd o're,
Or hollow places spue their wat'ry Store.
Nor yet the Ploughman, nor the lab'ring Steer,
Sustain alone the hazards of the Year:
But glutton Geese, and the *Strymonian* Crane,
180 With foreign Troops, invade the tender Grain:
And tow'ring Weeds malignant Shadows yield;
And spreading Succ'ry choaks the rising Field.
The Sire of Gods and Men, with hard Decrees,
Forbids our Plenty to be bought with Ease:
And wills that Mortal Men, inur'd to toil,
Shou'd exercise, with pains, the grudging Soil:
Himself invented first the shining Share,
And whetted Humane Industry by Care:
Himself did Handy-Crafts and Arts ordain;

---

162   Field:] ∼. F1-2.          170   Field:] ∼. F1-2.
182   Succ'ry] *Succ'ry* F1-2.          186   Soil:] ∼. F1-2.

190 Nor suffer'd Sloath to rust his active Reign.
E're this, no Peasant vex'd the peaceful Ground;
Which only Turfs and Greens for Altars found:
No Fences parted Fields, nor Marks nor Bounds
Distinguish'd Acres of litigious Grounds:
But all was common, and the fruitful Earth
Was free to give her unexacted Birth.
*Jove* added Venom to the Viper's Brood,
And swell'd, with raging Storms, the peaceful Flood:
Commission'd hungry Wolves t' infest the Fold,
200 And shook from Oaken Leaves the liquid Gold:
Remov'd from Humane reach the chearful Fire,
And from the Rivers bade the Wine retire:
That studious Need might useful Arts explore;
From furrow'd Fields to reap the foodful Store:
And force the Veins of clashing Flints t' expire
The lurking Seeds of their Cœlestial Fire.
Then first on Seas the hollow'd Alder swam;
Then Sailers quarter'd Heav'n, and found a Name
For ev'ry fix'd and ev'ry wandring Star:
210 The *Pleiads, Hyads,* and the Northern Car.
Then Toils for Beasts, and Lime for Birds were found,
And deep-mouth Dogs did Forrest Walks surround:
And casting Nets were spread in shallow Brooks,
Drags in the Deep, and Baits were hung on Hooks.
Then Saws were tooth'd, and sounding Axes made;
(For Wedges first did yielding Wood invade.)
And various Arts in order did succeed,
(What cannot endless Labour urg'd by need?)
First *Ceres* taught, the Ground with Grain to sow,
220 And arm'd with Iron Shares the crooked Plough;
When now *Dodonian* Oaks no more supply'd
Their Mast, and Trees their Forrest-fruit deny'd.
Soon was his Labour doubl'd to the Swain,
And blasting Mildews blackned all his Grain.
Tough Thistles choak'd the Fields, and kill'd the Corn,
And an unthrifty Crop of Weeds was born.

---

200   Gold:] ∼. F1–2.

To Sr. John Hawles: of Lincolns Inn in the
County of Midlesex Knt. His Majestyes Solicitor Genll.

Geor: 1 L: 240.

Then Burrs and Brambles, an unbidden Crew
Of graceless Guests, th' unhappy Field subdue:
And Oats unblest, and Darnel domineers,
230 And shoots its head above the shining Ears:
So that unless the Land with daily Care
Is exercis'd, and with an Iron War,
Of Rakes and Harrows, the proud Foes expell'd,
And Birds with clamours frighted from the Field;
Unless the Boughs are lopp'd that shade the Plain,
And Heav'n invok'd with Vows for fruitful Rain,
On other Crops you may with envy look,
And shake for Food the long abandon'd Oak.
Nor must we pass untold what Arms they wield,
240 Who labour Tillage and the furrow'd Field:
Without whose aid the Ground her Corn denys,
And nothing can be sown, and nothing rise.
The crooked Plough, the Share, the tow'ring height
Of Waggons, and the Cart's unweildy weight;
The Sled, the Tumbril, Hurdles and the Flail,
The Fan of *Bacchus*, with the flying Sail:
These all must be prepar'd, if Plowmen hope
The promis'd Blessing of a Bounteous Crop.
Young Elms with early force in Copses bow,
250 Fit for the Figure of the crooked Plough.
Of eight Foot long a fastned Beam prepare, ⎫
On either side the Head produce an Ear, ⎬
And sink a Socket for the shining Share: ⎭
Of Beech the Plough-tail, and the bending Yoke;
Or softer Linden harden'd in the Smoke.
I cou'd be long in Precepts, but I fear
So mean a Subject might offend your Ear.
Delve of convenient Depth your thrashing Floor;
With temper'd Clay, then fill and face it o're:
260 And let the weighty Rowler run the round,
To smooth the Surface of th' unequal Ground;
Lest crack'd with Summer Heats the flooring flies,

230  Ears:] ~. F1–2.          243  tow'ring] F2; towr'ing F1.
246  Sail:] ~. F1–2.          253  Share:] ~. F1–2.

Or sinks, and thro' the Crannies Weeds arise.
For sundry Foes the Rural Realm surround:
The Field-Mouse builds her Garner under ground,
For gather'd Grain the blind laborious Mole,
In winding Mazes works her hidden Hole.
In hollow Caverns Vermine make abode,
The hissing Serpent, and the swelling Toad:
270 The Corn-devouring Weezel here abides,
And the wise Ant her wintry Store provides.
    Mark well the flowring Almonds in the Wood;
If od'rous Blooms the bearing Branches load,
The Glebe will answer to the Sylvan Reign,
Great Heats will follow, and large Crops of Grain.
But if a Wood of Leaves o're-shade the Tree,
Such and so barren will thy Harvest be:
In vain the Hind shall vex the thrashing Floor,
For empty Chaff and Straw will be thy Store.
280 Some steep their Seed, and some in Cauldrons boil
With vigorous Nitre, and with Lees of Oyl,
O're gentle Fires; th' exuberant Juice to drain,
And swell the flatt'ring Husks with fruitful Grain.
Yet is not the Success for Years assur'd,
Tho chosen is the Seed, and fully cur'd;
Unless the Peasant, with his Annual Pain,
Renews his Choice, and culls the largest Grain.
Thus all below, whether by Nature's Curse,
Or Fates Decree, degen'rate still to worse.
290 So the Boats brawny Crew the Current stem,
And, slow advancing, struggle with the Stream:
But if they slack their hands, or cease to strive,
Then down the Flood with headlong haste they drive.
    Nor must the Ploughman less observe the Skies,
When the Kidds, Dragon, and *Arcturus* rise,
Than Saylors homeward bent, who cut their Way
Thro' *Helle*'s stormy Streights, and Oyster-breeding Sea.
But when *Astrea*'s Ballance, hung on high,

---

270  Corn-devouring] *the hyphen failed to print in some copies of F1.*
295  Kidds, Dragon] *Kidds, Dragon* F1–2.

Betwixt the Nights and Days divides the Sky,
300 Then Yoke your Oxen, sow your Winter Grain;
'Till cold December comes with driving Rain.
Lineseed and fruitful Poppy bury warm,
In a dry Season, and prevent the Storm.
Sow Beans and Clover in a rotten Soyl,
And Millet rising from your Annual Toyl;
When with his Golden Horns, in full Cariere,
The Bull beats down the Barriers of the Year;
And *Argo* and the Dog forsake the Northern Sphere.
   But if your Care to Wheat alone extend,
310 Let *Maja* with her Sisters first descend,
And the bright *Gnosian* Diadem downward bend:
Before you trust in Earth your future Hope;
Or else expect a listless lazy Crop.
Some Swains have sown before, but most have found
A husky Harvest, from the grudging Ground.
Vile Vetchcs wou'd you sow, or Lentils lean,
The Growth of *Egypt,* or the Kidney-bean?
Begin when the slow Waggoner descends,
Nor cease your sowing till Mid-winter ends:
320 For this, thro' twelve bright Signs *Apollo* guides
The Year, and Earth in sev'ral Climes divides.
Five Girdles bind the Skies, the torrid Zone
Glows with the passing and repassing Sun.
Far on the right and left, th' extreams of Heav'n,
To Frosts and Snows, and bitter Blasts are giv'n.
Betwixt the midst and these, the Gods assign'd
Two habitable Seats for Humane Kind:
And cross their limits cut a sloping way,
Which the twelve Signs in beauteous order sway.
330 Two Poles turn round the Globe; one seen to rise
O're *Scythian* Hills, and one in *Lybian* Skies:
The first sublime in Heav'n, the last is whirl'd
Below the Regions of the nether World.
Around our Pole the spiry Dragon glides,

301  December] *December* F1–2.      308  *Argo*] *Argos* F1–2.
331  Skies:] ~. F1–2.

And like a winding Stream the Bears divides;
The less and greater, who by Fates Decree
Abhor to dive beneath the Southern Sea:
There, as they say, perpetual Night is found
In silence brooding on th' unhappy ground:
340 Or when *Aurora* leaves our Northern Sphere,
She lights the downward Heav'n, and rises there.
And when on us she breaths the living Light,
Red *Vesper* kindles there the Tapers of the Night.
From hence uncertain Seasons we may know;
And when to reap the Grain, and when to sow:
Or when to fell the Furzes, when 'tis meet
To spread the flying Canvass for the Fleet.
Observe what Stars arise or disappear;
And the four Quarters of the rolling Year.
350 But when cold Weather and continu'd Rain,
The lab'ring Husband in his House restrain:
Let him forecast his Work with timely care,
Which else is huddl'd, when the Skies are fair:
Then let him mark the Sheep, or whet the shining Share:
Or hollow Trees for Boats, or number o're
His Sacks, or measure his increasing Store:
Or sharpen Stakes, or head the Forks, or twine
The Sallow Twigs to tye the stragling Vine:
Or wicker Baskets weave, or aire the Corn,
360 Or grinded Grain betwixt two Marbles turn.
No Laws, Divine or Human, can restrain
From necessary Works, the lab'ring Swain.
Ev'n Holy-days and Feasts permission yield,
To float the Meadows, or to fence the Field,
To Fire the Brambles, snare the Birds, and steep
In wholsom Water-falls the woolly Sheep.
And oft the drudging Ass is driv'n, with Toyl,
To neighb'ring Towns with Apples and with Oyl:
Returning late, and loaden home with Gain

354   Share:] ∼. F1–2.
356   Store:] F1 (*corrected state*), F2; ∼; F1 (*uncorrected state*).
364   To float the Meadows, or] F2; The Meads to water, and F1.

To Joseph Jekyll
of the Middle Temple Esq.

Geo: L. 1711

370 Of barter'd Pitch, and Hand-mills for the Grain.
       The lucky Days, in each revolving Moon,
    For Labour chuse: The Fifth be sure to shun;
    That gave the Furies and pale *Pluto* Birth,
    And arm'd, against the Skies, the Sons of Earth.
    With Mountains pil'd on Mountains, thrice they strove
    To scale the steepy Battlements of *Jove:*
    And thrice his Lightning and red Thunder play'd,
    And their demolish'd Works in Ruin laid.
    The Sev'nth is, next the Tenth, the best to joyn
380 Young Oxen to the Yoke, and plant the Vine.
    Then Weavers stretch your Stays upon the Weft:
    The Ninth is good for Travel, bad for Theft.
    Some Works in dead of Night are better done;
    Or when the Morning Dew prevents the Sun.
    Parch'd Meads and Stubble mow, by *Phœbe*'s Light;
    Which both require the Coolness of the Night:
    For Moisture then abounds, and Pearly Rains
    Descend in Silence to refresh the Plains.
    The Wife and Husband equally conspire,
390 To work by Night, and rake the Winter Fire:
    He sharpens Torches in the glim'ring Room,
    She shoots the flying Shuttle through the Loom:
    Or boils in Kettles Must of Wine, and skims
    With Leaves, the Dregs that overflow the Brims.
    And till the watchful Cock awakes the Day,
    She sings to drive the tedious hours away.
    But in warm Weather, when the Skies are clear,
    By Daylight reap the Product of the Year:
    And in the Sun your golden Grain display,
400 And thrash it out, and winnow it by Day.
    Plough naked, Swain, and naked sow the Land,
    For lazy Winter numbs the lab'ring Hand.

---

379   is, next the Tenth,] F1 (*corrected state*), F2; ~ʌ ~, ~ ~ʌ F1 (*uncorrected state*).
382   bad] F1 (*corrected state*), F2; ill F1 (*uncorrected state*).
393   Wine, and skims] F1 (*corrected state*) [skims *is from the errata list; the text has* Skins], F2; Wine and Skins, F1 (*uncorrected state*).
394   Leaves, the Dregs] F1 (*corrected state*), F2; ~ʌ ~ ~, F1 (*uncorrected state*).

In Genial Winter, Swains enjoy their Store,
Forget their Hardships, and recruit for more.
The Farmer to full Bowls invites his Friends,
And what he got with Pains, with Pleasure spends.
So Saylors, when escap'd from stormy Seas,
First crown their Vessels, then indulge their Ease.
Yet that's the proper Time to thrash the Wood
410 For Mast of Oak, your Fathers homely Food:
To gather Laurel-berries, and the Spoil
Of bloody Myrtles, and to press your Oyl:
For stalking Cranes to set the guileful Snare,
T' inclose the Stags in Toyls, and hunt the Hare:
With *Balearick* Slings, or *Gnossian* Bow,
To persecute from far the flying Doe:
Then, when the Fleecy Skies new cloath the Wood,
And cakes of rustling Ice come rolling down the Flood.
    Now sing we stormy Stars, when Autumn weighs ⎫
420 The Year, and adds to Nights, and shortens Days; ⎬
And Suns declining shine with feeble Rays: ⎭
What Cares must then attend the toiling Swain; ⎫
Or when the low'ring Spring, with lavish Rain, ⎬
Beats down the slender Stem and bearded Grain: ⎭
While yet the Head is green, or lightly swell'd
With Milky-moisture, over-looks the Field.
Ev'n when the Farmer, now secure of Fear,
Sends in the Swains to spoil the finish'd Year:
Ev'n while the Reaper fills his greedy hands,
430 And binds the golden Sheafs in brittle bands:
Oft have I seen a sudden Storm arise,
From all the warring Winds that sweep the Skies:
The heavy Harvest from the Root is torn,
And whirl'd aloft the lighter Stubble born;
With such a force the flying rack is driv'n;
And such a Winter wears the face of Heav'n:
And oft whole sheets descend of slucy Rain,

---

410  Fathers] F2; Father's F1.
412  Oyl:] ~. F1–2.
416  Doe:] ~. F1–2.

410  Food:] ~. F1–2.
414  Hare:] ~. F1–2.

Inviting Plenty to their crowded Floors.
Thus in the Spring, and thus in Summer's Heat,
Before the Sickles touch the ripening Wheat,
On *Ceres* call; and let the lab'ring Hind
480 With Oaken Wreaths his hollow Temples bind:
On *Ceres* let him call, and *Ceres* praise,
With uncouth Dances, and with Country Lays.
    And that by certain signs we may presage
Of Heats and Rains, and Wind's impetuous rage,
The Sov'reign of the Heav'ns has set on high
The Moon, to mark the Changes of the Skye:
When Southern blasts shou'd cease, and when the Swain
Shou'd near their Folds his feeding Flocks restrain.
For e're the rising Winds begin to roar,
490 The working Seas advance to wash the Shoar:
Soft whispers run along the leavy Woods,
And Mountains whistle to the murm'ring Floods:
Ev'n then the doubtful Billows scarce abstain
From the toss'd Vessel on the troubled Main:
When crying Cormorants forsake the Sea,
And stretching to the Covert wing their way:
When sportful Coots run skimming o're the Strand;
When watchful Herons leave their watry Stand,
And mounting upward, with erected flight,
500 Gain on the Skyes, and soar above the sight.
And oft before tempest'ous Winds arise,
The seeming Stars fall headlong from the Skies;
And, shooting through the darkness, guild the Night
With sweeping Glories, and long trails of Light:
And Chaff with eddy Winds is whirl'd around,
And dancing Leaves are lifted from the Ground;
And floating Feathers on the Waters play.
But when the winged Thunder takes his way
From the cold North, and East and West ingage,
510 And at their Frontiers meet with equal rage,
The Clouds are crush'd, a glut of gather'd Rain  ⎞
The hollow Ditches fills, and floats the Plain,  ⎬
And Sailors furl their dropping Sheets amain.  ⎠

Wet weather seldom hurts the most unwise,
So plain the Signs, such Prophets are the Skies:
The wary Crane foresees it first, and sails
Above the Storm, and leaves the lowly Vales:
The Cow looks up, and from afar can find
The change of Heav'n, and snuffs it in the Wind.
520  The Swallow skims the River's watry Face,
The Frogs renew the Croaks of their loquacious Race.
The careful Ant her secret Cell forsakes,
And drags her Eggs along the narrow Tracks.
At either Horn the Rainbow drinks the Flood, ⎞
Huge Flocks of rising Rooks forsake their Food, ⎬
And, crying, seek the Shelter of the Wood. ⎠
Besides, the sev'ral sorts of watry Fowls,
That swim the Seas, or haunt the standing Pools:
The Swans that sail along the Silver Flood,
530  And dive with stretching Necks to search their Food,
Then lave their Backs with sprinkling Dews in vain,
And stem the Stream to meet the promis'd Rain.
The Crow with clam'rous Cries the Show'r demands,
And single stalks along the Desart Sands.
The nightly Virgin, while her Wheel she plies,
Foresees the Storm impending in the Skies,
When sparkling Lamps their sputt'ring Light advance,
And in the Sockets Oyly Bubbles dance.
       Then after Show'rs, 'tis easie to descry
540  Returning Suns, and a serener Sky:
The Stars shine smarter, and the Moon adorns,
As with unborrow'd Beams, her sharpen'd Horns.
The filmy Gossamer now flitts no more,
Nor Halcyons bask on the short Sunny Shoar:
Their Litter is not toss'd by Sows unclean,
But a blue droughty Mist descends upon the Plain.
And Owls, that mark the setting Sun, declare
A Star-light Evening, and a Morning fair.

523  Eggs] Egs F1-2.
532  stem the] F2; ∼ tke F1.
544  Halcyons] *Halcyons* F1-2.

530  Food,] F2; ∼. F1.
543  Gossamer] *Gossamer* F1-2.

Tow'ring aloft, avenging *Nisus* flies,
550 While dar'd below the guilty *Scylla* lies.
Where-ever frighted *Scylla* flies away,
Swift *Nisus* follows, and pursues his Prey.
Where injur'd *Nisus* takes his Airy Course,
Thence trembling *Scylla* flies and shuns his Force.
This punishment pursues th' unhappy Maid,
And thus the purple Hair is dearly paid.
Then, thrice the Ravens rend the liquid Air,
And croaking Notes proclaim the settled fair.
Then, round their Airy Palaces they fly,
560 To greet the Sun; and seis'd with secret Joy,
When Storms are over-blown, with Food repair
To their forsaken Nests, and callow Care:
Not that I think their Breasts with Heav'nly Souls
Inspir'd, as Man, who Destiny controls;
But with the changeful Temper of the Skies,
As  Rains condense, and Sun-shine rarifies;
So turn the Species in their alter'd Minds,
Compos'd by Calms, and discompos'd by Winds.
From hence proceeds the Birds harmonious Voice:
570 From hence the Cows exult, and frisking Lambs rejoice.
Observe the daily Circle of the Sun,
And the short Year of each revolving Moon:
By them thou shalt foresee the following day;
Nor shall a starry Night thy Hopes betray.
When first the Moon appears, if then she shrouds
Her silver Crescent, tip'd with sable Clouds;
Conclude she bodes a Tempest on the Main,
And brews for Fields impetuous Floods of Rain.
Or if her Face with fiery Flushing glow,
580 Expect the ratling Winds aloft to blow.
But four Nights old, (for that's the surest Sign,)
With sharpen'd Horns if glorious then she shine:
Next Day, nor only that, but all the Moon,

557   Then,] F1 *(corrected state)*, F2; ~∧ F1 *(uncorrected state)*.
562   Care:] ~. F1–2.
564   controls;] ~. F1–2.
581   (for . . . Sign,)] F1 *(corrected state)*, F2; ∧~ . . . ~,∧ F1 *(uncorrected state)*.

Till her revolving Race be wholly run;
Are void of Tempests, both by Land and Sea,
And Saylors in the Port their promis'd Vow shall pay.
Above the rest, the Sun, who never lies;
Foretels the change of Weather in the Skies:
For if he rise, unwilling to his Race,
590 Clouds on his Brows, and Spots upon his Face;
Or if thro' Mists he shoots his sullen Beams,
Frugal of Light, in loose and stragling Streams:
Suspect a drisling Day, with Southern Rain,
Fatal to Fruits, and Flocks, and promis'd Grain.
Or if *Aurora*, with half open'd Eyes,
And a pale sickly Cheek, salute the Skies;
How shall the Vine, with tender Leaves, defend
Her teeming Clusters, when the Storms descend,
When ridgy Roofs and Tiles can scarce avail,
600 To barr the Ruin of the ratling Hail?
But more than all, the setting Sun survey,
When down the Steep of Heav'n he drives the Day.
For oft we find him finishing his Race,
With various Colours erring on his Face;
If fiery red his glowing Globe descends,
High Winds and furious Tempests he portends.
But if his Cheeks are swoln with livid blue,
He bodes wet Weather by his watry Hue.
If dusky Spots are vary'd on his Brow,
610 And, streak'd with red, a troubl'd Colour show;
That sullen Mixture shall at once declare
Winds, Rain, and Storms, and Elemental War:
What desp'rate Madman then wou'd venture o're
The Frith, or haul his Cables from the Shoar?
But if with Purple Rays he brings the Light,
And a pure Heav'n resigns to quiet Night:
No rising Winds, or falling Storms, are nigh: ⎫
But Northern Breezes through the Forrest fly: ⎬
And drive the rack, and purge the ruffl'd Sky. ⎭

---

598  descend,] ∼? F1-2.                    600  Hail?] ∼. F1-2.
614  Frith] *Frith* F1-2.

To William Dobyns
of Lincolns Inn Esq.

Geo 1: 625

620 Th' unerring Sun by certain Signs declares,
What the late Ev'n, or early Morn prepares:
And when the South projects a stormy Day,
And when the clearing North will puff the Clouds away.
   The Sun reveals the Secrets of the Sky;
And who dares give the Source of Light the Lye?
The change of Empires often he declares,
Fierce Tumults, hidden Treasons, open Wars.
He first the Fate of *Cæsar* did foretel,
And pity'd *Rome,* when *Rome* in *Cæsar* fell:
630 In Iron Clouds conceal'd the Publick Light:
And Impious Mortals fear'd Eternal Night.
   Nor was the Fact foretold by him alone:
Nature her self stood forth, and seconded the Sun.
Earth, Air, and Seas, with Prodigies were sign'd,
And Birds obscene, and howling Dogs divin'd.
What Rocks did *Ætna*'s bellowing Mouth expire
From her torn Entrails! and what Floods of Fire!
What Clanks were heard, in *German* Skies afar,
Of Arms and Armies, rushing to the War!
640 Dire Earthquakes rent the solid *Alps* below,
And from their Summets shook th' Eternal Snow.
Pale Specters in the close of Night were seen;
And Voices heard of more than Mortal Men.
In silent Groves, dumb Sheep and Oxen spoke;
And Streams ran backward, and their Beds forsook:
The yawning Earth disclos'd th' Abyss of Hell: ⎫
The weeping Statues did the Wars foretel; ⎬
And Holy Sweat from Brazen Idols fell. ⎭
Then rising in his Might, the King of Floods,
650 Rusht thro' the Forrests, tore the lofty Woods;
And rolling onward, with a sweepy Sway,
Bore Houses, Herds, and lab'ring Hinds away.
Blood sprang from Wells, Wolfs howl'd in Towns by Night,
And boding Victims did the Priests affright.
Such Peals of Thunder never pour'd from high;

---

629  fell:] ~. F1–2.

Nor forky Light'nings flash'd from such a sullen Sky.
Red Meteors ran a-cross th' Etherial Space;
Stars disappear'd, and Comets took their place.
For this, th' *Emathian* Plains once more were strow'd ⎫
660 With *Roman* Bodies, and just Heav'n thought good ⎬
To fatten twice those Fields with *Roman* Blood. ⎭
Then, after length of Time, the lab'ring Swains,
Who turn the Turfs of those unhappy Plains,
Shall rusty Piles from the plough'd Furrows take,
And over empty Helmets pass the Rake:
Amaz'd at Antick Titles on the Stones,
And mighty Relicks of Gygantick Bones.
   Ye home-born Deities, of Mortal Birth!
Thou Father *Romulus,* and Mother Earth,
670 Goddess unmov'd! whose Guardian Arms extend
O're *Thuscan Tiber*'s Course, and *Roman* Tow'rs defend;
With youthful *Cæsar* your joint Pow'rs ingage,
Nor hinder him to save the sinking Age.
O! let the Blood, already spilt, atone
For the past Crimes of curst *Laomedon!*
Heav'n wants thee there, and long the Gods, we know,
Have grudg'd thee, *Cæsar,* to the World below:
Where Fraud and Rapine, Right and Wrong confound; ⎫
Where impious Arms from ev'ry part resound, ⎬
680 And monstrous Crimes in ev'ry Shape are crown'd. ⎭
The peaceful Peasant to the Wars is prest;
The Fields lye fallow in inglorious Rest.
The Plain no Pasture to the Flock affords,
The crooked Scythes are streightned into Swords:
And there *Euphrates* her soft Off-spring Arms,
And here the *Rhine* rebellows with Alarms:

---

656  forky Light'nings flash'd from such a sullen] F2; Light'ning flash'd from so
serene a F1.
657  a-cross] F2; along F1.
665  Rake:] ∼. F1–2.
671  defend;] F1 (*corrected state*), F2; ∼: F1 (*uncorrected state*).
677  below:] ∼. F1–2.
686  rebellows] F1 (*corrected state*), F2; rebellious F1 (*uncorrected state*).

The neighb'ring Cities range on sev'ral sides, ⎞
Perfidious *Mars* long plighted Leagues divides, ⎬
And o're the wasted World in Triumph rides. ⎠
690 So four fierce Coursers starting to the Race,
Scow'r thro' the Plain, and lengthen ev'ry Pace:
Nor Reins, nor Curbs, nor threat'ning Cries they fear,
But force along the trembling Charioteer.

---

692  Reins] F2; Reigns F1.

To S.ʳ William                    Bowyer Baronet
of Denham Court        in the County of Bucks.

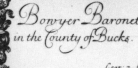

*Geor: 2. L. 1.*

## The Second Book of the Georgics

### THE ARGUMENT.

*The Subject of the following Book is Planting: In handling of which Argument, the Poet shews all the different Methods of raising Trees: Describes their Variety; and gives Rules for the management of each in particular. He then points out the Soils in which the several Plants thrive best: And thence takes occasion to run out into the Praises of* Italy: *After which he gives some Directions for discovering the Nature of every Soil; prescribes Rules for the Dressing of Vines, Olives, &c. And concludes the Georgic with a Panegyric on a Country Life.*

THUS far of Tillage, and of Heav'nly Signs;
  Now sing my Muse the growth of gen'rous Vines:
  The shady Groves, the Woodland Progeny,
And the slow Product of *Minerva*'s Tree.
 Great Father *Bacchus!* to my Song repair;
For clustring Grapes are thy peculiar Care:
For thee large Bunches load the bending Vine,
And the last Blessings of the Year are thine.
To thee his Joys the jolly Autumn owes,
10 When the fermenting Juice the Vat o'reflows.
Come strip with me, my God, come drench all o're
Thy Limbs in Must of Wine, and drink at ev'ry Pore.
 Some Trees their birth to bounteous Nature owe:
For some without the pains of Planting grow.
With Osiers thus the Banks of Brooks abound,
Sprung from the watry Genius of the Ground:
From the same Principles grey Willows come;

---

1 *Planting:*] ∼. F1–2.
6 Italy:] ∼. F1–2.
7 load] F1 (*corrected state*), F2; lade F1 (*uncorrected state*).
13 *not indented in some copies of F1.*
13 owe:] F1 (*corrected state*), F2; ∼, F1 (*uncorrected state*).

*Herculean* Poplar, and the tender Broom.
But some from Seeds inclos'd in Earth arise:
20 For thus the mastful Chesnut mates the Skies.
Hence rise the branching Beech and vocal Oke,
Where *Jove* of old Oraculously spoke.
Some from the Root a rising Wood disclose;
Thus Elms, and thus the salvage Cherry grows.
Thus the green Bays, that binds the Poet's Brows,
Shoots and is shelter'd by the Mother's Boughs.
    These ways of Planting, Nature did ordain,
For Trees and Shrubs, and all the Sylvan Reign.
Others there are, by late Experience found:
30 Some cut the Shoots, and plant in furrow'd ground:
Some cover rooted Stalks in deeper Mold:
Some cloven Stakes, and (wond'rous to behold,)
Their sharpen'd ends in Earth their footing place,
And the dry Poles produce a living Race.
Some bowe their Vines, which bury'd in the Plain,
Their tops in distant Arches rise again.
Others no Root require, the Lab'rer cuts
Young Slips, and in the Soil securely puts.
Ev'n Stumps of Olives, bar'd of Leaves, and dead,
40 Revive, and oft redeem their wither'd head.
'Tis usual now, an Inmate Graff to see,
With Insolence invade a Foreign Tree:
Thus Pears and Quinces from the Crabtree come;
And thus the ruddy Cornel bears the Plum.
    Then let the Learned Gard'ner mark with care
The Kinds of Stocks, and what those Kinds will bear:
Explore the Nature of each sev'ral Tree;
And known, improve with artful Industry:
And let no spot of idle Earth be found,
50 But cultivate the Genius of the Ground.
For open *Ismarus* will *Bacchus* please;
*Taburnus* loves the shade of Olive Trees.
    The Virtues of the sev'ral Soils I sing,
*Mæcenas*, now thy needful Succour bring!

54  *Mæcenas*] *Mecænas* F1–2.

O thou! the better part of my Renown,
Inspire thy Poet, and thy Poem crown:
Embarque with me, while I new Tracts explore,
With flying sails and breezes from the shore:
Not that my song, in such a scanty space,
60 So large a Subject fully can embrace:
Not tho I were supply'd with Iron Lungs,
A hundred Mouths, fill'd with as many Tongues:
But steer my Vessel with a steady hand,
And coast along the Shore in sight of Land.
Nor will I tire thy Patience with a train
Of Preface, or what ancient Poets feign.
The Trees, which of themselves advance in Air,
Are barren kinds, but strongly built and fair:
Because the vigour of the Native Earth
70 Maintains the Plant, and makes a Manly Birth.
Yet these, receiving Graffs of other Kind,
Or thence transplanted, change their salvage Mind:
Their Wildness lose, and quitting Nature's part,
Obey the Rules and Discipline of Art.
The same do Trees, that, sprung from barren Roots
In open fields, transplanted bear their Fruits.
For where they grow the Native Energy
Turns all into the Substance of the Tree,
Starves and destroys the Fruit, is only made
80 For brawny bulk, and for a barren shade.
The Plant that shoots from Seed, a sullen Tree
At leisure grows, for late Posterity;
The gen'rous flavour lost, the Fruits decay,
And salvage Grapes are made the Birds ignoble prey.
Much labour is requir'd in Trees, to tame
Their wild disorder, and in ranks reclaim.
Well must the ground be dig'd, and better dress'd,
New Soil to make, and meliorate the rest.
Old Stakes of Olive Trees in Plants revive;      ⎫
90 By the same Methods *Paphian* Myrtles live:     ⎬
But nobler Vines by Propagation thrive.          ⎭
From Roots hard Hazles, and from Cyens rise

Tall Ash, and taller Oak that mates the Skies:
Palm, Poplar, Firr, descending from the Steep
Of Hills, to try the dangers of the Deep.
The thin-leav'd Arbute, Hazle graffs receives,
And Planes huge Apples bear, that bore but Leaves.
Thus Mastful Beech the bristly Chesnut bears,
And the wild Ash is white with blooming Pears.
100 And greedy Swine from grafted Elms are fed,
With falling Acorns, that on Oaks are bred.
　　But various are the ways to change the state
Of Plants, to Bud, to Graff, t' Inoculate.
For where the tender Rinds of Trees disclose
Their shooting Gems, a swelling Knot there grows;
Just in that space a narrow Slit we make,
Then other Buds from bearing Trees we take:
Inserted thus, the wounded Rind we close,
In whose moist Womb th' admitted Infant grows.
110 But when the smoother Bole from Knots is free,
We make a deep Incision in the Tree,
And in the solid Wood the Slip inclose;
The bat'ning Bastard shoots again and grows:
And in short space the laden Boughs arise,
With happy Fruit advancing to the Skies.
The Mother Plant admires the Leaves unknown,
Of Alien Trees, and Apples not her own.
　　Of vegetable Woods are various Kinds,
And the same Species are of sev'ral Minds.
120 Lotes, Willows, Elms, have diff'rent Forms allow'd,
So fun'ral Cypress rising like a Shrowd.
Fat Olive Trees of sundry Sorts appear:
Of sundry Shapes their unctuous Berries bear.
Radij long Olives, Orchits round produce,
And bitter Pausia, pounded for the Juice.
*Alcinous* Orchard various Apples bears:
Unlike are Bergamotes and pounder Pears.

---

96　Arbute, Hazle] F1 *errata*, F2 (*Arbute* F2); *Arbute* Hazle, F1.
111　Tree,] ~; F1–2.
112　inclose;] ~, F1–2.
124–125　Radij . . . Orchits . . . Pausia] *Radij . . . Orchit's . . . Pausia* F1–2.

To Gilbert Dolbin of Thindon
in Northampton-Shire Esq

Geo: L: 145.

Such large increase the Land that joins *Vesuvius* yields.
And such a Country cou'd *Acerra* boast,
Till *Clanius* overflow'd th' unhappy Coast.
    I teach thee next the diff'ring Soils to know;
310 The light for Vines, the heavyer for the Plough.
Chuse first a place for such a purpose fit,
There dig the solid Earth, and sink a Pit:
Next fill the hole with its own Earth agen,
And trample with thy Feet, and tread it in:
Then if it rise not to the former height
Of superfice, conclude that Soil is light;
A proper Ground for Pasturage and Vines.
But if the sullen Earth, so press'd, repines
Within its native Mansion to retire,
320 And stays without, a heap of heavy Mire;
'Tis good for Arable, a Glebe that asks
Tough Teams of Oxen, and laborious Tasks.
    Salt Earth and bitter are not fit to sow,
Nor will be tam'd or mended with the Plough.
Sweet Grapes degen'rate there, and Fruits declin'd
From their first flav'rous Taste, renounce their Kind.
This Truth by sure Experiment is try'd;
For first an Osier Colendar provide
Of Twigs thick wrought, (such toiling Peasants twine,
330 When thro' streight Passages they strein their Wine;)
In this close Vessel place that Earth accurs'd,
But fill'd brimful with wholsom Water first;
Then run it through, the Drops will rope around,
And by the bitter Taste disclose the Ground.
The fatter Earth by handling we may find,
With Ease distinguish'd from the meagre Kind:
Poor Soil will crumble into Dust, the Rich
Will to the Fingers cleave like clammy Pitch:
Moist Earth produces Corn and Grass, but both
340 Too rank and too luxuriant in their Growth.
Let not my Land so large a Promise boast,

---

306    the Land that joins *Vesuvius* yields.] F2; *Vesuvian Nola* yields: F1.
338    Will] F2; will F1.

Lest the lank Ears in length of Stem be lost.
The heavier Earth is by her Weight betray'd,
The lighter in the poising Hand is weigh'd:
'Tis easy to distinguish by the Sight
The Colour of the Soil, and black from white.
But the cold Ground is difficult to know, ⎫
Yet this the Plants that prosper there, will show; ⎬
Black Ivy, Pitch Trees, and the baleful Yeugh. ⎭
350 These Rules consider'd well, with early Care,
The Vineyard destin'd for thy Vines prepare:
But, long before the Planting, dig the Ground,
With Furrows deep that cast a rising Mound:
The Clods, expos'd to Winter Winds, will bake:
For putrid Earth will best in Vineyards take,
And hoary Frosts, after the painful Toyl
Of delving Hinds, will rot the Mellow Soil.
    Some Peasants, not t' omit the nicest Care,
Of the same Soil their Nursery prepare,
360 With that of their Plantation; lest the Tree
Translated, should not with the Soil agree.
Beside, to plant it as it was, they mark
The Heav'ns four Quarters on the tender Bark;
And to the North or South restore the Side,
Which at their Birth did Heat or Cold abide.
So strong is Custom; such Effects can Use
In tender Souls of pliant Plants produce.
    Chuse next a Province, for thy Vineyards Reign,
On Hills above, or in the lowly Plain:
370 If fertile Fields or Valleys be thy Choice,
Plant thick, for bounteous *Bacchus* will rejoice
In close Plantations there: But if the Vine
On rising Ground be plac'd, or Hills supine,
Extend thy loose Battalions largely wide,
Opening thy Ranks and Files on either Side:
But marshall'd all in order as they Stand,
And let no Souldier straggle from his Band.
As Legions in the Field their Front display,
To try the Fortune of some doubtful Day,

Unhurt by Southern Show'rs or Northern Hail.
They spread their Gems the genial Warmth to share:
And boldly trust their Buds in open Air.
In this soft Season (Let me dare to sing,)
The World was hatch'd by Heav'ns Imperial King:
In prime of all the Year, and Holydays of Spring.
460 Then did the new Creation first appear;
Nor other was the Tenour of the Year:
When laughing Heav'n did the great Birth attend,
And Eastern Winds their Wintry Breath suspend:
Then Sheep first saw the Sun in open Fields;
And salvage Beasts were sent to Stock the Wilds:
And Golden Stars flew up to Light the Skies,
And Man's relentless Race, from Stony Quarries rise.
Nor cou'd the tender, new Creation, bear
Th' excessive Heats or Coldness of the Year:
470 But chill'd by Winter, or by Summer fir'd,
The middle Temper of the Spring requir'd:
When Warmth and Moisture did at once abound,
And Heav'ns Indulgence brooded on the Ground.
    For what remains, in depth of Earth secure
Thy cover'd Plants, and dung with hot Manure;
And Shells and Gravel in the Ground inclose;
For thro' their hollow Chinks the Water flows:
Which, thus imbib'd, returns in misty Dews,
And steeming up, the rising Plant renews.
480 Some Husbandmen, of late, have found the Way,
A hilly Heap of Stones above to lay,
And press the Plants with Sherds of Potters Clay.

---

457  Let me dare to sing,] F2; so sweet Poets sing F1.
460–464  *in F1 as follows:*
        Earth knew no Season then, but Spring alone:
        On the moist Ground the Sun serenely shone:
        Then Winter Winds their blustring Rage forbear,
        And in a silent Pomp proceeds the mighty Year.
        Sheep soon were sent to people flow'ry Fields,
465  sent to Stock the Wilds:] F2; banish'd into Wilds. F1.
466–467  *in F1 as follows:*
        Then Heav'n was lighted up with Stars; and Man,
        A hard relentless Race, from Stones began.
471  requir'd:] ~. F1–2.
472  *in F1 as follows:* When Infant Nature was with Quiet crown'd,

This Fence against immod'rate Rain they found:
Or when the Dog-star cleaves the thirsty Ground.
Be mindful when thou hast intomb'd the Shoot,
With Store of Earth around to feed the Root;
With Iron Teeth of Rakes and Prongs, to move
The crusted Earth, and loosen it above.
Then exercise thy sturdy Steers to plough
490 Betwixt thy Vines, and teach thy feeble Row
To mount on Reeds, and Wands, and, upward led,
On Ashen Poles to raise their forky Head.
On these new Crutches let them learn to walk,
Till swerving upwards, with a stronger Stalk,
They brave the Winds, and, clinging to their Guide,
On tops of Elms at length triumphant ride.
But in their tender Nonage, while they spread
Their Springing Leafs, and lift their Infant Head,
And upward while they shoot in open Air,
500 Indulge their Child-hood, and the Nurseling spare.
Nor exercise thy Rage on new-born Life,
But let thy Hand supply the Pruning-knife;
And crop luxuriant Straglers, nor be loath
To strip the Branches of their leafy Growth:
But when the rooted Vines, with steady Hold,
Can clasp their Elms, then Husbandman be bold
To lop the disobedient Boughs, that stray'd
Beyond their Ranks: let crooked Steel invade
The lawless Troops, which Discipline disclaim,
510 And their superfluous Growth with Rigour tame.
Next, fenc'd with Hedges and deep Ditches round,
Exclude th' incroaching Cattle from thy Ground,
While yet the tender Gems but just appear,
Unable to sustain th' uncertain Year;
Whose Leaves are not alone foul Winter's Prey,
But oft by Summer Suns are scorch'd away;
And worse than both, become th' unworthy Browze ⎫
Of Buffalo's, salt Goats, and hungry Cows. ⎬
For not December's Frost that burns the Boughs, ⎭

489  sturdy] F2; strugling F1.  518  Buffalo's] F2; Buffal'os F1.
519  December's] *December's* F1–2.

To John Loving Esq. of Little Ealing
in the County of Middlesex.

F. Cleyn. Lombart Sculpsit. Londini.

520 Nor Dog-days parching Heat that splits the Rocks, )
Are half so harmful as the greedy Flocks: }
Their venom'd Bite, and Scars indented on the Stocks. )
For this the Malefactor Goat was laid
On *Bacchus* Altar, and his forfeit paid.
At *Athens* thus old Comedy began,
When round the Streets the reeling Actors ran;
In Country Villages, and crossing ways,
Contending for the Prizes of their Plays:
And glad, with *Bacchus,* on the grassie soil,
530 Leapt o're the Skins of Goats besmear'd with Oyl.
Thus *Roman* Youth deriv'd from ruin'd *Troy,*
In rude *Saturnian* Rhymes express their Joy:
With Taunts, and Laughter loud, their Audience please,
Deform'd with Vizards, cut from Barks of Trees:
In jolly Hymns they praise the God of Wine, )
Whose Earthen Images adorn the Pine; }
And there are hung on high, in honour of the Vine: )
A madness so devout the Vineyard fills.
In hollow Valleys and on rising Hills;
540 On what e're side he turns his honest face,
And dances in the Wind, those Fields are in his grace.
To *Bacchus* therefore let us tune our Lays,
And in our Mother Tongue resound his Praise.
Thin Cakes in Chargers, and a Guilty Goat,
Dragg'd by the Horns, be to his Altars brought;
Whose offer'd Entrails shall his Crime reproach,
And drip their Fatness from the Hazle Broach.
To dress thy Vines new labour is requir'd,
Nor must the painful Husbandman be tir'd:
550 For thrice, at least, in Compass of the Year,
Thy Vineyard must employ the sturdy Steer,
To turn the Glebe; besides thy daily pain
To break the Clods, and make the Surface plain:
T' unload the Branches or the Leaves to thin,
That suck the Vital Moisture of the Vine.
Thus in a Circle runs the Peasant's Pain,

---

524  *Bacchus*] *Bacchus's* F1–2.        538  Vineyard] F2; Vineyards F1.

And the Year rowls within it self again.
Ev'n in the lowest Months, when Storms have shed
From Vines the hairy Honours of their Head;
560 Not then the drudging Hind his Labour ends;
But to the coming Year his Care extends:
Ev'n then the naked Vine he persecutes;
His Pruning Knife at once Reforms and Cuts.
Be first to dig the Ground, be first to burn
The Branches lopt, and first the Props return
Into thy House, that bore the burden'd Vines;
But last to reap the Vintage of thy Wines.
Twice in the Year luxuriant Leaves o'reshade
Th' incumber'd Vine; rough Brambles twice invade:
570 Hard Labour both! commend the large excess
Of spacious Vineyards; cultivate the less.
Besides, in Woods the Shrubs of prickly Thorn,
Sallows and Reeds, on Banks of Rivers born,
Remain to cut; for Vineyards useful found, ⎫
To stay thy Vines, and fence thy fruitful Ground. ⎬
Nor when thy tender Trees at length are bound; ⎭
When peaceful Vines from Pruning Hooks are free, ⎫
When Husbands have survey'd the last degree, ⎬
And utmost Files of Plants, and order'd ev'ry Tree; ⎭
580 Ev'n when they sing at ease in full Content,
Insulting o're the Toils they underwent;
Yet still they find a future Task remain;
To turn the Soil, and break the Clods again:
And after all, their Joys are unsincere,
While falling Rains on ripening Grapes they fear.
Quite opposite to these are Olives found,
No dressing they require, and dread no wound;
Nor Rakes nor Harrows need, but fix'd below,
Rejoyce in open Air, and unconcerndly grow.
590 The Soil it self due Nourishment supplies:
Plough but the Furrows, and the Fruits arise:
Content with small Endeavours, 'till they spring, ⎫
Soft Peace they figure, and sweet Plenty bring: ⎬
Then Olives plant, and Hymns to *Pallas* sing. ⎭

592 spring,] ∼. F1–2.

Thus Apple Trees, whose Trunks are strong to bear
Their spreading Boughs, exert themselves in Air:
Want no supply, but stand secure alone,
Not trusting foreign Forces, but their own:
'Till with the ruddy freight the bending Branches groan.
600 Thus Trees of Nature, and each common Bush,
Uncultivated thrive, and with red Berries blush.
Vile Shrubs are shorn for Browze: the tow'ring hight
Of unctuous Trees, are Torches for the Night.
And shall we doubt, (indulging easie Sloath,)
To sow, to set, and to reform their growth?
To leave the lofty Plants; the lowly kind,
Are for the Shepherd, or the Sheep design'd.
Ev'n humble Broom and Osiers have their use,
And Shade for Sleep, and Food for Flocks produce;
610 Hedges for Corn, and Honey for the Bees:
Besides the pleasing Prospect of the Trees.
How goodly looks *Cytorus,* ever green
With Boxen Groves, with what delight are seen
*Narycian* Woods of Pitch, whose gloomy shade,
Seems for retreat of heav'nly Muses made!
But much more pleasing are those Fields to see,
That need not Ploughs, nor Human Industry.
Ev'n cold *Caucasean* Rocks with Trees are spread,
And wear green Forests on their hilly Head.
620 Tho' bending from the blast of Eastern Storms,
Tho' shent their Leaves, and shatter'd are their Arms;
Yet Heav'n their various Plants for use designs:
For Houses Cedars, and for Shipping Pines:
Cypress provides for Spokes, and Wheels of Wains:
And all for Keels of Ships, that scour the watry Plains.
Willows in Twigs are fruitful, Elms in Leaves,
The War, from stubborn Myrtle Shafts receives:
From Cornels Jav'lins, and the tougher Yeugh
Receives the bending Figure of a Bow.
630 Nor Box, nor Limes, without their use are made,
Smooth-grain'd, and proper for the Turner's Trade:
Which curious Hands may kerve, and Steel with Ease invade.

---

615  heav'nly] F2; thoughtful F1.          623  Pines:] ~. F1–2.

Whose Mind, unmov'd, the Bribes of Courts can see;
Their glitt'ring Baits, and Purple Slavery:
Nor hopes the People's Praise, nor fears their Frown, ⎫
Nor, when contending Kindred tear the Crown, ⎬
Will set up one, or pull another down. ⎭
    Without Concern he hears, but hears from far,
710 Of Tumults and Descents, and distant War:
Nor with a Superstitious Fear is aw'd,
For what befals at home, or what abroad.
Nor envies he the Rich their heapy Store,
Nor his own Peace disturbs, with Pity for the Poor.
He feeds on Fruits, which, of their own accord,
The willing Ground, and laden Trees afford.
From his lov'd Home no Lucre him can draw; ⎫
The Senates mad Decrees he never saw; ⎬
Nor heard, at bawling Bars, corrupted Law. ⎭
720 Some to the Seas, and some to Camps resort,
And some with Impudence invade the Court.
In foreign Countries others seek Renown,
With Wars and Taxes others waste their own:
And Houses burn, and houshold Gods deface,
To drink in Bowls which glitt'ring Gems enchase:
To loll on Couches, rich with Cytron Steds,
And lay their guilty Limbs in *Tyrian* Beds.
This Wretch in Earth intombs his Golden Ore,
Hov'ring and brooding on his bury'd Store.
730 Some Patriot Fools to pop'lar Praise aspire,
By Publick Speeches, which worse Fools admire:
While from both Benches, with redoubl'd Sounds,
Th' Applause of Lords and Commoners abounds.
Some through Ambition, or thro' Thirst of Gold,

---

705   Slavery:] ∼. F1–2.
714   his own Peace disturbs, with Pity for] F2; with a helpless Hand condoles F1.
723   own:] ∼. F1–2.
726   Cytron] *Cytron* F1–2.
730   pop'lar] F1 (*corrected state*); popular F1 (*uncorrected state*), F2.
731   By] F1 (*corrected state*); Or F1 (*uncorrected state*), F2.
731   admire:] ∼. F1–2.
734   through Ambition] F1 (*corrected state*); thro' Ambition F1 (*uncorrected state*), F2.
734   Gold,] ∼; F1–2.

To William Walsh of Abberley
in Worcester = shire Esq.

Geo. VM.768.

To the most Noble and        Illustrious Prince
Charles Duke of Richmond    and Lenox Earl of March
and Darnley Baron of        Sitrington Knight of the
Most noble Order             of the Garter.

# The Third Book of the Georgics

THE ARGUMENT.

*This Book begins with an Invocation of some Rural Deities, and a Compliment to* Augustus: *After which* Virgil *directs himself to* Mæcenas, *and enters on his Subject. He lays down Rules for the Breeding and Management of Horses, Oxen, Sheep, Goats, and Dogs: And interweaves several pleasant Descriptions of a Chariot-Race, of the Battel of the Bulls, of the Force of Love, and of the* Scythian *Winter. In the latter part of the Book he relates the Diseases incident to Cattel; and ends with the Description of a fatal Murrain that formerly rag'd among the* Alps.

THY Fields, propitious *Pales,* I reherse;
And sing thy Pastures in no vulgar Verse,
*Amphrysian* Shepherd; the *Lycæan* Woods;
*Arcadia's* flow'ry Plains, and pleasing Floods.
All other Themes, that careless Minds invite,
Are worn with use; unworthy me to write.
*Busiris* Altars, and the dire Decrees
Of hard *Eurystheus,* ev'ry Reader sees:
*Hylas* the Boy, *Latona's* erring Isle,
10 And *Pelops* Iv'ry Shoulder, and his Toil
For fair *Hippodamè,* with all the rest
Of *Grecian* Tales, by Poets are exprest:
New ways I must attempt, my groveling Name
To raise aloft, and wing my flight to Fame.
I, first of *Romans* shall in Triumph come
From conquer'd *Greece,* and bring her Trophies home:
With Foreign Spoils adorn my native place;
And with *Idume's* Palms, my *Mantua* grace.
Of *Parian* Stone a Temple will I raise,

---

3  Mæcenas] Mecænas F1–2; *no Argument in* O.
7  *Busiris*] *Busiri's* O, F1–2.          8  *Eurystheus*] *Euristheus* O, F1–2.
10  *Pelops*] *Pelop's* O, F1–2.          11  *Hippodamè*] *Hippodamé* O, F1–2.

20 Where the slow *Mincius* through the Vally strays:
Where cooling Streams invite the Flocks to drink:
And Reeds defend the winding Waters Brink.
Full in the midst shall mighty *Cæsar* stand:
Hold the chief Honours; and the Dome command.
Then I, conspicuous in my *Tyrian* Gown,
(Submitting to his Godhead my Renown)
A hundred Coursers from the Goal will drive;
The rival Chariots in the Race shall strive.
All *Greece* shall flock from far, my Games to see; )
30 The Whorlbat, and the rapid Race, shall be          }
Reserv'd for *Cæsar,* and ordain'd by me.            )
My self, with Olive crown'd, the Gifts will bear: )
Ev'n now methinks the publick shouts I hear:      }
The passing Pageants, and the Pomps appear.      )
I, to the Temple will conduct the Crew:
The Sacrifice and Sacrificers view;
From thence return, attended with my Train,
Where the proud Theatres disclose the Scene:
Which interwoven *Britains* seem to raise,
40 And shew the Triumph which their Shame displays.
High o're the Gate, in Elephant and Gold,
The Crowd shall *Cæsar's Indian* War behold;
The *Nile* shall flow beneath; and on the side,
His shatter'd Ships on Brazen Pillars ride.
Next him *Niphates* with inverted Urn,               )
And dropping Sedge, shall his *Armenia* mourn;  }
And *Asian* Cities in our Triumph born.             )
With backward Bows the *Parthians* shall be there;
And, spurring from the Fight confess their Fear.
50 A double Wreath shall crown our *Cæsar's* Brows;
Two differing Trophies, from two different Foes.
*Europe* with *Africk* in his Fame shall join;
But neither Shoar his Conquest shall confine.
The *Parian* Marble, there, shall seem to move,
In breathing Statues, not unworthy *Jove:*

---

40  Triumph . . . Shame] *Triumph . . . Shame* O, F1-2.
55  *Jove:*] ~. O, F1-2.

Resembling Heroes, whose Etherial Root,
Is *Jove* himself, and *Cæsar* is the Fruit.
*Tros* and his Race the Sculptor shall employ;
And he the God, who built the Walls of *Troy*.
60 Envy her self at last, grown pale and dumb;
(By *Cæsar* combated and overcome)
Shall give her Hands; and fear the curling Snakes
Of lashing Furies, and the burning Lakes:
The Pains of famisht *Tantalus* shall feel; ⎫
And *Sisyphus* that labours up the Hill ⎬
The rowling Rock in vain; and curst *Ixion*'s Wheel. ⎭
   Mean time we must pursue the Sylvan Lands; ⎫
(Th' abode of Nymphs,) untouch'd by former Hands: ⎬
For such, *Mæcenas*, are thy hard Commands. ⎭
70 Without thee nothing lofty can I sing;
Come then, and with thy self thy Genius bring:
With which inspir'd, I brook no dull delay. ⎫
*Cytheron* loudly calls me to my way; ⎬
Thy Hounds, *Taygetus*, open and pursue their Prey. ⎭
High *Epidaurus* urges on my speed,
Fam'd for his Hills, and for his Horses breed:
From Hills and Dales the chearful Cries rebound:
For Eccho hunts along; and propagates the sound.
   A time will come, when my maturer Muse,
80 In *Cæsar*'s Wars, a Nobler Theme shall chuse:
And through more Ages bear my Soveraign's Praise;
Than have from *Tithon* past to *Cæsar*'s Days.
   The Generous Youth, who studious of the Prize,
The Race of running Coursers multiplies;
Or to the Plough the sturdy Bullock breeds,
May know that from the Dam the worth of each proceeds:
The Mother Cow must wear a low'ring look,
Sour headed, strongly neck'd, to bear the Yoke.
Her double Dew-lap from her Chin descends:
90 And at her Thighs the pondrous burthen ends.
Long are her sides and large, her Limbs are great;

---

67  Sylvan] *Sylvan* O, F1–2.
80  chuse:] ∼. O, F1–2.

Rough are her Ears, and broad her horny Feet.
Her Colour shining Black, but fleck'd with white;
She tosses from the Yoke; provokes the Fight:
She rises in her Gate, is free from Fears;
And in her Face a Bull's Resemblance bears:
Her ample Forehead with a Star is crown'd;
And with her length of Tail she sweeps the Ground.
The Bull's Insult at Four she may sustain;
100 But, after Ten, from Nuptial Rites refrain.
Six Seasons use; but then release the Cow,
Unfit for Love, and for the lab'ring Plough.
    Now while their Youth is fill'd with kindly Fire,
Submit thy Females to the lusty Sire:
Watch the quick motions of the frisking Tail, ⎫
Then serve their fury with the rushing Male, ⎬
Indulging Pleasure lest the Breed shou'd fail. ⎭
    In Youth alone, unhappy Mortals live;
But, ah! the mighty Bliss is fugitive;
110 Discolour'd Sickness, anxious Labours come,
And Age, and Death's inexorable Doom.
    Yearly thy Herds in vigour will impair;
Recruit and mend 'em with thy Yearly care:
Still propagate, for still they fall away,
'Tis Prudence to prevent th' entire decay.
    Like Diligence requires the Courser's Race;
In early Choice; and for a longer space.
The Colt, that for a Stallion is design'd, ⎫
By sure Presages shows his generous Kind, ⎬
120 Of able Body, sound of Limb and Wind. ⎭
Upright he walks, on Pasterns firm and straight;
His Motions easy; prancing in his Gate:
The first to lead the Way, to tempt the Flood;
To pass the Bridge unknown, nor fear the trembling Wood:
Dauntless at empty Noises; lofty neck'd;
Sharp headed, Barrel belly'd, broadly back'd:

---

122   Gate:] ∼. O, F1–2.
124   Wood:] ∼. O, F1–2.
126   back'd:] ∼. O, F1–2.

Brawny his Chest, and deep, his Colour gray; ⎫
For Beauty dappled, or the brightest Bay: ⎬
Faint white and Dun will scarce the Rearing pay. ⎭
130  The fiery Courser, when he hears from far,
The sprightly Trumpet, and the shouts of War,
Pricks up his Ears; and trembling with Delight,
Shifts place, and paws; and hopes the promis'd Fight.
On his right Shoulder his thick Mane reclin'd,
Ruffles at speed; and dances in the Wind.
His horny Hoofs are jetty black, and round; ⎫
His Chine is double; starting, with a bound ⎬
He turns the Turf, and shakes the solid Ground. ⎭
Fire from his Eyes, Clouds from his Nostrils flow:
140  He bears his Rider headlong on the Foe.
Such was the Steed in *Græcian* Poets fam'd,
Proud *Cyllarus,* by *Spartan Castor* tam'd:
Such Coursers bore to Fight the God of *Thrace;*
And such, *Achilles,* was thy warlike Race.
In such a Shape, old *Saturn* did restrain
His Heav'nly Limbs, and flow'd with such a Mane:
When, half surpriz'd, and fearing to be seen,
The Leacher gallop'd from his Jealous Queen:
Ran up the ridges of the Rocks amain;
150  And with shrill Neighings fill'd the Neighb'ring Plain.
But worn with Years, when dire Diseases come,
Then hide his not Ignoble Age, at Home:
In Peace t' enjoy his former Palms and Pains;
And gratefully be kind to his Remains.
For when his Blood no Youthful Spirits move,
He languishes and labours in his Love.
And when the sprightly Seed shou'd swiftly come,
Dribling he drudges, and defrauds the Womb.
In vain he burns, like fainty Stubble Fires;

---

131   Trumpet] F1 (*corrected state*); Trumpets O, F1 (*uncorrected state*), F2.
142   *Castor*] F1 (*corrected state*); *Pollux* O, F1 (*uncorrected state*), F2.
145   old] F1 (*corrected state*); grim O, F1 (*uncorrected state*), F2.
146   Mane:] ~. O, F1–2.
150   Neighb'ring] Neighbouring O, F2; Neigbouring F1 (*uncorrected state*); Neigbo'ring F1 (*corrected state*).
159   fainty] F1 (*corrected state*); hasty O, F1 (*uncorrected state*), F2.

160 And in himself his former self requires.
  His Age and Courage weigh: Nor those alone,
But note his Father's Virtues with his own;
Observe if he disdains to yield the Prize;
Of Loss impatient, proud of Victories.
  Hast thou beheld, when from the Goal they start,
The Youthful Charioteers with heaving Heart,
Rush to the Race; and panting, scarcely bear
Th' extreams of feaverish hope, and chilling Fear;
Stoop to the Reins, and lash with all their force;
170 The flying Chariot kindles in the Course:
And now aloft; and now alow they fly,
Now seem to sink in Earth, and now to touch the Sky;
No stop, no stay, but Clouds of Sand arise;
Spurn'd, and cast backward on the Follower's Eyes.
The hindmost blows the foam upon the first:
Such is the love of Praise, an Honourable Thirst.
  Bold *Ericthonius* was the first, who join'd
Four Horses for the rapid Race design'd;
And o're the dusty Wheels presiding sate;
180 The *Lapithæ* to Chariots, added State
Of Bits and Bridles; taught the Steed to bound;
To run the Ring, and trace the mazy round:
To stop, to fly, the Rules of War to know:
T' obey the Rider; and to dare the Foe.
  To chuse a Youthful Steed, with Courage fir'd;
To breed him, break him, back him, are requir'd
Experienc'd Masters; and in sundry Ways:
Their Labours equal, and alike their Praise.
But once again the batter'd Horse beware,
190 The weak old Stallion will deceive thy care.

---

162 with] F1 (*corrected state*); and O, F1 (*uncorrected state*), F2.
166 heaving] F2; beating O, F1.
171 aloft . . . alow] F1 (*corrected state*); a-low . . . aloft O, F1 (*uncorrected state*), F2.
172 Now seem to sink in Earth, and now] F1 (*corrected state*); As born through Air,
and seem O, F1 (*uncorrected state*), F2.
172 Sky;] F1 (*corrected state*); ~. O, F1 (*uncorrected state*), F2.
180 *Lapithæ*] *Lapythæ* O, F1–2.
180 added] F1 (*corrected state*); add the O, F1 (*uncorrected state*), F2.
182 round:] ~. O, F1–2.

Though Famous in his Youth for force and speed,
Or was of *Argos* or *Epirian* breed,
Or did from *Neptune*'s Race, or from himself proceed.
 These things premis'd, when now the Nuptial time
Approaches for the stately Steed to climb;
With Food inable him, to make his Court;
Distend his Chine, and pamper him for sport.
Feed him with Herbs, whatever thou can'st find,
Of generous warmth; and of salacious kind.
200 Then Water him, and (drinking what he can)
Encourage him to thirst again, with Bran.
Instructed thus, produce him to the Faire;
And joyn in Wedlock to the longing Mare.
For if the Sire be faint, or out of case,
He will be copied in his famish'd Race:
And sink beneath the pleasing Task assign'd;
(For all's too little for the craving Kind.)
 As for the Females, with industrious care
Take down their Mettle, keep 'em lean and bare;
210 When conscious of their past delight, and keen
To take the leap, and prove the sport agen;
With scanty measure then supply their food;
And, when athirst, restrain 'em from the flood:
Their Bodies harrass, sink 'em when they run;
And fry their melting Marrow in the Sun.
Starve 'em, when Barns beneath their burthen groan,
And winnow'd Chaff, by western winds is blown:
For Fear the rankness of the swelling Womb
Shou'd scant the passage, and confine the room:
220 Lest the Fat Furrows shou'd the sense destroy
Of Genial Lust; and dull the Seat of Joy.
But let 'em suck the Seed with greedy force;
And close involve the Vigour of the Horse.
 The Male has done; thy care must now proceed

---

217 blown:] ~. O, F1–2.    219 room:] ~. O, F1–2.
223 close involve] F2; there enclose O, F1.
224–225 *so in O, F1 (corrected state), F2; F1 (uncorrected state) has:*
  No more of Coursers yet: We now proceed
  To teeming Kine; and their laborious breed.

To teeming Females; and the promis'd breed.
First let 'em run at large; and never know
The taming Yoak, or draw the crooked Plough.
Let 'em not leap the Ditch, or swim the Flood;
Or lumber o're the Meads; or cross the Wood:
230 But range the Forrest, by the silver side
Of some cool Stream, where Nature shall provide
Green Grass and fat'ning Clover for their fare;
And Mossy Caverns for their Noontide lare:
With Rocks above, to shield the sharp Nocturnal air.
    About th' *Alburnian* Groves, with Holly green,
Of winged Insects mighty swarms are seen:
This flying Plague (to mark its quality;)
*Oestros* the *Grecians* call: *Asilus*, we:
A fierce loud buzzing Breez; their stings draw blood;
240 And drive the Cattel gadding through the Wood.
Seiz'd with unusual pains, they loudly cry,
*Tanagrus* hastens thence; and leaves his Channel dry.
This Curse the jealous *Juno* did invent;
And first imploy'd for *Io*'s Punishment.
To shun this Ill, the cunning Leach ordains
In Summer's Sultry Heats (for then it reigns)
To feed the Females, e're the Sun arise,
Or late at Night, when Stars adorn the Skies.
    When she has calv'd, then set the Dam aside;
250 And for the tender Progeny provide.
Distinguish all betimes, with branding Fire;
To note the Tribe, the Lineage, and the Sire:
Whom to reserve for Husband of the Herd;
Or who shall be to Sacrifice preferr'd;
Or whom thou shalt to turn thy Glebe allow;
To smooth the Furrows, and sustain the Plough:

---

229  Wood:] ∼. O, F1–2.        232  fare;] O; ∼! F1–2.
233  Noontide] O, F1 (*corrected state*), F2; Evening F1 (*uncorrected state*).
235  *not indented in O, F1–2, but preceded by a blank line in O.*
238  *Asilus*] *Asylus* O, F1–2.
249  *not indented in O, F1–2, but preceded by a blank line in O.*
252  and the] O, F2; and The F1.
252  Sire:] ∼. O, F1–2.        256  smooth the] F2; harrow O, F1.

The rest, for whom no Lot is yet decreed,
May run in Pastures, and at pleasure feed.
The Calf, by Nature and by Genius made
260 To turn the Glebe, breed to the Rural Trade.
Set him betimes to School; and let him be
Instructed there in Rules of Husbandry:
While yet his youth is flexible and green;
Nor bad Examples of the World has seen.
Early begin the stubborn Child to break;
For his soft Neck, a supple Collar make
Of bending Osiers; and (with time and care
Enur'd that easie Servitude to bear)
Thy flattering Method on the Youth pursue:
270 Join'd with his School-Fellows, by two and two,
Perswade 'em first to lead an empty Wheel,
That scarce the dust can raise; or they can feel:
In length of Time produce the lab'ring Yoke
And shining Shares, that make the Furrow smoak.
E're the licentious Youth be thus restrain'd,
Or Moral Precepts on their Minds have gain'd;
Their wanton appetites not only feed
With delicates of Leaves, and marshy Weed,
But with thy Sickle reap the rankest land:
280 And minister the blade, with bounteous hand.
Nor be with harmful parsimony won
To follow what our homely Sires have done;
Who fill'd the Pail with Beestings of the Cow:
But all her Udder to the Calf allow.
  If to the Warlike Steed thy Studies bend,
Or for the Prize in Chariots to contend;
Near *Pisa*'s Flood the rapid Wheels to guide,
Or in *Olympian* Groves aloft to ride,
The generous Labours of the Courser, first
290 Must be with sight of Arms and sounds of Trumpets nurst:
Inur'd the groaning Axle-tree to bear;
And let him clashing Whips in Stables hear.
Sooth him with Praise, and make him understand
The loud Applauses of his Master's Hand:

This from his Weaning, let him well be taught;
And then betimes in a soft Snaffle wrought:
Before his tender Joints with Nerves are knit;
Untry'd in Arms, and trembling at the Bit.
But when to four full Springs his years advance,
300 Teach him to run the round, with Pride to prance;
And (rightly manag'd) equal time to beat;
To turn, to bound in measure; and Curvet.
Let him, to this, with easie pains be brought:
And seem to labour, when he labours not.
Thus, form'd for speed, he challenges the Wind;
And leaves the *Scythian* Arrow far behind:
He scours along the Field, with loosen'd Reins;
And treads so light, he scarcely prints the Plains:
Like *Boreas* in his Race, when rushing forth,
310 He sweeps the Skies, and clears the cloudy North:
The waving Harvest bends beneath his blast;
The Forest shakes, the Groves their Honours cast;
He flies aloft, and with impetuous roar
Pursues the foaming Surges to the Shoar.
Thus o're th' *Elean* Plains, thy well-breath'd Horse
Impels the flying Carr, and wins the Course:
Or, bred to *Belgian* Waggons, leads the Way;
Untir'd at night, and chearful all the Day.
When once he's broken, feed him full and high:
320 Indulge his Growth, and his gaunt sides supply.
Before his Training, keep him poor and low;
For his stout Stomach with his Food will grow;
The pamper'd Colt will Discipline disdain,
Impatient of the Lash, and restiff to the Rein.
Wou'dst thou their Courage and their Strength improve,
Too soon they must not feel the stings of Love.
Whether the Bull or Courser be thy Care,
Let him not leap the Cow, nor mount the Mare.
The youthful Bull must wander in the Wood;

298    Untry'd in] F2; Guiltless of O, F1.
308    Plains:] ~. O, F1–2.
316    Impels the flying Carr] F2; Sustains the goring Spurs O, F1.
316    Course:] ~. O, F1–2.

330 Behind the Mountain, or beyond the Flood:
Or, in the Stall at home his Fodder find;
Far from the Charms of that alluring Kind.
With two fair Eyes his Mistress burns his Breast;
He looks, and languishes, and leaves his Rest;
Forsakes his Food, and pining for the Lass,
Is joyless of the Grove, and spurns the growing grass.
The soft Seducer, with enticing Looks,
The bellowing Rivals to the Fight provokes.
A beauteous Heifer in the Woods is bred;
340 The stooping Warriours, aiming Head to Head,
Engage their clashing Horns; with dreadful Sound
The Forest rattles, and the Rocks rebound.
They fence, they push, and pushing loudly roar;
Their Dewlaps and their Sides are bath'd in Gore.
Nor when the War is over, is it Peace;
Nor will the vanquish'd Bull his Claim release:
But feeding in his Breast his ancient Fires,
And cursing Fate, from his proud Foe retires.
Driv'n from his Native Land, to foreign Grounds,
350 He with a gen'rous Rage resents his Wounds;
His ignominious Flight, the Victor's boast,
And more than both, the Loves, which unreveng'd he lost.
Often he turns his Eyes, and, with a Groan,
Surveys the pleasing Kingdoms, once his own.
And therefore to repair his Strength he tries: ⎫
Hardning his Limbs with painful Exercise, ⎬
And rough upon the flinty Rock he lies. ⎭
On prickly Leaves, and on sharp Herbs he feeds,
Then to the Prelude of a War proceeds.
360 His Horns, yet sore, he tries against a Tree:
And meditates his absent Enemy.
He snuffs the Wind, his heels the Sand excite; ⎫
But, when he stands collected in his might, ⎬
He roars, and promises a more successful Fight. ⎭
Then, to redeem his Honour at a blow,
He moves his Camp, to meet his careless Foe.
Not with more Madness, rolling from afar,

The spumy Waves proclaim the watry War:
And mounting upwards, with a mighty Roar,
370 March onwards, and insult the rocky shoar.
They mate the middle Region with their height;
And fall no less, than with a Mountain's weight;
The Waters boil, and belching from below
Black Sands, as from a forceful Engine throw.
　　Thus every Creature, and of every Kind,
The secret Joys of sweet Coition find:
Not only Man's Imperial Race; but they
That wing the liquid Air; or swim the Sea,
Or haunt the Desart, rush into the flame:
380 For Love is Lord of all; and is in all the same.
　　'Tis with this rage, the Mother Lion stung,
Scours o're the Plain; regardless of her young:
Demanding Rites of Love, she sternly stalks;
And hunts her Lover in his lonely Walks.
'Tis then the shapeless Bear his Den forsakes;
In Woods and Fields a wild destruction makes.
Boars whet their Tusks; to battel Tygers move;
Enrag'd with Hunger, more enrag'd with Love.
Then wo to him, that in the desart Land
390 Of *Lybia* travels, o're the burning Sand.
The Stallion snuffs the well-known Scent afar;
And snorts and trembles for the distant Mare:
Nor Bits nor Bridles can his Rage restrain;
And rugged Rocks are interpos'd in vain:
He makes his way o're Mountains, and contemns
Unruly Torrents, and unfoorded Streams.
The bristled Boar, who feels the pleasing Wound,
New grinds his arming Tusks, and digs the Ground.
The sleepy Leacher shuts his little Eyes;
400 About his churning Chaps the frothy bubbles rise:
He rubs his sides against a Tree; prepares
And hardens both his Shoulders for the Wars.
　　What did the Youth, when Love's unerring Dart

---

368　War:] ∼. O, F1–2.　　　　383　Love,] ∼; O, F1–2.
403　*not indented in O, F1–2.*　　403　Youth] *Youth* O, F1–2.

The Shepherd knows it well; and calls by Name
*Hippomanes,* to note the Mother's Flame.
This, gather'd in the Planetary Hour,
With noxious Weeds, and spell'd with Words of pow'r,
Dire Stepdames in the Magick Bowl infuse;
And mix, for deadly Draughts, the poys'nous Juice.
But time is lost, which never will renew, ⎞
While we too far the pleasing Path pursue; ⎬
450 Surveying Nature, with too nice a view. ⎠
 Let this suffice for Herds: our following Care
Shall woolly Flocks, and shaggy Goats declare.
Nor can I doubt what Oyl I must bestow,
To raise my Subject from a Ground so low:
And the mean Matter which my Theme affords,
T' embellish with Magnificence of Words.
But the commanding Muse my Chariot guides;
Which o're the dubious Cliff securely rides:
And pleas'd I am, no beaten Road to take:
460 But first the way to new Discov'ries make.
 Now, sacred *Pales,* in a lofty strain,
I sing the Rural Honours of thy Reign.
First with assiduous care, from Winter keep
Well fodder'd in the Stalls, thy tender Sheep.
Then spread with Straw, the bedding of thy Fold;
With Fern beneath, to fend the bitter Cold:
That free from Gouts thou may'st preserve thy Care:
And clear from Scabs, produc'd by freezing Air.
Next let thy Goats officiously be nurs'd;
470 And led to living Streams; to quench their Thirst.
Feed 'em with Winter-brouze, and for their lare
A Cot that opens to the South prepare:
Where basking in the Sun-shine they may lye,
And the short Remnants of his Heat enjoy.
This during Winter's drisly Reign be done:
'Till the new Ram receives th' exalted Sun:
For hairy Goats of equal profit are
With woolly Sheep, and ask an equal Care.

---

466 Cold:] ∼. O, F1–2.

'Tis true, the Fleece, when drunk with *Tyrian* Juice,
480 Is dearly sold; but not for needful use:
For the sallacious Goat encreases more;
And twice as largely yields her milky Store.
The still distended Udders never fail;
But when they seem exhausted swell the Pail.
Mean time the Pastor shears their hoary Beards;
And eases of their Hair, the loaden Herds.
Their Camelots, warm in Tents, the Souldier hold;
And shield the shiv'ring Mariner from Cold.
On Shrubs they brouze, and on the bleaky Top
490 Of rugged Hills, the thorny Bramble crop.
Attended with their bleating Kids they come
At Night unask'd, and mindful of their home;
And scarce their swelling Bags the threshold overcome.
So much the more thy diligence bestow
In depth of Winter, to defend the Snow:
By how much less the tender helpless Kind,
For their own ills, can fit Provision find.
Then minister the browze, with bounteous hand;
And open let thy Stacks all Winter stand.
500 But when the Western Winds with vital pow'r
Call forth the tender Grass, and budding Flower;
Then, at the last, produce in open Air
Both Flocks; and send 'em to their Summer fare.
Before the Sun, while *Hesperus* appears;
First let 'em sip from Herbs the pearly tears
Of Morning Dews: And after break their Fast
On Green-sword Ground; (a cool and grateful taste:)
But when the day's fourth hour has drawn the Dews,
And the Sun's sultry heat their thirst renews;
510 When creaking Grashoppers on Shrubs complain,
Then lead 'em to their wat'ring Troughs again.
In Summer's heat, some bending Valley find,
Clos'd from the Sun, but open to the Wind:
Or seek some ancient Oak, whose Arms extend

---

488   shiv'ring] F2; wretched O, F1.          491   bleating Kids] F2; Family O, F1.
499   Stacks] O, F1 (*corrected state*), F2; Staks F1 (*uncorrected state*).

In ample breadth, thy Cattle to defend:
Or solitary Grove, or gloomy Glade:
To shield 'em with its venerable Shade.
Once more to wat'ring lead; and feed again
When the low Sun is sinking to the Main:
520 When rising *Cynthia* sheds her silver Dews;
And the cool Evening-breeze the Meads renews:
When Linnets fill the Woods with tuneful sound,
And hollow shoars the Halcyons Voice rebound.

Why shou'd my Muse enlarge on *Lybian* Swains;
Their scatter'd Cottages, and ample Plains?
Where oft the Flocks, without a Leader stray; ⎞
Or through continu'd Desarts take their way; ⎬
And, feeding, add the length of Night to day. ⎠
Whole Months they wander, grazing as they go;
530 Nor Folds, nor hospitable Harbour know:
Such an extent of Plains, so vast a space
Of Wilds unknown, and of untasted Grass
Allures their Eyes: The Shepherd last appears,
And with him all his Patrimony bears:
His House and household Gods! his trade of War,
His Bow and Quiver; and his trusty Cur.
Thus, under heavy Arms, the Youth of *Rome*
Their long laborious Marches overcome;
Chearly their tedious Travels undergo:
540 And pitch their sudden Camp before the Foe.

Not so the *Scythian* Shepherd tends his Fold;
Nor he who bears in *Thrace* the bitter cold:
Nor he, who treads the bleak *Meotian* Strand;
Or where proud *Ister* rouls his yellow Sand.
Early they stall their Flocks and Herds; for there
No Grass the Fields, no Leaves the Forests wear.
The frozen Earth lies buried there, below ⎞
A hilly heap, sev'n Cubits deep in Snow: ⎬
And all the West Allies of stormy *Boreas* blow. ⎠

519  Main:] ∼. O, F1–2.
523  Halcyons] *Halcyons* O, F1–2.
530  know:] ∼. O, F1–2.
549  West Allies] *West* Allies F1–2; *Western* Sons O.

To John Dormer of Rousham
in the County of Oxford Esq.

Geo: 3 : L 570.

550    The Sun from far, peeps with a sickly face;
       Too weak the Clouds, and mighty Fogs to chace;
       When up the Skies, he shoots his rosie Head;
       Or in the ruddy Ocean seeks his Bed.
       Swift Rivers, are with sudden Ice constrain'd;
       And studded Wheels are on its back sustain'd:
       An Hostry now for Waggons; which before
       Tall Ships of burthen, on its Bosom bore.
       The brazen Cauldrons, with the Frost are flaw'd;
       The Garment, stiff with Ice, at Hearths is thaw'd;
560  With Axes first they cleave the Wine, and thence
       By weight, the solid portions they dispence.
       From Locks uncomb'd, and from the frozen Beard,
       Long Isicles depend, and crackling Sounds are heard.
       Mean time perpetual Sleet, and driving Snow,
       Obscure the Skies, and hang on Herds below.
       The starving Cattle perish in their Stalls,
       Huge Oxen stand enclos'd in wint'ry Walls
       Of Snow congeal'd; whole Herds are bury'd there
       Of mighty Stags, and scarce their Horns appear.
570  The dext'rous Huntsman wounds not these afar,
       With Shafts, or Darts, or makes a distant War
       With Dogs; or pitches Toyls to stop their Flight:
       But close engages in unequal Fight:
       And while they strive in vain to make their way
       Through hills of Snow, and pitifully bray;
       Assaults with dint of Sword, or pointed Spears,
       And homeward, on his Back, the joyful burthen bears.
       The Men to subterranean Caves retire;
       Secure from Cold; and crowd the chearful Fire:
580  With Trunks of Elms and Oaks, the Hearth they load,
       Nor tempt th' inclemency of Heav'n abroad.
       Their jovial Nights, in frollicks and in play
       They pass, to drive the tedious Hours away:
       And their cold Stomachs with crown'd Goblets cheer,
       Of windy Cider, and of barmy Beer.

---

555   sustain'd:] ~. O, F1–2.                    559   thaw'd;] F2; ~. O, F1.
573   Fight:] ~. O, F1–2.                         583   away:] ~. O, F1–2.

Such are the cold *Riphæan* Race; and such
The savage *Scythian,* and unwarlike *Dutch:*
Where Skins of Beasts, the rude Barbarians wear;
The spoils of Foxes, and the furry Bear.
590    Is Wool thy care? Let not thy Cattle go
Where Bushes are, where Burs and Thistles grow;
Nor in too rank a Pasture let 'em feed:
Then of the purest white select thy Breed.
Ev'n though a snowy Ram thou shalt behold,
Prefer him not in haste, for Husband to thy Fold:
But search his Mouth; and if a swarthy Tongue
Is underneath his humid Pallat hung;
Reject him, lest he darken all the Flock;
And substitute another from thy Stock.
600    Twas thus with Fleeces milky white (if we
May trust report,) *Pan* God of *Arcady*
Did bribe thee *Cynthia;* nor didst thou disdain
When call'd in woody shades, to cure a Lover's pain.
If Milk be thy design; with plenteous hand
Bring Clover-grass; and from the marshy Land
Salt Herbage for the fodd'ring Rack provide;
To fill their Bags, and swell the milky Tide:
These raise their Thirst, and to the Taste restore
The savour of the Salt, on which they fed before.
610    Some, when the Kids their Dams too deeply drain,
With gags and muzzles their soft Mouths restrain.
Their morning Milk, the Peasants press at Night:
Their Evening Meal, before the rising Light
To Market bear: or sparingly they steep
With seas'ning Salt, and stor'd, for Winter keep.
Nor last, forget thy faithful Dogs: but feed
With fat'ning Whey the Mastiffs gen'rous breed;
And *Spartan* Race: who for the Folds relief
Will prosecute with Cries the Nightly Thief:
620 Repulse the prouling Wolf, and hold at Bay

586   *Riphæan*] *Ryphæan* O; *Ryphean* F1-2.
587   *Dutch:*] ~. O, F1-2.
588   Barbarians] *Barbarians* O, F1-2.          595   Fold:] ~. O, F1-2.
612   Peasants] *Peasants* O, F1-2.          620   Bay] ~, O, F1-2.

The Mountain Robbers, rushing to the Prey.
With cries of Hounds, thou may'st pursue the fear
Of flying Hares, and chace the fallow Deer;
Rouze from their desart Dens, the brisl'd Rage
Of Boars, and beamy Stags in Toyls engage.
  With smoak of burning Cedar scent thy Walls:
And fume with stinking Galbanum thy Stalls:
With that rank Odour from thy dwelling Place
To drive the Viper's brood, and all the venom'd Race.
630 For often under Stalls unmov'd, they lye,
Obscure in shades, and shunning Heav'ns broad Eye.
And Snakes, familiar, to the Hearth succeed,
Disclose their Eggs, and near the Chimny breed:
Whether, to roofy Houses they repair,
Or Sun themselves abroad in open Air,
In all abodes of pestilential Kind,
To Sheep and Oxen, and the painful Hind.
Take, Shepherd take, a plant of stubborn Oak;
And labour him with many a sturdy stroak:
640 Or with hard Stones, demolish from a-far
His haughty Crest, the seat of all the War.
Invade his hissing Throat, and winding spires;
'Till stretch'd in length, th' unfolded Foe retires.
He drags his Tail; and for his Head provides:
And in some secret cranny slowly glides;
But leaves expos'd to blows, his Back and batter'd sides.
  In fair *Calabria*'s Woods, a Snake is bred,
With curling Crest, and with advancing Head:
Waving he rolls, and makes a winding Track;
650 His Belly spotted, burnisht is his Back:
While Springs are broken, while the Southern Air
And dropping Heav'ns, the moisten'd Earth repair,
He lives on standing Lakes, and trembling Bogs,
And fills his Maw with Fish, or with loquacious Frogs.
But when, in muddy Pools, the water sinks;
And the chapt Earth is furrow'd o're with Chinks;

---

627  Galbanum] *Galbanum* O, F1–2.        633  breed:] ~. O, F1–2.
651  Southern] *Southern* O, F1–2.

He leaves the Fens, and leaps upon the Ground;
And hissing, rowls his glaring Eyes around.
With Thirst inflam'd, impatient of the heats,
660 He rages in the Fields, and wide Destruction threats.
Oh let not Sleep, my closing Eyes invade,
In open Plains, or in the secret Shade,
When he, renew'd in all the speckl'd Pride
Of pompous Youth, has cast his slough aside:
And in his Summer Liv'ry rowls along:
Erect, and brandishing his forky Tongue,
Leaving his Nest, and his imperfect Young;
And thoughtless of his Eggs, forgets to rear
The hopes of Poyson, for the foll'wing Year.
670    The Causes and the Signs shall next be told,
Of ev'ry Sickness that infects the Fold.
A scabby Tetter on their pelts will stick,
When the raw Rain has pierc'd them to the quick:
Or searching Frosts, have eaten through the Skin,
Or burning Isicles are lodg'd within:
Or when the Fleece is shorn, if sweat remains
Unwash'd, and soaks into their empty Veins:
When their defenceless Limbs, the Brambles tear;
Short of their Wool, and naked from the Sheer.
680    Good Shepherds after sheering, drench their Sheep,
And their Flocks Father (forc'd from high to leap)
Swims down the Stream, and plunges in the deep.
They oint their naked Limbs with mother'd Oyl;
Or from the Founts where living Sulphurs boyl,
They mix a Med'cine to foment their Limbs;
With Scum that on the molten Silver swims.
Fat Pitch, and black Bitumen, add to these,
Besides, the waxen labour of the Bees:
And Hellebore, and Squills deep rooted in the Seas.
690 Receits abound; but searching all thy Store,
The best is still at hand, to launch the Sore:

---

668   Eggs] O, F2; Egs F1.                   673   them] F2; 'em O, F1.
689   Hellebore . . . Squills] *Hellebore . . . Squills* O, F1–2.
689   Seas.] O; ~, F1–2.

F. Clein inv.    W. Hollar fecit.

To Fredrick Tilney        of Tilney Hall
in Hant     Shire Esq.

Geo 3. L721.

And cut the Head; for till the Core be found,
The secret Vice is fed, and gathers Ground:
While making fruitless Moan, the Shepherd stands, ⎫
And, when the launching Knife requires his hands, ⎬
Vain help, with idle Pray'rs from Heav'n demands. ⎭
Deep in their Bones when Feavers fix their seat,
And rack their Limbs; and lick the vital heat;
The ready Cure to cool the raging Pain,
700 Is underneath the Foot to breath a Vein.
This remedy the *Scythian* Shepherds found:
Th' Inhabitants of *Thracia*'s hilly Ground,
And *Gelons* use it; when for Drink and Food
They mix their cruddl'd Milk with Horses Blood.
    But where thou seest a single Sheep remain
In shades aloof, or couch'd upon the Plain;
Or listlesly to crop the tender Grass;
Or late to lag behind, with truant pace;
Revenge the Crime; and take the Traytor's head,
710 E're in the faultless Flock the dire Contagion spread.
    On Winter Seas we fewer Storms behold,
Than foul Diseases that infect the Fold.
Nor do those ills, on single Bodies prey; ⎫
But oft'ner bring the Nation to decay; ⎬
And sweep the present Stock, and future Hope away. ⎭
    A dire Example of this Truth appears:
When, after such a length of rowling Years,
We see the naked *Alps,* and thin Remains ⎫
Of scatter'd Cotts, and yet unpeopl'd Plains: ⎬
720 Once fill'd with grazing Flocks, the Shepherds happy Reigns. ⎭
    Here from the vicious Air, and sickly Skies,
A Plague did on the dumb Creation rise:
During th' Autumnal Heats th' Infection grew,
Tame Cattle, and the Beasts of Nature slew:
Poys'ning the Standing Lakes; and Pools Impure:
Nor was the foodful Grass in Fields secure.
Strange Death! For when the thirsty fire had drunk
Their vital Blood, and the dry Nerves were shrunk;

724  slew:] ∼. O, F1–2.

When the contracted Limbs were cramp'd, ev'n then
730 A wat'rish Humour swell'd and ooz'd agen:
Converting into Bane the kindly Juice,
Ordain'd by Nature for a better use.
The Victim Ox, that was for Altars prest,
Trim'd with white Ribbons, and with Garlands drest,
Sunk of himself, without the Gods Command:
Preventing the slow Sacrificer's Hand.
Or, by the holy Butcher, if he fell,
Th' inspected Entrails, cou'd no Fates foretel.
Nor, laid on Altars, did pure Flames arise;
740 But Clouds of smouldring Smoke, forbad the Sacrifice.
Scarcely the Knife was redden'd with his Gore,
Or the black Poyson stain'd the sandy Floor.
The thriven Calves in Meads their Food forsake,
And render their sweet Souls before the plenteous Rack.
The fawning Dog runs mad; the wheasing Swine
With Coughs is choak'd; and labours from the Chine:
The Victor Horse, forgetful of his Food,
The Palm renounces, and abhors the Flood.
He paws the Ground, and on his hanging Ears ⎞
750 A doubtful Sweat in clammy drops appears: ⎬
Parch'd is his Hide, and rugged are his Hairs. ⎠
Such are the Symptoms of the young Disease;
But in time's process, when his pains encrease,
He rouls his mournful Eyes, he deeply groans
With patient sobbing, and with manly Moans.
He heaves for Breath: which, from his Lungs supply'd,
And fetch'd from far, distends his lab'ring side.
To his rough Palat, his dry Tongue succeeds;
And roapy Gore, he from his Nostrils bleeds.
760 A Drench of Wine has with success been us'd;
And through a Horn, the gen'rous Juice infus'd:
Which timely taken op'd his closing Jaws;
But, if too late, the Patient's death did cause.
For the too vig'rous Dose, too fiercely wrought;
And added Fury to the Strength it brought.

---

765  Strength] O, F2; Srength F1.

Recruited into Rage, he grinds his Teeth
In his own Flesh, and feeds approaching Death.
Ye Gods, to better Fate, good Men dispose;
And turn that Impious Errour on our Foes!
770   The Steer, who to the Yoke was bred to bow,
(Studious of Tillage; and the crooked Plough)
Falls down and dies; and dying spews a Flood
Of foamy Madness, mix'd with clotted Blood.
The Clown, who cursing Providence repines,
His Mournful Fellow from the Team disjoyns:
With many a groan, forsakes his fruitless care;
And in th' unfinish'd Furrow, leaves the Share.
The pineing Steer, no Shades of lofty Woods,
Nor flow'ry Meads can ease; nor Crystal floods
780 Roul'd from the Rock: His flabby Flanks decrease;
His Eyes are settled in a stupid peace.
His bulk too weighty for his Thighs is grown;
And his unweildy Neck, hangs drooping down.
Now what avails his well-deserving Toil
To turn the Glebe; or smooth the rugged Soil?
And yet he never supt in solemn State,
Nor undigested Feasts did urge his Fate;
Nor day, to Night, luxuriously did joyn;
Nor surfeited on rich *Campanian* Wine.
790 Simple his Bev'rage; homely was his Food;
The wholsom Herbage, and the running Flood:
No dreadful Dreams awak'd him with affright;
His Pains by Day, secur'd his Rest by Night.
  'Twas then that Buffalo's, ill pair'd, were seen
To draw the Carr of *Jove*'s Imperial Queen
For want of Oxen: and the lab'ring Swain
Scratch'd with a Rake, a Furrow for his Grain:
And cover'd, with his hand, the shallow Seed again.
He Yokes himself, and up the Hilly height,
800 With his own Shoulders, draws the Waggon's weight.
  The nightly Wolf, that round th' Enclosure proul'd

---

785   Soil?] ∼! O, F1–2.
794   Buffalo's] *Buffolo*'s O; *Buffalo*'s F1–2.

To leap the Fence; now plots not on the Fold,
Tam'd with a sharper Pain. The fearful Doe
And flying Stag, amidst the Grey-Hounds go:
And round the Dwellings roam of Man, their fiercer Foe.
The scaly Nations of the Sea profound,
Like Shipwreck'd Carcasses are driv'n aground:
And mighty Phocæ, never seen before
In shallow Streams, are stranded on the shore.
810 The Viper dead, within her Hole is found:
Defenceless was the shelter of the ground.
The water-Snake, whom Fish and Paddocks fed,
With staring Scales lies poyson'd in his Bed:
To Birds their Native Heav'ns contagious prove,
From Clouds they fall, and leave their Souls above.
    Besides, to change their Pasture 'tis in vain:
Or trust to Physick; Physick is their Bane.
The Learned Leaches in despair depart:
And shake their Heads, desponding of their Art.
820     *Tisiphone,* let loose from under ground,
Majestically pale, now treads the round:
Before her drives Diseases, and affright;
And every moment rises to the sight:
Aspiring to the Skies; encroaching on the light.
The Rivers and their Banks, and Hills around,
With lowings, and with dying Bleats resound.
At length, she strikes an Universal Blow;
To Death at once whole Herds of Cattle go:
Sheep, Oxen, Horses fall; and, heap'd on high,
830 The diff'ring Species in Confusion lie:
'Till warn'd by frequent ills, the way they found,
To lodge their loathsom Carrion underground.
For, useless to the Currier were their Hides:
Nor cou'd their tainted Flesh with Ocean Tides
Be freed from Filth; nor cou'd *Vulcanian* Flame
The Stench abolish; or the Savour tame.
Nor safely cou'd they shear their fleecy Store;

---

802    Fold,] ~. O, F1–2.                    808    Phocæ] *Phocæ* F1–2; Sea-Calves O.
830    lie:] ~. O, F1–2.

(Made drunk with poys'nous Juice, and stiff with Gore:)
Or touch the Web: But if the Vest they wear,
840 Red Blisters rising on their Paps appear,
And flaming Carbuncles; and noisom Sweat,
And clammy Dews, that loathsom Lice beget:
'Till the slow creeping Evil eats his way,
Consumes the parching Limbs; and makes the Life his prey.

To Richard ⟨crest⟩ Norton of Southwick
in Hant= shire Esq.

Gen 4:1.

# The Fourth Book of the Georgics

### THE ARGUMENT.

Virgil *has taken care to raise the Subject of each Georgic: In the First he has only dead Matter on which to work. In the second he just steps on the World of Life, and describes that degree of it which is to be found in Vegetables. In the third he advances to Animals: And in the last, singles out the Bee, which may be reckon'd the most sagacious of 'em, for his Subject.*

*In this Georgic he shews us what Station is most proper for the Bees, and when they begin to gather Honey: how to call 'em home when they swarm; and how to part 'em when they are en-gag'd in Battel. From hence he takes occasion to discover their different Kinds; and, after an Excursion, relates their prudent and politick Administration of Affairs, and the several Diseases that often rage in their Hives, with the proper Symptoms and Remedies of each Disease. In the last place he lays down a method of repairing their Kind, supposing their whole Breed lost; and gives at large the History of its Invention.*

THE Gifts of Heav'n my foll'wing Song pursues,
Aerial Honey, and Ambrosial Dews.
*Mæcenas*, read this other part, that sings ⎫
Embattel'd Squadrons and advent'rous Kings: ⎬
A mighty Pomp, tho' made of little Things. ⎭
Their Arms, their Arts, their Manners I disclose,
And how they War, and whence the People rose:
Slight is the Subject, but the Praise not small,
If Heav'n assist, and *Phœbus* hear my Call.
10   First, for thy Bees a quiet Station find,
And lodge 'em under Covert of the Wind:
For Winds, when homeward they return, will drive
The loaded Carriers from their Ev'ning Hive.

---

5   *Animals:*] ∼. F1–2.                    4   Squadrons] F2; Sqadrons F1.

Far from the Cows and Goats insulting Crew,
That trample down the Flow'rs, and brush the Dew:
The painted Lizard, and the Birds of Prey,
Foes of the frugal Kind, be far away.
The Titmouse, and the Peckers hungry Brood,
And *Progne,* with her Bosom stain'd in Blood:
20 These rob the trading Citizens, and bear ⎞
The trembling Captives thro' the liquid Air; ⎬
And for their callow young a cruel Feast prepare. ⎠
But near a living Stream their Mansion place,
Edg'd round with Moss, and tufts of matted Grass:
And plant (the Winds impetuous rage to stop,)
Wild Olive Trees, or Palms, before the buisy Shop:
That when the youthful Prince, with proud allarm,
Calls out the vent'rous Colony to swarm;
When first their way thro' yielding Air they wing,
30 New to the Pleasures of their native Spring;
The Banks of Brooks may make a cool retreat
For the raw Souldiers from the scalding Heat:
And neighb'ring Trees, with friendly Shade invite
The Troops unus'd to long laborious Flight.
Then o're the running Stream, or standing Lake,
A Passage for thy weary People make;
With Osier Floats the standing Water strow;
Of massy Stones make Bridges, if it flow:
That basking in the Sun thy Bees may lye,
40 And resting there, their flaggy Pinions dry:
When late returning home, the laden Host,
By raging Winds is wreck'd upon the Coast.
Wild Thyme and Sav'ry set around their Cell,
Sweet to the Taste, and fragrant to the Smell:
Set rows of Rosemary with flow'ring Stem,
And let the purple Vi'lets drink the Stream.
    Whether thou build the Palace of thy Bees
With twisted Osiers, or with Barks of Trees;
Make but a narrow Mouth: for as the Cold

---

27  proud] F2; loud F1.

50 Congeals into a Lump the liquid Gold;
So 'tis again dissolv'd by Summer's heat,
And the sweet Labours both Extreams defeat.
And therefore, not in vain, th' industrious Kind
With dawby Wax and Flow'rs the Chinks have lin'd:
And, with their Stores of gather'd Glue, contrive
To stop the Vents, and Crannies of their Hive.
Not Birdlime, or *Idean* Pitch produce
A more tenacious Mass of clammy Juice.
    Nor Bees are lodg'd in Hives alone, but found
60 In Chambers of their own, beneath the Ground:
Their vaulted Roofs are hung in Pumices,
And in the rotten Trunks of hollow Trees.
    But plaister thou the chinky Hives with Clay,
And leafy Branches o're their Lodgings lay.
Nor place them where too deep a Water flows,
Or where the Yeugh their pois'nous Neighbour grows:
Nor rost red Crabs t' offend the niceness of their Nose:
Nor near the steaming Stench of muddy Ground;
Nor hollow Rocks that render back the Sound,
70 And doubled Images of Voice rebound.
    For what remains, when Golden Suns appear,
And under Earth have driv'n the Winter Year:
The winged Nation wanders thro' the Skies,
And o're the Plains, and shady Forrest flies:
Then stooping on the Meads and leafy Bow'rs;
They skim the Floods, and sip the purple Flow'rs.
Exalted hence, and drunk with secret Joy,
Their young Succession all their Cares employ:
They breed, they brood, instruct and educate,
80 And make Provision for the future State:
They work their waxen Lodgings in their Hives,
And labour Honey to sustain their Lives.
But when thou seest a swarming Cloud arise,
That sweeps aloft, and darkens all the Skies:

---

54 lin'd:] ∼. F1–2.          67 Nose:] ∼. F1–2.
81 their waxen] *some copies of F1 have* ther waxen.

Their friends encourage, and amaze the Foe.
With mighty Souls in narrow Bodies prest,
They challenge, and encounter Breast to Breast;
So fix'd on Fame, unknowing how to fly,
And obstinately bent to win or dye;
That long the doubtful Combat they maintain,
Till one prevails (for one can only Reign.)
130 Yet all those dreadful deeds, this deadly fray, ⎫
A cast of scatter'd Dust will soon alay,        ⎬
And undecided leave the Fortune of the day. ⎭
When both the Chiefs are sund'red from the Fight,
Then to the lawful King restore his Right.
And let the wastful Prodigal be slain,
That he, who best deserves, alone may reign.
With ease distinguish'd is the Regal Race,
One Monarch wears an honest open Face;
Shap'd to his Size, and Godlike to behold,
140 His Royal Body shines with specks of Gold,
And ruddy Skales; for Empire he design'd,
Is better born, and of a Nobler Kind.
That other looks like Nature in disgrace,        ⎫
Gaunt are his sides, and sullen is his face:     ⎬
And like their grizly Prince appears his gloomy Race: ⎭
Grim, ghastly, rugged, like a thirsty train      ⎫
That long have travel'd through a desart plain,  ⎬
And spet from their dry Chaps the gather'd dust again. ⎭
The better Brood, unlike the Bastard Crew,
150 Are mark'd with Royal streaks of shining hue;
Glitt'ring and ardent, though in Body less:
From these at pointed Seasons hope to press
Huge heavy Honey-Combs, of Golden Juice,
Not only sweet, but pure, and fit for use:
T' allay the Strength and Hardness of the Wine,
And with old *Bacchus,* new Metheglin join.
     But when the Swarms are eager of their play,
And loath their empty Hives, and idly stray,
Restrain the wanton Fugitives, and take

139  Shap'd to his Size] F2; Large are his Limbs F1.

160 A timely Care to bring the Truants back.
The Task is easy: but to clip the Wings
Of their high-flying Arbitrary Kings:
At their Command, the People swarm away;
Confine the Tyrant, and the Slaves will stay.

   Sweet Gardens, full of Saffron Flow'rs, invite
The wandring Gluttons, and retard their Flight:
Besides, the God obscene, who frights away,
With his Lath Sword, the Thiefs and Birds of Prey.
With his own hand, the Guardian of the Bees,
170 For Slips of Pines, may search the Mountain Trees:
And with wild Thyme and Sav'ry, plant the Plain,
'Till his hard horny Fingers ake with Pain:
And deck with fruitful Trees the Fields around,
And with refreshing Waters drench the Ground.

   Now, did I not so near my Labours end,   &#125;
Strike Sail, and hast'ning to the Harbour tend;  &#125;
My Song to Flow'ry Gardens might extend:    &#125;
To teach the vegetable Arts, to sing
The *Pæstan* Roses, and their double Spring:
180 How Succ'ry drinks the running Streams, and how
Green Beds of Parsley near the River grow;
How Cucumers along the Surface creep,
With crooked Bodies, and with Bellies deep:
The late *Narcissus,* and the winding Trail
Of Bears-foot, Myrtles green, and Ivy pale.
For where with stately Tow'rs *Tarentum* stands,
And deep *Galesus* soaks the yellow Sands,
I chanc'd an Old *Corycian* Swain to know,   &#125;
Lord of few Acres, and those barren too;   &#125;
190 Unfit for Sheep or Vines, and more unfit to sow: &#125;
Yet lab'ring well his little Spot of Ground,
Some scatt'ring Potherbs here and there he found:
Which cultivated with his daily Care,
And bruis'd with Vervain, were his frugal Fare.
Sometimes white Lyllies did their Leaves afford,

---

166  Flight:] ∼. F1–2.            177   extend:] ∼. F1–2.
183  deep:] ∼. F1–2.

With wholsom Poppy-flow'rs, to mend his homely Board:
For late returning home he sup'd at ease,
And wisely deem'd the Wealth of Monarchs less:
The little of his own, because his own, did please.
200  To quit his Care, he gather'd first of all
In Spring the Roses, Apples in the Fall:
And when cold Winter split the Rocks in twain,
And Ice the running Rivers did restrain,
He strip'd the Bears-foot of its leafy growth;
And, calling Western Winds, accus'd the Spring of sloath.
He therefore first among the Swains was found,
To reap the Product of his labour'd Ground,
And squeese the Combs with Golden Liquor Crown'd.
His Limes were first in Flow'rs, his lofty Pines,
210  With friendly Shade, secur'd his tender Vines.
For ev'ry Bloom his Trees in Spring afford,
An Autumn Apple was by tale restor'd.
He knew to rank his Elms in even rows;
For Fruit the grafted Peartree to dispose:
And tame to Plums, the sourness of the Sloes.
With spreading Planes he made a cool retreat,
To shade good Fellows from the Summer's heat.
But streighten'd in my space, I must forsake
This Task; for others afterwards to take.
220      Describe we next the Nature of the Bees,
Bestow'd by *Jove* for secret Services:
When by the tinkling Sound of Timbrels led,
The King of Heav'n in *Cretan* Caves they fed.
Of all the Race of Animals, alone
The Bees have common Cities of their own:
And common Sons, beneath one Law they live,
And with one common Stock their Traffick drive.
Each has a certain home, a sev'ral Stall:
All is the States, the State provides for all.
230  Mindful of coming Cold, they share the Pain:
And hoard, for Winter's use, the Summer's gain.
Some o're the Publick Magazines preside,

---

197–199  *No brace in F1.*                221  Bestow'd] F2; bestow'd F1.

And some are sent new Forrage to provide:
These drudge in Fields abroad, and those at home ⎫
Lay deep Foundations for the labour'd Comb, ⎬
With dew, *Narcissus* Leaves, and clammy Gum. ⎭
To pitch the waxen Flooring some contrive:
Some nurse the future Nation of the Hive:
Sweet Honey some condense, some purge the Grout;
240 The rest, in Cells apart, the liquid Nectar shut.
All, with united Force, combine to drive
The lazy Drones from the laborious Hive.
With Envy stung, they view each others Deeds:
With Diligence the fragrant Work proceeds:
As when the *Cyclops,* at th' Almighty Nod,
New Thunder hasten for their angry God:
Subdu'd in Fire the Stubborn Mettal lyes,
One brawny Smith the puffing Bellows plyes;
And draws, and blows reciprocating Air:
250 Others to quench the hissing Mass prepare:
With lifted Arms they order ev'ry Blow, ⎫
And chime their sounding Hammers in a Row; ⎬
With labour'd Anvils *Ætna* groans below. ⎭
Strongly they strike, huge Flakes of Flames expire,
With Tongs they turn the Steel, and vex it in the Fire.
If little things with great we may compare,
Such are the Bees, and such their busie Care:
Studious of Honey, each in his Degree,
The youthful Swain, the grave experienc'd Bee:
260 That in the Field; this in Affairs of State,
Employ'd at home, abides within the Gate:
To fortify the Combs, to build the Wall,
To prop the Ruins lest the Fabrick fall:
But late at Night, with weary Pinions come
The lab'ring Youth, and heavy laden home.
Plains, Meads, and Orchards all the day he plies,
The gleans of yellow Thime distend his Thighs:

---

240  Nectar] *Nectar* F1–2.                 244  proceeds:] ∼. F1–2.
253  labour'd] F2; strokes of F1.
257  busie] F2; native F1.
265  lab'ring] F2; labr'ring F1.

He spoils the Saffron Flow'rs, he sips the blues
Of Vi'lets, wilding Blooms, and Willow Dews.
270 Their Toyl is common, common is their Sleep;
They shake their Wings when Morn begins to peep;
Rush through the City Gates without delay,
Nor ends their Work, but with declining Day:
Then having spent the last remains of Light,
They give their Bodies due repose at Night:
When hollow Murmurs of their Ev'ning Bells,
Dismiss the sleepy Swains, and toll 'em to their Cells.
When once in Beds their weary Limbs they steep,
No buzzing Sounds disturb their Golden Sleep.
280 'Tis sacred Silence all. Nor dare they stray,
When Rain is promis'd, or a stormy Day:
But near the City Walls their Watring take,
Nor Forrage far, but short Excursions make.
     And as when empty Barks on Billows float,
With sandy Ballast Sailors trim the Boat;
So Bees bear Gravel Stones, whose poising Weight
Steers thro' the whistling Winds their steddy Flight.
     But what's more strange, their modest Appetites,
Averse from *Venus*, fly the nuptial Rites.
290 No lust enervates their Heroic Mind,
Nor wasts their Strength on wanton Woman-Kind.
But in their Mouths reside their Genial Pow'rs,
They gather Children from the Leaves and Flow'rs.
Thus make they Kings to fill the Regal Seat;  )
And thus their little Citizens create:  }
And waxen Cities build, and Palaces of State.  )
And oft on Rocks their tender Wings they tear,
And sink beneath the Burthens which they bear.
Such Rage of Honey in their Bosom beats:
300 And such a Zeal they have for flow'ry Sweets.
     Thus tho' the race of Life they quickly run;
Which in the space of sev'n short Years is done,

275   their] F2; thir F1.          279   their] F2; thir F1.
302   sev'n] F2; seven F1.

Th' immortal Line in sure Succession reigns,  }
The Fortune of the Family remains:  }
And Grandsires Grandsons the long List contains.  }
   Besides, not *Egypt, India, Media* more
With servile Awe, their Idol King adore:
While he survives, in Concord and Content  }
The Commons live, by no Divisions rent;  }
310 But the great Monarch's Death dissolves the Government.  }
All goes to Ruin, they themselves contrive
To rob the Honey, and subvert the Hive.
The King presides, his Subjects Toil surveys;
The servile Rout their careful *Cæsar* praise:
Him they extol, they worship him alone,
They crowd his Levees, and support his Throne:
They raise him on their shoulders with a Shout:
And when their Sov'raigns Quarrel calls 'em out,
His Foes to mortal Combat they defy,
320 And think it honour at his feet to die.
   Induc'd by such Examples, some have taught
That Bees have Portions of Etherial Thought:
Endu'd with Particles of Heavenly Fires:
For God the whole created Mass inspires;
Thro' Heav'n, and Earth, and Oceans depth he throws
His Influence round, and kindles as he goes.
Hence Flocks, and Herds, and Men, and Beasts, and Fowls
With Breath are quicken'd; and attract their Souls:
Hence take the Forms his Prescience did ordain,
330 And into him at length resolve again.
No room is left for Death, they mount the Sky,
And to their own congenial Planets fly.
   Now when thou hast decreed to seize their Stores,
And by Prerogative to break their Doors:
With sprinkl'd Water first the City choak,
And then pursue the Citizens with Smoak.
Two Honey Harvests fall in ev'ry Year:
First, when the pleasing *Pleiades* appear,

---

328  Souls:]  ∼.  F1–2.

And springing upward spurn the briny Seas:
340 Again, when their affrighted Quire surveys
The watry Scorpion mend his Pace behind,
With a black Train of Storms, and winter Wind;
They plunge into the Deep, and safe Protection find.
Prone to Revenge, the Bees, a wrathful Race,
When once provok'd assault th' Agressor's Face:
And through the purple Veins a passage find;
There fix their Stings, and leave their Souls behind.
    But if a pinching Winter thou foresee,
And woud'st preserve thy famish'd Family;
350 With fragrant Thyme the City fumigate,
And break the waxen Walls to save the State.
For lurking Lizards often lodge, by Stealth,
Within the Suburbs, and purloyn their Wealth.
And Lizards shunning Light, a dark Retreat
Have found in Combs, and undermin'd the Seat.
Or lazy Drones, without their Share of Pain;
In Winter Quarters free, devour the Gain:
Or Wasps infest the Camp with loud Alarms,
And mix in Battel with unequal Arms:
360 Or secret Moaths are there in Silence fed;
Or Spiders in the Vault, their snary Webs have spred.
    The more oppress'd by Foes, or Famine pin'd;
The more increase thy Care to save the sinking Kind.
With Greens and Flow'rs recruit their empty Hives,
And seek fresh Forrage to sustain their Lives.
    But since they share with Man one common Fate,
In Health and Sickness, and in Turns of State;
Observe the Symptoms when they fall away,
And languish with insensible Decay.
370 They change their Hue, with hagger'd Eyes they stare,
Lean are their Looks, and shagged is their Hair:

---

341   Scorpion] *Scorpion* F1–2.
350   fragrant] F2; fragant F1.
354   Lizards shunning] F1 *errata*, F2; Worms that shun the F1.
366   Man] F2; us F1.

And Crowds of dead, that never must return  
To their lov'd Hives, in decent Pomp are born:  
Their Friends attend the Herse, the next Relations Mourn.  
The sick, for Air before the Portal gasp,  
Their feeble Legs within each other clasp:  
Or idle in their empty Hives remain,  
Benum'd with Cold, and listless of their Gain.  
Soft Whispers then, and broken Sounds are heard,  
380  As when the Woods by gentle Winds are stir'd:  
Such stifled noise as the close Furnace hides,  
Or dying Murmurs of departing Tides.  
This when thou seest, Galbanean Odours use,  
And Honey in the sickly Hive infuse.  
Thro' reeden Pipes convey the Golden Flood,  
T' invite the People to their wonted Food.  
Mix it with thicken'd Juice of sodden Wines,  
And Raisins from the Grapes of Psythian Vines:  
To these add pounded Galls, and Roses dry,  
390  And with *Cecropian* Thyme, strong scented Centaury.  
    A Flow'r there is that grows in Meadow Ground,  
*Amellus* call'd, and easy to be found;  
For from one Root the rising Stem bestows  
A Wood of Leaves, and vi'let-purple Boughs:  
The Flow'r it self is glorious to behold,  
And shines on Altars like refulgent Gold:  
Sharp to the Taste, by Shepherds near the Stream  
Of *Mella* found, and thence they gave the Name.  
Boyl this restoring Root in gen'rous Wine,  
400  And set beside the Door, the sickly Stock to dine.  
But if the lab'ring Kind be wholly lost,  
And not to be retriev'd with Care or Cost;  
'Tis time to touch the Precepts of an Art,  
Th' *Arcadian* Master did of old impart:  
And how he stock'd his empty Hives again;  
Renew'd with putrid Gore of Oxen slain.  

---

376  clasp:] ~. F1–2.  
383  Galbanean] *Galbanean* F1–2.  
380  stir'd:] ~. F1–2.  
388  Psythian] *Psythian* F1–2.

An ancient Legend I prepare to sing,
And upward follow Fame's immortal Spring.
   For where with sev'n-fold Horns mysterious *Nile*
410 Surrounds the Skirts of *Egypt*'s fruitful Isle,
And where in Pomp the Sun-burnt People ride
On painted Barges, o're the teeming Tide,
Which pouring down from *Ethiopian* Lands,
Makes green the Soyl with Slime, and black prolific Sands;
That length of Region, and large Tract of Ground,
In this one Art a sure relief have found.
First, in a place, by Nature closs, they build
A narrow Flooring, gutter'd, wall'd, and til'd.
In this, four Windows are contriv'd, that strike
420 To the four Winds oppos'd, their Beams oblique.
A Steer of two Years old they take, whose Head
Now first with burnish'd Horns begins to spread:
They stop his Nostrils, while he strives in vain
To breath free Air, and struggles with his Pain.
Knock'd down, he dyes: his Bowels bruis'd within,
Betray no Wound on his unbroken Skin.
Extended thus, in this obscene Abode,
They leave the Beast; but first sweet Flow'rs are strow'd
Beneath his Body, broken Boughs and Thyme,
430 And pleasing Cassia just renew'd in prime.
This must be done, e're Spring makes equal Day,
When Western Winds on curling Waters play:
E're painted Meads produce their Flow'ry Crops,
Or Swallows twitter on the Chimney Tops.
The tainted Blood, in this close Prison pent,
Begins to boyl and through the Bones ferment.
Then, wondrous to behold, new Creatures rise,
A moving Mass at first, and short of Thighs;
'Till shooting out with Legs, and imp'd with Wings,
440 The Grubs proceed to Bees with pointed Stings:
And more and more affecting Air, they try
Their tender Pinions, and begin to fly:
At length, like Summer Storms from spreading Clouds,

432  Western] *Western* F1–2.

That burst at once, and pour impetuous Floods;
Or Flights of Arrows from the *Parthian* Bows,
When from afar they gaul embattel'd Foes;
With such a Tempest thro' the Skies they Steer;
And such a form the winged Squadrons bear.
    What God, O Muse! this useful Science taught?
450 Or by what Man's Experience was it brought?
    Sad *Aristæus* from fair *Tempe* fled, ⎫
His Bees with Famine, or Diseases dead: ⎬
On *Peneus* Banks he stood, and near his holy Head: ⎭
And while his falling Tears the Stream supply'd,
Thus mourning, to his Mother Goddess cry'd.
Mother *Cyrene,* Mother, whose abode
Is in the depth of this immortal Flood:
What boots it, that from *Phœbus* Loyns I spring,
The third by him and thee, from Heav'ns high King?
460 O! Where is all thy boasted Pity gone,
And Promise of the Skies to thy deluded Son?
Why didst thou me, unhappy me, create?
Odious to Gods, and born to bitter Fate:
Whom, scarce my Sheep, and scarce my painful Plough, ⎫
The needful Aids of Human Life allow; ⎬
So wretched is thy Son, so hard a Mother thou. ⎭
Proceed, inhuman Parent in thy Scorn; ⎫
Root up my Trees, with Blites destroy my Corn; ⎬
My Vineyards Ruin, and my Sheepfolds burn. ⎭
470 Let loose thy Rage, let all thy Spite be shown,
Since thus thy Hate persues the Praises of thy Son.
But from her Mossy Bow'r below the Ground, ⎫
His careful Mother heard the Plaintive sound; ⎬
Encompass'd with her Sea-green Sisters round. ⎭
One common Work they ply'd: their Distaffs full
With carded Locks of blue *Milesian* Wool:
*Spio* with *Drymo* brown, and *Xanthe* fair,

---

453  *Peneus . . .* Head:] *Peneus's . . . ∼.* F1–2.
458  *Phœbus*] *Phœbus's* F1–2.
463  Fate:] ∼. F1–2.
471  thy Hate persues] F2; thou hat'st F1.
476  Wool:] ∼. F1–2.

And sweet *Phyllodoce* with long dishevel'd Hair:
*Cydippe* with *Lycorias,* one a Maid,
480 And one that once had call'd *Lucina*'s Aid:
*Clio* and *Beroe,* from one Father both,
Both girt with Gold, and clad in particolour'd Cloth:
*Opis* the meek, and *Deiopeia* proud;
*Nisæa* softly, with *Ligæa* loud;
*Thalia* joyous, *Ephyre* the sad,            ⎫
And *Arethusa* once *Diana*'s Maid,           ⎬
But now, her Quiver left, to Love betray'd.   ⎭
To these, *Clymene* the sweet Theft declares,
Of *Mars;* and *Vulcans* unavailing Cares:
490 And all the Rapes of Gods, and ev'ry Love,
From antient *Chaos* down to youthful *Jove.*
  Thus while she sings, the Sisters turn the Wheel,
Empty the wooly Rock, and fill the Reel.
A mournful Sound, agen the Mother hears;
Agen the mournful Sound invades the Sisters Ears:
Starting at once from their green Seats, they rise;
Fear in their Heart, Amazement in their Eyes.
But *Arethusa* leaping from her Bed,          ⎫
First lifts above the Waves her beauteous Head; ⎬
500 And, crying from afar, thus to *Cyrene* said. ⎭
O Sister! not with causeless Fear possest,
No Stranger Voice disturbs thy tender Breast.
'Tis *Aristæus,* 'tis thy darling Son,
Who to his careless Mother makes his Moan.
Near his Paternal Stream he sadly stands,
With down-cast Eyes, wet Cheeks, and folded Hands:
Upbraiding Heav'n from whence his Lineage came,
And cruel calls the Gods, and cruel thee, by Name.
  *Cyrene* mov'd with Love, and seiz'd with Fear,
510 Cries out, Conduct my Son, conduct him here:
'Tis lawful for the Youth, deriv'd from Gods,

---

479  *Lycorias*] *Licorias* F1–2.          480  Aid:] ∼. F1–2.
482  Cloth:] ∼. F1–2.                       488  *Clymene*] *Climene* F1–2.
489  *Mars;*] F2; ∼∧ F1.                    495  Sisters] Sister's F1–2.
503  *Aristæus*] *Aristeus* F1–2.           510  out, Conduct] ∼, conduct F1–2.

To S.<sup>r</sup> Bartholomew Shower of the Midle Temple. Kn.<sup>t</sup>

Gol. l. 550.

To view the Secrets of our deep Abodes.
At once she wav'd her Hand on either side,
At once the Ranks of swelling Streams divide.
Two rising Heaps of liquid Crystal stand,
And leave a Space betwixt, of empty Sand.
Thus safe receiv'd, the downward track he treads,
Which to his Mother's watry Palace leads.
With wond'ring Eyes he views the secret Store
520 Of Lakes, that pent in hollow Caverns, roar.
He hears the crackling Sound of Coral Woods,
And sees the secret Source of subterranean Floods:
And where, distinguish'd in their sev'ral Cells,
The Fount of *Phasis,* and of *Lycus* dwells;
Where swift *Enipeus* in his Bed appears,
And *Tiber* his Majestick Forehead rears:
Whence *Anio* flows, and *Hypanis,* profound,
Breaks through th' opposing Rocks with raging Sound:
Where *Po* first issues from his dark abodes,
530 And, awful in his Cradle, rules the Floods.
Two Golden Horns on his large Front he wears,
And his grim Face a Bull's Resemblance bears.
With rapid Course he seeks the sacred Main,
And fattens, as he runs, the fruitful Plain.
      Now to the Court arriv'd, th' admiring Son
Beholds the vaulted Roofs of Pory Stone;
Now to his Mother Goddess tells his Grief,
Which she with Pity hears, and promises Relief.
Th' officious Nymphs, attending in a Ring,
540 With Waters drawn from their perpetual Spring,
From earthly dregs his Body purify,
And rub his Temples, with fine Towels, dry:
Then load the Tables with a lib'ral Feast,
And honour with full Bowls their friendly Guest.
The sacred Altars are involv'd in Smoak,
And the bright Quire their kindred Gods invoke.

522   Floods:] ∼. F1–2.                    526   rears:] ∼. F1–2.
528   Sound:] ∼. F1–2.                    536   Pory] *Pory* F1–2.

Two Bowls the Mother fills with *Lydian* Wine;
Then thus, Let these be pour'd, with Rites divine,
To the great Authors of our wat'ry Line.
550 To Father Ocean, this; and this, she said,
Be to the Nymphs his sacred Sisters paid,
Who rule the wat'ry Plains, and hold the woodland Shade.
She sprinkl'd thrice, with Wine, the Vestal Fire,
Thrice to the vaulted Roof the Flames aspire.
Rais'd with so blest an Omen, she begun,
With Words like these, to chear her drooping Son.
In the *Carpathian* Bottom makes abode
The Shepherd of the Seas, a Prophet and a God;
High o're the Main in wat'ry Pomp he rides,
560 His azure Carr and finny Coursers guides:
*Proteus* his Name: to his *Pallenian* Port,
I see from far the weary God resort.
Him, not alone, we River Gods adore,
But aged *Nereus* hearkens to his Lore.
With sure foresight, and with unerring Doom,
He sees what is, and was, and is to come.
This *Neptune* gave him, when he gave to keep
His scaly Flocks, that graze the wat'ry deep.
Implore his Aid, for *Proteus* onely knows
570 The secret Cause, and Cure of all thy Woes.
But first the wily Wizard must be caught,
For unconstrain'd he nothing tells for naught;
Nor is with Pray'rs, or Bribes, or Flatt'ry bought.
Surprise him first, and with hard Fetters bind;
Then all his Frauds will vanish into Wind.
I will my self conduct thee on thy Way,
When next the Southing Sun inflames the Day:
When the dry Herbage thirsts for Dews in vain,
And Sheep, in Shades, avoid the parching Plain.
580 Then will I lead thee to his secret Seat;
When weary with his Toyl, and scorch'd with Heat,
The wayward Sire frequents his cool Retreat.
His Eyes with heavy Slumber overcast;

With Force invade his Limbs, and bind him fast:
Thus surely bound, yet be not over bold,
The slipp'ry God will try to loose his hold:
And various Forms assume, to cheat thy sight;
And with vain Images of Beasts affright:
With foamy Tusks will seem a bristly Boar,
590 Or imitate the Lion's angry Roar;
Break out in crackling Flames to shun thy Snare,
Or hiss a Dragon, or a Tyger stare:
Or with a Wile, thy Caution to betray,
In fleeting Streams attempt to slide away.
But thou, the more he varies Forms, beware
To strain his Fetters with a stricter Care:
'Till tiring all his Arts, he turns agen
To his true Shape, in which he first was seen.
This said, with Nectar she her Son anoints:
600 Infusing Vigour through his mortal Joynts:
Down from his Head the liquid Odours ran;
He breath'd of Heav'n, and look'd above a Man.
Within a Mountain's hollow Womb, there lies
A large Recess, conceal'd from Human Eyes;
Where heaps of Billows, driv'n by Wind and Tide, ⎫
In Form of War, their wat'ry Ranks divide; ⎬
And there, like Centries set, without the Mouth abide: ⎭
A Station safe for Ships, when Tempests roar,
A silent Harbour, and a cover'd Shoar.
610 Secure within resides the various God,
And draws a Rock upon his dark Abode.
Hether with silent Steps, secure from Sight, ⎫
The Goddess guides her Son, and turns him from the Light: ⎬
Her self, involv'd in Clouds, precipitates her Flight. ⎭
'Twas Noon; the sultry Dog-star from the Sky
Scorch'd *Indian* Swains, the rivell'd Grass was dry;

588  affright:] ∼. F1–2.                      589  will seem] F2; he seems F1.
590  imitate] F2; imitates F1.               591  Break] F2; Breaks F1.
591  Snare] Snares F1–2.
592  Or hiss a Dragon] F2; A Dragon hisses F1.
592  stare] stares F1–2.                      594  attempt] F2; attempts F1.
599  Nectar] *Nectar* F1–2.

To Simon Harcourt of Stanton Harcourt
in the County of Oxon Esq.

Non Timet Vendita

Geo 4: L: 635.

The Sun with flaming Arrows pierc'd the Flood,
And, darting to the bottom, bak'd the Mud:
When weary *Proteus,* from the briny Waves,
620 Retir'd for Shelter to his wonted Caves:
His finny Flocks about their Shepherd play,
And rowling round him, spirt the bitter Sea.
Unweildily they wallow first in Ooze,
Then in the shady Covert seek Repose.
Himself their Herdsman, on the middle Mount,
Takes of his muster'd Flocks a just Account.
So, seated on a Rock, a Shepherd's Groom
Surveys his Ev'ning Flocks returning Home:
When lowing Calves, and bleating Lambs, from far,
630 Provoke the prouling Wolf to nightly War.
Th' Occasion offers, and the Youth complies:
For scarce the weary God had clos'd his Eyes;
When rushing on, with shouts, he binds in Chains
The drowzy Prophet, and his Limbs constrains.
He, not unmindful of his usual Art,
First in dissembled Fire attempts to part:
Then roaring Beasts, and running Streams he tryes,
And wearies all his Miracles of Lies:
But having shifted ev'ry Form to scape,
640 Convinc'd of Conquest, he resum'd his shape:
And thus, at length, in human Accent spoke.
Audacious Youth, what madness cou'd provoke
A Mortal Man t' invade a sleeping God?
What Buis'ness brought thee to my dark abode?
    To this, th' audacious Youth; Thou know'st full well
My Name, and Buis'ness, God, nor need I tell:
No Man can *Proteus* cheat; but *Proteus* leave
Thy fraudful Arts, and do not thou deceive.
Foll'wing the Gods Command, I come t' implore
650 Thy Help, my perish'd People to restore.
    The Seer, who could not yet his Wrath asswage,
Rowl'd his green Eyes, that sparkl'd with his Rage;
And gnash'd his Teeth, and cry'd, No vulgar God
Pursues thy Crimes, nor with a Common Rod.

Thy great Misdeeds have met a due Reward,
And *Orpheus* dying Pray'rs at length are heard.
For Crimes, not his, the Lover lost his Life,
And at thy Hands requires his murther'd Wife:
Nor (if the Fates assist not) canst thou scape
660 The just Revenge of that intended Rape.
To shun thy lawless Lust, the dying Bride,
Unwary, took along the River's side:
Nor, at her Heels perceiv'd the deadly Snake,
That kept the Bank, in Covert of the Brake.
But all her fellow Nymphs the Mountains tear
With loud Laments, and break the yielding Air:
The Realms of *Mars* remurmur'd all around,
And Echoes to th' *Athenian* Shoars rebound.
Th' unhappy Husband, Husband now no more, ⎫
670 Did on his tuneful Harp his Loss deplore, ⎬
And sought, his mournful Mind with Musick to restore. ⎭
On thee, dear Wife, in Desarts all alone, ⎫
He call'd, sigh'd, sung, his Griefs with Day begun, ⎬
Nor were they finish'd with the setting Sun. ⎭
Ev'n to the dark Dominions of the Night,
He took his way, thro' Forrests void of Light:
And dar'd amidst the trembling Ghosts to sing,
And stood before th' inexorable King.
Th' Infernal Troops like passing Shadows glide,
680 And, list'ning, crowd the sweet Musician's side.
Not flocks of Birds when driv'n by Storms, or Night,
Stretch to the Forest with so thick a flight.
Men, Matrons, Children, and th' unmarry'd Maid, ⎫
* The mighty Heroes more Majestic shade; ⎬
And Youths on Fun'ral Piles before their Parents laid: ⎭
All these *Cocytus* bounds with squalid Reeds,
With Muddy Ditches, and with deadly Weeds:
And baleful *Styx* encompasses around,
With Nine slow circling Streams, th' unhappy ground.

---

* *This whole Line is taken from the Marquess of* Normanby's *Translation.*
[Dryden's note.]

---

656 *Orpheus*] Orpheus's F1–2.          685 laid:] ∼. F1–2.

Wash'd by the Waters, was on *Hebrus* born;
Ev'n then his trembling Tongue invok'd his Bride; }
With his last Voice, *Eurydice,* he cry'd, }
*Eurydice,* the Rocks and River-banks reply'd. }
This answer *Proteus* gave, nor more he said, }
But in the Billows plung'd his hoary Head; }
And where he leap'd, the Waves in Circles widely spread. }
   The Nymph return'd, her drooping Son to chear,
And bade him banish his superfluous fear:
770 For now, said she, the Cause is known, from whence
Thy Woe succeeded, and for what Offence:
The Nymphs, Companions of th' unhappy Maid,
This punishment upon thy Crimes have laid;
And sent a Plague among thy thriving Bees.
With Vows and suppliant Pray'rs their Pow'rs appease:
The soft Napæan Race will soon repent
Their Anger, and remit the Punishment.
The secret in an easy Method lies;
Select four Brawny Bulls for Sacrifice,
780 Which on *Lycæus* graze, without a Guide;
Add four fair Heifars yet in Yoke untry'd:
For these, four Altars in their Temple rear,
And then adore the Woodland Pow'rs with Pray'r.
From the slain Victims pour the streaming Blood,
And leave their Bodies in the shady Wood:
Nine Mornings thence, *Lethean* Poppy bring,
T' appease the *Manes* of the Poets King:
And to propitiate his offended Bride,
A fatted Calf, and a black Ewe provide:
790 This finish'd, to the former Woods repair. }
His Mother's Precepts he performs with care; }
The Temple visits, and adores with Pray'r: }
Four Altars raises, from his Herd he culls,
For Slaughter, four the fairest of his Bulls;
Four Heifars from his Female Store he took,
All fair, and all unknowing of the Yoke.
Nine Mornings thence, with Sacrifice and Pray'rs,

776 Napæan] *Napæan* F1–2.        792 Pray'r:] ~. F1–2.

To the Hon.ble John                    Granville second Son
to John Earl of Bath                   one of the Com.rs appointed
by Act of Parliam.t for                Examining Taking & Stating
the Publick Accounts                   of the Kingdome

Geor: 4: l: 701.

The Pow'rs aton'd, he to the Grove repairs.
Behold a Prodigy! for from within
800 The broken Bowels, and the bloated Skin,
A buzzing noise of Bees his Ears alarms,
Straight issue through the Sides assembling Swarms:
Dark as a Cloud they make a wheeling Flight,
Then on a neighb'ring Tree, descending, light:
Like a large Cluster of black Grapes they show,
And make a large dependance from the Bough.
    Thus have I sung of Fields, and Flocks, and Trees,
And of the waxen Work of lab'ring Bees;
While mighty *Cæsar,* thund'ring from afar,
810 Seeks on *Euphrates* Banks the Spoils of War:
With conq'ring Arms asserts his Country's Cause,
With Arts of Peace the willing People draws:
On the glad Earth the Golden Age renews,
And his great Father's Path to Heav'n pursues:
While I at *Naples* pass my peaceful Days,
Affecting Studies of less noisy Praise;
And bold, through Youth, beneath the Beechen Shade,
The Lays of Shepherds, and their Loves have plaid.

---

801   his] F2; their F1.                814   pursues:] ~. F1–2.

VIRGIL READING FROM THE *Æneid* TO AUGUSTUS
ILLUSTRATED HALF-TITLE TO *Æneis*
CLARK LIBRARY LARGE-PAPER COPY OF THE FIRST EDITION
(MACDONALD 33A)

TO THE MOST HONOURABLE
*John,* Lord Marquess of *Normanby,*
EARL of *MULGRAVE,* &c. and
Knight of the *Most Noble Order of the Garter.*

A heroick Poem, truly such, is undoubedly the greatest Work which the Soul of Man is capable to perform. The Design of it, is to form the Mind to Heroick Virtue by Example; 'tis convey'd in Verse, that it may delight, while it instructs: The Action of it is always one, entire, and great. The least and most trivial Episodes, or under-Actions, which are interwoven in it, are parts either necessary, or convenient to carry on the main Design: Either so necessary, that without them the Poem must be Imperfect, or so convenient, that no others can be imagin'd more suitable to the place in which they are. There is nothing to be left void in a firm Building; even the Cavities ought not to be fill'd with Rubbish, which is of a perishable kind, destructive to the strength: But with Brick or Stone, though of less pieces, yet of the same Nature, and fitted to the Cranies. Even the least portions of them must be of the Epick kind; all things must be Grave, Majestical, and Sublime: Nothing of a Foreign Nature, like the trifling Novels, which *Ariosto* and others have inserted in their Poems: By which the Reader is miss-led into another sort of Pleasure, opposite to that which is design'd in an Epick Poem. One raises the Soul and hardens it to Virtue, the other softens it again and unbends it into Vice. One conduces to the Poet's aim, the compleating of his Work; which he is driving on, labouring and hast'ning in every Line: the other slackens his pace, diverts him from his Way, and locks him up like a Knight Errant in an Enchanted Castle, when he should be pursuing his first Adventure. *Statius,* as *Bossu* has well observ'd, was ambitious of trying his strength with his Master *Virgil,* as *Virgil* had before try'd his with *Homer.* The *Grecian* gave the

---

8 Design:] ~. F1–2.
17 *Ariosto*] *Aristotle* F1–2.

17 Novels] *Novels* F1–2.
18 Poems:] ~. F1–2.

Beauty were omitted. To raise, and afterwards to calm the Passions, to purge the Soul from Pride, by the Examples of Humane Miseries, which befall the greatest; in few words, to expel Arrogance, and introduce Compassion, are the great effects of Tragedy: Great, I must confess, if they were altogether as true as they are pompous. But are Habits to be introduc'd at three Hours warning? Are radical Diseases so suddenly remov'd? A Mountebank may promise such a Cure, but a skilful Physician will not undertake it. An Epick Poem is not in so much haste;
10 it works leisurely; the Changes which it makes are slow; but the Cure is likely to be more perfect. The effects of Tragedy, as I said, are too violent to be lasting. If it be answer'd that for this Reason Tragedies are often to be seen, and the Dose to be repeated; this is tacitely to confess, that there is more Virtue in one Heroick Poem than in many Tragedies. A Man is humbled one Day, and his Pride returns the next. Chymical Medicines are observ'd to Relieve oft'ner than to Cure: For 'tis the nature of Spirits to make swift impressions, but not deep. *Galenical* Decoctions, to which I may properly compare an Epick Poem, have
20 more of Body in them; they work by their substance and their weight. It is one Reason of *Aristotle*'s to prove, that Tragedy is the more Noble, because it turns in a shorter Compass; the whole Action being circumscrib'd within the space of Four-and-Twenty Hours. He might prove as well that a Mushroom is to be preferr'd before a Peach, because it shoots up in the compass of a Night. A Chariot may be driven round the Pillar in less space than a large Machine, because the Bulk is not so great: Is the Moon a more Noble Planet than *Saturn,* because she makes her Revolution in less than Thirty Days, and He in little less than Thirty
30 Years? Both their Orbs are in proportion to their several Magnitudes; and, consequently, the quickness or slowness of their Motion, and the time of their circumvolutions, is no Argument of the greater or less Perfection. And besides, what Virtue is there in a Tragedy, which is not contain'd in an Epick Poem: Where Pride is humbled, Vertue rewarded, and Vice punish'd; and those more amply treated, than the narrowness of the Drama can

---

5    Tragedy:] ∼. F1–2.                    27   Moon] *Moon* F1–2.
34   Poem:] ∼? F1–2.                    36   Drama] *Drama* F1–2.

admit? The shining Quality of an Epick Heroe, his Magnanim-
ity, his Constancy, his Patience, his Piety, or whatever Char-
acteristical Virtue his Poet gives him, raises first our Admiration:
We are naturally prone to imitate what we admire: And frequent
Acts produce a habit. If the Hero's chief quality be vicious, as
for Example, the Choler and obstinate desire of Vengeance in
*Achilles,* yet the Moral is Instructive: And besides, we are in-
form'd in the very proposition of the *Iliads,* that this anger was
pernicious: That it brought a thousand ills on the *Grecian*
10 Camp. The Courage of *Achilles* is propos'd to imitation, not his
Pride and Disobedience to his General, nor his brutal Cruelty
to his dead Enemy, nor the selling his Body to his Father. We
abhor these Actions while we read them, and what we abhor we
never imitate: The Poet only shews them like Rocks or Quick-
Sands, to be shun'd.

By this Example the Criticks have concluded that it is not
necessary the Manners of the Heroe should be virtuous. They
are Poetically good if they are of a Piece: Though where a
Character of perfect Virtue is set before us, 'tis more lovely: for
20 there the whole Heroe is to be imitated. This is the *Æneas* of our
Author: this is that Idea of perfection in an Epick Poem, which
Painters and Statuaries have only in their minds; and which no
hands are able to express. These are the Beauties of a God
in a Humane Body. When the Picture of *Achilles* is drawn in
Tragedy, he is taken with those Warts, and Moles, and hard
Features, by those who represent him on the Stage, or he is no
more *Achilles:* for his Creatour *Homer* has so describ'd him.
Yet even thus he appears a perfect Heroe, though an imperfect
Character of Vertue. *Horace* Paints him after *Homer,* and de-
30 livers him to be Copied on the Stage with all those imperfec-
tions. Therefore they are either not faults in a Heroick Poem,
or faults common to the Drama. After all, on the whole merits
of the Cause, it must be acknowledg'd that the Epick Poem is
more for the Manners, and Tragedy for the Passions. The Pas-
sions, as I have said, are violent: and acute Distempers require
Medicines of a strong and speedy operation. Ill habits of the

---

1   Quality] F2; Qualitiy F1.          18   Piece:] ~. F1–2.
32   Drama] *Drama* F1–2.

Mind are like Chronical Diseases, to be corrected by degrees, and Cur'd by Alteratives: wherein though Purges are sometimes necessary, yet Diet, good Air, and moderate Exercise, have the greatest part. The Matter being thus stated, it will appear that both sorts of Poetry are of use for their proper ends. The Stage is more active, the Epick Poem works at greater leisure, yet is active too, when need requires. For Dialogue is imitated by the Drama, from the more active parts of it. One puts off a Fit like the Quinquina, and relieves us only for a time; the other
10 roots out the Distemper, and gives a healthful habit. The Sun enlightens and chears us, dispels Fogs, and warms the ground with his daily Beams; but the Corn is sow'd, increases, is ripen'd, and is reap'd for use in process of time, and in its proper Season. I proceed from the greatness of the Action, to the Dignity of the Actours, I mean to the Persons employ'd in both Poems. There likewise Tragedy will be seen to borrow from the *Epopee;* and that which borrows is always of less Dignity, because it has not of its own. A Subject, 'tis true, may lend to his Soveraign, but the act of borrowing makes the King inferiour, because he wants,
20 and the Subject supplies. And suppose the Persons of the Drama wholly Fabulous, or of the Poet's Invention, yet Heroick Poetry gave him the Examples of that Invention, because it was first, and *Homer* the common Father of the Stage. I know not of any one advantage, which Tragedy can boast above Heroick Poetry, but that it is represented to the view, as well as read: and instructs in the Closet, as well as on the Theatre. This is an uncontended Excellence, and a chief Branch of its Prerogative; yet I may be allow'd to say without partiality, that herein the Actors share the Poet's praise. Your Lordship knows some Modern Tragedies
30 which are beautiful on the Stage, and yet I am confident you wou'd not read them. *Tryphon* the Stationer complains they are seldom ask'd for in his Shop. The Poet who Flourish'd in the Scene, is damn'd in the *Ruelle;* nay more, he is not esteem'd a good Poet by those who see and hear his Extravagancies with delight. They are a sort of stately Fustian, and lofty Childishness. Nothing but Nature can give a sincere pleasure; where that is

---

8   Drama] *Drama* F1–2.                    9   Quinquina] *Quinquina* F1–2.
20   Drama] *Drama* F1–2.

not imitated, 'tis Grotesque Painting, the fine Woman ends in a Fishes Tail.

I might also add, that many things, which not only please, but are real Beauties in the reading, wou'd appear absurd upon the Stage: and those not only the *Speciosa Miracula,* as *Horace* calls them; of Transformations, of *Scylla, Antiphates,* and the *Lestrigons,* which cannot be represented even in Opera's; but the prowess of *Achilles* or *Æneas* wou'd appear ridiculous in our Dwarf-Heroes of the Theatre. We can believe they routed Armies in *Homer* or in *Virgil,* but *ne Hercules contra duos* in the Drama. I forbear to instance in many things which the Stage cannot or ought not to represent. For I have said already more than I intended on this Subject, and shou'd fear it might be turn'd against me; that I plead for the pre-eminence of Epick Poetry, because I have taken some pains in translating *Virgil;* if this were the first time that I had deliver'd my Opinion in this Dispute. But I have more than once already maintain'd the Rights of my two Masters against their Rivals of the Scene, even while I wrote Tragedies my self, and had no thoughts of this present Undertaking. I submit my Opinion to your Judgment, who are better qualified than any Man I know to decide this Controversie. You come, my Lord, instructed in the Cause, and needed not that I shou'd open it. Your *Essay on Poetry,* which was publish'd without a Name, and of which I was not honour'd with the Confidence, I read over and over with much delight, and as much instruction: and, without flattering you, or making my self more Moral than I am, not without some Envy. I was loath to be inform'd how an Epick Poem shou'd be written, or how a Tragedy shou'd be contriv'd and manag'd in better Verse and with more judgment than I cou'd teach others. A Native of *Parnassus,* and bred up in the Studies of its Fundamental Laws, may receive new Lights from his Contemporaries, but 'tis a grudging kind of praise which he gives his Benefactors. He is more oblig'd than he is willing to acknowledge: there is a tincture of Malice in his Commendations. For where I own I am taught, I confess my want of Knowledge. A Judge upon the Bench, may, out of good Nature, or at least interest, encourage the Pleadings of a puny

---

*Saint Louis;* and *Scudery* with his *Alaric,* for a godly King, and
a *Gothick* Conquerour; and *Chapelain* wou'd take it ill that his
*Maid* shou'd be refus'd a place with *Helen* and *Lavinia. Spencer*
has a better plea for his *Fairy-Queen,* had his action been finish'd,
or had been one: And *Milton,* if the Devil had not been his
Heroe instead of *Adam,* if the Gyant had not foil'd the Knight,
and driven him out of his strong hold, to wander through the
World with his Lady Errant: and if there had not been more
Machining Persons than Humane, in his Poem. After these, the
10  rest of our *English* Poets shall not be mention'd. I have that
Honour for them which I ought to have: but if they are Wor-
thies, they are not to be rank'd amongst the three whom I have
nam'd, and who are establish'd in their Reputation.

Before I quitted the Comparison betwixt Epick Poetry and
Tragedy, I shou'd have acquainted my Judge with one advan-
tage of the former over the latter, which I now casually remem-
ber out of the Preface of *Segrais* before his Translation of the
*Æneis,* or out of *Bossu,* no matter which. The stile of the Heroick
Poem is and ought to be more lofty than that of the Drama. The
20  Critick is certainly in the right, for the Reason already urg'd:
The work of Tragedy is on the Passions, and in Dialogue; both
of them abhor strong Metaphors, in which the *Epopee* delights.
A Poet cannot speak too plainly on the Stage: for *Volat irre-
vocabile verbum;* the sense is lost if it be not taken flying: but
what we read alone we have leisure to digest. There an Author
may beautifie his Sense by the boldness of his Expression, which
if we understand not fully at the first, we may dwell upon it,
'till we find the secret force and excellence. That which cures
the Manners by alterative Physick, as I said before, must pro-
30  ceed by insensible degrees; but that which purges the Passions,
must do its business all at once, or wholly fail of its effect, at
least in the present Operation, and without repeated Doses. We
must beat the Iron while 'tis hot, but we may polish it at leisure.
Thus, my Lord, you pay the Fine of my forgetfulness, and yet the
merits of both Causes are where they were, and undecided, 'till

1   *Saint*] Saint F1–2.                    3   *Maid*] Maid F1–2.
5   one:] ∼. F1–2.                          19  Drama] *Drama* F1–2.
21  Dialogue;] ∼, F1–2.

you declare whether it be more for the benefit of Mankind to
have their Manners in general corrected, or their Pride and hard-
heartedness remov'd.

I must now come closer to my present business: and not think
of making more invasive Wars abroad, when like *Hannibal,* I
am call'd back to the defence of my own Country. *Virgil* is at-
tack'd by many Enemies: He has a whole Confederacy against
him, and I must endeavour to defend him as well as I am able.
But their principal Objections being against his Moral, the
duration or length of time taken up in the action of the Poem,
and what they have to urge against the Manners of his Hero, I
shall omit the rest as meer Cavils of Grammarians: at the worst
but casual slips of a Great Man's Pen, or inconsiderable faults
of an admirable Poem, which the Author had not leisure to re-
view before his Death. *Macrobius* has answer'd what the An-
cients cou'd urge against him: and some things I have lately read
in *Tanneguy le Fèvre, Valois,* and another whom I name not,
which are scarce worth answering. They begin with the Moral
of his Poem, which I have elsewhere confess'd, and still must
own not to be so Noble as that of *Homer.* But let both be fairly
stated, and without contradicting my first Opinion, I can shew
that *Virgil's* was as useful to the *Romans* of his Age, as *Homer's*
was to the *Grecians* of his; in what time soever he may be sup-
pos'd to have liv'd and flourish'd. *Homer's* Moral was to urge
the necessity of Union, and of a good understanding betwixt
Confederate States and Princes engag'd in a War with a Mighty
Monarch: as also of Discipline in an Army, and obedience in the
several Chiefs, to the Supream Commander of the joynt Forces.
To inculcate this, he sets forth the ruinous Effects of Discord in
the Camp of those Allies, occasion'd by the quarrel betwixt the
General, and one of the next in Office under him. *Agamemnon*
gives the provocation, and *Achilles* resents the injury. Both Par-
ties are faulty in the Quarrel, and accordingly they are both
punish'd: the Aggressor is forc'd to sue for peace to his Inferiour,
on dishonourable Conditions; the Deserter refuses the satisfac-
tion offer'd, and his Obstinacy costs him his best Friend. This
works the Natural Effect of Choler, and turns his Rage against

17　*Fèvre*] *Fevrè* F1–2.　　　　　34　Aggressor] F2; Agressor F1.

him, by whom he was last Affronted, and most sensibly. The greater Anger expels the less; but his Character is still preserv'd. In the mean time the *Grecian* Army receives Loss on Loss, and is half destroy'd by a Pestilence into the Bargain.

*Quicquid delirant Reges plectuntur Achivi.*

As the Poet, in the first part of the Example, had shewn the bad effects of Discord, so after the Reconcilement, he gives the good effects of Unity. For *Hector* is slain, and then *Troy* must fall. By this, 'tis probable, that *Homer* liv'd when the *Median* Monarchy
10 was grown formidable to the *Grecians:* and that the joint Endeavours of his Country-men, were little enough to preserve their common Freedom, from an encroaching Enemy. Such was his Moral, which all Criticks have allow'd to be more Noble than that of *Virgil:* though not adapted to the times in which the *Roman* Poet liv'd. Had *Virgil* flourish'd in the Age of *Ennius,* and address'd to *Scipio,* he had probably taken the same Moral, or some other not unlike it. For then the *Romans* were in as much danger from the *Carthaginian* Commonwealth, as the *Grecians* were from the *Assyrian,* or *Median* Monarchy. But we are to
20 consider him as writing his Poem in a time when the Old Form of Government was subverted, and a new one just Established by *Octavius Cæsar:* In effect by force of Arms, but seemingly by the Consent of the *Roman* People. The Commonwealth had receiv'd a deadly Wound in the former Civil Wars betwixt *Marius* and *Sylla.* The Commons, while the first prevail'd, had almost shaken off the Yoke of the Nobility; and *Marius* and *Cinna,* like the Captains of the Mobb, under the specious Pretence of the Publick Good, and of doing Justice on the Oppressours of their Liberty, reveng'd themselves, without Form of Law, on their
30 private Enemies. *Sylla,* in his turn, proscrib'd the Heads of the adverse Party: He too had nothing but Liberty and Reformation in his Mouth; (for the Cause of Religion is but a Modern Motive to Rebellion, invented by the Christian Priesthood, refining on the Heathen:) *Sylla,* to be sure, meant no more good to the

---

2   Character] F2; Caracter F1.         9   *Median*] F2; *Persian* F1.
19   *Assyrian,* or *Median*] F2; *Persian* F1.

*Roman* People than *Marius* before him, whatever he declar'd; but Sacrific'd the Lives, and took the Estates of all his Enemies, to gratifie those who brought him into Power: Such was the Reformation of the Government by both Parties. The Senate and the Commons were the two Bases on which it stood; and the two Champions of either Faction, each destroy'd the Foundations of the other side: So the Fabrique of consequence must fall betwixt them: And Tyranny must be built upon their Ruines. This comes of altering Fundamental Laws and Constitutions:
Like him, who being in good Health, lodg'd himself in a Physician's House, and was over-perswaded by his Landlord to take Physick, of which he dyed, for the benefit of his Doctor. *Stavo ben* (was written on his Monument) *ma, per star meglio, sto qui.*

After the Death of those two Usurpers, the Commonwealth seem'd to recover, and held up its Head for a little time: But it was all the while in a deep Consumption, which is a flattering Disease. *Pompey, Crassus,* and *Cæsar,* had found the Sweets of Arbitrary Power; and each being a check to the others growth, struck up a false Friendship amongst themselves; and divided the Government betwixt them, which none of them was able to assume alone. These were the publick Spirited Men of their Age, that is, Patriots for their own Interest. The Commonwealth look'd with a florid Countenance in their Management, spread in Bulk, and all the while was wasting in the Vitals. Not to trouble your Lordship with the Repetition of what you know: After the death of *Crassus, Pompey* found himself out-witted by *Cæsar;* broke with him, over-power'd him in the Senate, and caus'd many unjust Decrees to pass against him: *Cæsar* thus injur'd, and unable to resist the Faction of the Nobles, which was now uppermost (for he was a *Marian*) had recourse to Arms; and his Cause was just against *Pompey,* but not against his Country, whose Constitution ought to have been sacred to him; and never to have been Violated on the account of any private Wrong. But he prevail'd, and Heav'n declaring for him, he became a Providential Monarch, under the Title of *Perpetual Dictator.* He being Murther'd by his own Son, whom I neither dare commend,

8   betwixt] F2; betwxt F1.          9   Constitutions:] ∼. F1–2.
13   *per star*] *perstar* F1–2.

nor can justly blame (though *Dante* in his *Inferno,* has put him and *Cassius,* and *Judas Iscariot* betwixt them, into the great Devil's Mouth) the Commonwealth popp'd up its Head for the third time, under *Brutus* and *Cassius,* and then sunk for ever.

Thus the *Roman* People were grosly gull'd twice or thrice over and as often enslav'd in one Century, and under the same pretence of Reformation. At last the two Battles of *Philippi,* gave the decisive stroak against Liberty; and not long after, the Commonwealth was turn'd into a Monarchy, by the Conduct and good Fortune of *Augustus.* 'Tis true, that the despotick Power could not have fallen into better Hands, than those of the first and second *Cæsar.* Your Lordship well knows what Obligations *Virgil* had to the latter of them: He saw, beside, that the Commonwealth was lost without ressource: The Heads of it destroy'd; the Senate new moulded, grown degenerate; and either bought off, or thrusting their own Necks into the Yoke, out of fear of being forc'd. Yet I may safely affirm for our great Author (as Men of good Sense are generally Honest) that he was still of Republican principles in his Heart.

*Secretisque Piis, his dantem jura Catonem.*

I think, I need use no other Argument to justify my Opinion, than that of this one Line, taken from the Eighth Book of the *Æneis.* If he had not well studied his Patron's Temper, it might have Ruin'd him with another Prince. But *Augustus* was not discontented, at least that we can find, that *Cato* was plac'd, by his own Poet, in *Elysium;* and there giving Laws to the Holy Souls, who deserv'd to be separated from the Vulgar sort of good Spirits. For his Conscience could not but whisper to the Arbitrary Monarch, that the Kings of *Rome* were at first Elective, and Govern'd not without a Senate: That *Romulus* was no Hereditary Prince, and though, after his Death, he receiv'd Divine Honours, for the good he did on Earth, yet he was but a God of their own making: that the last *Tarquin* was Expell'd

5–6   gull'd ... over] ∼: ... ∼: F1; ∼; ... ∼: F2.
18–19   Republican] F1 *errata,* F2; Republick F1.
19   his Heart] F1 *errata;* Heart F1–2.
23   *Æneis*] Eneis F1–2.          26   *Elysium*] Elisium F1–2.

justly, for Overt Acts of Tyranny, and Male-Administration; for
such are the Conditions of an Elective Kingdom: And I meddle
not with others: being, for my own Opinion, of *Montaign's*
Principles, that an Honest Man ought to be contented with that
Form of Government, and with those Fundamental Constitu-
tions of it, which he receiv'd from his Ancestors, and under which
himself was Born: Though at the same time he confess'd freely,
that if he could have chosen his Place of Birth, it shou'd have
been at *Venice:* Which for many Reasons I dislike, and am
10 better pleas'd to have been born an *English* Man.

But to return from my long rambling: I say that *Virgil* having
maturely weigh'd the Condition of the Times in which he liv'd:
that an entire Liberty was not to be retriev'd: that the present
Settlement had the prospect of a long continuance in the same
Family, or those adopted into it: that he held his Paternal Estate
from the Bounty of the Conqueror, by whom he was likewise en-
rich'd, esteem'd and cherish'd: that this Conquerour, though of
a bad kind, was the very best of it: that the Arts of Peace flour-
ish'd under him: that all Men might be happy if they would
20 be quiet: that now he was in possession of the whole, yet he
shar'd a great part of his Authority with the Senate: That he
would be chosen into the Ancient Offices of the Commonwealth,
and Rul'd by the Power which he deriv'd from them; and Pro-
rogu'd his Government from time to time: Still, as it were,
threatning to dismiss himself from Publick Cares, which he ex-
ercis'd more for the common Good, than for any delight he took
in greatness: These things, I say, being consider'd by the Poet,
he concluded it to be the Interest of his Country to be so Gov-
ern'd: To infuse an awful Respect into the People, towards such
30 a Prince: By that respect to confirm their Obedience to him;
and by that Obedience to make them Happy. This was the Moral
of his Divine Poem: Honest in the Poet: Honourable to the Em-
perour, whom he derives from a Divine Extraction; and reflect-
ing part of that Honour on the *Roman* People, whom he derives
also from the *Trojans;* and not only profitable, but necessary to
the present Age; and likely to be such to their Posterity. That it
was the receiv'd Opinion, that the *Romans* were descended from

---

1   Overt Acts] Overt-Acts F1–2.          3   *Montaign's*] F2; *Montaigns* F1.

the *Trojans,* and *Julius Cæsar* from *Iulus* the Son of *Æneas,* was enough for *Virgil;* tho' perhaps he thought not so himself: Or that *Æneas* ever was in *Italy,* which *Bochartus* manifestly proves. And *Homer,* where he says that *Jupiter* hated the House of *Priam,* and was resolv'd to transfer the Kingdom to the Family of *Æneas,* yet mentions nothing of his leading a Colony into a Foreign Country, and setling there: But that the *Romans* valued themselves on their *Trojan* Ancestry, is so undoubted a Truth, that I need not prove it. Even the Seals which we have remaining
10 of *Julius Cæsar,* which we know to be Antique, have the Star of *Venus* over them, though they were all graven after his Death, as a Note that he was Deifi'd. I doubt not but one Reason, why *Augustus* should be so passionately concern'd for the preservation of the *Æneis,* which its Author had Condemn'd to be Burnt, as an Imperfect Poem, by his last Will and Testament; was, because it did him a real Service as well as an Honour; that a Work should not be lost where his Divine Original was Celebrated in Verse, which had the Character of Immortality stamp'd upon it.
20      Neither were the great *Roman* Families which flourish'd in his time, less oblig'd by him than the Emperour. Your Lordship knows with what Address he makes mention of them, as Captains of Ships, or Leaders in the War; and even some of *Italian* Extraction are not forgotten. These are the single Stars which are sprinkled through the *Æneis:* But there are whole Constellations of them in the Fifth Book. And I could not but take notice, when I Translated it, of some Favourite Families to which he gives the Victory, and awards the Prizes, in the Person of his Heroe, at the Funeral Games which were Celebrated in Honour
30 of *Anchises.* I insist not on their Names: But am pleas'd to find the *Memmii* amongst them, deriv'd from *Mnestheus,* because *Lucretius* Dedicates to one of that Family, a Branch of which destroy'd *Corinth.* I likewise either found or form'd an Image to my self of the contrary kind; that those who lost the Prizes, were such as had disoblig'd the Poet, or were in disgrace with *Augustus,* or Enemies to *Mæcenas:* And this was the Poetical Revenge

---

1  *Iulus*] *Julus* F1–2.                    12  one] it was one F1–2.
30  I insist] F2; I, Insist F1.              36  *Mæcenas*] *Mecenas* F1; *Mecænas* F2.

he took. For *genus irritabile Vatum,* as *Horace* says. When a
Poet is throughly provok'd, he will do himself Justice, however
dear it cost him, *Animamque, in Vulnere ponit.* I think these
are not bare Imaginations of my own, though I find no trace of
them in the Commentatours: But one Poet may judge of another
by himself. The Vengeance we defer, is not forgotten. I hinted
before, that the whole *Roman* People were oblig'd by *Virgil,* in
deriving them from *Troy;* an Ancestry which they affected. We,
and the *French* are of the same Humour: They would be thought
10  to descend from a Son, I think, of *Hector:* And we wou'd have
our *Britain,* both Nam'd and Planted by a descendant of *Æneas.*
*Spencer* favours this Opinion what he can. His Prince *Arthur,*
or whoever he intends by him, is a *Trojan.* Thus the Heroe of
*Homer* was a *Grecian,* of *Virgil* a *Roman,* of *Tasso* an *Italian.*
I have transgress'd my Bounds, and gone farther than the
Moral led me. But if your Lordship is not tir'd, I am safe enough.
Thus far, I think, my Author is defended. But as *Augustus*
is still shadow'd in the Person of *Æneas,* of which I shall say more,
when I come to the Manners which the Poet gives his Hero: I
20  must prepare that Subject by shewing how dext'rously he man-
nag'd both the Prince and People, so as to displease neither, and
to do good to both, which is the part of a Wise and an Honest
Man: And proves that it is possible for a Courtier not to be a
Knave. I shall continue still to speak my Thoughts like a free-
born Subject as I am; though such things, perhaps, as no *Dutch*
Commentator cou'd, and I am sure no *French*-man durst. I have
already told your Lordship my Opinion of *Virgil;* that he was no
Arbitrary Man. Oblig'd he was to his Master for his Bounty,
and he repays him with good Counsel, how to behave himself in
30  his new Monarchy, so as to gain the Affections of his Subjects,
and deserve to be call'd the Father of his Country. From this
Consideration it is, that he chose for the ground-work of his
Poem, one Empire destroy'd, and another rais'd from the Ruins
of it. This was just the Parallel. *Æneas* cou'd not pretend to be
*Priam*'s Heir in a Lineal Succession: For *Anchises* the Heroe's
Father, was only of the second Branch of the Royal Family: And
*Helenus,* a Son of *Priam,* was yet surviving, and might lawfully

24  Knave.] F2; ~: F1.

claim before him. It may be *Virgil* mentions him on that Account. Neither has he forgotten *Priamus,* in the Fifth of his *Æneis,* the Son of *Polites,* youngest Son to *Priam;* who was slain by *Pyrrhus,* in the Second Book. *Æneas* had only Married *Creusa, Priam*'s Daughter, and by her could have no Title, while any of the Male Issue were remaining. In this case, the Poet gave him the next Title, which is, that of an Elective King. The remaining *Trojans* chose him to lead them forth, and settle them in some Foreign Country. *Ilioneus* in his Speech to *Dido,* calls him ex-
10 presly by the Name of King. Our Poet, who all this while had *Augustus* in his Eye, had no desire he should seem to succeed by any right of Inheritance, deriv'd from *Julius Cæsar;* such a Title being but one degree remov'd from Conquest. For what was introduc'd by force, by force may be remov'd. 'Twas better for the People that they should give, than he should take: Since that Gift was indeed no more at bottom than a Trust. *Virgil* gives us an Example of this, in the Person of *Mezentius.* He Govern'd Arbitrarily, he was expell'd: And came to the deserv'd End of all Tyrants. Our Author shews us another sort of Kingship in the
20 Person of *Latinus.* He was descended from *Saturn,* and as I remember, in the Third Degree. He is describ'd a just and a gracious Prince; solicitous for the Welfare of his People; always Consulting with his Senate to promote the common Good. We find him at the head of them, when he enters into the Council-Hall: Speaking first, but still demanding their Advice, and steering by it as far as the Iniquity of the Times wou'd suffer him. And this is the proper Character of a King by Inheritance, who is born a Father of his Country. *Æneas,* tho' he Married the Heiress of the Crown, yet claim'd no Title to it during the Life
30 of his Father-in-Law. *Pater arma Latinus habeto,* &c. are *Virgil*'s Words. As for himself, he was contented to take care of his Country Gods, who were not those of *Latium:* Wherein our

---

2   *Priamus*] F1 *errata,* F2; *Atis* F1.
4   Book.] F2; *F1 continues: Atis,* then, the Favourite Companion of *Ascanius,* had a better Right than he; tho' I know he was introduc'd by *Virgil,* to do Honour to the Family, from which *Julius Cæsar* was descended by the Mothers side.
15   take:] ∼. F1–2.
24–25   Council-Hall:] ∼. F1–2.
32   *Latium:*] ∼. F1–2.

Divine Author seems to relate to the after practice of the *Romans,* which was to adopt the Gods of those they Conquer'd, or receiv'd as Members of their Commonwealth. Yet withal, he plainly touches at the Office of the High Priesthood, with which *Augustus* was invested: And which made his Person more Sacred and inviolable, than even the Tribunitial Power. It was not therefore for nothing, that the most Judicious of all Poets, made that Office vacant, by the Death of *Panthus,* in the Second Book of the *Æneis,* for his Heroe to succeed in it; and consequently for *Augustus* to enjoy. I know not that any of the Commentatours have taken notice of that passage. If they have not, I am sure they ought: And if they have, I am not indebted to them for the Observation: The words of *Virgil* are very plain.

*Sacra, suosque tibi, commendat Troja Penates.*

As for *Augustus,* or his Uncle *Julius,* claiming by descent from *Æneas;* that Title is already out of doors. *Æneas* succeeded not, but was Elected. *Troy* was fore-doom'd to fall for ever.

*Postquam res Asiæ, Priamique evertere Regnum,*
*Immeritum, visum superis.—*Æneis, lib. III. lin. 1.

*Augustus* 'tis true, had once resolv'd to re-build that City, and there to make the Seat of Empire: But *Horace* writes an Ode on purpose to deter him from that Thought; declaring the place to be accurs'd, and that the Gods would as often destroy it as it shou'd be rais'd. Hereupon the Emperour laid aside a Project so ungrateful to the *Roman* People: But by this, my Lord, we may conclude that he had still his Pedigree in his Head; and had an Itch of being thought a Divine King, if his Poets had not given him better Counsel.

I will pass by many less material Objections, for want of room to Answer them: What follows next is of great Importance, if the Criticks can make out their Charge; for 'tis levell'd at the Manners which our Poet gives his Heroe; and which are the same

9  to] F2; ro F1.
19  —Æneis, lib. III. lin. 1.] F2; ₍Æneis the 3*d,* line the 1*st.* F1.

which were eminently seen in his *Augustus.* Those Manners
were Piety to the Gods, and a dutiful Affection to his Father;
Love to his Relations; Care of his People; Courage and Conduct
in the Wars; Gratitude to those who had oblig'd him; and Jus-
tice in general to Mankind.

Piety, as your Lordship sees, takes place of all, as the chief part
of his Character: And the word in *Latin* is more full than it can
possibly be exprest in any Modern Language; for there it com-
prehends not only Devotion to the Gods, but Filial Love and
10 tender Affection to Relations of all sorts. As instances of this,
the Deities of *Troy* and his own *Penates* are made the Com-
panions of his Flight: They appear to him in his Voyage, and
advise him; and at last he re-places them in *Italy,* their Native
Country. For his Father, he takes him on his Back: He leads his
little Son, his Wife follows him; but losing his Footsteps through
Fear or Ignorance, he goes back into the midst of his Enemies
to find her; and leaves not his pursute 'till her Ghost appears,
to forbid his farther search. I will say nothing of his Duty to his
Father while he liv'd; his Sorrow for his Death; of the Games
20 instituted in Honour of his Memory; or seeking him, by his
Command, even after Death, in the *Elysian* Fields. I will not
mention his Tenderness for his Son, which every where is visi-
ble; Of his raising a Tomb for *Polydorus,* the Obsequies for
*Misenus,* his pious remembrance of *Deiphobus:* The Funerals
of his Nurse: His Grief for *Pallas,* and his Revenge taken on his
Murtherer; whom, otherwise by his Natural Compassion, he had
forgiven: And then the Poem had been left imperfect: For we
could have had no certain prospect of his Happiness, while the
last Obstacle to it was unremov'd. Of the other parts which com-
30 pose his Character, as a King, or as a General, I need say nothing:
The whole *Æneis* is one continued Instance, of some one or
other of them: And where I find any thing of them tax'd, it shall
suffice me, as briefly as I can, to vindicate my Divine Master to
your Lordship, and by you to the Reader. But herein, *Segrais,*
in his admirable Preface to his Translation of the *Æneis,* as the
Author of the *Dauphin's Virgil* justly calls it, has prevented me.

---

7   *Latin*] Latin F1–2.  14   Father,] F2; ∼∧ F1.
36   it,] F2; ∼; F1.

Him I follow; and what I borrow from him, am ready to acknowledge to him. For, impartially speaking, the *French* are as much better Criticks than the *English,* as they are worse Poets. Thus we generally allow that they better understand the management of a War, than our Islanders; but we know we are superiour to them, in the day of Battel. They value themselves on their Generals; we on our Souldiers. But this is not the proper place to decide that Question, if they make it one. I shall say perhaps as much of other Nations, and their Poets, excepting
10 only *Tasso:* and hope to make my Assertion good, which is but doing Justice to my Country: Part of which Honour will reflect on your Lordship, whose Thoughts are always just; your Numbers harmonious; your Words chosen; your Expressions strong and manly; your Verse flowing, and your turns as happy as they are easie. If you wou'd set us more Copies, your Example would make all Precepts needless. In the mean time, that little you have Written is own'd, and that particularly by the Poets, (who are a Nation not over-lavish of praise to their Contemporaries,) as a principal Ornament of our Language: But the sweetest Es-
20 sences are always confin'd in the smallest Glasses.

When I speak of your Lordship, 'tis never a digression, and therefore I need beg no pardon for it; but take up *Segrais* where I left him: And shall use him less often than I have occasion for him. For his Preface is a perfect piece of Criticism, full and clear, and digested into an exact Method; mine is loose, and, as I intended it, Epistolary. Yet I dwell on many things which he durst not touch: For 'tis dangerous to offend an Arbitrary Master: And every Patron who has the Power of *Augustus,* has not his Clemency. In short, my Lord, I wou'd not Translate him,
30 because I wou'd bring you somewhat of my own. His Notes and Observations on every Book, are of the same Excellency; and for the same Reason I omit the greater part.

He takes notice that *Virgil* is Arraign'd for placing Piety before Valour; and making that Piety the chief Character of his Heroe. I have said already from *Bossu,* that a Poet is not oblig'd to make his Heroe a Virtuous Man: Therefore neither *Homer* nor *Tasso* are to be blam'd, for giving what predominant quality

---

5  know] F2; kuow F1.          11  Country:] ∼. F1; ∼; F2.

they pleas'd to their first Character. But *Virgil,* who design'd to
form a perfect Prince, and would insinuate, that *Augustus,* whom
he calls *Æneas* in his Poem, was truly such, found himself oblig'd
to make him without blemish; thoroughly Virtuous; and a thor-
ough Virtue both begins and ends in Piety. *Tasso,* without ques-
tion, observ'd this before me; and therefore split his Heroe in
two. He gave *Godfrey* Piety, and *Rinaldo* Fortitude; for their
chief Qualities or Manners. *Homer,* who had chosen another
Moral, makes both *Agamemnon* and *Achilles* vicious: For his
10 design was to instruct in Virtue, by shewing the deformity of
Vice. I avoid repetition of that I have said above. What follows
is Translated literally from *Segrais.*

    *Virgil* had consider'd that the greatest Virtues of *Augustus*
consisted in the perfect Art of Governing his People; which
caus'd him to Reign for more than Forty Years in great Felicity.
He consider'd that his Emperour was Valiant, Civil, Popular,
Eloquent, Politick, and Religious. He has given all these Quali-
ties to *Æneas.* But knowing that Piety alone comprehends the
whole Duty of Man towards the Gods; towards his Country, and
20 towards his Relations, he judg'd, that this ought to be his first
Character, whom he would set for a Pattern of Perfection. In
reality, they who believe that the Praises which arise from Val-
our, are superiour to those, which proceed from any other Vir-
tues, have not consider'd (as they ought), that Valour, destitute
of other Virtues, cannot render a Man worthy of any true es-
teem. That Quality which signifies no more than an intrepid
Courage, may be separated from many others which are good,
and accompany'd with many which are ill. A Man may be very
Valiant, and yet Impious and Vicious. But the same cannot be
30 said of Piety; which excludes all ill Qualities, and comprehends
even Valour it self, with all other Qualities which are good. Can
we, for Example, give the praise of Valour to a Man who shou'd
see his Gods prophan'd, and shou'd want the Courage to defend
them? To a Man who shou'd abandon his Father, or desert his
King in his last Necessity?

    Thus far *Segrais,* in giving the preference to Piety before Val-
our. I will now follow him, where he considers this Valour, or

---

11   repetition] F2; repetitione F1.        19   Country] F2; County F1.

intrepid Courage, singly in it self; and this also *Virgil* gives to his *Æneas,* and that in a Heroical Degree.

Having first concluded, that our Poet did for the best in taking the first Character of his Heroe, from that Essential Vertue on which the rest depend, he proceeds to tell us, that in the Ten Years war of *Troy,* he was consider'd as the second Champion of his Country; allowing *Hector* the first place; and this, even by the Confession of *Homer,* who took all occasions of setting up his own Countrymen the *Grecians,* and of undervaluing the
10 *Trojan* Chiefs. But *Virgil,* (whom *Segrais* forgot to cite,) makes *Diomede* give him a higher Character for Strength and Courage. His Testimony is this in the Eleventh Book.

> ————*stetimus tela aspera contra,*
> *Contulimusque manus: Experto, credite, quantus*
> *In clypeum assurgat, quo turbine torqueat hastam.*
> *Si duo præterea tales Idæa tulisset*
> *Terra viros; ultro Inachias venisset ad Urbes*
> *Dardanus, & versis lugeret Græcia fatis.*
> *Quicquid apud duræ cessatum est mœnia Trojæ,*
> 20 *Hectoris, Æneæque manu victoria Grajûm*
> *Hæsit; & in decumum vestigia rettulit annum.*
> *Ambo animis, ambo insignes præstantibus armis:*
> *Hic pietate prior.————*

I give not here my Translation of these Verses; though I think I have not ill succeeded in them; because your Lordship is so great a Master of the Original, that I have no reason to desire you shou'd see *Virgil* and me so near together: But you may please, my Lord, to take notice, that the *Latin* Author refines upon the *Greek;* and insinuates, That *Homer* had done his Heroe
30 Wrong, in giving the advantage of the Duel to his own Countryman: Though *Diomedes* was manifestly the second Champion of the *Grecians:* And *Ulysses* preferr'd him before *Ajax,* when

---

6    *Troy,*] *some copies of F1 read* Troy'.
20    *Æneæque*] F2; *Æeneæque* F1.
23    *prior.————*] F2; ~.∧ F1.
28–29    *Latin . . . Greek*] Latin . . . Greek F1–2.

he chose him for the Companion of his Nightly Expedition: For he had a Head-piece of his own; and wanted only the fortitude of another, to bring him off with safety; and that he might compass his Design with Honour.

The *French* Translator thus proceeds: They who accuse *Æneas* for want of Courage, either understand not *Virgil*, or have read him slightly; otherwise they would not raise an Objection so easie to be Answer'd. Hereupon he gives so many instances of the Heroe's Valour, that to repeat them after him would tire your Lordship, and put me to the unnecessary trouble of Transcribing the greatest part of the three last *Æneids*. In short, more could not be expected from an *Amadis*, a Sir *Lancelot*, or the whole Round Table, than he performs. *Proxima quæque metit gladio,* is the perfect Account of a Knight Errant. If it be reply'd, continues *Segrais*, that it was not difficult for him to undertake and atchieve such hardy Enterprizes, because he wore Enchanted Arms: That Accusation, in the first place, must fall on *Homer* e're it can reach *Virgil. Achilles* was as well provided with them as *Æneas*, though he was invulnerable without them: And *Ariosto*, the two *Tasso's, Bernardo* and *Torquato,* even our own *Spencer;* in a word, all Modern Poets have Copied *Homer* as well as *Virgil:* He is neither the first nor last; but in the midst of them; and therefore is safe if they are so. Who knows, says *Segrais*, but that his fated Armour was only an Allegorical Defence, and signifi'd no more than that he was under the peculiar protection of the Gods; born, as the Astrologers will tell us out of *Virgil* (who was well vers'd in the *Chaldæan* Mysteries) under the favourable influence of *Jupiter, Venus,* and the Sun? But I insist not on this, because I know you believe not there is such an Art: though not only *Horace* and *Persius,* but *Augustus* himself, thought otherwise. But in defence of *Virgil,* I dare positively say, that he has been more cautious in this particular than either his Predecessour, or his Descendants. For *Æneas* was actually wounded, in the Twelfth of the *Æneis;* though he had the same God-Smith to Forge his Arms, as had

---

8  Answer'd.] F2; ~: F1.
15  continues] F2; *continues* F1.
20  And] F2; ~, F1.
29  Sun?] *Sun:* F1; *Sun.* F2.

13  Round] F2; round F1.
17  Arms:] ~. F1; ~; F2.
26  Astrologers] F2; *Astrologers* F1.

*Achilles*. It seems he was no War-luck, as the *Scots* commonly
call such Men, who they say, are Iron-free, or Lead-free. Yet after
this Experiment, that his Arms were not impenetrable, when he
was Cur'd indeed by his Mother's help, because he was that day
to conclude the War by the death of *Turnus*, the Poet durst not
carry the Miracle too far, and restore him wholy to his former
Vigour: He was still too weak to overtake his Enemy; yet we
see with what Courage he attacks *Turnus,* when he faces and
renews the Combate. I need say no more, for *Virgil* defends
10 himself, without needing my assistance; and proves his Heroe
truly to deserve that Name. He was not then a Second-rate Cham-
pion, as they would have him, who think Fortitude the first Ver-
tue in a Heroe. But being beaten from this hold, they will not
yet allow him to be Valiant; because he wept more often, as they
think, than well becomes a Man of Courage.

In the first place, if Tears are Arguments of Cowardise, What
shall I say of *Homer*'s Heroe? shall *Achilles* pass for timorous
because he wept? and wept on less occasions than *Æneas?* Herein
*Virgil* must be granted to have excell'd his Master. For once both
20 Heroes are describ'd lamenting their lost Loves: *Briseis* was
taken away by force from the *Grecian: Creusa* was lost for ever
to her Husband. But *Achilles* went roaring along the salt Sea-
shore, and like a Booby, was complaining to his Mother, when
he shou'd have reveng'd his Injury by Arms. *Æneas* took a Nob-
ler Course; for having secur'd his Father and his Son, he repeated
all his former Dangers to have found his Wife, if she had been
above ground. And here your Lordship may observe the Address
of *Virgil;* it was not for nothing, that this Passage was related
with all these tender Circumstances. *Æneas* told it; *Dido* heard
30 it: That he had been so affectionate a Husband, was no ill Argu-
ment to the coming Dowager, that he might prove as kind to her.
*Virgil* has a thousand secret Beauties, tho' I have not leisure to
remark them.

*Segrais* on this Subject of a Heroe's shedding Tears, observes
that Historians commend *Alexander* for weeping, when he read
the mighty Actions of *Achilles*. And *Julius Cæsar* is likewise
prais'd, when out of the same Noble Envy, he wept at the Vic-

21   *Creusa*] F2; *Cerusa* F1.          29   heard] F2; hear'd F1.

tories of *Alexander*. But if we observe more closely, we shall find, that the tears of *Æneas* were always on a laudable Occasion. Thus he weeps out of Compassion, and tenderness of Nature, when in the Temple of *Carthage* he beholds the Pictures of his Friends, who Sacrific'd their Lives in Defence of their Country. He deplores the lamentable End of his Pilot *Palinurus;* the untimely death of young *Pallas* his Confederate; and the rest, which I omit. Yet even for these Tears his wretched Criticks dare condemn him. They make *Æneas* little better than a kind of a St.
10 *Swithen* Heroe, always raining. One of these Censors is bold enough to argue him of Cowardise; when in the beginning of the First Book, he not only weeps, but trembles at an approaching Storm.

> *Extemplò Æneæ solvuntur frigore Membra:*
> *Ingemit & duplices tendens ad sydera palmas,* &c.

But to this I have answer'd formerly; that his fear was not for himself, but for his People. And who can give a Soveraign a better Commendation, or recommend a Heroe more to the affection of the Reader? They were threatned with a Tempest,
20 and he wept; he was promis'd *Italy,* and therefore he pray'd for the accomplishment of that Promise: All this in the beginning of a Storm; therefore he shew'd the more early Piety, and the quicker sense of Compassion. Thus much I have urg'd elsewhere in the defence of *Virgil;* and since I have been inform'd, by Mr. *Moyl,* a young Gentleman, whom I can never sufficiently commend, that the Ancients accounted drowning an accursed Death: So that if we grant him to have been afraid, he had just occasion for that fear, both in relation to himself, and to his Subjects. I think our Adversaries can carry this Argument no
30 farther, unless they tell us that he ought to have had more confidence in the promise of the Gods: But how was he assur'd that he had understood their Oracles aright? *Helenus* might be mistaken, *Phœbus* might speak doubtfully, even his Mother might flatter him, that he might prosecute his Voyage, which if it succeeded happily, he shou'd be the Founder of an Empire. For that

---

15  *sydera*] F2; *syderas* F1.          21-22  Promise: ... Storm;] ~. ... ~, F1-2.
27  Death:] ~. F1-2.

she her self was doubtful of his Fortune, is apparent by the Address she made to *Jupiter* on his behalf: To which the God makes answer in these words:

> *Parce metu, Citherea, manent immota tuorum*
> *Fata tibi,* &c.

Notwithstanding which, the Goddess, though comforted, was not assur'd: For even after this, through the course of the whole *Æneis,* she still apprehends the interest which *Juno* might make with *Jupiter* against her Son. For it was a moot Point in Heaven, whether he cou'd alter Fate or not. And indeed, some passages in *Virgil* wou'd make us suspect, that he was of Opinion, *Jupiter* might deferr Fate, though he cou'd not alter it. For in the latter end of the Tenth Book, he introduces *Juno* begging for the Life of *Turnus,* and flattering her Husband with the power of changing Destiny. *Tua qui potes, orsa reflectas.* To which he graciously answers:

> *Si mora præsentis lethi tempusq; caduco*
> *Oratur Juveni, meq; hoc ita ponere sentis,*
> *Tolle fugâ Turnum, atq; instantibus Eripe fatis.*
> *Hactenus indulsisse vacat. Sin altior istis*
> *Sub precibus venia ulla latet, totumq; moveri,*
> *Mutarive putas bellum, spes pascis inanis.*

But that he cou'd not alter those Decrees, the King of Gods himself confesses, in the Book above cited: when he comforts *Hercules,* for the death of *Pallas,* who had invok'd his aid, before he threw his Lance at *Turnus.*

> ———*Trojæ sub mœnibus altis,*
> *Tot Nati Cecidere Deûm; quin occidit unâ*
> *Sarpedon mea progenies: etiam sua Turnum*
> *Fata manent: metasq; dati pervenit ad ævi.*

---

2  behalf:] ∼. F1–2.  
6  Notwithstanding] indented in *F1–2.*  
4  *tuorum*] F2; ∼, F1.  
22  *inanis*] *inaneis* F1–2.

Where he plainly acknowledges, that he cou'd not save his own Son, or prevent the death which he foresaw. Of his power to deferr the blow, I once occasionally discours'd with that Excellent Person Sir *Robert Howard:* who is better conversant than any Man that I know, in the Doctrine of the Stoicks, and he set me right, from the concurrent testimony of Philosophers and Poets, that *Jupiter* cou'd not retard the effects of Fate, even for a moment. For when I cited *Virgil* as favouring the contrary opinion in that Verse,

10        *Tolle fugâ Turnum, atq; instantibus eripe fatis;*

he reply'd, and I think with an exact Judgment, that when *Jupiter* gave *Juno* leave to withdraw *Turnus* from the present danger, it was because he certainly fore-knew that his Fatal hour was not come: that it was in Destiny for *Juno* at that time to save him; and that he himself obey'd Destiny, in giving her that leave.

I need say no more in justification of our Heroe's Courage, and am much deceiv'd, if he ever be attack'd on this side of his Character again. But he is Arraign'd with more shew of Reason by the Ladies; who will make a numerous Party against him,
20 for being false to Love, in forsaking *Dido.* And I cannot much blame them; for to say the truth, 'tis an ill Precedent for their Gallants to follow. Yet if I can bring him off, with Flying Colours, they may learn experience at her cost; and for her sake, avoid a Cave, as the worst shelter they can chuse from a shower of Rain, especially when they have a Lover in their Company.

In the first place, *Segrais* observes with much acuteness, that they who blame *Æneas* for his insensibility of Love, when he left *Carthage,* contradict their former accusation of him, for being always Crying, Compassionate, and Effeminately sensible of those
30 Misfortunes which befell others. They give him two contrary Characters, but *Virgil* makes him of a piece, always grateful, always tender-hearted. But they are impudent enough to discharge themselves of this blunder, by laying the Contradiction

---

1  Where] *indented in F1–2.*          5  Man that] F2; Man F1.
6  right,] F2; ~; F1.                  10  *fatis;*] ~. F1–2.
11  he] F2; He F1 (*indented*).        26  acuteness] F2; accuteness F1.

at *Virgil's* door. He, they say, has shewn his Heroe with these inconsistent Characters: Acknowledging, and Ungrateful, Compassionate, and Hard-harted; but at the bottom, Fickle, and Self-interested. For *Dido* had not only receiv'd his weather-beaten Troops before she saw him, and given them her protection, but had also offer'd them an equal share in her Dominion.

> *Vultis & his mecum pariter considere Regnis?*
> *Urbem quam statuo, vestra est.*————

This was an obligement never to be forgotten: and the more
10 to be consider'd, because antecedent to her Love. That passion, 'tis true, produc'd the usual effects of Generosity, Gallantry, and care to please, and thither we referr them. But when she had made all these advances, it was still in his power to have refus'd them: After the Intrigue of the Cave, call it Marriage, or Enjoyment only, he was no longer free to take or leave; he had accepted the favour, and was oblig'd to be Constant, if he wou'd be grateful.

My Lord, I have set this Argument in the best light I can, that the Ladies may not think I write booty: and perhaps it may
20 happen to me, as it did to Doctor *Cudworth*, who has rais'd such strong Objections against the being of a God, and Providence, that many think he has not answer'd them. You may please at least to hear the adverse Party. *Segrais* pleads for *Virgil*, that no less than an Absolute Command from *Jupiter*, cou'd excuse this insensibility of the Heroe, and this abrupt departure, which looks so like extream ingratitude. But at the same time, he does wisely to remember you, that *Virgil* had made Piety the first Character of *Æneas:* And this being allow'd, as I am afraid it must, he was oblig'd, antecedent to all other Considerations, to
30 search an Asylum for his Gods in *Italy:* For those very Gods, I say, who had promis'd to his Race the Universal Empire. Cou'd a Pious Man dispence with the Commands of *Jupiter* to satisfie his passion; or take it in the strongest sense, to comply with the obligations of his gratitude? Religion, 'tis true, must have Moral

8   *est.*————] F2; ~·ʌ F1.          14–15   Enjoyment] F2; Enjoment F1.
30   Asylum ... *Italy:*] *Asylum* ... ~. F1–2.

Honesty for its groundwork, or we shall be apt to suspect its truth; but an immediate Revelation dispenses with all Duties of Morality. All Casuists agree, that Theft is a breach of the Moral Law: yet if I might presume to mingle Things Sacred with Prophane, the *Israelites* only spoil'd the *Egyptians,* not rob'd them; because the propriety was transferr'd, by a Revelation to their Law-giver. I confess *Dido* was a very Infidel in this Point: for she wou'd not believe, as *Virgil* makes her say, that ever *Jupiter* wou'd send *Mercury* on such an Immoral Errand. But this needs
10 no Answer; at least no more than *Virgil* gives it:

*Fata obstant, placidasq; viri Deus obstruit aures.*

This notwithstanding, as *Segrais* confesses, he might have shewn a little more sensibility when he left her; for that had been according to his Character.

But let *Virgil* answer for himself; he still lov'd her, and struggled with his inclinations, to obey the Gods.

———*Curam sub Corde premebat,*
*Multa gemens; magnoq; animum labefactus Amore.*

Upon the whole Matter, and humanely speaking, I doubt
20 there was a fault somewhere; and *Jupiter* is better able to bear the blame, than either *Virgil* or *Æneas.* The Poet it seems had found it out, and therefore brings the deserting Heroe and the forsaken Lady to meet together in the lower Regions; where he excuses himself when 'tis too late, and accordingly she will take no satisfaction, nor so much as hear him. Now *Segrais* is forc'd to abandon his defence, and excuses his Author, by saying that the *Æneis* is an imperfect Work, and that Death prevented the Divine Poet from reviewing it; and for that Reason he had condemn'd it to the fire; though at the same time, his two Transla-
30 tors must acknowledge, that the Sixth Book is the most Correct of the whole *Æneis.* Oh, how convenient is a Machine sometimes in a Heroick Poem! This of *Mercury* is plainly one, and *Virgil*

---

5–6   them; . . . transferr'd,] F2; ∼, . . . ∼; F1.
17   ———*Curam*] F2; ∧∼ F1.

was constrain'd to use it here, or the honesty of his Heroe wou'd be ill-defended. And the Fair Sex however, if they had the Desertour in their power, wou'd certainly have shewn him no more mercy, than the *Bacchanals* did *Orpheus*. For if too much Constancy may be a fault sometimes, then want of Constancy, and Ingratitude after the last Favour, is a Crime that never will be forgiven. But of Machines, more in their proper place: where I shall shew, with how much judgment they have been us'd by *Virgil;* and in the mean time pass to another Article of his de-
10 fence on the present Subject: where if I cannot clear the Heroe, I hope at least to bring off the Poet; for here I must divide their Causes. Let *Æneas* trust to his Machine, which will only help to break his Fall, but the Address is incomparable. *Plato,* who borrow'd so much from *Homer,* and yet concluded for the Banishment of all Poets, wou'd at least have Rewarded *Virgil,* before he sent him into Exile. But I go farther, and say, that he ought to be acquitted, and deserv'd beside, the Bounty of *Augustus,* and the gratitude of the *Roman* People. If after this, the Ladies will stand out, let them remember, that the Jury is not all agreed;
20 for *Octavia* was of his Party, and was of the first Quality in *Rome;* she was also present at the reading of the Sixth *Æneid,* and we know not that she condemn'd *Æneas;* but we are sure she presented the Poet, for his admirable Elegy on her Son *Marcellus*.

But let us consider the secret Reasons which *Virgil* had, for thus framing this Noble Episode, wherein the whole passion of Love is more exactly describ'd than in any other Poet. Love was the Theme of his Fourth Book; and though it is the shortest of the whole *Æneis,* yet there he has given its beginning, its progress, its traverses, and its conclusion: And had exhausted so en-
30 tirely this Subject, that he cou'd resume it but very slightly in the Eight ensuing Books.

She was warm'd with the graceful appearance of the Heroe, she smother'd those Sparkles out of decency, but Conversation blew them up into a Flame. Then she was forc'd to make a Confident of her whom she best might trust, her own Sister, who approves the passion, and thereby augments it; then succeeds her

20    and was of] F2; and was also of F1.    21    was also present] F2; was present F1.
29    conclusion:] F2; ∼. F1.    36    augments it;] ∼ ∼, F1–2.

publick owning it; and after that, the consummation. Of *Venus* and *Juno, Jupiter* and *Mercury* I say nothing, for they were all Machining work; but possession having cool'd his Love, as it increas'd hers, she soon perceiv'd the change, or at least grew suspicious of a change; this suspicion soon turn'd to Jealousie, and Jealousie to Rage; then she disdains and threatens, and again is humble, and intreats; and nothing availing, despairs, curses, and at last becomes her own Executioner. See here the whole process of that passion, to which nothing can be added. I dare go no farther, lest I shou'd lose the connection of my Discourse.

To love our Native Country, and to study its Benefit and its Glory, to be interessed in its Concerns, is Natural to all Men, and is indeed our common Duty. A Poet makes a farther step; for endeavouring to do honour to it, 'tis allowable in him even to be partial in its Cause; for he is not ty'd to truth, or fetter'd by the Laws of History. *Homer* and *Tasso* are justly prais'd for chusing their Heroes out of *Greece* and *Italy; Virgil* indeed made his a *Trojan,* but it was to derive the *Romans,* and his own *Augustus* from him; but all the three Poets are manifestly partial to their Heroes, in favour of their Country. For *Dares Phrygius* reports of *Hector,* that he was slain Cowardly; *Æneas* according to the best account, slew not *Mezentius,* but was slain by him: and the Chronicles of *Italy* tell us little of that *Rinaldo d'Estè* who Conquers *Jerusalem* in *Tasso.* He might be a Champion of the Church; but we know not that he was so much as present at the Siege. To apply this to *Virgil,* he thought himself engag'd in Honour to espouse the Cause and Quarrel of his Country against *Carthage.* He knew he cou'd not please the *Romans* better, or oblige them more to Patronize his Poem, than by disgracing the Foundress of that City. He shews her ungrateful to the Memory of her first Husband, doting on a Stranger; enjoy'd, and afterwards forsaken by him. This was the Original, says he, of the immortal hatred betwixt the two Rival Nations. 'Tis true, he colours the falsehood of *Æneas* by an express Command from *Jupiter,* to forsake the Queen, who had oblig'd him: but he knew the *Romans* were to be his Readers, and them he brib'd, perhaps at the expence of his Heroe's honesty, but he gain'd his Cause however; as Pleading before Corrupt Judges. They were content

to see their Founder false to Love, for still he had the advantage
of the Amour: It was their Enemy whom he forsook, and she
might have forsaken him, if he had not got the start of her: she
had already forgotten her Vows to her *Sichæus;* and *varium &*
*mutabile semper femina,* is the sharpest Satire in the fewest
words that ever was made on Womankind; for both the Adjec-
tives are Neuter, and *Animal* must be understood, to make them
Grammar. *Virgil* does well to put those words into the mouth of
*Mercury. If a God had not spoken them, neither durst he have*
10 *written them, nor I translated them.* Yet the Deity was forc'd to
come twice on the same Errand: and the second time, as much a
Heroe as *Æneas* was, he frighted him. It seems he fear'd not *Jupi-*
*ter* so much as *Dido.* For your Lordship may observe, that as
much intent as he was upon his Voyage, yet he still delay'd it, 'till
the Messenger was oblig'd to tell him plainly, that if he weigh'd
not Anchor in the Night, the Queen wou'd be with him in the
Morning. *Notumq; furens quid femina possit;* she was Injur'd,
she was Revengeful, she was Powerful. The Poet had likewise
before hinted, that her People were naturally perfidious: For
20 he gives their Character in their Queen, and makes a Proverb
of *Punica fides,* many Ages before it was invented.

Thus I hope, my Lord, that I have made good my Promise,
and justify'd the Poet, whatever becomes of the false Knight.
And sure a Poet is as much priviledg'd to lye, as an Ambassador,
for the Honour and Interest of his Country; at least as Sir *Henry*
*Wootton* has defin'd.

This naturally leads me to the defence of the Famous Ana-
chronism, in making *Æneas* and *Dido* Contemporaries. For 'tis
certain that the Heroe liv'd almost two hundred years before
30 the Building of *Carthage.* One who imitates *Bocaline,* says that
*Virgil* was accus'd before *Apollo* for this Error. The God soon
found that he was not able to defend his Favourite by Reason,
for the Case was clear: he therefore gave this middle Sentence;
That any thing might be allow'd to his Son *Virgil* on the account
of his other Merits; That being a Monarch he had a dispensing
Power, and pardon'd him. But that this special Act of Grace

---

6   ever was] F2; was ever F1.
27–28   Anachronism] *Anachronism* F1–2.

might never be drawn into Example, or pleaded by his puny
Successors, in justification of their ignorance; he decreed for the
future, No Poet shou'd presume to make a Lady die for Love
two hundred years before her Birth. To Moralize this Story,
*Virgil* is the *Apollo,* who has this Dispensing Power. His great
Judgment made the Laws of Poetry, but he never made himself
a Slave to them: Chronology at best is but a Cobweb-Law, and
he broke through it with his weight. They who will imitate him
wisely, must chuse as he did, an obscure and a remote Æra,
10 where they may invent at pleasure, and not be easily contra-
dicted. Neither he, nor the *Romans* had ever read the Bible, by
which only his false computation of times can be made out
against him: this *Segrais* says in his defence, and proves it from
his Learned Friend *Bochartus,* whose Letter on this Subject, he
has Printed at the end of the Fourth *Æneid,* to which I referr
your Lordship, and the Reader. Yet the Credit of *Virgil* was so
great, that he made this Fable of his own Invention pass for an
Authentick History, or at least as credible as any thing in *Homer.*
*Ovid* takes it up after him, even in the same Age, and makes an
20 ancient Heroine of *Virgil*'s new-created *Dido;* Dictates a Letter
for her just before her death, to the ingrateful Fugitive; and
very unluckily for himself, is for measuring a Sword with a Man
so much superiour in force to him on the same subject. I think
I may be Judge of this, because I have Translated both. The
Famous Author of the *Art of Love* has nothing of his own, he
borrows all from a greater Master in his own profession; and
which is worse, improves nothing which he finds. Nature fails
him, and being forc'd to his old shift, he has recourse to Wit-
ticism. This passes indeed with his Soft Admirers, and gives him
30 the preference to *Virgil* in their esteem. But let them like for
themselves, and not prescribe to others, for our Author needs
not their Admiration.

The Motives that induc'd *Virgil* to Coyn this Fable, I have
shew'd already; and have also begun to shew that he might
make this Anachronism, by superseding the mechanick Rules of

---

9    Æra] *Æra* F1–2.
25   *Art of Love*] Art of Love F1–2.
35   Anachronism] *Anacronism* F1; *Anachronism* F2.

Poetry, for the same Reason, that a Monarch may dispense with, or suspend his own Laws, when he finds it necessary so to do; especially if those Laws are not altogether fundamental. Nothing is to be call'd a fault in Poetry, says *Aristotle*, but what is against the Art; therefore a Man may be an admirable Poet, without being an exact Chronologer. Shall we dare, continues *Segrais*, to condemn *Virgil*, for having made a Fiction against the order of time, when we commend *Ovid* and other Poets who have made many of their Fictions against the Order of Nature?

10 For what else are the splendid Miracles of the *Metamorphoses?* Yet these are Beautiful as they are related; and have also deep Learning and instructive Mythologies couch'd under them: But to give, as *Virgil* does in this Episode, the Original Cause of the long Wars betwixt *Rome* and *Carthage,* to draw Truth out of Fiction, after so probable a manner, with so much Beauty, and so much for the Honour of his Country, was proper only to the Divine Wit of *Maro;* and *Tasso* in one of his Discourses, admires him for this particularly. 'Tis not lawful indeed, to contradict a Point of History, which is known to all the World; as for Exam-

20 ple, to make *Hannibal* and *Scipio* Contemporaries with *Alexander;* but in the dark Recesses of Antiquity, a great Poet may and ought to feign such things as he finds not there, if they can be brought to embelish that Subject which he treats. On the other side, the pains and diligence of ill Poets is but thrown away, when they want the Genius to invent and feign agreeably. But if the Fictions be delightful, which they always are, if they be natural, if they be of a piece; if the beginning, the middle, and the end be in their due places, and artfully united to each other, such Works can never fail of their deserv'd Success. And such is

30 *Virgil's* Episode of *Dido* and *Æneas;* where the sourest Critick must acknowledge, that if he had depriv'd his *Æneis* of so great an Ornament, because he found no traces of it in Antiquity, he had avoided their unjust Censure, but had wanted one of the greatest Beauties of his Poem. I shall say more of this, in the next Article of their Charge against him, which is want of Inven-

---

10    else are] F2; are else F1.
10    *Metamorphoses*] F2; Metamorphoses F1.
31    acknowledge,] *some copies of F1 read* acknowledge'.

him. But in the first place, if Invention is to be taken in so strict a sense, that the Matter of a Poem must be wholly new, and that in all its Parts; then *Scaliger* has made out, says *Segrais,* that the History of *Troy* was no more the Invention of *Homer,* than of *Virgil.* There was not an Old Woman, or almost a Child, but had it in their Mouths, before the *Greek* Poet or his Friends digested it into this admirable order in which we read it. At this rate, as *Solomon* has told us, there is nothing new beneath the Sun: Who then can pass for an Inventor, if *Homer,* as well as
10 *Virgil* must be depriv'd of that Glory? Is *Versailles* the less a New Building, because the Architect of that Palace has imitated others which were built before it? Walls, Doors and Windows, Apartments, Offices, Rooms of convenience and Magnificence, are in all great Houses. So Descriptions, Figures, Fables, and the rest, must be in all Heroick Poems. They are the Common Materials of Poetry, furnish'd from the Magazine of Nature: Every Poet has as much right to them, as every Man has to Air or Water. *Quid prohibetis Aquas? Usus communis aquarum est.* But the Argument of the Work, that is to say, its principal Action, the
20 Oeconomy and Disposition of it; these are the things which distinguish Copies from Originals. The Poet, who borrows nothing from others, is yet to be Born. He and the *Jews* Messias will come together. There are parts of the *Æneis,* which resemble some parts both of the *Ilias* and of the *Odysses;* as for Example, *Æneas* descended into Hell, and *Ulysses* had been there before him: *Æneas* lov'd *Dido,* and *Ulysses* lov'd *Calypso:* In few words, *Virgil* has imitated *Homer's Odysses* in his first six Books, and in his six last the *Ilias.* But from hence can we infer, that the two Poets write the same History? Is there no invention in some other parts
30 of *Virgil's Æneis?* The disposition of so many various matters, is not that his own? From what Book of *Homer* had *Virgil* his Episode of *Nysus* and *Euryalus,* of *Mezentius* and *Lausus?* From whence did he borrow his Design of bringing *Æneas* into *Italy,* of Establishing the *Roman* Empire on the Foundations of a *Trojan* Colony? to say nothing of the honour he did his Patron, not

6   *Greek*] Greek F1–2.                    14   Descriptions,] F2; ~∧ F1.
27   *Odysses*] F2; Odysses F1.            32   Episode] F2; *Episode* F1.
35   Colony?] ~; F1; ~: F2.

only in his descent from *Venus,* but in making him so like him
in his best Features, that the Goddess might have mistaken
*Augustus* for her Son. He had indeed the Story from common
Fame, as *Homer* had his from the *Egyptian* Priestess. *Æneadum*
*Genetrix* was no more unknown to *Lucretius* than to him. But
*Lucretius* taught him not to form his Heroe; to give him Piety
or Valour for his Manners; and both in so eminent a degree, that
having done what was possible for Man, to save his King and
Country; his Mother was forc'd to appear to him and restrain his
10 Fury, which hurry'd him to death in their Revenge. But the Poet
made his Piety more successful; he brought off his Father and his
Son; and his Gods witness'd to his Devotion, by putting them-
selves under his Protection; to be re-plac'd by him in their prom-
is'd *Italy.* Neither the Invention, nor the Conduct of this great
Action, were owing to *Homer* or any other Poet. 'Tis one thing
to Copy, and another thing to imitate from Nature. The Copyer
is that servile Imitator, to whom *Horace* gives no better a Name
than that of Animal: He will not so much as allow him to be a
Man. *Raphael* imitated Nature: They who Copy one of *Raphael's*
20 Pieces, imitate but him, for his Work is their Original. They
Translate him as I do *Virgil;* and fall as short of him as I of
*Virgil.* There is a kind of Invention in the imitation of *Raphael;*
for though the thing was in Nature, yet the Idea of it was his own.
*Ulysses* Travell'd, so did *Æneas;* but neither of them were the
first Travellers; for *Cain* went into the Land of *Nod,* before they
were born: And neither of the Poets ever heard of such a Man.
If *Ulysses* had been kill'd at *Troy,* yet *Æneas* must have gone to
Sea, or he could never have arriv'd in *Italy.* But the designs of
the two Poets were as different as the Courses of their Heroes;
30 one went Home, and the other sought a Home. To return to
my first similitude: Suppose *Apelles* and *Raphael* had each of
them Painted a burning *Troy;* might not the Modern Painter
have succeeded as well as the Ancient, tho' neither of them had
seen the Town on Fire? For the draughts of both were taken
from the Idea's which they had of Nature. Cities had been burnt
before either of them were in Being. But to Close the Simile as
I begun it; they wou'd not have design'd after the same manner.
*Apelles* wou'd have distinguish'd *Pyrrhus* from the rest of all the

*Grecians,* and shew'd him forcing his entrance into *Priam's* Palace; there he had set him in the fairest Light, and given him the chief place of all his Figures, because he was a *Grecian,* and he wou'd do Honour to his Country. *Raphael,* who was an *Italian,* and descended from the *Trojans,* wou'd have made *Æneas* the Heroe of his piece: And perhaps not with his Father on his Back; his Son in one hand, his Bundle of Gods in the other, and his Wife following; (for an Act of Piety, is not half so graceful in a Picture as an Act of Courage:) He would rather have drawn him killing *Androgeos,* or some other, Hand to Hand; and the blaze of the Fires shou'd have darted full upon his Face, to make him conspicuous amongst his *Trojans.* This I think is a just Comparison betwixt the two Poets in the Conduct of their several designs. *Virgil* cannot be said to copy *Homer:* The *Grecian* had only the advantage of writing first. If it be urg'd that I have granted a resemblance in some parts; yet therein *Virgil* has excell'd him: For what are the Tears of *Calypso* for being left, to the Fury and Death of *Dido?* Where is there the whole process of her Passion, and all its violent Effects to be found, in the languishing Episode of the *Odysses?* If this be to Copy, let the Criticks shew us the same Disposition, Features, or Colouring in their Original. The like may be said of the Descent to Hell; which was not of *Homer's* Invention neither: He had it from the Story of *Orpheus* and *Eurydice.* But to what end did *Ulysses* make that Journey? *Æneas* undertook it by the express Commandment of his Father's Ghost: There he was to shew him all the succeeding Heroes of his Race; and next to *Romulus,* (mark, if you please, the Address of *Virgil*) his own Patron *Augustus Cæsar. Anchises* was likewise to instruct him, how to manage the *Italian* War; and how to conclude it with his Honour: That is, in other words, to lay the Foundations of that Empire which *Augustus* was to Govern. This is the Noble Invention of our Author: But it has been Copied by so many Sign-post Daubers, that now 'tis grown fulsom; rather by their want of Skill, than by the Commonness.

In the last place I may safely grant, that by reading *Homer,*

---

20  Episode] *Episode* F1–2.          30  Honour:] ~. F1–2.
33–34  Daubers, . . . fulsom;] F2; ~; . . . ~, F1.

*Virgil* was taught to imitate his Invention: That is, to imitate like him; which is no more, than if a Painter studied *Raphael,* that he might learn to design after his manner. And thus I might imitate *Virgil,* if I were capable of writing an Heroick Poem, and yet the Invention be my own: But I shou'd endeavour to avoid a servile Copying. I would not give the same Story under other Names: With the same Characters, in the same Order, and with the same Sequel: For every common Reader to find me out at the first sight for a Plagiary: And cry, This I read before in
10 *Virgil,* in a better Language, and in better Verse: This is like *Merry-Andrew* on the low Rope, copying lubberly the same Tricks, which his Master is so dextrously performing on the high.

I will trouble your Lordship but with one Objection more; which I know not whether I found in *Le Fèvre* or *Valois,* but I am sure I have read it in another *French* Critick, whom I will not name, because I think it is not much for his Reputation. *Virgil,* in the heat of Action, suppose for Example, in describing the fury of his Heroe in a Battel, when he is endeavouring
20 to raise our concernments to the highest pitch, turns short on the sudden into some similitude, which diverts, say they, your attention from the main Subject, and mispends it on some trivial Image. He pours cold Water into the Caldron when his business is to make it boil.

This Accusation is general against all who wou'd be thought Heroick Poets; but I think it touches *Virgil* less than any. He is too great a Master of his Art, to make a Blott which may so easily be hit. Similitudes, as I have said, are not for Tragedy, which is all violent, and where the Passions are in a perpetual
30 ferment; for there they deaden where they should animate; they are not of the nature of Dialogue, unless in Comedy: A Metaphor is almost all the Stage can suffer, which is a kind of Similitude comprehended in a word. But this Figure has a contrary effect in Heroick Poetry: There 'tis employ'd to raise the Admiration, which is its proper business. And Admiration is not of so violent a nature as Fear or Hope, Compassion or Horrour,

---

9    This] F2; this F1.          11    *Merry-Andrew*] F2; merry *Andrew* F1.
12    is so] F2; is F1.          15    *Fèvre*] *Fevre* F1-2.

or any Concernment we can have for such or such a Person on the Stage. Not but I confess, that Similitudes and Descriptions, when drawn into an unreasonable length, must needs nauseate the Reader. Once I remember, and but once; *Virgil* makes a Similitude of fourteen Lines; and his description of Fame is about the same number. He is blam'd for both; and I doubt not but he would have contracted them, had he liv'd to have review'd his Work: But Faults are no Precedents. This I have observ'd of his Similitudes in general, that they are not plac'd, as
10 our unobserving Criticks tell us, in the heat of any Action: But commonly in its declining: When he has warm'd us in his Description, as much as possibly he can; then, lest that warmth should languish, he renews it by some apt Similitude, which illustrates his Subject, and yet palls not his Audience. I need give your Lordship but one Example of this kind, and leave the rest to your Observation, when next you review the whole *Æneis* in the Original unblemish'd by my rude Translation. 'Tis in the first Book, where the Poet describes *Neptune* composing the Ocean, on which *Æolus* had rais'd a Tempest, without his per-
20 mission. He had already chidden the Rebellious Winds for obeying the Commands of their Usurping Master: He had warn'd them from the Seas: He had beaten down the Billows with his Mace; dispell'd the Clouds, restor'd the Sun-shine, while *Triton* and *Cymothoe* were heaving the Ships from off the Quick-Sands; before the Poet wou'd offer at a Similitude for illustration.

> *Ac, veluti magno in populo cùm sæpe coorta est*
> *Seditio, sævitque animis ignobile vulgus,*
> *Jamque faces, & saxa volant, furor arma ministrat;*
> *Tum, pietate gravem, ac meritis si forte virum quem*
> 30 *Conspexere, silent, arrectisque auribus adstant:*
> *Ille regit dictis animos, & pectora mulcet:*
> *Sic cunctus pelagi cecidit fragor, æquora postquam*
> *Prospiciens genitor, cæloque invectus aperto*
> *Flectit equos, currúque volans dat lora secundo.*

This is the first Similitude which *Virgil* makes in this Poem: And one of the longest in the whole; for which Reason I the rather cite it. While the Storm was in its fury, any Allusion had been improper: For the Poet cou'd have compar'd it to nothing more impetuous than it self; consequently he could have made no Illustration. If he cou'd have illustrated, it had been an ambitious Ornament out of season, and would have diverted our Concernment: *Nunc, non erat hisce locus;* and therefore he deferr'd it to its proper place.

These are the Criticisms of most moment which have been made against the *Æneis,* by the Ancients or Moderns. As for the particular Exceptions against this or that passage, *Macrobius* and *Pontanus* have answer'd them already. If I desir'd to appear more Learned than I am, it had been as easie for me to have taken their Objections and Solutions, as it is for a Country Parson to take the Expositions of the Fathers out of *Junius* and *Tremellius:* Or not to have nam'd the Authors from whence I had them: For so *Ruæus,* otherwise a most judicious Commentator on *Virgil's* Works, has us'd *Pontanus,* his greatest Benefactor, of whom, he is very silent, and I do not remember that he once cites him.

What follows next, is no Objection; for that implies a Fault: And it had been none in *Virgil,* if he had extended the time of his Action beyond a Year. At least *Aristotle* has set no precise limits to it. *Homer's,* we know, was within two Months: *Tasso* I am sure exceeds not a Summer: And if I examin'd him, perhaps he might be reduc'd into a much less compass. *Bossu* leaves it doubtful whether *Virgil's* Action were within the Year, or took up some Months beyond it. Indeed the whole Dispute is of no more concernment to the common Reader, than it is to a Ploughman, whether *February* this Year had 28 or 29 Days in it. But for the satisfaction of the more Curious, of which number, I am sure your Lordship is one; I will Translate what I think convenient out of *Segrais,* whom perhaps you have not read: For he has made it highly probable, that the Action of the *Æneis* began in the Spring, and was not extended beyond the Autumn. And we have known Campaigns that have begun sooner, and have ended later.

*Ronsard* and the rest whom *Segrais* names, who are of Opinion

34  Autumn] F2; *Autumn* F1.

that the Action of this Poem takes up almost a Year and half; ground their Calculation thus. *Anchises* dyed in *Sicily* at the end of Winter, or beginning of the Spring. *Æneas,* immediately after the Interment of his Father, puts to Sea for *Italy:* He is sur-priz'd by the Tempest describ'd in the beginning of the first Book; and there it is that the Scene of the Poem opens; and where the Action must Commence. He is driven by this Storm on the Coasts of *Affrick:* He stays at *Carthage* all that Summer, and al-most all the Winter following: Sets Sail again for *Italy* just be-
10 fore the beginning of the Spring; meets with contrary Winds, and makes *Sicily* the second time: This part of the Action com-pleats the Year. Then he celebrates the Anniversary of his Fa-ther's Funerals, and shortly after arrives at *Cumæs,* and from thence his time is taken up in his first Treaty with *Latinus;* the Overture of the War; the Siege of his Camp by *Turnus;* his going for Succours to relieve it: His return: The raising of the Siege by the first Battel: The twelve days Truce: The second Battel: The Assault of *Laurentum,* and the single Fight with *Turnus;* all which, they say, cannot take up less than four or five
20 Months more; by which Account we cannot suppose the entire Action to be contain'd in a much less compass than a Year and half.

*Segrais* reckons another way; and his computation is not con-demn'd by the learned *Ruæus,* who compil'd and Publish'd the Commentaries on our Poet, which we call the *Dauphin's Virgil.*

He allows the time of Year when *Anchises* dyed; to be in the latter end of Winter, or the beginning of the Spring; he ac-knowledges that when *Æneas* is first seen at Sea afterwards, and is driven by the Tempest on the Coast of *Affrick,* is the time
30 when the Action is naturally to begin: He confesses farther, that *Æneas* left *Carthage* in the latter end of Winter; for *Dido* tells him in express terms, as an Argument for his longer stay,

*Quinetiam Hyberno moliris sydere Classem.*

But whereas *Ronsard's* Followers suppose that when *Æneas* had buried his Father, he set Sail immediately for *Italy,* (tho' the

12   Anniversary] F2; Aniversary F1.          13   *Cumæs*] *Cumes* F1–2.
25   *Virgil*] F2; Virgil F1.

Tempest drove him on the Coast of *Carthage*,) *Segrais* will by no means allow that Supposition; but thinks it much more probable that he remain'd in *Sicily* 'till the midst of *July* or the beginning of *August*; at which time he places the first appearance of his Heroe on the Sea; and there opens the Action of the Poem: From which beginning, to the Death of *Turnus*, which concludes the Action, there need not be suppos'd above ten Months of intermediate time: For arriving at *Carthage* in the latter end of Summer, staying there the Winter following; departing thence
10 in the very beginning of the Spring; making a short abode in *Sicily* the second time, landing in *Italy*, and making the War, may be reasonably judg'd the business but of ten Months. To this the *Ronsardians* reply, that having been for Seven Years before in quest of *Italy*, and having no more to do in *Sicily*, than to interr his Father; after that Office was perform'd, what remain'd for him, but, without delay, to pursue his first Adventure? To which *Segrais* answers, that the Obsequies of his Father, according to the Rites of the *Greeks* and *Romans*, would detain him for many days: That a longer time must be taken
20 up in the refitting of his Ships, after so tedious a Voyage; and in refreshing his Weather-beaten Souldiers on a friendly Coast. These indeed are but Suppositions on both sides, yet those of *Segrais* seem better grounded. For the Feast of *Dido*, when she entertain'd *Æneas* first, has the appearance of a Summer's Night, which seems already almost ended, when he begins his Story: Therefore the Love was made in Autumn; the Hunting follow'd properly when the Heats of that scorching Country were declining: The Winter was pass'd in jollity, as the Season and their Love requir'd; and he left her in the latter end of Winter,
30 as is already prov'd. This Opinion is fortify'd by the Arrival of *Æneas* at the Mouth of *Tyber*; which marks the Season of the Spring, that Season being perfectly describ'd by the singing of the Birds, saluting the dawn; and by the Beauty of the place, which the Poet seems to have painted expresly in the Seventh *Æneid*.

---

1   *Carthage*,] F2; ∼. F1.
5   Poem:] ∼. F1–2.
12   ten] F1 *errata*, F2; three F1.

*Aurora in roseis fulgebat lutea bigis:*
*Cùm venti posuere; variæ circumque, supræque*
*Assuetæ ripis volucres, & fluminis alveo,*
*Æthera mulcebant cantu.*————

The remainder of the Action requir'd but three Months more;
for when *Æneas* went for Succour to the *Tuscans,* he found their
Army in a readiness to march; and wanting only a Commander:
So that according to this Calculation, the *Æneis* takes not up
above a Year compleat, and may be comprehended in less com-
10  pass.

This, amongst other Circumstances, treated more at large by
*Segrais,* agrees with the rising of *Orion,* which caus'd the Tem-
pest, describ'd in the beginning of the first Book. By some pas-
sages in the Pastorals, but more particularly in the *Georgicks,* our
Poet is found to be an exact Astronomer, according to the Knowl-
edge of that Age. Now *Ilioneus* (whom *Virgil* twice employs in
Embassies, as the best Speaker of the *Trojans*) attributes that
Tempest to *Orion* in his Speech to *Dido.*

*Cum subito, assurgens fluctu nimbosus Orion.*

20  He must mean either the *Heliacal* or *Achronical* rising of that
Sign. The *Heliacal* rising of a Constellation, is when it comes
from under the Rays of the Sun, and begins to appear before
Day-light. The *Achronical* rising, on the contrary, is when it
appears at the close of Day, and in opposition of the Sun's di-
urnal Course.

The *Heliacal* rising of *Orion,* is at present computed to be
about the sixth of *July;* and about that time it is, that he either
causes, or presages Tempests on the Seas.

*Segrais* has observ'd farther, that when *Anna* Counsels *Dido*
30  to stay *Æneas* during the Winter; she speaks also of *Orion;*

*Dum pelago desævit hyems, & aquosus Orion.*

If therefore *Ilioneus,* according to our Supposition, under-
stand the *Heliacal* rising of *Orion: Anna* must mean the *Achroni-*

———
4  *cantu.*————] F2;  ∼.∧ F1.

*cal,* which the different Epithetes given to that Constellation, seem to manifest. *Ilioneus* calls him *nimbosus, Anna aquosus.* He is tempestuous in the Summer when he rises *Heliacally,* and Rainy in the Winter when he rises *Achronically.* Your Lordship will pardon me for the frequent repetition of these cant words; which I cou'd not avoid in this abbreviation of *Segrais;* who I think deserves no little commendation in this new Criticism. I have yet a word or two to say of *Virgil's* Machines, from my own observation of them. He has imitated those of *Homer,* but not
10 Copied them. It was establish'd long before this time, in the *Roman* Religion as well as in the *Greek;* that there were Gods; and both Nations, for the most part, worshipp'd the same Deities; as did also the *Trojans:* From whom the *Romans,* I suppose, wou'd rather be thought to derive the Rites of their Religion, than from the *Grecians;* because they thought themselves descended from them. Each of those Gods had his proper Office, and the chief of them their particular Attendants. Thus *Jupiter* had in propriety, *Ganimede* and *Mercury;* and *Juno* had *Iris.* It was not for *Virgil* then to create new Ministers; he must take
20 what he found in his Religion. It cannot therefore be said that he borrow'd them from *Homer,* any more than *Apollo, Diana,* and the rest, whom he uses as he finds occasion for them, as the *Grecian* Poet did: But he invents the occasions for which he uses them. *Venus,* after the destruction of *Troy,* had gain'd *Neptune* entirely to her Party; therefore we find him busie in the beginning of the *Æneis,* to calm the Tempest rais'd by *Æolus,* and afterwards conducting the *Trojan* Fleet to *Cumæs* in safety, with the loss only of their Pilot; for whom he Bargains. I name those two Examples amongst a hundred which I omit; to prove
30 that *Virgil,* generally speaking, employ'd his Machines in performing those things, which might possibly have been done without them. What more frequent then a Storm at Sea, upon the rising of *Orion?* What wonder, if amongst so many Ships there shou'd one be overset, which was commanded by *Orontes;* though half the Winds had not been there, which *Æolus* employ'd?

---

19   for *Virgil* then] F2; then for *Virgil* F1.
27   *Cumæs*] *Cumes* F1–2.
28   Pilot;] *the semicolon prints as a comma in some copies of F1.*

Might not *Palinurus*, without a Miracle, fall asleep, and drop into the Sea, having been over-wearied with watching, and secure of a quiet passage, by his observation of the Skies? At least *Æneas*, who knew nothing of the Machine of *Somnus*, takes it plainly in this Sense.

> *O nimium Cælo & Pelago confise sereno,*
> *Nudus in ignotâ Palinure jacebis arenâ.*

But Machines sometimes are specious things to amuse the Reader, and give a colour of probability to things otherwise in-
10 credible. And besides, it sooth'd the vanity of the *Romans,* to find the Gods so visibly concern'd in all the Actions of their Predecessors. We who are better taught by our Religion, yet own every wonderful Accident which befalls us for the best, to be brought to pass by some special Providence of Almighty God; and by the care of guardian Angels: And from hence I might infer, that no Heroick Poem can be writ on the *Epicuræan* Prin-ciples: Which I cou'd easily demonstrate, if there were need to prove it, or I had leisure.

When *Venus* opens the Eyes of her Son *Æneas*, to behold the
20 Gods who Combated against *Troy,* in that fatal Night when it was surpriz'd; we share the pleasure of that glorious Vision, (which *Tasso* has not ill Copied in the sacking of *Jerusalem.*) But the *Greeks* had done their business; though neither *Nep-tune, Juno,* or *Pallas,* had given them their Divine assistance. The most crude Machine which *Virgil* uses, is in the Episode of *Camilla,* where *Opis* by the command of her Mistress, kills *Aruns.* The next is in the Twelfth *Æneid,* where *Venus* cures her Son *Æneas.* But in the last of these, the Poet was driven to a necessity; for *Turnus* was to be slain that very day: And *Æneas,* wounded
30 as he was, cou'd not have Engag'd him in single Combat, unless his Hurt had been miraculously heal'd. And the Poet had con-sider'd that the Dittany which she brought from *Crete,* cou'd not have wrought so speedy an effect, without the Juice of Am-brosia, which she mingled with it. After all, that his Machine

might not seem too violent, we see the Heroe limping after
*Turnus.* The Wound was skin'd; but the strength of his Thigh
was not restor'd. But what Reason had our Author to wound
*Æneas* at so critical a time? And how came the Cuisses to be
worse temper'd than the rest of his Armour, which was all
wrought by *Vulcan* and his Journey-men? These difficulties are
not easily to be solv'd, without confessing that *Virgil* had not
life enough to correct his Work: Tho' he had review'd it, and
found those Errours which he resolv'd to mend: But being pre-
10 vented by Death, and not willing to leave an imperfect work
behind him, he ordain'd, by his last Testament, that his *Æneis*
should be burn'd. As for the death of *Aruns,* who was shot by
a Goddess, the Machine was not altogether so outragious, as the
wounding *Mars* and *Venus* by the Sword of *Diomede.* Two
Divinities, one wou'd have thought, might have pleaded their
Prerogative of Impassibility, or, at least not have been wounded
by any mortal Hand: Beside that the ἰχώρ which they shed, was
so very like our common Blood, that it was not to be distin-
guish'd from it, but only by the Name and Colour. As for what
20 *Horace* says in his *Art of Poetry;* that no Machines are to be us'd,
unless on some extraordinary occasion,

*Nec Deus intersit, nisi dignus vindice nodus;*

That Rule is to be apply'd to the Theatre, of which he is then
speaking, and means no more than this, that when the Knot of
the Play is to be unty'd, and no other way is left, for making
the discovery; then and not otherwise, let a God descend upon
a Rope, and clear the Business to the Audience: But this has no
relation to the Machines which are us'd in an Epick Poem.

In the last place, for the *Dira,* or Flying-Pest, which flapping
30 on the Shield of *Turnus,* and fluttering about his Head, dis-
hearten'd him in the Duel, and presag'd to him his approaching
Death, I might have plac'd it more properly amongst the Objec-

16   not] F2; not to F1.
17   Hand:] ∼. F1–2.
17   ἰχώρ] ἔικωρ F1; ἔιχωρ F2.
20   *Art of Poetry*] Art of Poetry F1; Art Poetry F2.
22   *nodus;*] ∼. F1–2.

tions. For the Criticks, who lay want of Courage to the Charge
of *Virgil's* Heroe, quote this Passage as a main proof of their
Assertion. They say our Author had not only secur'd him before
the Duel, but also in the beginning of it, had given him the
advantage in impenetrable Arms, and in his Sword: (for that of
*Turnus* was not his own, which was forg'd by *Vulcan* for his
Father, but a Weapon which he had snatch'd in haste, and by
mistake, belonging to his Charioteer *Metiscus*). That after all
this, *Jupiter*, who was partial to the *Trojan*, and distrustful of
the Event, though he had hung the Ballance, and given it a jog
of his hand to weigh down *Turnus*, thought convenient to give
the Fates a collateral Security, by sending the Screech-Owl to
discourage him: For which they quote these words of *Virgil*.

> ————*Non me tua turbida virtus*
> *Terret, ait; Dii me terrent, & Jupiter Hostis.*

In answer to which, I say, that this Machine is one of those which
the Poet uses only for Ornament, and not out of Necessity. Noth-
ing can be more Beautiful, or more Poetical than his description
of the three *Diræ*, or the setting of the Balance, which our *Milton*
has borrow'd from him, but employ'd to a different end: For
first he makes God Almighty set the Scales for St. *Gabriel* and
*Sathan*, when he knew no Combat was to follow; then he makes
the good Angel's Scale descend, and the Devils mount; quite
contrary to *Virgil*, if I have Translated the three Verses, accord-
ing to my Author's Sense.

> *Jupiter ipse duas, æquato Examine lances*
> *Sustinet; & fata imponit diversa duorum:*
> *Quem damnet labor, & quo vergat pondere lethum.*

For I have taken these words *Quem damnet labor,* in the Sense
which *Virgil* gives them in another place; *Damnabis tu quoque
votis;* to signifie a prosperous Event. Yet I dare not condemn so

---

2  Heroe,] ~; F1–2.                    7–8  Father,... *Metiscus*).] ~) ... ~. F1–2.
13  him:] ~. F1–2.                     14  ————*Non*] F2; ∧~ F1.
14–15  *virtus* / *Terret,*] F2; ~, / ~∧ F1.
16  In] indented in *F1–2.*            21  *Gabriel*] F2; *Michael* F1.

great a Genius as *Milton:* For I am much mistaken if he alludes
not to the Text in *Daniel,* where *Belshazzar* was put into the
Balance, and found too light: This is digression, and I return
to my Subject. I said above, that these two Machines of the
Balance, and the *Dira,* were only Ornamental, and that the suc-
cess of the Duel had been the same without them. For when
*Æneas* and *Turnus* stood fronting each other before the Altar,
*Turnus* look'd dejected, and his Colour faded in his Face, as
if he desponded of the Victory before the Fight; and not only
10 he, but all his Party, when the strength of the two Champions
was judg'd by the proportion of their Limbs, concluded it was
*impar pugna,* and that their Chief was over-match'd: Where-
upon *Juturna* (who was of the same Opinion) took this oppor-
tunity to break the Treaty and renew the War. *Juno* her self had
plainly told the Nymph beforehand, that her Brother was to
Fight

> *Imparibus fatis; nec Diis, nec viribus æquis;*

So that there was no need of an Apparition to fright *Turnus.* He
had the presage within himself of his impending Destiny. The
20 *Dira* only serv'd to confirm him in his first Opinion, that it was
his Destiny to die in the ensuing Combat. And in this sense are
those words of *Virgil* to be taken;

> ————*Non me tua turbida virtus*
> *Terret ait; Dii me terrent, & Jupiter Hostis.*

I doubt not but the Adverb (*solùm*) is to be understood; 'tis
not your Valour only that gives me this concernment; but I find
also, by this portent, that *Jupiter* is my Enemy. For *Turnus* fled
before, when his first Sword was broken, 'till his Sister supply'd
him with a better; which indeed he cou'd not use; because *Æneas*
30 kept him at a distance with his Spear. I wonder *Ruæus* saw not
this, where he charges his Author so unjustly, for giving *Turnus*
a second Sword, to no purpose. How cou'd he fasten a blow, or

---

13  this] F1 *errata,* F2; his F1.        22  taken;] F2; ∼. F1.
23  ————*Non*] F2; ∧∼ F1.

Versification beside, he may learn from *Virgil,* if he will take him for his Guide. If he be above *Virgil,* and is resolv'd to follow his own *Verve* (as the *French* call it,) the Proverb will fall heavily upon him; *Who teaches himself, has a Fool for his Master.*

*Virgil* employ'd Eleven Years upon his *Æneis,* yet he left it as he thought himself imperfect: Which when I seriously consider, I wish, that instead of three years which I have spent in the Translation of his Works, I had four years more allow'd me to correct my Errours, that I might make my Version somewhat
10 more tolerable than it is. For a Poet cannot have too great a reverence for his Readers, if he expects his Labours shou'd survive him. Yet I will neither plead my Age nor Sickness in excuse of the faults which I have made: That I wanted time is all I have to say. For some of my Subscribers grew so clamorous, that I cou'd no longer deferr the Publication. I hope from the Candour of your Lordship, and your often experienc'd goodness to me, that if the faults are not too many, you will make allowances with *Horace.*

20
*Si plura nitent in Carmine, non ego paucis*
*Offendar maculis, quas aut incuria fudit,*
*Aut humana parùm cavit Natura.*————

You may please also to observe, that there is not, to the best of my remembrance, one Vowel gaping on another for want of a Cæsura, in this whole Poem. But where a Vowel ends a word, the next begins either with a Consonant, or what is its equivalent; for our *W* and *H* aspirate, and our Diphthongues are plainly such: The greatest latitude I take, is in the Letter *Y,* when it concludes a word, and the first Syllable of the next begins with a Vowel. Neither need I have call'd this a latitude, which is only
30 an explanation of this general Rule: That no Vowel can be cut off before another, when we cannot sink the Pronunciation of it: As *He, She, Me, I,* &c. *Virgil* thinks it sometimes a Beauty,

————

6   imperfect:] ∼. F1–2.                    21   *Natura.*————] F2; ∼.ₐ F1.
24   Cæsura] *Cæsura* F1–2.
26   Diphthongues] F2; Dipthongues F1.
30   Rule:] F2; ∼. F1.

to imitate the License of the *Greeks,* and leave two Vowels open-
ing on each other, as in that Verse of the Third *Pastoral,*

*Et succus pecori & lac subducitur Agnis.*

But *nobis non licet, esse tam disertis:* At least if we study to
refine our Numbers. I have long had by me the Materials of an
*English Prosodia,* containing all the Mechanical Rules of Versi-
fication, wherein I have treated with some exactness of the Feet,
the Quantities, and the Pauses. The *French* and *Italians* know
nothing of the two first; at least their best Poets have not practis'd
them. As for the Pauses, *Malherb* first brought them into *France,*
within this last Century: And we see how they adorn their *Alex-
andrins.* But as *Virgil* propounds a Riddle which he leaves un-
solv'd:

*Dic quibus in terris, inscripti nomina Regum*
*Nascantur flores, & Phyllida solus habeto:*

So I will give your Lordship another, and leave the Exposition of
it to your acute Judgment. I am sure there are few who make
Verses, have observ'd the sweetness of these two Lines in *Coopers
Hill.*

*Tho' deep, yet clear; though gentle, yet not dull;*
*Strong without rage, without o'reflowing, full.*

And there are yet fewer who can find the Reason of that sweet-
ness. I have given it to some of my Friends in Conversation, and
they have allow'd the Criticism to be just. But since the evil of
false quantities is difficult to be cur'd in any Modern Language;
since the *French* and the *Italians* as well as we, are yet ignorant
what feet are to be us'd in Heroick Poetry; since I have not
strictly observ'd those Rules my self, which I can teach others;
since I pretend to no Dictatorship among my Fellow-Poets; since
if I shou'd instruct some of them to make well-running Verses,
they want Genius to give them strength as well as sweetness; and

2   *Pastoral*] Pastoral F1–2.  
6   *English*] English F1–2.  
4   *disertis:*] ∼. F1–2.  
15   *habeto:*] ∼. F1–2.

above all, since your Lordship has advis'd me not to publish that little which I know, I look on your Counsel as your Command, which I shall observe inviolably, 'till you shall please to revoke it, and leave me at liberty to make my thoughts publick. In the mean time, that I may arrogate nothing to my self, I must acknowledge that *Virgil* in *Latine,* and *Spencer* in *English,* have been my Masters. *Spencer* has also given me the boldness to make use sometimes of his *Alexandrin* Line, which we call, though improperly, the *Pindarick;* because Mr. *Cowley* has often em-
10 ploy'd it in his *Odes.* It adds a certain Majesty to the Verse, when 'tis us'd with Judgment, and stops the sense from overflowing into another Line. Formerly the *French,* like us, and the *Italians,* had but five Feet, or ten Syllables in their Heroick Verse: but since *Ronsard*'s time, as I suppose, they found their Tongue too weak to support their Epick Poetry, without the addition of another Foot. That indeed has given it somewhat of the run, and measure of a Trimeter; but it runs with more activity than strength: Their Language is not strung with Sinews like our *English.* It has the nimbleness of a Greyhound, but not the bulk
20 and body of a Mastiff. Our Men and our Verses over-bear them by their weight; and *Pondere non Numero,* is the *British* Motto. The *French* have set up Purity for the Standard of their Language; and a Masculine Vigour is that of ours. Like their Tongue is the Genius of their Poets, light and trifling in comparison of the *English;* more proper for Sonnets, Madrigals, and Elegies, than Heroick Poetry. The turn on Thoughts and Words is their chief Talent, but the Epick Poem is too stately to receive those little Ornaments. The Painters draw their Nymphs in thin and airy Habits, but the weight of Gold and of Embroideries is re-
30 serv'd for Queens and Goddesses. *Virgil* is never frequent in those Turns, like *Ovid,* but much more sparing of them in his *Æneis,* than in his *Pastorals* and *Georgicks.*

*Ignoscenda quidem, scirent si ignoscere Manes.*

---

6   *Latine . . . English*] Latine . . . English F1–2.
16   somewhat of the run] F1 *(corrected state),* F2; the run F1 *(uncorrected state).*
17   Trimeter] *Trimeter* F1–2.
19, 25   *English*] F2; English F1.

That turn is Beautiful indeed; but he employs it in the Story of *Orpheus* and *Eurydice,* not in his great Poem. I have us'd that License in his *Æneis* sometimes: but I own it as my fault. 'Twas given to those who understand no better. 'Tis like *Ovid*'s

*Semivirumq; bovem, semibovemq; virum.*

The Poet found it before his Criticks, but it was a darling Sin which he wou'd not be perswaded to reform. The want of Genius, of which I have accus'd the *French,* is laid to their Charge by one of their own great Authors, though I have forgotten his Name,
10 and where I read it. If Rewards cou'd make good Poets, their great Master has not been wanting on his part in his bountiful Encouragements: For he is wise enough to imitate *Augustus,* if he had a *Maro.* The *Triumvir* and *Proscriber* had descended to us in a more hideous form than they now appear, if the Emperour had not taken care to make Friends of him and *Horace.* I confess the Banishment of *Ovid* was a Blot in his Escutcheon, yet he was only Banish'd, and who knows but his Crime was Capital, and then his Exile was a Favour? *Ariosto,* who with all his faults, must be acknowledg'd a great Poet, has put these words
20 into the mouth of an Evangelist, but whether they will pass for Gospel now, I cannot tell.

*Non fu si santo ni benigno Augusto,*
*Come la tuba di Virgilio suona;*
*L'haver havuto, in poesia buon gusto*
*La proscrittione, iniqua gli perdona.*

But Heroick Poetry is not of the growth of *France,* as it might be of *England,* if it were Cultivated. *Spencer* wanted only to have read the Rules of *Bossu:* for no Man was ever Born with a greater Genius, or had more Knowledge to support it. But the
30 performance of the *French* is not equal to their Skill; and hitherto we have wanted Skill to perform better. *Segrais,* whose Preface is so wonderfully good, yet is wholly destitute of Elevation; though his Version is much better than that of the two

Brothers, or any of the rest who have attempted *Virgil. Hannibal Caro* is a great Name amongst the *Italians,* yet his Translation of the *Æneis* is most scandalously mean, though he has taken the advantage of writing in Blank Verse, and freed himself from the shackles of modern Rhime: (if it be modern, for *Le Clerc* has told us lately, and I believe has made it out, that *David's* Psalms were written in as errant Rhime as they are Translated.) Now if a Muse cannot run when she is unfetter'd, 'tis a sign she has but little speed. I will not make a digression here, though I am
10 strangely tempted to it; but will only say, that he who can write well in Rhime, may write better in Blank Verse. Rhime is certainly a constraint even to the best Poets, and those who make it with most ease; though perhaps I have as little reason to complain of that hardship as any Man, excepting *Quarles,* and *Withers.* What it adds to sweetness, it takes away from sense; and he who loses the least by it, may be call'd a gainer: it often makes us swerve from an Author's meaning: As, if a Mark be set up for an Archer at a great distance, let him aim as exactly as he can, the least wind will take his Arrow, and divert it from the White.
20 I return to our *Italian* Translatour of the *Æneis:* He is a Foot-Poet, he Lacquies by the side of *Virgil* at the best, but never mounts behind him. Doctor *Morelli,* who is no mean Critick in our Poetry, and therefore may be presum'd to be a better in his own Language, has confirm'd me in this Opinion by his Judgment, and thinks withall, that he has often mistaken his Master's Sense. I wou'd say so, if I durst, but I am afraid I have committed the same fault more often, and more grosly: For I have forsaken *Ruæus,* (whom generally I follow) in many places, and made Expositions of my own in some, quite contrary to him:
30 Of which I will give but two Examples, because they are so near each other in the Tenth *Æneid.*

————*Sorti Pater æquus utrique.*

*Pallas* says it to *Turnus* just before they Fight. *Ruæus* thinks that the word *Pater* is to be referr'd to *Evander* the Father of *Pallas.* But how cou'd he imagine that it was the same thing to

---

17   meaning: As,] ∼. ∼ₐ F1–2.          29   him:] ∼. F1–2.

*Evander,* if his Son were slain, or if he overcame? The Poet certainly intended *Jupiter* the common Father of Mankind; who, as *Pallas* hop'd, wou'd stand an impartial Spectatour of the Combat, and not be more favourable to *Turnus,* than to him. The Second is not long after it, and both before the Duel is begun. They are the words of *Jupiter,* who comforts *Hercules* for the death of *Pallas,* which was immediately to ensue, and which *Hercules* cou'd not hinder (though the young Heroe had address'd his Prayers to him for his assistance:) Because the Gods cannot
10 controul Destiny————the Verse follows.

> *Sic ait; atq; oculos Rutulorum rejicit arvis.*

Which the same *Ruæus* thus construes. *Jupiter* after he had said this, immediately turns his eyes to the *Rutulian* Fields, and beholds the Duel. I have given this place another Exposition, that he turn'd his Eyes from the Field of Combat, that he might not behold a fight so unpleasing to him. The word *Rejicit* I know will admit of both senses; but *Jupiter* having confess'd that he could not alter Fate, and being griev'd he cou'd not, in consideration of *Hercules,* it seems to me that he shou'd avert his Eyes,
20 rather than take pleasure in the Spectacle. But of this I am not so confident as the other, though I think I have follow'd *Virgil's* sense.

What I have said, though it has the face of arrogance, yet is intended for the honour of my Country; and therefore I will boldly own, that this *English* Translation has more of *Virgil's* Spirit in it, than either the *French,* or the *Italian.* Some of our Country-men have translated Episodes, and other parts of *Virgil,* with great Success: As particularly your Lordship, whose Version of *Orpheus* and *Eurydice,* is eminently good. Amongst
30 the dead Authors, the *Silenus* of my Lord *Roscommon* cannot be too much commended. I say nothing of Sir *John Denham,* Mr. *Waller,* and Mr. *Cowley;* 'tis the utmost of my Ambition to be thought their Equal, or not to be much inferiour to them, and some others of the Living. But 'tis one thing to take pains on a Fragment, and Translate it perfectly; and another thing

---

1  overcame?] ∼. F1–2.          28  Success:] ∼. F1–2.

to have the weight of a whole Author on my shoulders. They who believe the burthen light, let them attempt the Fourth, Sixth or Eighth *Pastoral,* the First or Fourth *Georgick;* and amongst the *Æneids,* the Fourth, the Fifth, the Seventh, the Ninth, the Tenth, the Eleventh, or the Twelfth; for in these I think I have succeeded best.

Long before I undertook this Work, I was no stranger to the Original. I had also studied *Virgil's* Design, his disposition of it, his Manners, his judicious management of the Figures, the
10 sober retrenchments of his Sense, which always leaves somewhat to gratifie our imagination, on which it may enlarge at pleasure; but above all, the Elegance of his Expressions, and the harmony of his Numbers. For, as I have said in a former Dissertation, the words are in Poetry, what the Colours are in Painting. If the Design be good, and the Draught be true, the Colouring is the first Beauty that strikes the Eye. *Spencer* and *Milton* are the nearest in *English* to *Virgil* and *Horace* in the *Latine;* and I have endeavour'd to form my Stile by imitating their Masters. I will farther own to you, my Lord, that my chief Ambition is to please
20 those Readers, who have discernment enough to prefer *Virgil* before any other Poet in the *Latine* Tongue. Such Spirits as he desir'd to please, such wou'd I chuse for my Judges, and wou'd stand or fall by them alone. *Segrais* has distinguish'd the Readers of Poetry, according to their capacity of judging, into three Classes: (He might have said the same of Writers too if he had pleas'd.) In the lowest Form he places those whom he calls *Les Petits Esprits:* such things as are our Upper-Gallery Audience in a Play-House; who like nothing but the Husk and Rhind of Wit; preferr a Quibble, a Conceit, an Epigram, before solid
30 Sense, and Elegant Expression: These are Mobb-Readers: If *Virgil* and *Martial* stood for Parliament-Men, we know already who wou'd carry it. But though they make the greatest appearance in the Field, and cry the loudest, the best on't is, they are but a sort of *French Hugonots,* or *Dutch Boors,* brought over in

---

16–17   the nearest in *English* to *Virgil* and *Horace* in the *Latine;*] F1 (*corrected state*), F2 (English . . . Latine); in English what *Virgil* and *Horace* are in Latine, F1. (*uncorrected state*).
17   I have] F1 (*uncorrected state*); have F1 (*corrected state*), F2.
21   *Latine*] Latine F1–2.

Herds, but not Naturaliz'd: who have not Land of two Pounds *per Annum* in *Parnassus,* and therefore are not priviledg'd to Poll. Their Authors are of the same level; fit to represent them on a Mountebank's-Stage, or to be Masters of the Ceremonies in a Bear-Garden. Yet these are they who have the most Admirers. But it often happens, to their mortification, that as their Readers improve their Stock of Sense, (as they may by reading better Books, and by Conversation with Men of Judgment,) they soon forsake them: And when the Torrent from the Mountains falls
10 no more, the swelling Writer is reduc'd into his shallow Bed, like the *Mançanares* at *Madrid,* with scarce water to moisten his own Pebbles. There are a middle sort of Readers (as we hold there is a middle state of Souls) such as have a farther insight than the former; yet have not the capacity of judging right; (for I speak not of those who are brib'd by a Party, and know better if they were not corrupted;) but I mean a Company of warm young Men, who are not yet arriv'd so far as to discern the difference betwixt Fustian, or ostentatious Sentences, and the true sublime. These are above liking *Martial,* or *Owen*'s Epigrams,
20 but they wou'd certainly set *Virgil* below *Statius,* or *Lucan.* I need not say their Poets are of the same Paste with their Admirers. They affect greatness in all they write, but 'tis a bladder'd greatness, like that of the vain Man whom *Seneca* describes: An ill habit of Body, full of Humours, and swell'd with Dropsie. Even these too desert their Authors, as their Judgment ripens. The young Gentlemen themselves are commonly miss-led by their Pedagogue at School, their Tutor at the University, or their Governour in their Travels. And many of those three sorts are the most positive Blockheads in the World. How many of
30 those flatulent Writers have I known, who have sunk in their Reputation, after Seven or Eight Editions of their Works? for indeed they are Poets only for young Men. They had great success at their first appearance; but not being of God, as a Wit said formerly, they cou'd not stand.

I have already nam'd two sorts of Judges, but *Virgil* wrote for neither of them: and by his Example, I am not ambitious of pleasing the lowest, or the middle form of Readers.

27  Pedagogue] *Pedagogue* F1–2.

He chose to please the most Judicious: Souls of the highest
Rank, and truest Understanding. These are few in number; but
whoever is so happy as to gain their approbation, can never lose
it, because they never give it blindly. Then they have a certain
Magnetism in their Judgment, which attracts others to their
Sense. Every day they gain some new Proselyte, and in time be-
come the Church. For this Reason, a well-weigh'd Judicious
Poem, which at its first appearance gains no more upon the
World than to be just receiv'd, and rather not blam'd, than
10 much applauded, insinuates it self by insensible degrees into the
liking of the Reader: The more he studies it, the more it grows
upon him; every time he takes it up, he discovers some new
Graces in it. And whereas Poems which are produc'd by the
vigour of Imagination only, have a gloss upon them at the first,
which Time wears off; the Works of Judgment, are like the
Diamond, the more they are polish'd, the more lustre they re-
ceive. Such is the difference betwixt *Virgil's Æneis,* and *Marini's
Adone.* And if I may be allow'd to change the Metaphor, I wou'd
say, that *Virgil* is like the Fame which he describes;

20              *Mobilitate viget, viresq; acquirit eundo.*

Such a sort of Reputation is my aim, though in a far inferiour
degree, according to my Motto in the Title Page: *Sequiturq;
Patrem, non passibus æquis;* and therefore I appeal to the High-
est Court of Judicature, like that of the Peers, of which your
Lordship is so great an Ornament.

Without this Ambition which I own, of desiring to please the
*Judices Natos,* I cou'd never have been able to have done any
thing at this Age, when the fire of Poetry is commonly extin-
guish'd in other Men. Yet *Virgil* has given me the Example of
30 *Entellus* for my Encouragement: When he was well heated, the
younger Champion cou'd not stand before him. And we find the
Elder contended not for the Gift, but for the Honour; *Nec dona
moror.* For *Dampier* has inform'd us, in his Voyages, that the
Air of the Country which produces Gold, is never wholsom.

---

3  never] F2; nover F1.                    5  Magnetism] *Magnetism* F1–2.
23  *passibus*] F1 (*corrected state*), F2; *passiibus* F1 (*uncorrected state*).

I had long since consider'd, that the way to please the best
Judges, is not to Translate a Poet literally; and *Virgil* least of
any other. For his peculiar Beauty lying in his choice of Words,
I am excluded from it by the narrow compass of our Heroick
Verse, unless I wou'd make use of Monosyllables only, and those
clog'd with Consonants, which are the dead weight of our
Mother-Tongue. 'Tis possible, I confess, though it rarely hap-
pens, that a Verse of Monosyllables may sound harmoniously;
and some Examples of it I have seen. My first Line of the *Æneis*
is not harsh:

> *Arms, and the Man I Sing, who forc'd by Fate,* &c.

But a much better instance may be given from the last Line
of *Manilius,* made *English* by our Learned and Judicious Mr.
*Creech.*

> *Nor could the World have born so fierce a Flame.*

Where the many Liquid Consonants are plac'd so Artfully, that
they give a pleasing sound to the Words, though they are all of
one Syllable.
    'Tis true, I have been sometimes forc'd upon it in other places
of this Work, but I never did it out of choice: I was either in
haste, or *Virgil* gave me no occasion for the Ornament of Words;
for it seldom happens but a Monosyllable Line turns Verse to
Prose, and even that Prose is rugged, and unharmonious. *Phil-
archus,* I remember, taxes *Balzac* for placing Twenty Mono-
syllables in file, without one dissyllable betwixt them. The way
I have taken, is not so streight as Metaphrase, nor so loose as
Paraphrase: Some things too I have omitted, and sometimes
have added of my own. Yet the omissions I hope, are but of Cir-
cumstances, and such as wou'd have no grace in *English;* and the
Additions, I also hope, are easily deduc'd from *Virgil's* Sense.
They will seem (at least I have the Vanity to think so), not stuck
into him, but growing out of him. He studies brevity more than

---

13   *English*] English F1–2.          16   Where] *indented in F1–2.*
29   *English*] English F1–2.

vated early, or we shall never Write it with any kind of Elegance. Thus by gaining abroad he lost at home: Like the Painter in the *Arcadia,* who going to see a Skirmish, had his Arms lop'd off: and return'd, says Sir *Philip Sydney,* well instructed how to draw a Battel, but without a Hand to perform his Work.

There is another thing in which I have presum'd to deviate from him and *Spencer.* They both make Hemysticks (or half Verses) breaking off in the middle of a Line. I confess there are not many such in the *Fairy Queen:* And even those few might
10 be occasion'd by his unhappy choice of so long a Stanza. Mr. *Cowley* had found out, that no kind of Staff is proper for an Heroick Poem; as being all too lirical: Yet though he wrote in Couplets, where Rhyme is freer from constraint, he frequently affects half Verses: of which we find not one in *Homer,* and I think not in any of the *Greek* Poets, or the *Latin,* excepting only *Virgil;* and there is no question but he thought, he had *Virgil's* Authority for that License. But I am confident, our Poet never meant to leave him or any other such a Precedent. And I ground my Opinion on these two Reasons. First, we find no Example
20 of a Hemystick in any of his *Pastorals* or *Georgicks.* For he had given the last finishing Strokes to both these Poems: But his *Æneis* he left so uncorrect, at least so short of that perfection at which he aim'd, that we know how hard a Sentence He pass'd upon it: And in the second place, I reasonably presume, that he intended to have fill'd up all those Hemysticks, because in one of them we find the sense imperfect:

*Quem tibi jam Trojâ*———

Which some foolish Grammarian, has ended for him, with a half Line of Nonsense:

30 ———*Peperit fumante Crëusa.*

For *Ascanius* must have been born some Years before the burning of that City; which I need not prove. On the other side we

15  *Latin*] F2; Latin F1.      20  *Pastorals*] F2; Pastorals F1.
25  Hemysticks] *Hemysticks* F1–2.     28  Grammarian] F2; Gramarian F1.
29  Nonsense:] ∼. F1; ∼; F2.     30  ———*Peperit*] ∧∼ F1–2.

find also, that he himself fill'd up one Line in the sixth *Æneid,* the Enthusiasm seizing him, while he was reading to *Augustus.*

> *Misenum Æolidem, quo non præstantior alter*
> *Ære, ciere viros.*————

To which he added in that transport, *Martemque accendere Cantu.* And never was any Line more nobly finish'd; for the reasons which I have given in the Book *Of Painting.* On these Considerations I have shun'd Hemysticks: Not being willing to imitate *Virgil* to a Fault; like *Alexander's* Courtiers, who af-
10 fected to hold their Necks awry, because he cou'd not help it: I am confident your Lordship is by this time of my Opinion; and that you will look on those half lines hereafter, as the imperfect products of a hasty Muse: Like the Frogs and Serpents in the *Nile;* part of them kindled into Life; and part a lump of un-form'd unanimated Mudd.

I am sensible that many of my whole Verses, are as imperfect as those halves; for want of time to digest them better: But give me leave to make the Excuse of *Boccace:* Who when he was up-braided, that some of his Novels had not the Spirit of the rest,
20 return'd this Answer; that *Charlemain* who made the Paladins, was never able to raise an Army of them. The Leaders may be Heroes, but the multitude must consist of Common Men.

I am also bound to tell your Lordship, in my own defence: That from the beginning of the first *Georgick* to the end of the last *Æneid;* I found the difficulty of Translation growing on me in every succeeding Book. For *Virgil,* above all Poets, had a stock, which I may call almost inexhaustible, of figurative, Ele gant, and sounding Words. I who inherit but a small portion of his Genius, and write in a Language so much inferiour to the
30 *Latin,* have found it very painful to vary Phrases, when the same sense returns upon me. Even he himself, whether out of neces-sity or choice, has often express'd the same thing in the same

neither borrow from the *Latin* or any other Language: But when
I want at home, I must seek abroad.

   If sounding Words are not of our growth and Manufacture,
who shall hinder me to Import them from a Foreign Country?
I carry not out the Treasure of the Nation, which is never to
return: but what I bring from *Italy,* I spend in *England:* Here
it remains, and here it circulates; for if the Coyn be good, it will
pass from one hand to another. I Trade both with the Living and
the Dead, for the enrichment of our Native Language. We have
enough in *England* to supply our necessity; but if we will have
things of Magnificence and Splendour, we must get them by
Commerce. Poetry requires Ornament, and that is not to be
had from our Old *Teuton* Monosyllables; therefore if I find any
Elegant Word in a Classick Author, I propose it to be Natu-
raliz'd, by using it my self: and if the Publick approves of it, the
Bill passes. But every Man cannot distinguish betwixt Pedantry
and Poetry: Every Man therefore is not fit to innovate. Upon
the whole matter, a Poet must first be certain that the Word he
wou'd Introduce is Beautiful in the *Latin;* and is to consider,
in the next place, whether it will agree with the *English* Idiom:
After this, he ought to take the Opinion of judicious Friends,
such as are Learned in both Languages: And lastly, since no Man
is infallible, let him use this License very sparingly; for if too
many Foreign Words are pour'd in upon us, it looks as if they
were design'd not to assist the Natives, but to Conquer them.

   I am now drawing towards a Conclusion, and suspect your
Lordship is very glad of it. But permit me first, to own what
Helps I have had in this Undertaking. The late Earl of *Lauder-
dail,* sent me over his new Translation of the *Æneis;* which he
had ended before I ingag'd in the same Design. Neither did I
then intend it: But some Proposals being afterwards made me
by my Bookseller, I desir'd his Lordship's leave, that I might
accept them, which he freely granted; and I have his Letter yet
to shew, for that permission. He resolv'd to have Printed his
Work; which he might have done two Years before I cou'd
Publish mine: and had perform'd it, if Death had not prevented
him. But having his Manuscript in my hands, I consulted it as

1, 19   *Latin*] F2; Latin F1.

often as I doubted of my Author's sense. For no Man understood *Virgil* better than that Learned Noble Man. His Friends, I hear, have yet another, and more Correct Copy of that Translation by them: which had they pleas'd to have given the Publick, the Judges must have been convinc'd, that I have not flatter'd him. Besides this help, which was not inconsiderable, Mr. *Congreve* has done me the Favour to review the *Æneis;* and compare my Version with the Original. I shall never be asham'd to own, that this Excellent Young Man, has shew'd me many Faults, which
10 I have endeavour'd to Correct. 'Tis true, he might have easily found more, and then my Translation had been more Perfect.

Two other Worthy Friends of mine, who desire to have their Names conceal'd, seeing me straitned in my time, took Pity on me, and gave me the Life of *Virgil,* the two Prefaces to the *Pastorals,* and the *Georgics,* and all the Arguments in Prose to the whole Translation: Which perhaps, has caus'd a Report that the two First Poems are not mine. If it had been true, that I had taken their Verses for my own, I might have glory'd in their Aid; and like *Terence,* have farther'd the Opinion, that *Scipio*
20 and *Lælius* join'd with me. But the same Style being continu'd thro' the whole, and the same Laws of Versification observ'd, are proofs sufficient, that this is one Man's Work: And your Lordship is too well acquainted with my manner, to doubt that any part of it is anothers.

That your Lordship may see I was in earnest, when I promis'd to hasten to an end, I will not give the Reasons, why I Writ not always in the proper terms of Navigation, Land-Service, or in the Cant of any Profession. I will only say, that *Virgil* has avoided those proprieties, because he Writ not to Mariners, Souldiers,
30 Astronomers, Gardners, Peasants, &c. but to all in general, and in particular to Men and Ladies of the first Quality: who have been better Bred than to be too nicely knowing in the Terms. In such cases, 'tis enough for a Poet to write so plainly, that he may be understood by his Readers: To avoid impropriety, and not affect to be thought Learn'd in all things.

I have omitted the Four Preliminary Lines of the First *Æneid:*

---

14–15  *Pastorals*] Pastorals F1–2.  16  Translation:] ~. F1–2.
16  caus'd] F2; occasion'd F1.

Because I think them inferiour to any Four others, in the whole Poem: and consequently, believe they are not *Virgil*'s. There is too great a gap betwixt the Adjective *vicina* in the Second Line, and the Substantive *Arva* in the latter end of the Third, which keeps his meaning in obscurity too long: And is contrary to the clearness of his Style.

*Ut quamvis avidis*

Is too ambitious an Ornament to be his, and

*Gratum opus Agricolis,*

10 Are all words unnecessary, and Independent of what he had said before.

*Horrentia Martis Arma,*

Is worse than any of the rest. *Horrentia* is such a flat Epithete, as *Tully* wou'd have given us in his Verses. 'Tis a meer filler; to stop a vacancy in the Hexameter, and connect the Preface to the Work of *Virgil*. Our Author seems to sound a Charge, and begins like the clangour of a Trumpet;

*Arma, virumque cano; Trojæ qui primus ab oris.*

Scarce a word without an *R,* and the Vowels for the greater 20 part sonorous. The Prefacer began with *Ille ego,* which He was constrain'd to patch up in the Fourth line with *At nunc,* to make the Sense cohere. And if both those words are not notorious botches, I am much deceiv'd, though the *French* Translator thinks otherwise. For my own part, I am rather of the Opinion, that they were added by *Tucca* and *Varius,* than Retrench'd.

I know it may be answer'd by such as think *Virgil* the Author of the four Lines; that he asserts his Title to the *Æneis,* in the beginning of this Work, as he did to the two former, in the last lines of the fourth *Georgic.* I will not reply otherwise to this, 30 than by desiring them to compare these four Lines with the

19   *R,*] F2; ∼. F1.                    24   of the] F2; of F1.

four others; which we know are his, because no Poet but he alone could write them. If they cannot distinguish Creeping from Flying, let them lay down *Virgil,* and take up *Ovid de Ponto* in his stead. My Master needed not the assistance of that Preliminary Poet to prove his Claim. His own Majestick Meen discovers him to be the King, amidst a Thousand Courtiers. It was a superfluous Office, and therefore I wou'd not set those Verses in the Front of *Virgil:* But have rejected them to my own Preface.

10
> *I, who before, with Shepherds in the Groves,*
> *Sung to my Oaten Pipe, their Rural Loves,*
> *And issuing thence, compell'd the Neighb'ring Field*
> *A plenteous Crop of rising Corn to yield,*
> *Manur'd the Glebe, and stock'd the fruitful Plain,*
> *(A Poem grateful to the greedy Swain.)* &c.

If there be not a tolerable Line in all these six, the Prefacer gave me no occasion to write better. This is a just Apology in this place. But I have done great Wrong to *Virgil* in the whole Translation: Want of Time, the Inferiority of our Language, the
20 inconvenience of Rhyme, and all the other Excuses I have made, may alleviate my Fault, but cannot justifie the boldness of my Undertaking. What avails it me to acknowledge freely, that I have not been able to do him right in any line? For even my own Confession makes against me; and it will always be return'd upon me, Why then did you attempt it? To which, no other Answer can be made, than that I have done him less Injury than any of his former Libellers.

What they call'd his Picture, had been drawn at length, so many times, by the Daubers of almost all Nations, and still so
30 unlike him, that I snatch'd up the Pencil with disdain: being satisfi'd before hand, that I cou'd make some small resemblance of him, though I must be content with a worse likeness. A Sixth *Pastoral,* a *Pharmaceutria,* a single *Orpheus,* and some other

---

8   *Virgil:*] ∼. F1; ∼; F2.        16   Prefacer] F2; ∼, F1.
19   Language,] F2; ∼; F1.         33   *Pastoral*] Pastoral F1–2.

Features, have been exactly taken: But those Holiday Authors writ for Pleasure; and only shew'd us what they cou'd have done, if they wou'd have taken pains, to perform the whole.

Be pleas'd, My Lord, to accept, with your wonted goodness, this unworthy Present, which I make you. I have taken off one trouble from you, of defending it, by acknowledging its Imperfections: And though some part of them are cover'd in the Verse; (as *Ericthonius* rode always in a Chariot, to hide his lameness) such of them as cannot be conceal'd, you will please to connive at, though in the strictness of your Judgment, you cannot Pardon. If *Homer* was allow'd to nod sometimes, in so long a Work, it will be no wonder if I often fall asleep. You took my *Aureng-Zebe* into your Protection, with all his faults: And I hope here cannot be so many, because I Translate an Author, who gives me such Examples of Correctness. What my Jury may be, I know not; but 'tis good for a Criminal to plead before a favourable Judge: If I had said Partial, wou'd your Lordship have forgiven me? Or will you give me leave to acquaint the World, that I have many times been oblig'd to your Bounty since the Revolution? Though I never was reduc'd to beg a Charity, nor ever had the Impudence to ask one, either of your Lordship, or your Noble Kinsman the Earl of *Dorset,* much less of any other, yet when I least expected it, you have both remember'd me. So inherent it is in your Family not to forget an Old Servant. It looks rather like Ingratitude on my part, that where I have been so often oblig'd, I have appear'd so seldom to return my thanks: and where I was also so sure of being well receiv'd. Somewhat of Laziness was in the case; and somewhat too of Modesty: But nothing of Disrespect, or of Unthankfulness. I will not say that your Lordship has encourag'd me to this Presumption, lest if my Labours meet with no success in Publick, I may expose your Judgment to be Censur'd. As for my own Enemies I shall never think them worth an Answer; and if your Lordship has any, they will not dare to Arraign you for want of Knowledge in this Art, till they can produce somewhat better of their own, than your

---

8–9  lameness) such] ∼.) Such F1–2.        12–13  *Aureng-Zebe*] *Aureng-zeb* F1–2.
19–20  Revolution?] ∼. F1–2.                  34  for] F2; for your F1.

*Essay on Poetry.* 'Twas on this Consideration, that I have drawn out my Preface to so great a length. Had I not address'd to a Poet, and a Critick of the first Magnitude, I had my self been tax'd for want of Judgment, and sham'd my Patron for want of Understanding. But neither will you, My Lord, so soon be tir'd as any other, because the Discourse is on your Art; Neither will the Learned Reader think it tedious, because it is *ad Clerum.* At least, when he begins to be weary, the Church Doors are open. That I may pursue the Allegory with a short Prayer, after a 10 long Sermon:

May you Live happily and long, for the Service of your Country, the Encouragement of good Letters and the Ornament of Poetry; which cannot be wish'd more earnestly by any Man, than by

Your Lordships, most Humble,

Most Obliged, and most Obedient Servant.

*John Dryden.*

---

1   *on Poetry*] on Poetry F1–2.

To his Royall Highness PRINCE
GEORGE of DENMARK.

# VIRGIL'S ÆNEIS

## The First Book of the Æneis

### THE ARGUMENT.

*The* Trojans, *after a seven Years Voyage, set sail for* Italy, *but are overtaken by a dreadful Storm, which* Æolus *raises at* Juno's *Request. The Tempest sinks one, and scatters the rest:* Neptune *drives off the Winds and calms the Sea.* Æneas *with his own Ship, and six more, arrives safe at an* Affrican *Port.* Venus *complains to* Jupiter *of her Son's Misfortunes.* Jupiter *comforts her, and sends* Mercury *to procure him a kind Reception among the* Carthaginians. Æneas *going out to discover the Country, meets his Mother in the Shape of an Huntress, who conveys him in a Cloud to* Carthage; *where he sees his Friends whom he thought lost, and receives a kind Entertainment from the Queen.* Dido *by a device of* Venus *begins to have a Passion for him, and after some Discourse with him, desires the History of his Adventures since the Siege of* Troy, *which is the Subject of the two following Books.*

ARMS, and the Man I sing, who, forc'd by Fate,
　　And haughty *Juno*'s unrelenting Hate,
　　Expell'd and exil'd, left the *Trojan* Shoar:
Long Labours, both by Sea and Land he bore,
And in the doubtful War, before he won
The *Latian* Realm, and built the destin'd Town:
His banish'd Gods restor'd to Rites Divine,
And setl'd sure Succession in his Line:
From whence the Race of *Alban* Fathers come,
10　And the long Glories of Majestick *Rome.*
　　O Muse! the Causes and the Crimes relate,
What Goddess was provok'd, and whence her hate:

---

2　Hate,] ∼; F1–2.　　　　4　bore,] ∼; F1–2.

For what Offence the Queen of Heav'n began
To persecute so brave, so just a Man!
Involv'd his anxious Life in endless Cares,
Expos'd to Wants, and hurry'd into Wars!
Can Heav'nly Minds such high resentment show;
Or exercise their Spight in Human Woe?
  Against the *Tiber*'s Mouth, but far away,
20 An ancient Town was seated on the Sea:
A *Tyrian* Colony; the People made
Stout for the War, and studious of their Trade:
*Carthage* the Name, belov'd by *Juno* more
Than her own *Argos,* or the *Samian* Shoar.
Here stood her Chariot, here, if Heav'n were kind,
The Seat of awful Empire she design'd.
Yet she had heard an ancient Rumour fly,
(Long cited by the People of the Sky;)
That times to come shou'd see the *Trojan* Race
30 Her *Carthage* ruin, and her Tow'rs deface:
Nor thus confin'd, the Yoke of Sov'raign Sway,
Should on the Necks of all the Nations lay.
She ponder'd this, and fear'd it was in Fate; ⎫
Nor cou'd forget the War she wag'd of late, ⎬
For conq'ring *Greece* against the *Trojan* State. ⎭
Besides long Causes working in her Mind,
And secret Seeds of Envy lay behind.
Deep graven in her Heart, the Doom remain'd
Of partial *Paris,* and her Form disdain'd:
40 The Grace bestow'd on ravish'd *Ganimed,*
*Electra*'s Glories, and her injur'd Bed.
Each was a Cause alone, and all combin'd
To kindle Vengeance in her haughty Mind.
For this, far distant from the *Latian* Coast,
She drove the Remnants of the *Trojan* Hoast:
And sev'n long Years th' unhappy wand'ring Train,
Were toss'd by Storms, and scatter'd through the Main.
Such Time, such Toil requir'd the *Roman* Name,
Such length of Labour for so vast a Frame.

---

22  Trade:] ∼. F1–2.

50 Now scarce the *Trojan* Fleet with Sails and Oars,
Had left behind the Fair *Sicilian* Shoars:
Ent'ring with chearful Shouts the wat'ry Reign,
And ploughing frothy Furrows in the Main:
When lab'ring still, with endless discontent,
The Queen of Heav'n did thus her Fury vent.
　　Then am I vanquish'd, must I yield, said she,
And must the *Trojans* reign in *Italy?*
So Fate will have it, and *Jove* adds his Force;
Nor can my Pow'r divert their happy Course.
60 Cou'd angry *Pallas*, with revengeful Spleen,
The *Grecian* Navy burn, and drown the Men?
She for the Fault of one offending Foe,
The Bolts of *Jove* himself presum'd to throw:
With Whirlwinds from beneath she toss'd the Ship,
And bare expos'd the Bosom of the deep:
Then, as an Eagle gripes the trembling Game,
The Wretch yet hissing with her Father's Flame,
She strongly seiz'd, and with a burning Wound,
Transfix'd and naked, on a Rock she bound.
70 But I, who walk in awful State above,
The Majesty of Heav'n, the Sister-wife of *Jove;*
For length of Years, my fruitless Force employ
Against the thin remains of ruin'd *Troy.*
What Nations now to *Juno*'s Pow'r will pray,
Or Off'rings on my slighted Altars lay?
　　Thus rag'd the Goddess, and with Fury fraught,
The restless Regions of the Storms she sought:
Where in a spacious Cave of living Stone,
The Tyrant *Æolus* from his Airy Throne,
80 With Pow'r Imperial curbs the strugling Winds,
And sounding Tempests in dark Prisons binds.
This Way, and that, th' impatient Captives tend,
And pressing for Release, the Mountains rend;
High in his Hall, th' undaunted Monarch stands,
And shakes his Scepter, and their Rage commands:
Which did he not, their unresisted Sway

---

77　sought:] ∼. F1–2.　　　　79　*Æolus*] *E'lus* F1; *Eolus* F1 errata, F2.

Wou'd sweep the World before them, in their Way:
Earth, Air, and Seas through empty Space wou'd rowl,
And Heav'n would fly before the driving Soul.
90 In fear of this, the Father of the Gods
Confin'd their Fury to those dark Abodes,
And lock'd 'em safe within, oppress'd with Mountain loads:
Impos'd a King, with arbitrary Sway,
To loose their Fetters, or their Force allay:
To whom the suppliant Queen her Pray'rs addrest,
And thus the tenour of her Suit express'd.
   O *Æolus!* for to thee the King of Heav'n
The Pow'r of Tempests, and of Winds has giv'n:
Thy Force alone their Fury can restrain,
100 And smooth the Waves, or swell the troubl'd Main.
A race of wand'ring Slaves, abhorr'd by me,
With prosp'rous Passage cut the *Thuscan* Sea:
To fruitful *Italy* their Course they steer,
And for their vanquish'd Gods design new Temples there.
Raise all thy Winds, with Night involve the Skies;
Sink, or disperse my fatal Enemies.
Twice sev'n, the charming Daughters of the Main,
Around my Person wait, and bear my Train:
Succeed my Wish, and second my Design,
110 The fairest, *Deiopea,* shall be thine;
And make thee Father of a happy Line.
   To this the God————'Tis yours, O Queen! to will
The Work, which Duty binds me to fulfil.
These airy Kingdoms, and this wide Command,
Are all the Presents of your bounteous Hand:
Yours is my Sov'raign's Grace, and, as your Guest,
I sit with Gods at their Cœlestial Feast:
Raise Tempests at your Pleasure, or subdue;
Dispose of Empire, which I hold from you.
120 He said, and hurld against the Mountain side,
His quiv'ring Spear; and all, the God apply'd.

---

93   arbitrary] F2; arbritrary F1.          94   allay:] ∼. F1–2.
97   *Æolus*] *E'lus* F1; *Eolus* F1 *errata,* F2.   110   *Deiopea*] *Deiopeia* F1–2.
117   Feast:] ∼. F1–2.                        121   Spear;] ∼, F1–2.

The raging Winds rush through the hollow Wound,
And dance aloft in Air, and skim along the Ground:
Then setling on the Sea, the Surges sweep;
Raise liquid Mountains, and disclose the deep.
South, East, and West, with mix'd Confusion roar,
And rowl the foaming Billows to the Shoar.
The Cables crack, the Sailors fearful Cries ⎫
Ascend; and sable Night involves the Skies; ⎬
130 And Heav'n it self is ravish'd from their Eyes. ⎭
Loud Peals of Thunder from the Poles ensue,
Then flashing Fires the transient Light renew:
The Face of things a frightful Image bears,
And present Death in various Forms appears.
Struck with unusual Fright, the *Trojan* Chief,
With lifted Hands and Eyes, invokes Relief.
And thrice, and four times happy those, he cry'd,
That under *Ilian* Walls before their Parents dy'd.
*Tydides,* bravest of the *Grecian* Train, ⎫
140 Why cou'd not I by that strong Arm be slain, ⎬
And lye by noble *Hector* on the Plain, ⎭
Or great *Sarpedon,* in those bloody Fields,
Where *Simois* rouls the Bodies, and the Shields
Of Heroes, whose dismember'd Hands yet bear
The Dart aloft, and clench the pointed Spear?
Thus while the Pious Prince his Fate bewails,
Fierce *Boreas* drove against his flying Sails,
And rent the Sheets: The raging Billows rise,
And mount the tossing Vessel to the Skies:
150 Nor can the shiv'ring Oars sustain the Blow;
The Galley gives her side, and turns her Prow:
While those astern descending down the Steep,
Thro' gaping Waves behold the boiling deep.
Three Ships were hurry'd by the Southern Blast,
And on the secret Shelves with Fury cast.
Those hidden Rocks, th' *Ausonian* Sailors knew,
They call'd them Altars, when they rose in view,
And show'd their spacious Backs above the Flood.
Three more, fierce *Eurus* in his angry Mood,

160 Dash'd on the Shallows of the moving Sand,
And in mid Ocean left them moor'd a-land.
*Orontes* Barque that bore the *Lycian* Crew,
(A horrid Sight) ev'n in the Hero's view,
From Stem to Stern, by Waves was overborn:
The trembling Pilot, from his Rudder torn,
Was headlong hurl'd; thrice round, the Ship was tost,
Then bulg'd at once, and in the deep was lost.
And here and there above the Waves were seen
Arms, Pictures, precious Goods, and floating Men.
170 The stoutest Vessel to the Storm gave way,
And suck'd through loosen'd Planks the rushing Sea.
*Ilioneus* was her Chief: *Alethes* old,
*Achates* faithful, *Abas* young and bold
Endur'd not less: their Ships, with gaping Seams,
Admit the Deluge of the briny Streams.
   Mean time Imperial *Neptune* heard the Sound
Of raging Billows breaking on the Ground:
Displeas'd, and fearing for his Wat'ry Reign,
He reard his awful Head above the Main:
180 Serene in Majesty, then rowl'd his Eyes
Around the Space of Earth, and Seas, and Skies.
He saw the *Trojan* Fleet dispers'd, distress'd
By stormy Winds and wintry Heav'n oppress'd.
Full well the God his Sister's envy knew,
And what her Aims, and what her Arts pursue:
He summon'd *Eurus* and the western Blast,
And first an angry glance on both he cast:
Then thus rebuk'd; Audacious Winds! from whence
This bold Attempt, this Rebel Insolence?
190 Is it for you to ravage Seas and Land,
Unauthoriz'd by my supream Command?
To raise such Mountains on the troubl'd Main?
Whom I——But first 'tis fit, the Billows to restrain,
And then you shall be taught obedience to my Reign.
Hence, to your Lord my Royal Mandate bear,
The Realms of Ocean and the Fields of Air
Are mine, not his; by fatal Lot to me

The liquid Empire fell, and Trident of the Sea.
His Pow'r to hollow Caverns is confin'd,
200 There let him reign, the Jailor of the Wind:
With hoarse Commands his breathing Subjects call,
And boast and bluster in his empty Hall.
He spoke: And while he spoke, he smooth'd the Sea,
Dispell'd the Darkness, and restor'd the Day:
*Cymothoe, Triton,* and the Sea-green Train
Of beauteous Nymphs, the Daughters of the Main,
Clear from the Rocks the Vessels with their hands; )
The God himself with ready Trident stands, }
And opes the Deep, and spreads the moving sands; )
210 Then heaves them off the sholes: where e're he guides )
His finny Coursers, and in Triumph rides, }
The Waves unruffle and the Sea subsides. )
As when in Tumults rise th' ignoble Crowd,
Mad are their Motions, and their Tongues are loud;
And Stones and Brands in ratling Vollies fly,
And all the Rustick Arms that Fury can supply:
If then some grave and Pious Man appear,
They hush their Noise, and lend a list'ning Ear;
He sooths with sober Words their angry Mood,
220 And quenches their innate Desire of Blood:
So when the Father of the Flood appears,
And o're the Seas his Sov'raign Trident rears,
Their Fury falls: He skims the liquid Plains, )
High on his Chariot, and with loosen'd Reins, }
Majestick moves along, and awful Peace maintains. )
The weary *Trojans* ply their shatter'd Oars,
To nearest Land, and make the *Lybian* Shoars.
    Within a long Recess there lies a Bay,
An Island shades it from the rowling Sea,
230 And forms a Port secure for Ships to ride, )
Broke by the jutting Land on either side: }
In double Streams the briny Waters glide. )
Betwixt two rows of Rocks, a Sylvan Scene
Appears above, and Groves for ever green:

---

213  Crowd] Crow'd F1–2.          220  Blood:] F2; ~. F1.

Æ.1.l. 295

To her Royall Highness the
Princess Anne of Denmark

Earth, Air, and Shoars, and navigable Seas,
310 At length on *Lybian* Realms he fix'd his Eyes:
Whom, pond'ring thus on Human Miseries,
When *Venus* saw, she with a lowly Look,
Not free from Tears, her Heav'nly Sire bespoke.
   O King of Gods and Men, whose awful Hand, ⎫
Disperses Thunder on the Seas and Land;    ⎬
Disposing all with absolute Command:    ⎭
How cou'd my Pious Son thy Pow'r incense,
Or what, alas! is vanish'd *Troy*'s Offence?
Our hope of *Italy* not only lost,    ⎫
320 On various Seas, by various Tempests tost,  ⎬
But shut from ev'ry Shoar, and barr'd from ev'ry Coast. ⎭
   You promis'd once, a Progeny Divine,
Of *Romans,* rising from the *Trojan* Line,
In after-times shou'd hold the World in awe,
And to the Land and Ocean give the Law.
How is your Doom revers'd, which eas'd my Care;
When *Troy* was ruin'd in that cruel War?
Then Fates to Fates I cou'd oppose; but now,
When Fortune still pursues her former Blow,
330 What can I hope? what worse can still succeed?
What end of Labours has your Will decreed?
*Antenor,* from the midst of *Grecian* Hosts,
Could pass secure, and pierce th' *Illyrian* Coasts:
Where rowling down the Steep, *Timavus* raves,
And through nine Channels disembogues his Waves.
At length he founded *Padua*'s happy Seat,
And gave his *Trojans* a secure Retreat:
There fix'd their Arms, and there renew'd their Name,
And there in Quiet rules, and crown'd with Fame.
340 But we, descended from your sacred Line,
Entitled to your Heav'n, and Rites Divine,
Are banish'd Earth, and, for the Wrath of one,
Remov'd from *Latium,* and the promis'd Throne.
Are these our Scepters? These our due Rewards?
And is it thus that *Jove* his plighted Faith regards?
   To whom, the Father of th' immortal Race,

To her Grace Mary Dutchess of Ormond

Smiling with that serene indulgent Face,
With which he drives the Clouds, and clears the Skies:
First gave a holy Kiss, then thus replies.
350    Daughter, dismiss thy Fears: To thy desire
The Fates of thine are fix'd, and stand entire.
Thou shalt behold thy wish'd *Lavinian* Walls,
And, ripe for Heav'n, when Fate *Æneas* calls,
Then shalt thou bear him up, sublime, to me;
No Councils have revers'd my firm Decree.
And lest new Fears disturb thy happy State,
Know, I have search'd the Mystick Rolls of Fate:
Thy Son (nor is th' appointed Season far)
In *Italy* shall wage successful War:
360 Shall tame fierce Nations in the bloody Field,
And Sov'raign Laws impose, and Cities build.
'Till, after ev'ry Foe subdu'd, the Sun
Thrice through the Signs his Annual Race shall run:
This is his time prefix'd. *Ascanius* then,
Now called *Iulus,* shall begin his Reign.
He thirty rowling Years the Crown shall wear:
Then from *Lavinium* shall the Seat transfer:
And, with hard Labour, *Alba-longa* build;
The Throne with his Succession shall be fill'd,
370 Three hundred Circuits more: then shall be seen,
*Ilia* the fair, a Priestess and a Queen:
Who full of *Mars,* in time, with kindly Throws,
Shall at a Birth two goodly Boys disclose.
The Royal Babes a tawny Wolf shall drain,
Then *Romulus* his Grandsire's Throne shall gain,
Of Martial Tow'rs the Founder shall become,
The People *Romans* call, the City *Rome.*
To them, no Bounds of Empire I assign;
Nor term of Years to their immortal Line.
380 Ev'n haughty *Juno,* who, with endless Broils,
Earth, Seas, and Heav'n, and *Jove* himself turmoils;

365  *Iulus*] *Julus* F1–2.
368  *Alba-longa*] *the hyphen failed to print in some copies of F1.*
371  Queen:] ∼. F1–2.
375  gain,] F2; ∼. F1.

At length atton'd, her friendly Pow'r shall joyn,
To cherish and advance the *Trojan* Line.
The subject World shall *Rome*'s Dominion own,
And, prostrate, shall adore the Nation of the Gown.
An Age is ripening in revolving Fate,
When *Troy* shall overturn the *Grecian* State:
And sweet Revenge her conqu'ring Sons shall call,
To crush the People that conspir'd her Fall.
390 Then *Cæsar* from the *Julian* Stock shall rise,
Whose Empire Ocean, and whose Fame the Skies
Alone shall bound: Whom, fraught with Eastern Spoils,
Our Heav'n, the just Reward of Human Toyls,
Securely shall repay with Rites Divine;
And Incense shall ascend before his sacred Shrine.
Then dire Debate, and impious War shall cease,
And the stern Age be softned into Peace:
Then banish'd Faith shall once again return,
And Vestal Fires in hallow'd Temples burn;
400 And *Remus* with *Quirinus* shall sustain
The righteous Laws, and Fraud and Force restrain.
*Janus* himself before his Fane shall wait,
And keep the dreadful issues of his Gate,
With Bolts and Iron Bars: within remains
Imprison'd Fury, bound in brazen Chains:
High on a Trophie rais'd, of useless Arms,
He sits, and threats the World with vain Alarms.
   He said, and sent *Cyllenius* with Command
To free the Ports, and ope the *Punique* Land
410 To *Trojan* Guests; lest ignorant of Fate,
The Queen might force them from her Town and State.
Down from the Steep of Heav'n *Cyllenius* flies,
And cleaves with all his Wings the yielding Skies.
Soon on the *Lybian* Shoar descends the God;
Performs his Message, and displays his Rod:
The surly Murmurs of the People cease,
And, as the Fates requir'd, they give the Peace.

---

392   bound: . . . Eastern] ∼. . . . *Eastern* F₁-₂.
394   repay] F₂; reward F₁.                    400   sustain] ∼, F₁-₂.

The Queen her self suspends the rigid Laws,
The *Trojans* pities, and protects their Cause.
420    Mean time, in Shades of Night *Æneas* lies;
Care seiz'd his Soul, and Sleep forsook his Eyes.
But when the Sun restor'd the chearful Day,
He rose, the Coast and Country to survey,
Anxious and eager to discover more:
It look'd a wild uncultivated Shoar:
But whether Human Kind, or Beasts alone
Possess'd the new-found Region, was unknown.
Beneath a Ledge of Rocks his Fleet he hides;
Tall Trees surround the Mountains shady sides:
430 The bending Brow above, a safe Retreat provides.
Arm'd with two pointed Darts, he leaves his Friends,
And true *Achates* on his steps attends.
Loe, in the deep Recesses of the Wood,
Before his Eyes his Goddess Mother stood:
A Huntress in her Habit and her Meen;
Her dress a Maid, her Air confess'd a Queen.
Bare were her Knees, and knots her Garments bind;
Loose was her Hair, and wanton'd in the Wind;
Her Hand sustain'd a Bow, her Quiver hung behind.
440 She seem'd a Virgin of the *Spartan* Blood:
With such Array *Harpalice* bestrode
Her *Thracian* Courser, and outstrip'd the rapid Flood.
Ho! Strangers! have you lately seen, she said,
One of my Sisters, like my self array'd;
Who crost the Lawn, or in the Forest stray'd?
A Painted Quiver at her Back she bore;
Vary'd with Spots, a Lynx's Hide she wore:
And at full Cry pursu'd the tusky Boar?
Thus *Venus:* Thus her Son reply'd agen;
450 None of your Sisters have we heard or seen,
O virgin! or what other Name you bear
Above that stile; O more than mortal fair!
Your Voice and Meen Cœlestial birth betray!

---

428   Ledge of Rocks] F2 (ledge); hollow Rock F1.
447   Lynx's] *Linx's* F1–2.         452   Above] F2; A bove F1.

Cleyn in. Borrhart, sculpsit.                                              Æ. 2. L. 435.

If, as you seem, the Sister of the Day;
Or one at least of Chast *Diana*'s Train,
Let not an humble Suppliant sue in vain:
But tell a Stranger, long in Tempests tost,
What Earth we tread, and who commands the Coast?
Then on your Name shall wretched Mortals call;
460 And offer'd Victims at your Altars fall.
I dare not, she reply'd, assume the Name
Of Goddess, or Cœlestial Honours claim:
For *Tyrian* Virgins Bows and Quivers bear,
And Purple Buskins o're their Ankles wear.
Know, gentle Youth, in *Lybian* Lands you are:
A People rude in Peace, and rough in War.
The rising City, which from far you see,
Is *Carthage;* and a *Tyrian* Colony.
*Phœnician Dido* rules the growing State,
470 Who fled from *Tyre,* to shun her Brother's hate:
Great were her wrongs, her Story full of Fate;
Which I will sum in short. *Sicheus* known
For wealth, and Brother to the *Punic* Throne,
Possess'd fair *Dido*'s Bed: And either heart
At once was wounded with an equal Dart.
Her Father gave her, yet a spotless Maid;
*Pigmalion* then the *Tyrian* Scepter sway'd:
One who contemn'd Divine and Humane Laws:
Then Strife ensu'd, and cursed Gold the Cause.
480 The Monarch, blinded with desire of Wealth;
With Steel invades his Brother's life by stealth;
Before the sacred Altar made him bleed,
And long from her conceal'd the cruel deed.
Some Tale, some new Pretence, he daily coin'd,
To sooth his Sister, and delude her Mind.
At length, in dead of Night, the Ghost appears
Of her unhappy Lord: the Spectre stares,
And with erected Eyes his bloody Bosom bares.
The cruel Altars, and his Fate he tells,
490 And the dire Secret of his House reveals:

---

469 *Phœnician*] *Phenician* F1–2.          490 reveals:] ~. F1–2.

Then warns the Widdow, with her household Gods,
To seek a Refuge in remote abodes.
Last, to support her, in so long a way,
He shows her where his hidden Treasure lay.
Admonish'd thus, and seiz'd with mortal fright,
The Queen provides Companions of her flight:
They meet; and all combine to leave the State,
Who hate the Tyrant, or who fear his hate.
They seize a Fleet, which ready rigg'd they find:
500 Nor is *Pigmalion*'s Treasure left behind.
The Vessels, heavy laden, put to Sea
With prosprous winds; a Woman leads the way.
I know not, if by stress of Weather driv'n,
Or was their fatal Course dispos'd by Heav'n;
At last they landed, where from far your Eyes
May view the Turrets of new *Carthage* rise:
There bought a space of Ground, which *Byrsa* call'd
From the Bulls hide, they first inclos'd, and wall'd.
But whence are you, what Country claims your Birth?
510 What seek you, Strangers, on our *Lybian* Earth?
　　To whom, with sorrow streaming from his Eyes,
And deeply sighing, thus her Son replyes:
Cou'd you with Patience hear, or I relate,
O Nymph! the tedious Annals of our Fate!
Thro' such a train of Woes if I shou'd run,
The day wou'd sooner than the Tale be done!
From ancient *Troy,* by Force expell'd, we came,
If you by chance have heard the *Trojan* Name:
On various Seas by various Tempests tost,
520 At length we landed on your *Lybian* Coast.
The Good *Æneas* am I call'd, a Name,
While Fortune favour'd, not unknown to Fame:
My houshold Gods, Companions of my Woes,
With pious Care I rescu'd from our Foes.
To fruitful *Italy* my Course was bent,
And from the King of Heav'n is my Descent.
With twice ten Sail I crost the *Phrygian* Sea;
Fate, and my Mother Goddess, led my Way.

Scarce sev'n, the thin Remainders of my Fleet,
530 From Storms preserv'd, within your Harbour meet:
My self distress'd, an Exile, and unknown, ⎫
Debarr'd from *Europe,* and from *Asia* thrown, ⎬
In *Lybian* Desarts wander thus alone. ⎭
  His tender Parent could no longer bear;
But, interposing, sought to sooth his Care.
Who e're you are, not unbelov'd by Heav'n,
Since on our friendly Shoar your Ships are driv'n:
Have Courage: To the Gods permit the rest,
And to the Queen expose your just Request.
540 Now take this earnest of Success, for more:
Your scatter'd Fleet is join'd upon the Shoar;
The Winds are chang'd, your Friends from danger free,
Or I renounce my Skill in Augury.
Twelve Swans behold, in beauteous order move,
And stoop with closing Pinions from above:
Whom late the Bird of *Jove* had driv'n along,
And through the Clouds pursu'd the scatt'ring Throng:
Now all united in a goodly Team,
They skim the Ground, and seek the quiet Stream.
550 As they, with Joy returning, clap their Wings,
And ride the Circuit of the Skies in Rings:
Not otherwise your Ships, and ev'ry Friend,
Already hold the Port, or with swift Sails descend.
No more Advice is needful, but pursue
The Path before you, and the Town in view.
Thus having said, she turn'd, and made appear
Her Neck refulgent, and dishevel'd Hair;
Which flowing from her Shoulders, reach'd the Ground,
And widely spread Ambrosial Scents around:
560 In length of Train descends her sweeping Gown,
And by her graceful Walk, the Queen of Love is known.
The Prince pursu'd the parting Deity,
With Words like these: Ah! whither do you fly?
Unkind and cruel, to deceive your Son
In borrow'd Shapes, and his Embrace to shun:

563  whither] F1 (*corrected state*), F2; whether F1 (*uncorrected state*).

640 The Wars that Fame around the World had blown,
All to the Life, and ev'ry Leader known.
There *Agamemnon, Priam* here he spies,
And fierce *Achilles* who both Kings defies.
He stop'd, and weeping said, O Friend! ev'n here
The Monuments of *Trojan* Woes appear!
Our known Disasters fill ev'n foreign Lands:
See there, where old unhappy *Priam* stands!
Ev'n the Mute Walls relate the Warrior's Fame,
And *Trojan* Griefs the *Tyrians* Pity claim.
650 He said, his Tears a ready Passage find,       ⎫
Devouring what he saw so well design'd;           ⎬
And with an empty Picture fed his Mind.           ⎭
For there he saw the fainting *Grecians* yield,
And here the trembling *Trojans* quit the Field,
Pursu'd by fierce *Achilles* through the Plain,
On his high Chariot driving o're the Slain.
The Tents of *Rhesus* next, his Grief renew,
By their white Sails betray'd to nightly view:
And wakeful *Diomede,* whose cruel Sword
660 The Centries slew; nor spar'd their slumb'ring Lord:
Then took the fiery Steeds, e're yet the Food
Of *Troy* they taste, or drink the *Xanthian* Flood.
Elsewhere he saw where *Troilus* defy'd
*Achilles,* and unequal Combat try'd:
Then, where the Boy disarm'd with loosen'd Reins,
Was by his Horses hurry'd o're the Plains:
Hung by the Neck and Hair, and drag'd around,   ⎫
The hostile Spear yet sticking in his Wound;       ⎬
With tracks of Blood inscrib'd the dusty Ground.   ⎭
670     Mean time the *Trojan* Dames oppress'd with Woe,   ⎫
To *Pallas* Fane in long Procession goe,              ⎬
In hopes to reconcile their Heav'nly Foe:             ⎭
They weep, they beat their Breasts, they rend their Hair,⎫
And rich embroider'd Vests for Presents bear:           ⎬
But the stern Goddess stands unmov'd with Pray'r.       ⎭

640  Fame] F1 *errata*, F2; Fate F1.
658  view:] ∼. F1–2.
664  try'd:] ∼. F1–2.
660  Lord:] ∼. F1–2.
671  Procession] F2; Precession F1.

Thrice round the *Trojan* Walls *Achilles* drew
The Corps of *Hector,* whom in Fight he slew.
Here *Priam* sues, and there, for Sums of Gold,
The lifeless Body of his Son is sold.
680 So sad an Object, and so well express'd,
Drew Sighs and Groans from the griev'd Heroes Breast:
To see the Figure of his lifeless Friend,
And his old Sire his helpless Hand extend.
Himself he saw amidst the *Grecian* Train,
Mix'd in the bloody Battel on the Plain.
And swarthy *Memnon* in his Arms he knew,
His pompous Ensigns, and his *Indian* Crew.
*Penthesilea* there, with haughty Grace,
Leads to the Wars an *Amazonian* Race:
690 In their right Hands a pointed Dart they wield;
The left, for Ward, sustains the Lunar Shield.
Athwart her Breast a Golden Belt she throws, ⎫
Amidst the Press alone provokes a thousand Foes: ⎬
And dares her Maiden Arms to Manly Force oppose. ⎭
Thus, while the *Trojan* Prince employs his Eyes,
Fix'd on the Walls with wonder and surprise;
The Beauteous *Dido,* with a num'rous Train,
And pomp of Guards, ascends the sacred Fane.
Such on *Eurotas* Banks, or *Cynthus* hight,
700 *Diana* seems; and so she charms the sight,
When in the Dance the graceful Goddess leads
The Quire of Nymphs, and overtops their Heads.
Known by her Quiver, and her lofty Meen,
She walks Majestick, and she looks their Queen:
*Latona* sees her shine above the rest,
And feeds with secret Joy her silent Breast.
Such *Dido* was; with such becoming State,
Amidst the Crowd, she walks serenely great.
Their Labour to her future Sway she speeds,
710 And passing with a gracious Glance proceeds:
Then mounts the Throne, high plac'd before the Shrine;

---

686   knew,] ∼ₐ F1–2.
688   *Penthesilea*] Penthisilea F1–2.
699   *Eurotas . . . Cynthus*] Eurota's . . . Cynthus's F1–2.

That we to good *Acestes* may return,
And with our Friends our common Losses mourn.
Thus spoke *Ilioneus;* the *Trojan* Crew
With Cries and Clamours his Request renew.
The modest Queen a while, with down-cast Eyes,
Ponder'd the Speech; then briefly thus replies.
790   *Trojans* dismiss your Fears: my cruel Fate,
And doubts attending an unsetled State,
Force me to guard my Coast, from Foreign Foes.
Who has not heard the story of your Woes?
The Name and Fortune of your Native Place,
The Fame and Valour of the *Phrygian* Race?
We *Tyrians* are not so devoid of Sense,
Nor so remote from *Phœbus* influence.
Whether to *Latian* Shores your Course is bent, ⎫
Or driv'n by Tempests from your first intent,   ⎬
800 You seek the good *Acestes* Government;         ⎭
Your Men shall be receiv'd, your Fleet repair'd,
And sail, with Ships of Convoy for your guard;
Or, wou'd you stay, and joyn your friendly Pow'rs, ⎫
To raise and to defend the *Tyrian* Tow'rs;        ⎬
My Wealth, my City, and my Self are yours.          ⎭
And wou'd to Heav'n the Storm, you felt, wou'd bring
On *Carthaginian* Coasts your wand'ring King.
My People shall, by my Command, explore
The Ports and Creeks of ev'ry winding shore;
810 And Towns, and Wilds, and shady Woods, in quest
Of so renown'd and so desir'd a Guest.
Rais'd in his Mind the *Trojan* Heroe stood,
And long'd to break from out his Ambient Cloud;
*Achates* found it; and thus urg'd his way;
From whence, O Goddess born, this long delay?
What more can you desire, your Welcome sure,
Your Fleet in safety, and your Friends secure?
One only wants; and him we saw in vain
Oppose the Storm, and swallow'd in the Main.
820 *Orontes* in his Fate our Forfeit paid,

---

799   Tempests] F2; Tempest's F1.

The rest agrees with what your Mother said.
Scarce had he spoken, when the Cloud gave way,
The Mists flew upward, and dissolv'd in day.
The *Trojan* Chief appear'd in open sight,
August in Visage, and serenely bright.
His Mother Goddess, with her hands Divine,
Had form'd his Curling Locks, and made his Temples shine:
And giv'n his rowling Eyes a sparkling grace;
And breath'd a youthful vigour on his Face:
830 Like polish'd Iv'ry, beauteous to behold,
Or *Parian* Marble, when enchas'd in Gold:
Thus radiant from the circling Cloud he broke;
And thus with manly modesty he spoke.
    He whom you seek am I: by Tempests tost,
And sav'd from Shipwreck on your *Lybian* Coast:
Presenting, gracious Queen, before your Throne,
A Prince that ows his Life to you alone.
Fair Majesty, the Refuge and Redress
Of those whom Fate pursues, and Wants oppress;
840 You, who your pious Offices employ
To save the Reliques of abandon'd *Troy;*
Receive the Shipwreck'd on your friendly Shore,
With hospitable Rites relieve the Poor:
Associate in your Town a wandring Train,
And Strangers in your Palace entertain.
What thanks can wretched Fugitives return,
Who scatter'd thro' the World in exile mourn?
The Gods, (if Gods to Goodness are inclin'd,)
If Acts of mercy touch their Heav'nly Mind;
850 And more than all the Gods, your gen'rous heart,
Conscious of worth, requite its own desert!
In you this Age is happy, and this Earth:
And Parents more than Mortal gave you birth.
While rowling Rivers into Seas shall run,
And round the space of Heav'n the radiant Sun;
While Trees the Mountain tops with Shades supply,
Your Honour, Name, and Praise shall never dye.

839 oppress;] ~. F1–2.

Æ.ı.l: 875.

To the Right Hon.ble Elizabeth Countess
Dowager of Winchelsea &c.ct

What e're abode my Fortune has assign'd,
Your Image shall be present in my Mind.
860 Thus having said; he turn'd with pious hast, ⎫
And joyful his expecting Friends embrac'd: ⎬
With his right hand *Ilioneus* was grac'd, ⎭
*Serestus* with his left; then to his breast ⎫
*Cloanthus* and the Noble *Gyas* prest; ⎬
And so by turns descended to the rest. ⎭
　　The *Tyrian* Queen stood fix'd upon his Face,
Pleas'd with his motions, ravish'd with his grace:
Admir'd his Fortunes, more admir'd the Man;
Then recollected stood; and thus began.
870 　　What Fate, O Goddess born, what angry Pow'rs
Have cast you shipwrack'd on our barren Shores?
Are you the great *Æneas,* known to Fame,
Who from Cœlestial Seed your Lineage claim!
The same *Æneas* whom fair *Venus* bore
To fam'd *Anchises* on th' *Idæan* Shore?
It calls into my mind, tho' then a Child,
When *Teucer* came from *Salamis* exil'd;
And sought my Father's aid, to be restor'd:
My Father *Belus* then with Fire and Sword
880 Invaded *Cyprus,* made the Region bare,
And, Conqu'ring, finish'd the successful War.
From him the *Trojan* Siege I understood,
The *Grecian* Chiefs, and your Illustrious Blood.
Your Foe himself the *Dardan* Valour prais'd,
And his own Ancestry from *Trojans* rais'd.
Enter, my Noble Guest; and you shall find,
If not a costly welcome, yet a kind.
For I my self, like you, have been distress'd;
Till Heav'n afforded me this place of rest.
890 Like you an Alien in a Land unknown;
I learn to pity Woes, so like my own.
She said, and to the Palace led her Guest,
Then offer'd Incense, and proclaim'd a Feast.
Nor yet less careful for her absent Friends,
Twice ten fat Oxen to the Ships she sends:

Besides a hundred Boars, a hundred Lambs,
With bleating cries, attend their Milky Dams.
And Jars of gen'rous Wine, and spacious Bowls,
She gives to chear the Sailors drooping Souls.
900 Now Purple Hangings cloath the Palace Walls,
And sumptuous Feasts are made in splendid Halls:
On *Tyrian* Carpets, richly wrought, they dine;
With loads of Massy Plate the Side-boards shine:
And Antique Vases all of Gold Emboss'd;
(The Gold it self inferiour to the Cost:)
Of curious Work, where on the sides were seen )
The Fights and Figures of Illustrious Men; }
From their first Founder to the present Queen. )
The Good *Æneas,* whose Paternal Care
910 *Iulus* absence could no longer bear,
Dispatch'd *Achates* to the Ships in hast,
To give a glad Relation of the past;
And, fraught with precious Gifts, to bring the Boy
Snatch'd from the Ruins of unhappy *Troy:*
A Robe of Tissue, stiff with golden Wire;
An upper Vest, once *Helen's* rich Attire;
From *Argos* by the fam'd Adultress brought,
With Golden flow'rs and winding foliage wrought;
Her Mother *Leda's* Present, when she came
920 To ruin *Troy,* and set the World on flame:
The Scepter *Priam's* eldest Daughter bore,
Her orient Necklace, and the Crown she wore;
Of double texture, glorious to behold;
One order set with Gems, and one with Gold.
Instructed thus, the wise *Achates* goes:
And in his diligence his duty shows.
But *Venus,* anxious for her Son's Affairs,
New Councils tryes; and new Designs prepares:
That *Cupid* should assume the Shape and Face
930 Of sweet *Ascanius,* and the sprightly grace:
Shou'd bring the Presents, in her Nephews stead,

---

903  shine:] ~. F1–2.        916  *Helen's*] *Hellen's* F1–2.
919  *Leda's*] *Læda's* F1–2.    920  flame:] ~. F1–2.

And in *Elisa*'s Veins the gentle Poison shed.
For much she fear'd the *Tyrians,* double tongu'd,
And knew the Town to *Juno*'s care belong'd.
These thoughts by Night her Golden Slumbers broke;
And thus alarm'd, to winged Love she spoke.
My Son, my strength, whose mighty Pow'r alone
Controuls the Thund'rer, on his awful Throne;
To thee thy much afflicted Mother flies,
940 And on thy Succour, and thy Faith relies.
Thou know'st, my Son, how *Jove*'s revengeful Wife,
By force and Fraud, attempts thy Brother's life.
And often hast thou mourn'd with me his Pains: ⎫
Him *Dido* now with Blandishment detains; ⎬
But I suspect the Town where *Juno* reigns. ⎭
For this, 'tis needful to prevent her Art,
And fire with Love the proud *Phœnician*'s heart:
A Love so violent, so strong, so sure,
As neither Age can change, nor Art can cure.
950 How this may be perform'd, now take my mind:
*Ascanius,* by his Father is design'd
To come, with Presents, laden from the Port,
To gratifie the Queen, and gain the Court.
I mean to plunge the Boy in pleasing Sleep,
And, ravish'd, in *Idalian* Bow'rs to keep;
Or high *Cythæra:* That the sweet Deceipt
May pass unseen, and none prevent the Cheat,
Take thou his Form and Shape. I beg the Grace ⎫
But only for a Night's revolving Space; ⎬
960 Thy self a Boy, assume a Boy's dissembled Face: ⎭
That when amidst the fervour of the Feast,
The *Tyrian* hugs, and fonds thee on her Breast,
And with sweet Kisses in her Arms constrains,
Thou may'st infuse thy Venom in her Veins.
The God of Love obeys, and sets aside
His Bow, and Quiver, and his plumy Pride:

---

932 *Elisa's*] *Eliza's* F1–2.
948 strong] F2; fond F1.
960 Face:] ~. F1–2.

947 heart:] ~. F1–2.
949 As] F2; That F1.

Unhappy *Dido* little thought what Guest,
How dire a God she drew so near her Breast.
But he, not mindless of his Mother's Pray'r,
Works in the pliant Bosom of the Fair;
And moulds her Heart anew, and blots her former Care.
The dead is to the living Love resign'd,
1010　And all *Æneas* enters in her Mind.
　　Now, when the Rage of Hunger was appeas'd,
The Meat remov'd, and ev'ry Guest was pleas'd;
The Golden Bowls with sparkling Wine are crown'd,
And through the Palace chearful Cries resound.
From gilded Roofs depending Lamps display
Nocturnal Beams, that emulate the Day.
A Golden Bowl, that shone with Gems Divine,
The Queen commanded to be crown'd with Wine;
The Bowl that *Belus* us'd, and all the *Tyrian* Line.
1020　Then, Silence through the Hall proclaim'd, she spoke:
O hospitable *Jove!* we thus invoke,
With solemn Rites, thy sacred Name and Pow'r!
Bless to both Nations this auspicious Hour.
So may the *Trojan* and the *Tyrian* Line,
In lasting Concord, from this Day combine.
Thou, *Bacchus*, God of Joys and friendly Cheer,
And gracious *Juno*, both be present here:
And you, my Lords of *Tyre,* your Vows address
To Heav'n with mine, to ratifie the Peace.
1030　The Goblet then she took, with Nectar crown'd,
(Sprinkling the first Libations on the Ground,)
And rais'd it to her Mouth with sober Grace,
Then sipping, offer'd to the next in place.
'Twas *Bitias* whom she call'd, a thirsty Soul,
He took the Challenge, and embrac'd the Bowl:
With Pleasure swill'd the Gold, nor ceas'd to draw,
'Till he the bottom of the Brimmer saw.
The Goblet goes around: *Iopas* brought
His Golden Lyre, and sung what ancient *Atlas* taught:

---

1024　*Trojan*] F2; *Tojan* F1.　　　　1030　Nectar] *Nectar* F1–2.
1039　taught:] ∼. F1–2.

1040 The various Labours of the wand'ring Moon,
And whence proceed th' Eclipses of the Sun:
Th' Original of Men, and Beasts; and whence ⎫
The Rains arise, and Fires their Warmth dispence; ⎬
And fix'd, and erring Stars, dispose their Influence: ⎭
What shakes the solid Earth, what Cause delays
The Summer Nights, and shortens Winter Days.
With Peals of Shouts the *Tyrians* praise the Song;
Those Peals are echo'd by the *Trojan* Throng.
Th' unhappy Queen with Talk prolong'd the Night,
1050 And drank large Draughts of Love with vast Delight:
Of *Priam* much enquir'd, of *Hector* more; ⎫
Then ask'd what Arms the swarthy *Memnon* wore; ⎬
What Troops he landed on the *Trojan* Shore: ⎭
The Steeds of *Diomede* vary'd the Discourse,
And fierce *Achilles,* with his matchless Force:
At length, as Fate and her ill Stars requir'd,
To hear the Series of the War desir'd.
Relate at large, my God-like Guest, she said,
The *Grecian* Stratagems, the Town betray'd;
1060 The fatal Issue of so long a War,
Your Flight, your Wand'rings, and your Woes declare.
For since on ev'ry Sea, on ev'ry Coast,
Your Men have been distress'd, your Navy tost,
Sev'n times the Sun has either Tropick view'd,
The Winter banish'd, and the Spring renew'd.

---

1041  Sun:] ∼. F1–2.               1044  Influence:] ∼. F1–2.
1050  Delight:] ∼. F1–2.          1053  Shore:] ∼. F1–2.
1054  *Diomede*] F1 *errata,* F2; *Di'mede* F1.
1055  Force:] ∼. F1–2.

To y<sup>e</sup> most Illustrious Prince Charles
Duke of Somerset Knight of y<sup>e</sup> most
Noble Order of y<sup>e</sup> Garter.

FOY POUR DEVOIR

Lombart. sculp. à Londre.

# The Second Book of the Æneis

## The Second Book of the Æneis

### THE ARGUMENT.

Æneas *relates how the City of* Troy *was taken, after a Ten Years Siege, by the Treachery of* Sinon, *and the Stratagem of a wooden Horse. He declares the fixt Resolution he had taken not to survive the Ruins of his Country, and the various Adventures he met with in the Defence of it: at last having been before advis'd by* Hector's *Ghost, and now by the Appearance of his Mother* Venus, *he is prevail'd upon to leave the Town, and settle his Houshold-Gods in another Country. In order to this, he carries off his Father on his Shoulders, and leads his little Son by the Hand, his Wife following him behind. When he comes to the Place appointed for the general Rendevouze, he finds a great Confluence of People, but misses his Wife, whose Ghost afterwards appears to him, and tells him the Land which was design'd for him.*

A LL were attentive to the God-like Man;
  When from his lofty Couch he thus began.
  Great Queen, what you command me to relate,
Renews the sad remembrance of our Fate.
An Empire from its old Foundations rent,
And ev'ry Woe the *Trojans* underwent:
A Peopl'd City made a Desart Place;
All that I saw, and part of which I was:
Not ev'n the hardest of our Foes cou'd hear,
10 Nor stern *Ulysses* tell without a Tear.
And now the latter Watch of wasting Night,
And setting Stars to kindly Rest invite.
But since you take such Int'rest in our Woe,
And *Troy*'s disast'rous end desire to know:
I will restrain my Tears, and briefly tell

---

8 *In order*] F2; *in order* F1.
2 his] F1 *errata*, F2; the F1.

What in our last and fatal Night befel.
   By Destiny compell'd, and in Despair,
The *Greeks* grew weary of the tedious War:
And by *Minerva*'s Aid a Fabrick rear'd,
20 Which like a Steed of monstrous height appear'd;
The Sides were planck'd with Pine, they feign'd it made
For their Return, and this the Vow they paid.
Thus they pretend, but in the hollow Side,
Selected Numbers of their Souldiers hide:
And inward Arms the dire Machine they load,
With Iron Bowels stuff the dark Abode.
In sight of *Troy* lies *Tenedos,* an Isle,
(While Fortune did on *Priam*'s Empire smile)
Renown'd for Wealth, but since a faithless Bay,
30 Where Ships expos'd to Wind and Weather lay.
There was their Fleet conceal'd: We thought for *Greece*
Their Sails were hoisted, and our Fears release.
The *Trojans* coop'd within their Walls so long,
Unbar their Gates, and issue in a Throng,
Like swarming Bees, and with Delight survey
The Camp deserted, where the *Grecians* lay:
The Quarters of the sev'ral Chiefs they show'd, ⎞
Here *Phœnix,* here *Achilles* made abode, ⎬
Here join'd the Battels, there the Navy rode. ⎠
40 Part on the Pile their wond'ring Eyes employ,
(The Pile by *Pallas* rais'd to ruin *Troy.*)
*Thymœtes* first ('tis doubtful whether hir'd,
Or so the *Trojan* Destiny requir'd)
Mov'd that the Ramparts might be broken down,
To lodge the monster Fabrique in the Town.
But *Capys,* and the rest of sounder Mind,
The fatal Present to the Flames design'd;
Or to the watry deep: At least to bore
The hollow sides, and hidden Frauds explore:
50 The giddy Vulgar, as their Fancies guide,
With Noise say nothing, and in parts divide.

---

25  And] F2; With F1.          42  *Thymœtes*] *Thymætes* F1–2.
45  monster Fabrique] F2 (Monster); fatal Engine F1.

*Laocoon,* follow'd by a num'rous Crowd,
Ran from the Fort; and cry'd, from far, aloud;
O wretched Country-men! what Fury reigns?
What more than Madness has possess'd your Brains?
Think you the *Grecians* from your Coasts are gone,
And are *Ulysses* Arts no better known?
This hollow Fabrick either must inclose,
Within its blind Recess, our secret Foes;
60 Or 'tis an Engine rais'd above the Town,
T' o'relook the Walls, and then to batter down.
Somewhat is sure design'd; by Fraud or Force;
Trust not their Presents, nor admit the Horse.
Thus having said, against the Steed he threw
His forceful Spear, which, hissing as it flew,
Pierc'd through the yielding Planks of jointed Wood,
And trembling in the hollow Belly stood.
The sides transpierc'd, return a ratling Sound,
And Groans of *Greeks* inclos'd come issuing through the Wound.
70 And had not Heav'n the fall of *Troy* design'd, ⎫
Or had not Men been fated to be blind, ⎬
Enough was said and done, t' inspire a better Mind: ⎭
Then had our Lances pierc'd the treach'rous Wood,
And *Ilian* Tow'rs, and *Priam*'s Empire stood.
Mean time, with Shouts, the *Trojan* Shepherds bring
A captive *Greek* in Bands, before the King:
Taken, to take; who made himself their Prey,
T' impose on their Belief, and *Troy* betray:
Fix'd on his Aim, and obstinately bent
80 To die undaunted, or to circumvent.
About the Captive, tides of *Trojans* flow;
All press to see, and some insult the Foe.
Now hear how well the *Greeks* their Wiles disguis'd,
Behold a Nation in a Man compris'd.
Trembling the Miscreant stood, unarm'd and bound;
He star'd, and rowl'd his hagger'd Eyes around:
Then said, Alas! what Earth remains, what Sea
Is open to receive unhappy me?

78  betray:] ~. F1–2.          88   me?] ~! F1–2.

*Æ. 2. l. 290.*

To the Right *Hon.*ble *James*
*Earle of Salisbury* &

With Cables haul along th' unweildy Beast.
310 Each on his Fellow for Assistance calls:
At length the fatal Fabrick mounts the Walls,
Big with Destruction. Boys with Chaplets crown'd,
And Quires of Virgins sing, and dance around.
Thus rais'd aloft, and then descending down,
It enters o're our Heads, and threats the Town.
O sacred City! built by Hands Divine!
O valiant Heroes of the *Trojan* Line!
Four times he struck; as oft the clashing sound
Of Arms was heard, and inward Groans rebound.
320 Yet mad with Zeal, and blinded with our Fate,
We hawl along the Horse, in solemn state;
Then place the dire Portent within the Tow'r.
*Cassandra* cry'd, and curs'd th' unhappy Hour;
Foretold our Fate; but by the Gods decree
All heard, and none believ'd the Prophecy.
With Branches we the Fanes adorn, and wast
In jollity, the Day ordain'd to be the last.
Mean time the rapid Heav'ns rowl'd down the Light,
And on the shaded Ocean rush'd the Night:
330 Our Men secure, nor Guards nor Centries held,
But easie Sleep their weary Limbs compell'd.
The *Grecians* had embark'd their Naval Pow'rs
From *Tenedos,* and sought our well known Shoars:
Safe under Covert of the silent Night,
And guided by th' Imperial Galley's light:
When *Sinon,* favour'd by the Partial Gods,
Unlock'd the Horse, and op'd his dark abodes:
Restor'd to vital Air our hidden Foes,
Who joyful from their long Confinement rose.
340 *Tysander* bold, and *Sthenelus* their Guide,
And dire *Ulysses* down the Cable slide:
Then *Thoas, Athamas,* and *Pyrrhus* hast;
Nor was the *Podalyrian* Heroe last:
Nor injur'd *Menelaus,* nor the fam'd
*Epeus,* who the fatal Engine fram'd.

---

335   light:] ~. F1–2.

In smoaky Flames, and catches on his Friends.
*Ucalegon* burns next; the Seas are bright
420 With splendor, not their own; and shine with *Trojan* light.
New Clamours, and new Clangors now arise,
The sound of Trumpets mix'd with fighting cries.
With frenzy seiz'd, I run to meet th' Alarms,
Resolv'd on death, resolv'd to die in Arms:
But first to gather Friends, with them t' oppose,
If Fortune favour'd, and repel the Foes:
Spurr'd by my courage, by my Country fir'd;
With sense of Honour, and Revenge inspir'd.
    *Panthus, Apollo*'s Priest, a sacred Name,
430 Had scap'd the *Grecian* Swords, and pass'd the Flame;
With Reliques loaden, to my Doors he fled,
And by the hand his tender Grand-son led.
What hope, O *Panthus!* whither can we run?
Where make a stand? and what may yet be done?
Scarce had I said, when *Panthus*, with a groan,
*Troy* is no more, and *Ilium* was a Town!
The fatal Day, th' appointed Hour is come,
When wrathful *Jove*'s irrevocable doom
Transfers the *Trojan* State to *Grecian* hands.
440 The Fire consumes the Town, the Foe commands:
And armed Hosts, an unexpected Force,
Break from the Bowels of the Fatal Horse.
Within the Gates, proud *Sinon* throws about
The flames, and Foes for entrance press without:
With thousand others, whom I fear to name,
More than from *Argos*, or *Mycenæ* came.
To sev'ral Posts their Parties they divide;
Some block the narrow Streets, some scour the wide.
The bold they kill, th' unwary they surprise;
450 Who fights finds Death, and Death finds him who flies.
The Warders of the Gate but scarce maintain
Th' unequal Combat, and resist in vain.
I Heard; and Heav'n, that well-born Souls inspires,

---

424  Arms:] ∼. F1–2.        426  Foes:] ∼. F1–2.
429, 433, 435  *Panthus*] *Pantheus* F1–2.    444  without:] ∼. F1–2.

Prompts me, thro' lifted Swords, and rising Fires
To run, where clashing Arms and Clamour calls,
And rush undaunted to defend the Walls.
*Ripheus* and *Iphitus* by my side engage,
For Valour one Renown'd, and one for Age.
*Dymas* and *Hypanis* by Moonlight knew
460 My motions, and my Meen, and to my Party drew;
With young *Chorœbus,* who by Love was led
To win Renown, and fair *Cassandra's* Bed;
And lately brought his Troops to *Priam's* aid:
Forewarn'd in vain, by the Prophetic Maid:
Whom, when I saw, resolv'd in Arms to fall,
And that one Spirit animated all;
Brave Souls, said I, but Brave, alas! in vain:
Come, finish what our Cruel Fates ordain.
You see the desp'rate state of our Affairs;
470 And Heav'ns protecting Pow'rs are deaf to Pray'rs.
The passive Gods behold the *Greeks* defile
Their Temples, and abandon to the Spoil
Their own Abodes: we, feeble few, conspire
To save a sinking Town, involv'd in Fire.
Then let us fall, but fall amidst our Foes;
Despair of Life, the Means of Living shows.
So bold a Speech incourag'd their desire
Of Death, and added fuel to their fire.
    As hungry Wolves, with raging appetite,
480 Scour thro' the fields, nor fear the stormy Night;
Their Whelps at home expect the promis'd Food,
And long to temper their dry Chaps in Blood:
So rush'd we forth at once, resolv'd to die,
Resolv'd in Death the last Extreams to try.
We leave the narrow Lanes behind, and dare  )
Th' unequal Combat in the publick Square:    }
Night was our Friend, our Leader was Despair. )
What Tongue can tell the Slaughter of that Night?
What Eyes can weep the Sorrows and Affright?

---

457  *Iphitus*] *Iph'itus* F1; *Iph'itas* F2.        464  Maid:] ~. F1-2.
475  Foes;] ~, F1-2.                                  477  bold] F2; fierce F1.
489  Affright?] ~! F1-2.

Æ.2.l:546.

To the Right Hon.ble            William O'Bryen Earle
of Inchiquin in the            Kingdom of Ireland &

With Fury charge us, and renew the Fight.
The Brother-Kings with *Ajax* join their force,
And the whole Squadron of *Thessalian* Horse.
   Thus, when the Rival Winds their Quarrel try,
Contending for the Kingdom of the Skie;
South, East, and West, on airy Coursers born,
The Whirlwind gathers, and the Woods are torn:
Then *Nereus* strikes the deep, the Billows rise,
570 And, mix'd with Ooze and Sand, pollute the Skies.
The Troops we squander'd first, again appear
From sev'ral Quarters, and enclose the Rear.
They first observe, and to the rest betray
Our diff'rent Speech; our borrow'd Arms survey.
Oppress'd with odds, we fall; *Chorœbus* first,
At *Pallas* Altar, by *Peneleus* pierc'd.
Then *Ripheus* follow'd, in th' unequal Fight;
Just of his Word, observant of the right;
Heav'n thought not so: *Dymas* their Fate attends,
580 With *Hypanis,* mistaken by their Friends.
Nor *Panthus,* thee, thy Mitre nor the Bands
Of awful *Phœbus,* sav'd from impious Hands.
Ye *Trojan* Flames your Testimony bear,
What I perform'd, and what I suffer'd there:
No Sword avoiding in the fatal Strife,
Expos'd to Death, and prodigal of Life.
Witness, ye Heav'ns! I live not by my Fault,
I strove to have deserv'd the Death I sought.
But when I cou'd not fight, and wou'd have dy'd,
590 Born off to distance by the growing Tide,
Old *Iphitus* and I were hurry'd thence,
With *Pelias* wounded, and without Defence.
New Clamors from th' invested Palace ring;
We run to die, or disengage the King.
So hot th' Assault, so high the Tumult rose,
While ours defend, and while the *Greeks* oppose;
As all the *Dardan* and *Argolick* Race

---

575  *Chorœbus*] *Chorœbus* F1–2.      576  *Pallas*] *Pallas's* F1–2.
581  *Panthus*] *Pantheus* F1–2.

Had been contracted in that narrow Space:
Or as all *Ilium* else were void of Fear,
600 And Tumult, War, and Slaughter only there.
Their Targets in a Tortoise cast, the Foes
Secure advancing, to the Turrets rose:
Some mount the scaling Ladders, some more bold
Swerve upwards, and by Posts and Pillars hold:
Their left hand gripes their Bucklers, in th' ascent,
While with the right they seise the Battlement.
From their demolish'd Tow'rs the *Trojans* throw
Huge heaps of Stones, that falling, crush the Foe:
And heavy Beams, and Rafters from the sides,
610 (Such Arms their last necessity provides:)
And gilded Roofs come tumbling from on high,
The marks of State, and ancient Royalty.
The Guards below, fix'd in the Pass, attend
The Charge undaunted, and the Gate defend.
Renew'd in Courage with recover'd Breath,
A second time we ran to tempt our Death:
To clear the Palace from the Foe, succeed
The weary living, and revenge the dead.
A Postern door, yet unobserv'd and free,
620 Join'd by the length of a blind Gallery,
To the King's Closet led; a way well known
To *Hector*'s Wife, while *Priam* held the Throne:
Through which she brought *Astyanax*, unseen,
To chear his Grandsire, and his Grandsire's Queen.
Through this we pass, and mount the Tow'r, from whence
With unavailing Arms the *Trojans* make defence.
From this the trembling King had oft descry'd
The *Grecian* Camp, and saw their Navy ride.
Beams from its lofty height with Swords we hew;
630 Then wrenching with our hands, th' Assault renew.
And where the Rafters on the Columns meet,
We push them headlong with our Arms and Feet:
The Lightning flies not swifter than the Fall;
Nor Thunder louder than the ruin'd Wall:

632   Feet:] *the colon printed as a period in some copies of F1.*

Down goes the top at once; the *Greeks* beneath
Are piecemeal torn, or pounded into Death.
Yet more succeed, and more to death are sent;
We cease not from above, nor they below relent.
Before the Gate stood *Pyrrhus,* threat'ning loud,
640 With glitt'ring Arms conspicuous in the Crowd.
So shines, renew'd in Youth, the crested Snake,
Who slept the Winter in a thorny Brake:
And casting off his Slough, when Spring returns,
Now looks aloft, and with new Glory burns:
Restor'd with pois'nous Herbs, his ardent sides
Reflect the Sun, and rais'd on Spires he rides:
High o're the Grass, hissing he rowls along,
And brandishes by fits his forky Tongue.
Proud *Periphas,* and fierce *Automedon,*
650 His Father's Charioteer, together run
To force the Gate: The *Scyrian* Infantry
Rush on in Crowds, and the barr'd Passage free.
Ent'ring the Court, with Shouts the Skies they rend,
And flaming Firebrands to the Roofs ascend.
Himself, among the foremost, deals his Blows,
And with his Axe repeated Stroaks bestows
On the strong Doors: then all their Shoulders ply,
'Till from the Posts the brazen Hinges fly.
He hews apace, the double Bars at length
660 Yield to his Ax, and unresisted Strength.
A mighty Breach is made; the Rooms conceal'd
Appear, and all the Palace is reveal'd:
The Halls of Audience, and of publick State,
And where the lonely Queen in secret sate.
Arm'd Souldiers now by trembling Maids are seen,
With not a Door, and scarce a Space between.
The House is fill'd with loud Laments and Cries,
And Shrieks of Women rend the vaulted Skies.
The fearful Matrons run from place to place,
670 And kiss the Thresholds, and the Posts embrace.
The fatal work inhuman *Pyrrhus* plies,

662 reveal'd:] ~. F1–2.

And all his Father sparkles in his Eyes.
Nor Bars, nor fighting Guards his force sustain;
The Bars are broken, and the Guards are slain.
In rush the *Greeks,* and all th' Apartments fill;
Those few Defendants whom they find, they kill.
Not with so fierce a Rage, the foaming Flood
Roars, when he finds his rapid Course withstood:
Bears down the Dams with unresisted sway,
680 And sweeps the Cattle and the Cots away.
These Eyes beheld him, when he march'd between
The Brother-Kings: I saw th' unhappy Queen,
The hundred Wives, and where old *Priam* stood,
To stain his hallow'd Altar with his Blood.
The fifty Nuptial Beds: (such Hopes had he,
So large a Promise of a Progeny:)
The Posts of plated Gold, and hung with Spoils,
Fell the Reward of the proud Victor's Toils.
Where e're the raging Fire had left a space,
690 The *Grecians* enter, and possess the Place.
Perhaps you may of *Priam*'s Fate enquire.
He, when he saw his Regal Town on fire,
His ruin'd Palace, and his ent'ring Foes,
On ev'ry side inevitable woes;
In Arms, disus'd, invests his Limbs, decay'd
Like them, with Age; a late and useless aid.
His feeble shoulders scarce the weight sustain: ⎫
Loaded, not arm'd, he creeps along, with pain; ⎬
Despairing of Success; ambitious to be slain! ⎭
700 Uncover'd but by Heav'n, there stood in view
An Altar; near the hearth a Lawrel grew;
Dodder'd with Age, whose Boughs encompass round
The Household Gods, and shade the holy Ground.
Here *Hecuba,* with all her helpless Train
Of Dames, for shelter sought, but sought in vain.
Driv'n like a Flock of Doves along the skie,
Their Images they hugg, and to their Altars fly.

---

675   th' Apartments] the Apartments F1-2.
686   Progeny:)] ∼.) F1-2.                              695   Limbs,] ∼ˌ F1-2.

The Queen, when she beheld her trembling Lord,
And hanging by his side a heavy Sword,
710 What Rage, she cry'd, has seiz'd my Husband's mind;
What Arms are these, and to what use design'd?
These times want other aids: were *Hector* here,
Ev'n *Hector* now in vain, like *Priam* wou'd appear.
With us, one common shelter thou shalt find,
Or in one common Fate with us be join'd.
She said, and with a last Salute embrac'd
The poor old Man, and by the Lawrel plac'd.
Behold *Polites,* one of *Priam*'s Sons,
Pursu'd by *Pyrrhus,* there for safety runs.
720 Thro Swords, and Foes, amaz'd and hurt, he flies
Through empty Courts, and open Galleries:
Him *Pyrrhus,* urging with his Lance, pursues;
And often reaches, and his thrusts renews.
The Youth transfix'd, with lamentable Cries
Expires, before his wretched Parent's Eyes:
Whom, gasping at his feet, when *Priam* saw,
The Fear of death gave place to Nature's Law.
And shaking more with Anger, than with Age,
The Gods, said He, requite thy brutal Rage:
730 As sure they will, Barbarian, sure they must,
If there be Gods in Heav'n, and Gods be just:
Who tak'st in Wrongs an insolent delight;
With a Son's death t' infect a Father's sight.
Not He, whom thou and lying Fame conspire
To call thee his; Not He, thy vaunted Sire,
Thus us'd my wretched Age: The Gods he fear'd,
The Laws of Nature and of Nations heard.
He chear'd my Sorrows, and for Sums of Gold
The bloodless Carcass of my *Hector* sold:
740 Pity'd the Woes a Parent underwent,
And sent me back in safety from his Tent.
   This said, his feeble hand a Javelin threw,
Which flutt'ring, seem'd to loiter as it flew:
Just, and but barely, to the Mark it held,

725   Eyes:] ~. F1-2.          739   sold:] ~. F1-2.

That common Bane of *Greece* and *Troy*, I found.
780 For *Ilium* burnt, she dreads the *Trojan* Sword; ⎞
More dreads the Vengeance of her injur'd Lord; ⎬
Ev'n by those Gods, who refug'd her, abhorr'd. ⎠
Trembling with Rage, the Strumpet I regard;
Resolv'd to give her Guilt the due reward.
Shall she triumphant sail before the Wind,
And leave in Flames, unhappy *Troy* behind?
Shall she, her Kingdom and her Friends review,
In State attended with a Captive Crew;
While unreveng'd the good old *Priam* falls,
790 And *Grecian* Fires consume the *Trojan* Walls?
For this the *Phrygian* Fields, and *Xanthian* Flood
Were swell'd with Bodies, and were drunk with Blood?
'Tis true a Souldier can small Honour gain,
And boast no Conquest from a Woman slain:
Yet shall the Fact not pass without Applause,
Of Vengeance taken in so just a Cause.
The punish'd Crime shall set my Soul at ease:
And murm'ring *Manes* of my Friends appease.
Thus while I rave, a gleam of pleasing Light ⎞
800 Spread o're the Place, and shining Heav'nly bright, ⎬
My Mother stood reveal'd before my Sight. ⎠
Never so radiant did her Eyes appear;
Not her own Star confess'd a Light so clear.
Great in her Charms, as when on Gods above
She looks, and breaths her self into their Love,
She held my hand, the destin'd Blow to break:
Then from her rosie Lips began to speak.
My Son, from whence this Madness, this neglect
Of my Commands, and those whom I protect?
810 Why this unmanly Rage? Recall to mind
Whom you forsake, what Pledges leave behind.
Look if your helpless Father yet survive;
Or if *Ascanius*, or *Creusa* live.

798  *Manes*] Manes F1–2.
805  Love,] ∼. F1–2.

Around your House the greedy *Grecians* err; }
And these had perish'd in the nightly War, }
But for my Presence and protecting Care. }
Not *Helen's* Face, nor *Paris* was in fault;
But by the Gods was this Destruction brought.
Now cast your Eyes around; while I dissolve
820 The Mists and Films that mortal Eyes involve:
Purge from your sight the Dross, and make you see
The Shape of each avenging Deity.
Enlighten'd thus, my just Commands fulfill;
Nor fear Obedience to your Mother's Will.
Where yon disorder'd heap of Ruin lies,
Stones rent from Stones, where Clouds of dust arise,
Amid that smother, *Neptune* holds his place: }
Below the Wall's foundation drives his Mace: }
And heaves the Building from the solid Base. }
830 Look where, in Arms, Imperial *Juno* stands, }
Full in the *Scæan* Gate, with loud Commands; }
Urging on Shore the tardy *Grecian* Bands. }
See, *Pallas,* of her snaky Buckler proud,
Bestrides the Tow'r, refulgent through the Cloud:
See, *Jove* new Courage to the Foe supplies,
And arms against the Town, the partial Deities.
Haste hence, my Son; this fruitless Labour end: }
Haste where your trembling Spouse, and Sire attend: }
Haste, and a Mother's Care your Passage shall befriend. }
840 She said: and swiftly vanish'd from my Sight,
Obscure in Clouds, and gloomy Shades of Night.
I look'd, I listen'd; dreadful Sounds I hear;
And the dire Forms of hostile Gods appear.
*Troy* sunk in Flames I saw, nor could prevent;
And *Ilium* from its old Foundations rent:
Rent like a Mountain Ash, which dar'd the Winds;
And stood the sturdy Stroaks of lab'ring Hinds:
About the Roots the cruel Ax resounds,

---

833, 835  See,] ~‸ F1–2.
845  rent:] ~. F1–2.

F Clein inv.     W. Hollar fecit     E 2. l. 015.

To whom do you expose your Father's Life,
Your Son's, and mine, your now forgotten Wife?
While thus she fills the House with clam'rous Cries,
Our Hearing is diverted by our Eyes.
For while I held my Son, in the short space,
Betwixt our Kisses and our last Embrace;
930 Strange to relate, from young *Iulus* Head          )
A lambent Flame arose, which gently spread          }
Around his Brows, and on his Temples fed.          )
Amaz'd, with running Water we prepare
To quench the sacred Fire, and shake his Hair;
But old *Anchises,* vers'd in Omens, rear'd
His hands to Heav'n, and this request preferr'd.
If any Vows, Almighty *Jove,* can bend          )
Thy Will, if Piety can Pray'rs commend,          }
Confirm the glad Presage which thou art pleas'd to send. )
940 Scarce had he said, when, on our left, we hear
A peal of ratling Thunder rowl in Air:
There shot a streaming Lamp along the Sky,
Which on the winged Lightning seem'd to fly;
From o're the Roof the blaze began to move;
And trailing vanish'd in th' *Idean* Grove.
It swept a path in Heav'n, and shone a Guide;
Then in a steaming stench of Sulphur dy'd.
   The good old Man with suppliant hands implor'd
The Gods protection, and their Star ador'd.
950 Now, now, said he, my Son, no more delay,
I yield, I follow where Heav'n shews the way.
Keep (O my Country Gods) our dwelling Place,
And guard this Relick of the *Trojan* Race:
This tender Child; these Omens are your own;
And you can yet restore the ruin'd Town.
At least accomplish what your Signs foreshow:
I stand resign'd, and am prepar'd to go.
   He said; the crackling Flames appear on high,
And driving Sparkles dance along the Sky.
960 With *Vulcan*'s rage the rising Winds conspire;

925   Wife?] ∼! F1–2.

Cry'd out, Haste, haste my Son, the Foes are nigh;
Their Swords, and shining Armour I descry.
Some hostile God, for some unknown Offence,
Had sure bereft my Mind of better Sence:
1000 For while through winding Ways I took my Flight;
And sought the shelter of the gloomy Night;
Alas! I lost *Creusa:* hard to tell
If by her fatal Destiny she fell,
Or weary sate, or wander'd with affright,
But she was lost for ever to my sight.
I knew not, or reflected, 'till I meet
My Friends, at *Ceres* now deserted Seat:
We met: not one was wanting, only she
Deceiv'd her Friends, her Son, and wretched me.
1010 What mad expressions did my Tongue refuse?
Whom did I not of Gods or Men accuse?
This was the fatal Blow, that pain'd me more
Than all I felt from ruin'd *Troy* before.
Stung with my Loss, and raving with Despair,
Abandoning my now forgotten Care,
Of Counsel, Comfort, and of Hope bereft,
My Sire, my Son, my Country Gods, I left.
In shining Armour once again I sheath
My Limbs, not feeling Wounds, nor fearing Death.
1020 Then headlong to the burning Walls I run,
And seek the Danger I was forc'd to shun.
I tread my former Tracks: through Night explore
Each Passage, ev'ry Street I cross'd before.
All things were full of Horrour and Affright,
And dreadful ev'n the silence of the Night.
Then, to my Father's House I make repair,
With some small Glimps of hope to find her there:
Instead of her the cruel *Greeks* I met;
The house was fill'd with Foes, with Flames beset.
1030 Driv'n on the wings of Winds, whole sheets of Fire,
Through Air transported, to the Roofs aspire.

---

996   Haste, haste] haste, haste F1–2.          1010   expressions] F2; expessions F1.
1010   refuse?] ∼! F1–2.                         1011   accuse?] ∼! F1–2.

From thence to *Priam*'s Palace I resort;
And search the Citadel, and desart Court.
Then, unobserv'd, I pass by *Juno*'s Church;
A guard of *Grecians* had possess'd the Porch:
There *Phœnix* and *Ulysses* watch the Prey:
And thither all the Wealth of *Troy* convey:
The Spoils which they from ransack'd Houses brought;
And golden Bowls from burning Altars caught:
1040 The Tables of the Gods, the Purple Vests;
The People's Treasure, and the Pomp of Priests.
A ranck of wretched Youths, with pinion'd Hands,
And captive Matrons in long Order stands.
Then, with ungovern'd Madness, I proclaim,
Through all the silent Streets, *Creusa*'s Name.
*Creusa* still I call: At length she hears;
And suddain, through the Shades of Night appears:
Appears, no more *Creusa*, nor my Wife:
But a pale Spectre, larger than the Life.
1050 Aghast, astonish'd, and struck dumb with Fear,
I stood; like Bristles rose my stiffen'd Hair.
Then thus the Ghost began to sooth my Grief:
Nor Tears, nor Cries can give the dead Relief;
Desist, my much lov'd Lord, t' indulge your Pain:
You bear no more than what the Gods ordain.
My Fates permit me not from hence to fly;
Nor he, the great Comptroller of the Sky.
Long wandring Ways for you the Pow'rs decree:
On Land hard Labors, and a length of Sea.
1060 Then, after many painful Years are past,
On *Latium*'s happy Shore you shall be cast:
Where gentle *Tiber* from his Bed beholds
The flow'ry Meadows, and the feeding Folds.
There end your Toils: And there your Fates provide
A quiet Kingdom, and a Royal Bride:
There Fortune shall the *Trojan* Line restore;

1036 *Phœnix*] *Phænix* F1–2.          1037 convey:] ∼. F1–2.
1038 brought] F2; bronght F1.          1039 caught:] ∼. F1–2.
1047 appears:] ∼. F1–2.               1050 struck] F2; struk F1.

And you for lost *Creusa* weep no more.
Fear not that I shall watch with servile Shame,
Th' imperious Looks of some proud *Grecian* Dame:
1070 Or, stooping to the Victor's Lust, disgrace
My Goddess Mother, or my Royal Race.
And now, farewell: the Parent of the Gods
Restrains my fleeting Soul in her Abodes:
I trust our common Issue to your Care.
She said: And gliding pass'd unseen in Air.
I strove to speak, but Horror ty'd my Tongue; ⎫
And thrice about her Neck my Arms I flung; ⎬
And thrice deceiv'd, on vain Embraces hung. ⎭
Light as an empty Dream at break of Day,
1080 Or as a blast of Wind, she rush'd away.
     Thus, having pass'd the Night in fruitless Pain,
I, to my longing Friends, return again:
Amaz'd th' augmented Number to behold,
Of Men, and Matrons mix'd, of young and old:
A wretched Exil'd Crew together brought,
With Arms appointed, and With Treasure fraught:
Resolv'd, and willing under my Command,
To run all hazards both of Sea and Land.
The Morn began, from *Ida*, to display
1090 Her rosy Cheeks, and *Phosphor* led the day;
Before the Gates the *Grecians* took their Post:
And all pretence of late Relief was lost.
I yield to Fate, unwillingly retire;
And loaded, up the Hill convey my Sire.

------

1082   again:] ∼. F1–2.                    1086   fraught:] ∼. F1–2.

To the Right Hon.ble William Stanley
Earle of Derby &c.d L.d of Man & y Isles

SANS CHANGER

## The Third Book of the Æneis

### THE ARGUMENT.

*Æneas proceeds in his Relation: He gives an Account of the Fleet with which he sail'd, and the Success of his first Voyage to* Thrace; *from thence he directs his Course to* Delos, *and asks the Oracle what place the Gods had appointed for his Habitation? By a mistake of the Oracle's Answer, he settles in* Crete; *his household Gods give him the true sense of the Oracle, in a Dream. He follows their advice, and makes the best of his way for* Italy: *He is cast on several Shores, and meets with very surprising Adventures,'till at length he lands on* Sicily: *where his Father* Anchises *dies. This is the place which he was sailing from when the Tempest rose and threw him upon the* Carthaginian *Coast.*

WHEN Heav'n had overturn'd the *Trojan* State,
And *Priam*'s Throne, by too severe a Fate:
When ruin'd *Troy* became the *Grecians* Prey,
And *Ilium*'s lofty Tow'rs in Ashes lay:
Warn'd by Cœlestial Omens, we retreat,
To seek in foreign Lands a happier Seat.
Near old *Antandros,* and at *Ida*'s foot,
The Timber of the sacred Groves we cut:
And build our Fleet; uncertain yet to find
10 What place the Gods for our Repose assign'd.
Friends daily flock; and scarce the kindly Spring
Began to cloath the Ground, and Birds to sing;
When old *Anchises* summon'd all to Sea:
The Crew, my Father and the Fates obey.
With Sighs and Tears I leave my native Shore,
And empty Fields, where *Ilium* stood before.
My Sire, my Son, our less, and greater Gods,
All sail at once; and cleave the briny Floods.
  Against our Coast appears a spacious Land,

18   cleave] F2; tempt F1.

20 Which once the fierce *Lycurgus* did command:
*Thracia* the Name; the People bold in War;
Vast are their Fields, and Tillage is their Care:
A hospitable Realm while Fate was kind;
With *Troy* in friendship and Religion join'd.
I land; with luckless Omens, then adore
Their Gods, and draw a Line along the Shore:
I lay the deep Foundations of a Wall;
And *Ænos,* nam'd from me, the City call.
To *Dionæan Venus* Vows are paid,
30 And all the Pow'rs that rising Labours aid;
A Bull on *Jove*'s Imperial Altar laid.
Not far, a rising Hillock stood in view;
Sharp Myrtles, on the sides, and Cornels grew.
There, while I went to crop the Silvan Scenes,
And shade our Altar with their leafy Greens;
I pull'd a Plant; (with horror I relate
A Prodigy so strange, and full of Fate.)
The rooted Fibers rose; and from the Wound,
Black bloody Drops distill'd upon the Ground.
40 Mute, and amaz'd, my Hair with Terrour stood;
Fear shrunk my Sinews, and congeal'd my Blood.
Man'd once again, another Plant I try;
That other gush'd with the same sanguine Dye.
Then, fearing Guilt, for some Offence unknown,
With Pray'rs and Vows the Dryads I attone:
With all the Sisters of the Woods, and most
The God of Arms, who rules the *Thracian* Coast:
That they, or he, these Omens wou'd avert;
Release our Fears, and better signs impart.
50 Clear'd, as I thought, and fully fix'd at length
To learn the Cause, I tug'd with all my Strength;
I bent my knees against the Ground; once more
The violated Myrtle ran with Gore.

---

22  Care:] ∼. F1–2.
36–37  (with . . . Fate.)] F2; ∧∼ . . . ∼·∧ F1.
40  Terrour] F1 *errata,* F2; Horror F1.
45  Dryads] *Driads* F1–2.
28  *Ænos*] *Enos* F1–2.
53  with] F2; with purple F1.

Scarce dare I tell the Sequel: From the Womb
Of wounded Earth, and Caverns of the Tomb,
A Groan, as of a troubled Ghost, renew'd
My Fright, and then these dreadful Words ensu'd.
Why dost thou thus my bury'd Body rend?
O spare the Corps of thy unhappy Friend!
60 Spare to pollute thy pious Hands with Blood:
The Tears distil not from the wounded Wood;
But ev'ry drop this living Tree contains,
Is kindred Blood, and ran in *Trojan* Veins:
O fly from this unhospitable Shore,
Warn'd by my Fate; for I am *Polydore!*
Here loads of Lances, in my Blood embru'd,
Again shoot upward, by my Blood renew'd.
    My faultring Tongue, and shiv'ring Limbs declare
My Horror, and in Bristles rose my Hair.
70 When *Troy* with *Grecian* Arms was closely pent, )
Old *Priam,* fearful of the Wars Event,          }
This hapless *Polydore* to *Thracia* sent.       )
Loaded with Gold, he sent his Darling, far       )
From Noise and Tumults, and destructive War:     }
Commited to the faithless Tyrant's Care:         )
Who, when he saw the Pow'r of *Troy* decline,
Forsook the weaker, with the strong to join:
Broke ev'ry Bond of Nature, and of Truth;
And murder'd, for his Wealth, the Royal Youth.
80 O sacred Hunger of pernicious Gold,
What bands of Faith can impious Lucre hold?
Now, when my Soul had shaken off her Fears,
I call my Father, and the *Trojan* Peers:
Relate the Prodigies of Heav'n; require
What he commands, and their Advice desire.
All vote to leave that execrable Shore,
Polluted with the Blood of *Polydore:*
But e're we sail, his Fun'ral Rites prepare;

75  Care:] ~. F1–2.          77  join:] ~. F1–2.
81  hold?] ~! F1–2.          87  *Polydore:*] ~. F1–2.

Æ. 3 l: 110                    Lambert. fæ.l.A. la. ly

To the Right Hon:ble Nathanael Lord.
Bishop of Durham

Then, to his Ghost, a Tomb and Altars rear.
90 In mournful Pomp the Matrons walk the round: 
   With baleful Cypress, and blue Fillets crown'd;
   With Eyes dejected, and with Hair unbound.
Then Bowls of tepid Milk and Blood we pour,
And thrice invoke the Soul of *Polydore.*

   Now when the raging Storms no longer reign;
But Southern Gales invite us to the Main;
We launch our Vessels, with a prosp'rous Wind;
And leave the Cities and the Shores behind.
   An Island in th' *Ægean* Main appears:
100 *Neptune* and wat'ry *Doris* claim it theirs.
It floated once, till *Phœbus* fix'd the sides
To rooted Earth, and now it braves the Tides.
Here, born by friendly Winds, we come ashore; 
   With needful ease our weary Limbs restore;
   And the Sun's Temple, and his Town adore.
   *Anius* the Priest, and King, with Lawrel crown'd,
His hoary Locks with purple Fillets bound,
Who saw my Sire the *Delian* Shore ascend,
Came forth with eager haste to meet his Friend:
110 Invites him to his Palace; and in sign
Of ancient Love, their plighted Hands they join.
Then to the Temple of the God I went;
And thus, before the Shrine, my Vows present.
Give,' O *Thymbræus,* give a resting place,
To the sad Relicks of the *Trojan* Race:
A Seat secure, a Region of their own,
A lasting Empire, and a happier Town.
Where shall we fix, where shall our Labours end,
Whom shall we follow, and what Fate attend?
120 Let not my Pray'rs a doubtful Answer find,
But in clear Auguries unveil thy Mind.
Scarce had I said, He shook the holy Ground: 
   The Lawrels, and the lofty Hills around: 
   And from the Tripos rush'd a bellowing sound. 

---

89  rear.] ∼, F1–2.
109  Friend:] ∼. F1–2.
103  ashore;] ∼ₐ F1–2.
124  Tripos] *Tripos* F1–2.

Prostrate we fell; confess'd the present God,
Who gave this Answer from his dark Abode.
Undaunted Youths, go seek that Mother Earth
From which your Ancestors derive their Birth.
The Soil that sent you forth, her Ancient Race,
130   In her old Bosom, shall again embrace.
Through the wide World th' *Æneian* House shall reign,
And Childrens Children shall the Crown sustain.
Thus *Phœbus* did our future Fates disclose;
A mighty Tumult, mix'd with Joy, arose.
     All are concern'd to know what place the God
Assign'd, and where determind our abode.
My Father, long revolving in His Mind,
The Race and Lineage of the *Trojan* Kind,
Thus answer'd their demands: Ye Princes, hear
140   Your pleasing Fortune; and dispel your fear.
The fruitful Isle of *Crete* well known to Fame,
Sacred of old to *Jove*'s Imperial Name,
In the mid Ocean lies, with large Command;
And on its Plains a hundred Cities stand.
Another *Ida* rises there; and we
From thence derive our *Trojan* Ancestry.
From thence, as 'tis divulg'd by certain Fame,
To the *Rhœtean* Shores old *Teucrus* came:
There fix'd, and there the Seat of Empire chose,
150   E're *Ilium* and the *Trojan* Tow'rs arose.
In humble Vales they built their soft abodes:
Till *Cybele,* the Mother of the Gods,
With tinckling Cymbals charm'd th' *Idean* Woods.
She, secret Rites and Ceremonies taught,
And to the Yoke, the salvage Lions brought.
Let us the Land, which Heav'n appoints, explore;
Appease the Winds, and seek the *Gnossian* Shore.
If *Jove* assists the passage of our Fleet,

---

131   *Æneian*] F2; *Eneian* F1.
142   Imperial] F2; Immortal F1.
142   Name,] F1 *errata,* F2; ~. F1.
148   *Rhœtean* . . . came:] *Rhœtean* . . . came. F1–2.
158   the] F2; tht F1.

The third propitious dawn discovers *Creet*.
160 Thus having said, the Sacrifices laid
On smoking Altars, to the Gods He paid:
A Bull, to *Neptune* an Oblation due,
Another Bull to bright *Apollo* slew:
A milk white Ewe the Western Winds to please;
And one cole black to calm the stormy Seas.
E're this, a flying Rumour had been spred,
That fierce *Idomeneus* from *Crete* was fled;
Expell'd and exil'd; that the Coast was free
From Foreign or Domestick Enemy:
170 We leave the *Delian* Ports, and put to Sea:
By *Naxos,* fam'd for Vintage, make our way:
Then green *Donysa* pass; and Sail in sight
Of *Paros* Isle, with Marble Quarries white.
We pass the scatter'd Isles of *Cyclades;*
That, scarce distinguish'd, seem to stud the Seas.
The shouts of Saylors double near the shores;
They stretch their Canvass, and they ply their Oars.
All hands aloft, For *Creet* for *Creet* they cry,
And swiftly through the foamy Billows fly.
180 Full on the promis'd Land at length we bore,
With Joy descending on the *Cretan* Shore.
With eager haste a rising Town I frame,
Which from the *Trojan Pergamus* I name:
The Name it self was grateful; I exhort
To found their Houses, and erect a Fort.
Our Ships are haul'd upon the yellow strand,
The Youth begin to till the labour'd Land.
And I my self new Marriages promote,
Give Laws: and Dwellings I divide by Lot:
190 When rising Vapours choak the wholesom Air,
And blasts of noisom Winds corrupt the Year:
The Trees, devouring Caterpillers burn:

161 paid:] ∼. F1–2.
177 Canvass,] F2; ∼„ F1.
178 aloft, For] ∼, for F1–2.
181 descending] F2; desending F1.
189 Lot:] ∼. F1–2.

Parch'd was the Grass, and blited was the Corn.
Nor scape the Beasts: for *Syrius* from on high, ⎞
With pestilential Heat infects the Sky: ⎟
My Men, some fall, the rest in Feavers fry. ⎠
Again my Father bids me seek the Shore
Of sacred *Delos;* and the God implore:
To learn what end of Woes we might expect,
200 And to what Clime, our weary Course direct.
    'Twas Night, when ev'ry Creature, void of Cares,
The common gift of balmy Slumber shares:
The Statues of my Gods, (for such they seem'd)
Those Gods whom I from flaming *Troy* redeem'd,
Before me stood; Majestically bright,
Full in the Beams of *Phœbe*'s entring light.
Then thus they spoke; and eas'd my troubled Mind:
What from the *Delian* God thou go'st to find,
He tells thee here; and sends us to relate:
210 Those Pow'rs are we, Companions of thy Fate,
Who from the burning Town by thee were brought;
Thy Fortune follow'd, and thy safety wrought.
Through Seas and Lands, as we thy Steps attend,
So shall our Care thy Glorious Race befriend.
An ample Realm for thee thy Fates ordain;
A Town, that o're the conquer'd World shall reign.
Thou, mighty Walls for mighty Nations build;
Nor let thy weary Mind to Labours yield:
But change thy Seat; for not the *Delian* God,
220 Nor we, have giv'n thee *Crete* for our Abode.
A Land there is, *Hesperia* call'd of old,
The Soil is fruitful, and the Natives bold.
Th' *Oenotrians* held it once; by later Fame,
Now call'd *Italia* from the Leader's Name.
*Iäsius* there, and *Dardanus* were born:
From thence we came, and thither must return.
Rise, and thy Sire with these glad Tidings greet;
Search *Italy,* for *Jove* denies thee *Creet.*
    Astonish'd at their Voices, and their sight,

---

225   *indented in F1–2 (Jäsius).*          229   *not indented in F1–2.*

230 (Nor were they Dreams, but Visions of the Night;
I saw, I knew their Faces, and descry'd
In perfect View, their Hair with Fillets ty'd:)
I started from my Couch; a clammy Sweat
On all my Limbs, and shiv'ring Body sate.
To Heav'n I lift my Hands with pious haste,
And sacred Incense in the Flames I cast.
Thus to the Gods their perfect Honours done,
More chearful to my good old Sire I run:
And tell the pleasing News; in little space
240 He found his Error, of the double Race:
Not, as before he deem'd, deriv'd from *Creet;*
No more deluded by the doubtful Seat:
Then said, O Son, turmoil'd in *Trojan* Fate;
Such things as these *Cassandra* did relate.
This Day revives within my Mind, what she
Foretold of *Troy* renew'd in *Italy;*
And *Latian* Lands: but who cou'd then have thought, ⎫
That *Phrygian* Gods to *Latium* should be brought; ⎬
Or who believ'd what mad *Cassandra* taught? ⎭
250 Now let us go, where *Phœbus* leads the way.
He said, and we with glad Consent obey:
Forsake the Seat; and leaving few behind,
We spread our sails before the willing Wind.
Now from the sight of Land, our Gallies move,
With only Seas around, and Skies above:
When o're our Heads, descends a burst of Rain;
And Night, with sable Clouds involves the Main:
The ruffling Winds the foamy Billows raise:
The scatter'd Fleet is forc'd to sev'ral Ways:
260 The face of Heav'n is ravish'd from our Eyes,
And in redoubl'd Peals the roaring Thunder flys.
Cast from our Course, we wander in the Dark;
No Stars to guide, no point of Land to mark.
Ev'n *Palinurus* no distinction found

---

233  Couch;] ∼, F1–2.
242  Seat:] ∼. F1–2.
251  obey:] ∼. F1–2.

240  Race:] ∼. F1–2.
250  way.] ∼: F1–2.
255  above:] ∼. F1–2.

Betwixt the Night and Day; such Darkness reign'd around.
Three starless Nights the doubtful Navy strays
Without Distinction, and three Sunless Days.
The fourth renews the Light, and from our Shrowds
We view a rising Land like distant Clouds:
270 The Mountain tops confirm the pleasing Sight;
And curling Smoke ascending from their Height.
The Canvas falls; their Oars the Sailors ply;
From the rude strokes the whirling Waters fly.
At length I land upon the *Strophades;*
Safe from the danger of the stormy Seas:
Those Isles are compass'd by th' *Ionian* Main;
The dire Abode where the foul Harpies reign:
Forc'd by the winged Warriors to repair
To their old Homes, and leave their costly Fare.
280 Monsters more fierce, offended Heav'n ne're sent
From Hell's Abyss, for Human Punishment:
With Virgin-faces, but with Wombs obscene,      ⎞
Foul Paunches, and with Ordure still unclean:   ⎬
With Claws for Hands, and Looks for ever lean.  ⎠
    We landed at the Port; and soon beheld
Fat Herds of Oxen graze the flowry Field:
And wanton Goats without a Keeper stray'd:
With Weapons we the welcome Prey invade:
Then call the Gods, for Partners of our Feast:
290 And *Jove* himself the chief invited Guest.
We spread the Tables, on the greensword Ground:
We feed with Hunger, and the Bowls go round:
When from the Mountain tops, with hideous Cry,
And clatt'ring Wings, the hungry Harpies fly:
They snatch the Meat; defiling all they find:
And parting leave a loathsom Stench behind.
Close by a hollow Rock, again we sit;
New dress the Dinner, and the Beds refit:
Secure from Sight, beneath a pleasing Shade;
300 Where tufted Trees a native Arbour made.

---

277  Harpies] *Harpies* F1–2.              281  Punishment:] ∼. F1–2.
288  invade:] ∼. F1–2.                     292  round:] ∼. F1–2.

Again the Holy Fires on Altars burn:
And once again the rav'nous Birds return:
Or from the dark Recesses where they ly,
Or from another Quarter of the Sky:
With filthy Claws their odious Meal repeat,
And mix their loathsom Ordures with their Meat.
I bid my Friends for Vengeance then prepare;
And with the Hellish Nation wage the War.
They, as commanded, for the Fight provide,
310 And in the Grass their glitt'ring Weapons hide:
Then, when along the crooked Shoar we hear
Their clatt'ring Wings, and saw the Foes appear;
*Misenus* sounds a charge: We take th' Alarm;
And our strong hands with Swords and Bucklers arm.
In this new kind of Combat, all employ
Their utmost Force, the Monsters to destroy.
In vain; the fated Skin is proof to Wounds:
And from their Plumes the shining Sword rebounds.
At length rebuff'd, they leave their mangled Prey,
320 And their stretch'd Pinions to the Skies display.
Yet one remain'd, the Messenger of Fate; ⎫
High on a craggy Cliff *Celæno* sate,           ⎬
And thus her dismal Errand did relate.   ⎭
What, not contented with our Oxen slain,      ⎫
Dare you with Heav'n an impious War maintain, ⎬
And drive the Harpies from their Native Reign? ⎭
Heed therefore what I say; and keep in mind
What *Jove* decrees, what *Phœbus* has design'd:
And I, the Furys Queen, from both relate:
330 You seek th' *Italian* Shores, foredoom'd by Fate:
Th' *Italian* Shores are granted you to find:
And a safe Passage to the Port assign'd.
But know, that e're your promis'd Walls you build,
My Curses shall severely be fulfill'd.
Fierce Famine is your Lot, for this Misdeed,
Reduc'd to grind the Plates on which you feed.
She said; and to the neighb'ring Forest flew:

---

304  Sky:] ~. F1–2.                    329  Furys] Fury's F1–2.

172                                                          Æ.3.l.315.

To ỹ Right Reverend          Dᵣ John Hartstonge Bᵖ.
of Ossory in Kilkenny Son      of Sᵣ Standish Hartstonge Barᵗ.

Our Courage fails us, and our Fears renew.
Hopeless to win by War, to Pray'rs we fall:
340 And on th' offended Harpies humbly call:
And whether Gods, or Birds obscene they were,
Our Vows for Pardon, and for Peace prefer.
But old *Anchises,* off'ring Sacrifice,
And lifting up to Heav'n his Hands, and Eyes;
Ador'd the greater Gods: Avert, said he,   ⎫
These Omens, render vain this Prophecy:    ⎬
And from th' impending Curse, a Pious People free. ⎭
Thus having said, he bids us put to Sea;   ⎫
We loose from Shore our Haulsers, and obey: ⎬
350 And soon with swelling Sails, pursue the wat'ry Way. ⎭
Amidst our course *Zacynthian* Woods appear;
And next by rocky *Neritos* we steer:
We fly from *Ithaca's* detested Shore,
And curse the Land which dire *Ulysses* bore.
At length *Leucata's* cloudy top appears;
And the Sun's Temple, which the Sailor fears.
Resolv'd to breath a while from Labour past, ⎫
Our crooked Anchors from the Prow we cast; ⎬
And joyful to the little City haste.      ⎭
360 Here safe beyond our Hopes, our Vows we pay
To *Jove,* the Guide and Patron of our way.
The Customs of our Country we pursue;
And *Trojan* Games on *Actian* Shores renew.
Our Youth, their naked Limbs besmear with Oyl;
And exercise the Wrastlers noble Toil:
Pleas'd to have sail'd so long before the Wind;
And left so many *Grecian* Towns behind.
The Sun had now fulfill'd his Annual Course,
And *Boreas* on the Seas display'd his Force:
370 I fix'd upon the Temples lofty Door,
The brazen Shield which vanquish'd *Abas* bore:
The Verse beneath, my Name and Action speaks,
These Arms, *Æneas* took from Conqu'ring *Greeks.*

---

340  call:] ~. F1-2.           355  *Leucata's*] *Leucates* F1-2.
356  the Sun's] F2; *Phœbus* F1.      365  Toil:] ~. F1-2.

Then I command to weigh; the Seamen ply
Their sweeping Oars, the smokeing Billows fly.
The sight of high *Phæacia* soon we lost:
And skim'd along *Epirus* rocky Coast.
Then to *Chaonia*'s Port our Course we bend,
And landed, to *Buthrotus* heights ascend.
380 Here wond'rous things were loudly blaz'd by Fame;
How *Helenus* reviv'd the *Trojan* Name;
And raign'd in *Greece:* That *Priam*'s captive Son
Succeeded *Pyrrhus* in his Bed and Throne:
And fair *Andromache,* restor'd by Fate,
Once more was happy in a *Trojan* Mate.
I leave my Gallies riding in the Port;
And long to see the new *Dardanian* Court.
By chance, the mournful Queen, before the Gate,
Then solemniz'd her former Husbands Fate.
390 Green Altars rais'd of Turf, with Gifts she Crown'd; ⎫
And sacred Priests in order stand around; ⎬
And thrice the Name of hapless *Hector* sound. ⎭
The Grove it self resembles *Ida*'s Wood;
And *Simois* seem'd the well dissembl'd Flood.
But when, at nearer distance, she beheld
My shining Armour, and my *Trojan* Shield;
Astonish'd at the sight, the vital Heat
Forsakes her Limbs, her Veins no longer beat:
She faints, she falls, and scarce recov'ring strength,
400 Thus, with a falt'ring Tongue, she speaks at length.
    Are you alive, O Goddess born! she said,
Or if a Ghost, then where is *Hector*'s Shade?
At this, she cast a loud and frightful Cry:
With broken words, I made this brief Reply.
All of me that remains, appears in sight,
I live; if living be to loath the Light.
No Phantome; but I drag a wretched life;
My Fate resembling that of *Hector*'s Wife.
What have you suffer'd since you lost your Lord,
410 By what strange blessing are you now restor'd?

---

383  Throne:] ∼. F1-2.          410  restor'd?] ∼! F1-2.

Still are you *Hector*'s, or is *Hector* fled,
And his Remembrance lost in *Pyrrhus* Bed?
With Eyes dejected, in a lowly tone,
After a modest pause, she thus begun.
   Oh only happy Maid of *Priam*'s Race,
Whom Death deliver'd from the Foes embrace!
Commanded on *Achilles* Tomb to die, }
Not forc'd, like us, to hard Captivity: }
Or in a haughty Master's Arms to lie. }
420 In *Grecian* Ships unhappy we were born:
Endur'd the Victor's Lust, sustain'd the Scorn:
Thus I submitted to the lawless pride
Of *Pyrrhus*, more a Handmaid than a Bride.
Cloy'd with Possession, He forsook my Bed,
And *Helen*'s lovely Daughter sought to wed:
Then me, to *Trojan Helenus* resign'd:
And his two Slaves in equal Marriage join'd:
Till young *Orestes*, pierc'd with deep despair, }
And longing to redeem the promis'd Fair, }
430 Before *Apollo*'s Altar slew the Ravisher. }
By *Pyrrhus* death the Kingdom we regain'd:
At least one half with *Helenus* remain'd;
Our part, from *Chaon*, He *Chaonia* calls:
And names, from *Pergamus*, his rising Walls.
But you, what Fates have landed on our Coast,
What Gods have sent you, or what Storms have tost?
Does young *Ascanius* life and health enjoy,
Sav'd from the Ruins of unhappy *Troy*?
O tell me how his Mothers loss he bears, }
440 What hopes are promis'd from his blooming years, }
How much of *Hector* in his Face appears? }
She spoke: and mix'd her Speech with mournful Cries:
And fruitless Tears came trickling from her Eyes.
At length her Lord descends upon the Plain;
In pomp, attended with a num'rous Train:
Receives his Friends, and to the City leads;

---

425   wed:] ∼. F1–2.          427   join'd:] ∼. F1–2.
438   *Troy?*] ∼! F1–2.

Æ.3.l.415.
F. Clern inu:    W. Hollar fecit.

To The Honᵇˡᵉ Dᵣ Joʰⁿ Mountague Master of
Trinity College in Cambridge

And Tears of Joy amidst his Welcome sheds.
Proceeding on, another *Troy* I see;
Or, in less compass, *Troy*'s Epitome.
450 A Riv'let by the name of *Xanthus* ran:
And I embrace the *Scæan* Gate again.
My Friends in Portico's were entertain'd;
And Feasts and Pleasures through the City reign'd.
The Tables fill'd the spacious Hall around:
And Golden Bowls with sparkling Wine were crown'd.
Two days we pass'd in mirth, till friendly Gales,
Blown from the South, supply'd our swelling Sails.
Then to the Royal Seer I thus began:
O thou who know'st beyond the reach of Man,
460 The Laws of Heav'n, and what the Stars decree, ⎞
Whom *Phœbus* taught unerring Prophecy,       ⎬
From his own Tripod, and his holy Tree:       ⎠
Skill'd in the wing'd Inhabitants of Air,
What Auspices their notes, and flights declare:
O say; for all Religious Rites portend
A happy Voyage, and a prosp'rous End:
And ev'ry Pow'r and Omen of the Sky,
Direct my Course for destin'd *Italy:*
But only dire *Celæno*, from the Gods,
470 A dismal Famine fatally fore-bodes:
O say what Dangers I am first to shun:
What Toils to vanquish, and what Course to run.
  The Prophet first with Sacrifice adores
The greater Gods; their Pardon then implores:
Unbinds the Fillet from his holy Head;      ⎞
To *Phœbus* next, my trembling Steps he led: ⎬
Full of religious Doubts, and awful dread.   ⎠
Then with his God possess'd, before the Shrine,
These words proceeded from his Mouth Divine.
480 O Goddess-born, (for Heav'n's appointed Will,
With greater Auspices of good than ill,
Fore-shows thy Voyage, and thy Course directs;
Thy Fates conspire, and *Jove* himself protects:)

Of many things, some few I shall explain,    ⎞
Teach thee to shun the dangers of the Main,   ⎬
And how at length the promis'd Shore to gain. ⎠
The rest the Fates from *Helenus* conceal;
And *Juno*'s angry Pow'r forbids to tell.
First then, that happy Shore, that seems so nigh, ⎞
490 Will far from your deluded Wishes fly:               ⎬
Long tracts of Seas divide your hopes from *Italy*. ⎠
For you must cruise along *Sicilian* Shoars;
And stem the Currents with your struggling Oars:
Then round th' *Italian* Coast your Navy steer;
And after this to *Circe*'s Island veer:
And last, before your new Foundations rise,
Must pass the *Stygian* Lake, and view the neather Skies.
Now mark the Signs of future Ease and Rest;
And bear them safely treasur'd in thy Breast.
500 When in the shady Shelter of a Wood,
And near the Margin of a gentle Flood,
Thou shalt behold a Sow upon the Ground,
With thirty sucking young encompass'd round;
The Dam and Off-spring white as falling Snow: ⎞
These on thy City shall their Name bestow:    ⎬
And there shall end thy Labours and thy Woe.  ⎠
Nor let the threatned Famine fright thy Mind,
For *Phœbus* will assist; and Fate the way will find.
Let not thy Course to that ill Coast be bent,
510 Which fronts from far th' *Epirian* Continent;
Those parts are all by *Grecian* Foes possess'd:
The salvage *Locrians* here the Shores infest:
There fierce *Idomeneus* his City builds,
And guards with Arms the *Salentinian* Fields.
And on the Mountains brow *Petilia* stands,
Which *Philoctetes* with his Troops commands.
Ev'n when thy Fleet is landed on the Shore,
And Priests with holy Vows the Gods adore;
Then with a Purple Veil involve your Eyes,
520 Lest hostile Faces blast the Sacrifice.

---

495   veer:] ~. F1–2.

These Rites and Customs to the Rest commend;
That to your Pious Race they may descend.
   When parted hence, the Wind that ready waits
For *Sicily,* shall bear you to the Streights:
Where proud *Pelorus* opes a wider way,
Tack to the Larboord, and stand off to Sea:
Veer Star-board Sea and Land. Th' *Italian* Shore,
And fair *Sicilia*'s Coast were one, before
An Earthquake caus'd the Flaw, the roaring Tides ⎫
530 The Passage broke, that Land from Land divides: ⎬
And where the Lands retir'd, the rushing Ocean rides. ⎭
Distinguish'd by the Streights, on either hand,
Now rising Cities in long order stand;
And fruitful Fields: (So much can Time invade
The mouldring Work, that beauteous Nature made.)
Far on the right, her Dogs foul *Scylla* hides: ⎫
*Charibdis* roaring on the left presides; ⎬
And in her greedy Whirl-pool sucks the Tides: ⎭
Then Spouts them from below; with Fury driv'n,
540 The Waves mount up, and wash the face of Heav'n.
But *Scylla* from her Den, with open Jaws,
The sinking Vessel in her Eddy draws;
Then dashes on the Rocks: A Human Face,
And Virgin Bosom, hides her Tails disgrace.
Her Parts obscene below the Waves descend,
With Dogs inclos'd; and in a Dolphin end.
'Tis safer, then, to bear aloof to Sea,
And coast *Pachynus,* though with more delay;
Than once to view mishapen *Scylla* near,
550 And the loud yell of watry Wolves to hear.
   Besides, if Faith to *Helenus* be due,
And if Prophetick *Phœbus* tell me true;
Do not this Precept of your Friend forget;
Which therefore more than once I must repeat.
Above the rest, great *Juno*'s Name adore:
Pay Vows to *Juno; Juno*'s Aid implore.
Let Gifts be to the mighty Queen design'd;

534–535  (So . . . made.)] F2; ∧~ . . . ~·∧ F1.

And mollify with Pray'rs her haughty Mind.
Thus, at the length, your Passage shall be free,
560 And you shall safe descend on *Italy.*
Arriv'd at *Cumæ,* when you view the Flood
Of black *Avernus,* and the sounding Wood,
The mad prophetick Sibyl you shall find,
Dark in a Cave, and on a Rock reclin'd.
She sings the Fates, and in her frantick Fitts,
The Notes and Names inscrib'd, to Leafs commits.
What she commits to Leafs, in order laid,
Before the Caverns Entrance are display'd:
Unmov'd they lie, but if a Blast of Wind
570 Without, or Vapours issue from behind,
The Leafs are born aloft in liquid Air,
And she resumes no more her Museful Care:
Nor gathers from the Rocks her scatter'd Verse;
Nor sets in order what the Winds disperse.
Thus, many not succeeding, most upbraid    )
The Madness of the visionary Maid;          }
And with loud Curses leave the mystick Shade. )
    Think it not loss of time a while to stay;
Though thy Companions chide thy long delay:
580 Tho' summon'd to the Seas, tho' pleasing Gales
Invite thy Course, and stretch thy swelling Sails.
But beg the sacred Priestess to relate
With willing Words, and not to write thy Fate.
The fierce *Italian* People she will show;    )
And all thy Wars, and all thy Future Woe;     }
And what thou may'st avoid, and what must undergo. )
She shall direct thy Course, instruct thy Mind;
And teach thee how the happy Shores to find.
This is what Heav'n allows me to relate:     )
590 Now part in Peace; pursue thy better Fate,    }
And raise, by strength of Arms, the *Trojan* State. )
    This, when the Priest with friendly Voice declar'd,
He gave me Licence, and rich Gifts prepar'd:
Bounteous of Treasure, he supply'd my want

------

563   Sibyl] F2 *(Sibyl); Sybil* F1.

With heavy Gold, and polish'd Elephant:
Then *Dodonæan* Caldrons put on Bord,
And ev'ry Ship with Sums of Silver stor'd.
A trusty Coat of Mail to me he sent,
Thrice chain'd with Gold, for Use and Ornament:
600 The Helm of *Pyrrhus* added to the rest,
That flourish'd with a Plume and waving Crest.
Nor was my Sire forgotten, nor my Friends:
And large Recruits he to my Navy sends;
Men, Horses, Captains, Arms, and warlick Stores:
Supplies new Pilots, and new sweeping Oars.
Mean time, my Sire commands to hoist our Sails;
Lest we shou'd lose the first auspicious Gales.
The Prophet bless'd the parting Crew: and last,
With Words like these, his ancient Friend embrac'd.
610 Old happy Man, the Care of Gods above,
Whom Heav'nly *Venus* honour'd with her Love,
And twice preserv'd thy Life, when *Troy* was lost;
Behold from far the wish'd *Ausonian* Coast:
There land; but take a larger Compass round;
For that before is all forbidden Ground.
The Shore that *Phœbus* has design'd for you,
At farther distance lies, conceal'd from view.
Go happy hence, and seek your new Abodes;
Bless'd in a Son, and favour'd by the Gods:
620 For I with useless words prolong your stay;
When Southern Gales have summon'd you away.
    Nor less the Queen our parting thence deplor'd;
Nor was less bounteous than her *Trojan* Lord.
A noble Present to my Son she brought,
A Robe with Flow'rs on Golden Tissue wrought;
A *Phrygian* Vest; and loads, with Gifts beside
Of precious Texture, and of *Asian* Pride.
Accept, she said, these Monuments of Love;
Which in my Youth with happier Hands I wove:
630 Regard these Trifles for the Giver's sake;
Tis the last Present *Hector*'s Wife can make.

595   Elephant:] ~. F1–2.

Thou call'st my lost *Astyanax* to mind:
In thee his Features, and his Form I find.
His Eyes so sparkled with a lively Flame;
Such were his Motions, such was all his Frame;
And ah! had Heav'n so pleas'd, his Years had been the same. }

 With Tears I took my last adieu, and said,
Your Fortune, happy pair, already made,
Leaves you no farther Wish: My diff'rent state,
640 Avoiding one, incurs another Fate.
To you a quiet Seat the Gods allow,
You have no Shores to search, no Seas to plow,
Nor Fields of flying *Italy* to chase:
(Deluding Visions, and a vain Embrace!)
You see another *Simois,* and enjoy
The labour of your Hands, another *Troy;*
With better Auspice than her ancient Tow'rs:
And less obnoxious to the *Grecian* Pow'rs.
If e're the Gods, whom I with Vows adore,
650 Conduct my Steps to *Tiber*'s happy Shore:
If ever I ascend the *Latian* Throne,
And build a City I may call my own,
As both of us our Birth from *Troy* derive, }
So let our Kindred Lines in Concord live: }
And both in Acts of equal Friendship strive. }
Our Fortunes, good or bad, shall be the same,
The double *Troy* shall differ but in Name:
That what we now begin, may never end;
But long, to late Posterity descend.
660  Near the *Ceraunean* Rocks our Course we bore:
(The shortest passage to th' *Italian* shore:)
Now had the Sun withdrawn his radiant Light,
And Hills were hid in dusky Shades of Night:
We land; and on the bosom of the Ground
A safe Retreat, and a bare Lodging found;
Close by the Shore we lay; the Sailors keep
Their watches, and the rest securely sleep.

---

665 Lodging] *Lodging* F1–2.

The Night proceeding on with silent pace,  )
Stood in her noon; and view'd with equal Face,  }
670 Her steepy rise, and her declining Race.  )
    Then wakeful *Palinurus* rose, to spie  )
The face of Heav'n, and the Nocturnal Skie;  }
And listen'd ev'ry breath of Air to try:  )
Observes the Stars, and notes their sliding Course,
The *Pleiads, Hyads,* and their wat'ry force;
And both the Bears is careful to behold;
And bright *Orion* arm'd with burnish'd Gold.
Then when he saw no threat'ning Tempest Nigh,
But a sure promise of a settled Skie;
680 He gave the Sign to weigh; we break our sleep;
Forsake the pleasing Shore, and plow the deep.
And now the rising Morn, with rosie light
Adorns the Skies, and puts the Stars to flight:
When we from far, like bluish Mists, descry
The Hills, and then the Plains of *Italy.*
*Achates* first pronounc'd the Joyful sound;
Then *Italy* the chearful Crew rebound.
My Sire *Anchises* crown'd a Cup with Wine:
And off'ring, thus implor'd the Pow'rs Divine.
690 Ye Gods, presiding over Lands and Seas,
And you who raging Winds and Waves appease,
Breath on our swelling Sails a prosp'rous Wind:
And smooth our Passage to the Port assign'd.
The gentle Gales their flagging force renew;
And now the happy Harbour is in view.
*Minerva*'s Temple then salutes our sight;
Plac'd, as a Land-mark, on the Mountains height:
We furl our Sails, and turn the Prows to shore;
The curling Waters round the Galleys roar:
700 The Land lies open to the raging East,
Then, bending like a Bow, with Rocks compress'd,
Shuts out the Storms; the Winds and Waves complain,
And vent their malice on the Cliffs in vain.
The Port lies hid within; on either side
Two Tow'ring Rocks the narrow mouth divide.

The Temple, which aloft we view'd before,
To distance flies, and seems to shun the Shore.
Scarce landed, the first Omens I beheld
Were four white Steeds that crop'd the flow'ry Field.
710 War, War is threaten'd from this Forreign Ground,
(My Father cry'd) where warlike Steeds are found.
Yet, since reclaim'd to Chariots they submit,
And bend to stubborn Yokes, and champ the Bitt,
Peace may succeed to Warr. Our way we bend
To *Pallas,* and the sacred Hill ascend:
There, prostrate to the fierce Virago pray;
Whose Temple was the Land-Mark of our way.
Each with a *Phrygian* Mantle veil'd his Head; ⎫
And all Commands of *Helenus* obey'd; ⎬
720 And pious Rites to *Grecian Juno* paid. ⎭
These dues perform'd, we stretch our Sails, and stand
To Sea, forsaking that suspected Land.
From hence *Tarentum*'s Bay appears in view;
For *Hercules* renown'd, if Fame be true.
Just opposite, *Lacinian Juno* stands;
*Caulonian* Tow'rs and *Scylacæan* Strands,
For Shipwrecks fear'd: Mount *Ætna* thence we spy,
Known by the smoaky Flames which Cloud the Skie.
Far off we hear the Waves, with surly sound
730 Invade the Rocks, the Rocks their groans rebound.
The Billows break upon the sounding Strand;
And roul the rising Tide, impure with Sand.
Then thus *Anchises,* in Experience old,
'Tis that *Charibdis* which the Seer foretold:
And those the promis'd Rocks; bear off to Sea:
With haste the frighted Mariners obey.
First *Palinurus* to the Larboord veer'd;
Then all the Fleet by his Example steer'd.
To Heav'n aloft on ridgy Waves we ride;
740 Then down to Hell descend, when they divide.

---

715   ascend:] ∼. F1–2.                716   Virago] *Virago* F1–2.
726   Strands,] ∼. F1–2.              727   *Ætna*] F2; *Etna* F1.
737   Larboord] Larboor'd F1–2.

And thrice our Gallies knock'd the stony ground,
And thrice the hollow Rocks return'd the sound,
And thrice we saw the Stars, that stood with dews around.
The flagging Winds forsook us, with the Sun;
And weary'd, on *Cyclopean* Shores we run.
The Port capacious, and secure from Wind,
Is to the foot of thundring *Ætna* joyn'd.
By turns a pitchy Cloud she rowls on high;
By turns hot Embers from her entrails fly;
750 And flakes of mounting Flames, that lick the Skie.
Oft from her Bowels massy Rocks are thrown,
And shiver'd by the force come piece-meal down.
Oft liquid Lakes of burning Sulphur flow,
Fed from the fiery Springs that boil below.
*Enceladus* they say, transfix'd by *Jove*,
With blasted Limbs came tumbling from above:
And, where he fell, th' Avenging Father drew
This flaming Hill, and on his Body threw:
As often as he turns his weary sides,
760 He shakes the solid Isle, and smoke the Heavens hides.
In shady Woods we pass the tedious Night,
Where bellowing Sounds and Groans our Souls affright,
Of which no Cause is offer'd to the sight.
For not one Star was kindled in the Skie;
Nor cou'd the Moon her borrow'd Light supply:
For misty Clouds involv'd the Firmament;
The Stars were muffled, and the Moon was pent.
Scarce had the rising Sun the day reveal'd;
Scarce had his heat the pearly dews dispell'd;
770 When from the Woods there bolts, before our sight,
Somewhat, betwixt a Mortal and a Spright:
So thin, so ghastly meagre, and so wan,
So bare of flesh, he scarce resembled Man.
This thing, all tatter'd, seem'd from far t'implore
Our pious aid, and pointed to the Shore.
We look behind; then view his shaggy Beard;

---

747  *Ætna*] *Etna* F1–2.                  762  affright,] ~. F1–2.
766  involv'd] invovl'd F1–2.              771  Spright:] ~. F1–2.

His Cloaths were tagg'd with Thorns, and Filth his Limbs
  besmear'd:
The rest, in Meen, in habit, and in Face,
Appear'd a *Greek;* and such indeed he was.
780 He cast on us, from far, a frightful view,
Whom soon for *Trojans* and for Foes he knew:
Stood still, and paus'd; then all at once began
To stretch his Limbs, and trembled as he ran.
Soon as approach'd, upon his Knees he falls,
And thus with Tears and Sighs for pity calls.
Now by the Pow'rs above, and what we share
From Nature's common Gift, this vital Air,
O *Trojans* take me hence: I beg no more,
But bear me far from this unhappy Shore.
790 'Tis true I am a *Greek*, and farther own,
Among your Foes besieg'd th' Imperial Town;
For such Demerits if my death be due,
No more for this abandon'd life I sue:
This only Favour let my Tears obtain,
To throw me headlong in the rapid Main:
Since nothing more than Death my Crime demands,
I dye content, to dye by human Hands.
He said, and on his Knees my Knees embrac'd,
I bad him boldly tell his Fortune past;
800 His present State, his Lineage and his Name;
Th' occasion of his Fears, and whence he came.
The good *Anchises* rais'd him with his Hand;
Who, thus encourag'd, answer'd our Demand:
From *Ithaca* my native Soil I came
To *Troy*, and *Achæmenides* my Name.
Me, my poor Father, with *Ulysses* sent;
(Oh had I stay'd, with Poverty content!)
But fearful for themselves, my Country-men
Left me forsaken in the *Cyclops* Den.
810 The Cave, though large, was dark, the dismal Flore
Was pav'd with mangled Limbs and putrid Gore.
Our monstrous Host, of more than Human Size,

---

787 From] F2; As F1.        809 *Cyclops*] *Cyclop's* F1–2.

Erects his Head, and stares within the Skies.
Bellowing his Voice, and horrid in his Hue:
Ye Gods, remove this Plague from Mortal View!
The Joints of slaughter'd Wretches are his Food:
And for his Wine he quaffs the streaming Blood.
These Eyes beheld, when with his spacious Hand
He seiz'd two Captives of our *Grecian* Band;
820 Stretch'd on his Back, he dash'd against the Stones
Their broken Bodies, and their crackling Bones:
With spouting Blood the Purple Pavement swims,
While the dire Glutton grinds the trembling Limbs.
 Not unreveng'd, *Ulysses* bore their Fate,
Nor thoughtless of his own unhappy State:
For, gorg'd with Flesh, and drunk with Human Wine,
While fast asleep the Gyant lay supine;
Snoaring aloud, and belching from his Maw
His indigested Foam, and Morsels raw:
830 We pray, we cast the Lots, and then surround
The monstrous Body, stretch'd along the Ground:
Each, as he cou'd approach him, lends a hand
To bore his Eyeball with a flaming Brand.
Beneath his frowning Forehead lay his Eye,
(For onely one did the vast Frame supply;)
But that a Globe so large, his Front it fill'd,
Like the Sun's disk, or like a *Grecian* Shield.
The Stroke succeeds; and down the Pupil bends;
This Vengeance follow'd for our slaughter'd Friends.
840 But haste, unhappy Wretches, haste to fly;
Your Cables cut, and on your Oars rely.
Such, and so vast as *Polypheme* appears,
A hundred more this hated Island bears:
Like him in Caves they shut their woolly Sheep,
Like him, their Herds on tops of Mountains keep;
Like him, with mighty Strides, they stalk from Steep to Steep.
And now three Moons their sharpen'd Horns renew,
Since thus in Woods and Wilds, obscure from view,

---

814 Hue:] ~. F1–2.
847 renew,] *the comma failed to print in some copies of F1.*

I drag my loathsom Days with mortal Fright;
850 And in deserted Caverns lodge by Night:
Oft from the Rocks a dreadful Prospect see,
Of the huge *Cyclops,* like a walking Tree:
From far I hear his thund'ring Voice resound;
And trampling Feet that shake the solid Ground.
Cornels, and salvage Berries of the Wood,
And Roots and Herbs have been my meagre Food.
   While all around my longing Eyes I cast,
I saw your happy Ships appear at last.
On those I fix'd my hopes, to these I run,
860 'Tis all I ask this cruel Race to shun:
What other Death you please, your selves bestow.
Scarce had he said, when on the Mountain's brow,
We saw the Gyant-Shepherd stalk before
His following Flock, and leading to the Shore:
A monstrous Bulk, deform'd, depriv'd of Sight,
His Staff a trunk of Pine, to guide his steps aright.
His pondrous Whistle from his Neck descends; ⎞
His woolly Care their pensive Lord attends: ⎬
This onely Solace his hard Fortune sends. ⎠
870 Soon as he reach'd the Shore, and touch'd the Waves,
From his bor'd Eye the gutt'ring Blood he laves:
He gnash'd his Teeth and groan'd; thro' Seas he strides,
And scarce the topmost Billows touch'd his sides.
   Seiz'd with a sudden Fear, we run to Sea,
The Cables cut, and silent haste away:
The well deserving Stranger entertain;
Then, buckling to the Work, our Oars divide the Main.
The Gyant harken'd to the dashing Sound:
But when our Vessels out of reach he found,
880 He strided onward; and in vain essay'd
Th' *Ionian* Deep, and durst no farther wade.
With that he roar'd aloud; the dreadful Cry ⎞
Shakes Earth, and Air, and Seas; the Billows fly ⎬
Before the bellowing Noise, to distant *Italy.* ⎠

---

850  Night:] ~. F1–2.
864  Shore:] ~. F1–2.

861  please, your selves] ~∧ ~ ~, F1–2.

Æ. 3. l. 365.

To Wm Gibbons Dr in Physick

The neighb'ring *Ætna* trembled all around;
The winding Caverns echo to the sound.
His brother *Cyclops* hear the yelling Roar;
And, rushing down the Mountains, crowd the Shoar:
We saw their stern distorted looks, from far,
890 And one ey'd Glance, that vainly threatned War.
A dreadful Council, with their heads on high;
The misty Clouds about their Foreheads fly:
Not yielding to the tow'ring Tree of *Jove;*
Or tallest Cypress of *Diana*'s Grove.
New Pangs of mortal Fear our Minds assail, ⎞
We tug at ev'ry Oar, and hoist up ev'ry Sail; ⎬
And take th' Advantage of the friendly Gale. ⎠
Forewarn'd by *Helenus,* we strive to shun
*Charibdis* Gulph, nor dare to *Scylla* run.
900 An equal Fate on either side appears;
We, tacking to the left, are free from Fears.
For from *Pelorus* Point, the North arose,
And drove us back where swift *Pantagias* flows.
His Rocky Mouth we pass; and make our Way
By *Thapsus,* and *Megara*'s winding Bay;
This Passage *Achæmenides* had shown,
Tracing the Course which he before had run.
    Right o're-against *Plemmyrium*'s watry Strand,
There lies an Isle once call'd th' *Ortygian* Land:
910 *Alphëus,* as Old Fame reports, has found
From *Greece* a secret Passage under-ground:
By Love to beauteous *Arethusa* led,
And mingling here, they rowl in the same Sacred Bed.
As *Helenus* enjoyn'd, we next adore
*Diana*'s Name, Protectress of the Shore.
With prosp'rous Gales we pass the quiet Sounds
Of still *Elorus* and his fruitful Bounds.
Then doubling Cape *Pachynus,* we survey
The rocky Shore extended to the Sea.
920 The Town of *Camarine* from far we see;
And fenny Lake undrain'd by Fates decree.
In sight of the *Geloan* Fields we pass,

And the large Walls, where mighty *Gela* was:
Then *Agragas* with lofty Summets crown'd;
Long for the Race of warlike Steeds renown'd:
We pass'd *Selinus*, and the Palmy Land,
And widely shun the *Lilybæan* Strand,
Unsafe, for secret Rocks, and moving Sand.
At length on Shore the weary Fleet arriv'd;
930 Which *Drepanum's* unhappy Port receiv'd.
Here, after endless Labours, often tost
By raging Storms, and driv'n on ev'ry Coast,
My dear, dear Father, spent with Age, I lost.
Ease of my Cares, and Solace of my Pain,
Sav'd through a thousand Toils, but sav'd in vain:
The Prophet, who my future Woes reveal'd,
Yet this, the greatest and the worst, conceal'd.
And dire *Celæno,* whose foreboding Skill
Denounc'd all else, was silent of this Ill:
940 This my last Labour was. Some friendly God,
From thence convey'd us to your blest Abode.

    Thus to the listning Queen, the Royal Guest
His wand'ring Course, and all his Toils express'd;
And here concluding, he retir'd to rest.

938 *Celæno*] F2; *Celœno* F1.

## The Fourth Book of the Æneis

### THE ARGUMENT.

Dido *discovers to her Sister her Passion for* Æneas, *and her thoughts of marrying him. She prepares a Hunting-Match for his Entertainment.* Juno *by* Venus's *consent raises a Storm, which separates the Hunters, and drives* Æneas *and* Dido *into the same Cave, where their Marriage is suppos'd to be compleated.* Jupiter *dispatches* Mercury *to* Æneas, *to warn him from* Carthage; Æneas *secretly prepares for his Voyage:* Dido *finds out his Design, and to put a stop to it, makes use of her own, and her Sister's Entreaties, and discovers all the variety of Passions that are incident to a neglected Lover: When nothing wou'd prevail upon him, she contrives her own Death, with which this Book concludes.*

B UT anxious Cares already seiz'd the Queen:
 She fed within her Veins a Flame unseen:
 The Heroe's Valour, Acts, and Birth inspire
Her Soul with Love, and fann the secret Fire.
His Words, his Looks imprinted in her Heart,
Improve the Passion, and increase the Smart.
Now, when the Purple Morn had chas'd away
The dewy Shadows, and restor'd the Day;
Her Sister first, with early Care she sought,
10 And thus in mournful Accents eas'd her Thought.
My dearest *Anna*, what new Dreams affright
My lab'ring Soul; what Visions of the Night
Disturb my Quiet, and distract my Breast,
With strange Ideas of our *Trojan* Guest!
His Worth, his Actions, and Majestick Air,
A Man descended from the Gods declare:
Fear ever argues a degenerate kind,

---

14 Guest!] ∼? F1–2.
17–18 *as in F2; in F1 as follows:*
   Fear never harbours in a Noble Mind,
   But Modesty, with just Assurance join'd.

His Birth is well asserted by his Mind.
Then, what he suffer'd, when by Fate betray'd,
20 What brave Attempts for falling *Troy* he made!
Such were his Looks, so gracefully he spoke,
That were I not resolv'd against the Yoke
Of hapless Marriage; never to be curs'd
With second Love, so fatal was my first;
To this one Error I might yield again:
For since *Sichæus* was untimely slain,
This onely Man, is able to subvert
The fix'd Foundations of my stubborn Heart.
And to confess my Frailty, to my shame,      ⎫
30 Somewhat I find within, if not the same,     ⎬
Too like the Sparkles of my former Flame.     ⎭
    But first let yawning Earth a Passage rend;
And let me through the dark Abyss descend;
First let avenging *Jove,* with Flames from high, ⎫
Drive down this Body, to the neather Sky,         ⎬
Condemn'd with Ghosts in endless Night to lye;    ⎭
Before I break the plighted Faith I gave;     ⎫
No; he who had my Vows, shall ever have;      ⎬
For whom I lov'd on Earth, I worship in the Grave. ⎭
40    She said; the Tears ran gushing from her Eyes,
And stop'd her Speech: her Sister thus replies.
O dearer than the vital Air I breath,
Will you to Grief your blooming Years bequeath?
Condem'd to wast in Woes, your lonely Life,
Without the Joys of Mother, or of Wife?
Think you these Tears, this pompous Train of Woe,
Are known, or valu'd by the Ghosts below?
I grant, that while your Sorrows yet were green,
It well became a Woman, and a Queen,
50 The Vows of *Tyrian* Princes to neglect,
To scorn *Hyarbas,* and his Love reject,
With all the *Lybian* Lords of mighty Name;
But will you fight against a pleasing Flame?

---

45  Wife?] ~. F1–2.              51  reject,] ~; F1–2.
52  Name;] ~, F1–2.             53  Flame?] ~! F1–2.

This little Spot of Land, which Heav'n bestows,
On ev'ry side is hemm'd with warlike Foes:
*Getulian* Cities here are spread around;
And fierce *Numidians* there your Frontiers bound;
Here lies a barren Wast of thirsty Land,
And there the *Syrtes* raise the moving Sand:
60 *Barcæan* Troops besiege the narrow Shore;
And from the Sea *Pygmalion* threatens more.
Propitious Heav'n, and gracious *Juno,* lead
This wand'ring Navy to your needful Aid:
How will your Empire spread, your City rise
From such an Union, and with such Allies!
Implore the Favour of the Pow'rs above;
And leave the Conduct of the rest to Love.
Continue still your hospitable way,
And still invent occasions of their Stay;
70 'Till Storms, and winter Winds, shall cease to threat,
And Plancks and Oars, repair their shatter'd Fleet.
　　These Words, which from a Friend, and Sister came, ⎫
With Ease resolv'd the Scruples of her Fame; ⎬
And added Fury to the kindled Flame. ⎭
Inspir'd with Hope, the Project they pursue;
On ev'ry Altar Sacrifice renew;
A chosen Ewe of two Years old they pay
To *Ceres, Bacchus,* and the God of Day:
Preferring *Juno*'s Pow'r: For *Juno* ties
80 The Nuptial Knot, and makes the Marriage Joys.
The beauteous Queen before her Altar stands,
And holds the Golden Goblet in her Hands:
A milk-white Heifar she with Flow'rs adorns,
And pours the ruddy Wine betwixt her Horns;
And while the Priests with Pray'r the Gods invoke,
She feeds their Altars with *Sabæan* Smoke:
With hourly Care the Sacrifice renews,
And anxiously the panting Entrails Views.
What Priestly Rites, alas! what Pious Art,

---

61 *Pygmalion*] *Pigmalion* F1–2.　　　　86 Smoke:] ∼. F1–2.

The Mole is left unfinish'd to the Foe.
The Mounds, the Works, the Walls, neglected lye,
Short of their promis'd heigth that seem'd to threat the Sky.
　　But when Imperial *Juno*, from above,
130　Saw *Dido* fetter'd in the Chains of Love;
Hot with the Venom, which her Veins inflam'd,
And by no sense of Shame to be reclaim'd:
With soothing Words to *Venus* she begun.
High Praises, endless Honours you have won,
And mighty Trophees with your worthy Son:
Two Gods a silly Woman have undone.
Nor am I ignorant, you both suspect
This rising City, which my Hands erect:
But shall Cœlestial Discord never cease?
140　'Tis better ended in a lasting Peace.
You stand possess'd of all your Soul desir'd;
Poor *Dido* with consuming Love is fir'd:
Your *Trojan* with my *Tyrian* let us join, ⎫
So *Dido* shall be yours, *Æneas* mine: ⎬
One common Kingdom, one united Line. ⎭
*Elisa* shall a *Dardan* Lord obey,
And lofty *Carthage* for a Dow'r convey.
Then *Venus,* who her hidden Fraud descry'd, ⎫
(Which wou'd the Scepter of the World, misguide ⎬
150　To *Lybian* Shores,) thus artfully reply'd, ⎭
Who but a Fool, wou'd Wars with *Juno* chuse,
And such Alliance, and such Gifts refuse?
If Fortune with our joint Desires comply:
The Doubt is all from *Jove,* and Destiny:
Lest he forbid, with absolute Command,
To mix the People in one common Land.
Or will the *Trojan,* and the *Tyrian* Line,
In lasting Leagues, and sure Succession join?
But you, the Partner of his Bed and Throne,
160　May move his Mind; my Wishes are your own.

---

128　*as in F2; in F1 as follows:* And, left unbuilt, are shorter of the Sky.
154　Destiny:] ∼. F1–2.

Mine, said Imperial *Juno,* be the Care; ⎫
Time urges, now, to perfect this Affair:   ⎬
Attend my Counsel, and the Secret share. ⎭
When next the Sun his rising Light displays,
And guilds the World below, with Purple Rays;
The Queen, *Æneas,* and the *Tyrian* Court,
Shall to the shady Woods, for Silvan Game, resort.
There, while the Huntsmen pitch their Toils around,
And chearful Horns, from Side to Side, resound;
170 A Pitchy Cloud shall cover all the Plain
With Hail, and Thunder, and tempestuous Rain:
The fearful Train shall take their speedy Flight,
Dispers'd, and all involv'd in gloomy Night:
One Cave a grateful Shelter shall afford
To the fair Princess, and the *Trojan* Lord.
I will my self, the bridal Bed prepare,
If you, to bless the Nuptials, will be there:
So shall their Loves be crown'd with due Delights,
And *Hymen* shall be present at the Rites.
180 The Queen of Love consents, and closely smiles
At her vain Project, and discover'd Wiles.
  The rosy Morn was risen from the Main,
And Horns and Hounds awake the Princely Train:
They issue early through the City Gate,
Where the more wakeful Huntsmen ready wait,
With Nets, and Toils, and Darts, beside the force
Of *Spartan* Dogs, and swift *Massylian* Horse.
The *Tyrian* Peers, and Officers of State,
For the slow Queen, in Anti-Chambers wait:
190 Her lofty Courser, in the Court below,
(Who his Majestick Rider seems to know,)
Proud of his Purple Trappings, paws the Ground;
And champs the Golden Bitt; and spreads the Foam around.
The Queen at length appears: On either Hand
The brawny Guards in Martial Order stand.

163  Counsel] F1 *(corrected state),* F2; Councel F1 *(uncorrected state).*
169  chearful] F1 *(corrected state);* cheerful F1 *(uncorrected state).*

A wintry Deluge down; and sounding Show'rs.
The Company dispers'd, to Coverts ride,
And seek the homely Cotts, or Mountains hollow side.
The rapid Rains, descending from the Hills,
To rowling Torrents raise the creeping Rills.
The Queen and Prince, as Love or Fortune guides,
240 One common Cavern in her Bosom hides.
Then first the trembling Earth the signal gave;
And flashing Fires enlighten all the Cave:
Hell from below, and *Juno* from above,
And howling Nymphs, were conscious to their Love.
From this ill Omend Hour, in Time arose
Debate and Death, and all succeeding woes.
    The Queen whom sense of Honour cou'd not move
No longer made a Secret of her Love;
But call'd it Marriage, by that specious Name,
250 To veil the Crime and sanctifie the Shame.
    The loud Report through *Lybian* Cities goes;
Fame, the great Ill, from small beginnings grows:
Swift from the first; and ev'ry Moment brings
New Vigour to her flights, new Pinions to her wings.
Soon grows the Pygmee to Gygantic size;
Her Feet on Earth, her Forehead in the Skies:
Inrag'd against the Gods, revengeful Earth
Produc'd her last of the *Titanian* birth.
Swift is her walk, more swift her winged hast:
260 A monstrous Fantom, horrible and vast;
As many Plumes as raise her lofty flight,
So many piercing Eyes inlarge her sight:
Millions of opening Mouths to Fame belong;
And ev'ry Mouth is furnish'd with a Tongue:
And round with listning Ears the flying Plague is hung. )
She fills the peaceful Universe with Cries;
No Slumbers ever close her wakeful Eyes.
By Day from lofty Tow'rs her Head she shews;
And spreads through trembling Crowds disastrous News:

---

252   grows:] ∼. F1–2.                    257   revengeful] F2; revengful F1.
269   News:] ∼. F1–2.

270 With Court Informers haunts, and Royal Spies,
Things done relates, not done she feigns; and mingles Truth
with Lyes.
Talk is her business; and her chief delight
To tell of Prodigies, and cause affright.
She fills the Peoples Ears with *Dido*'s Name;
Who, lost to Honour, and the sense of Shame,
Admits into her Throne and Nuptial Bed
A wandring Guest, who from his Country fled:
Whole days with him she passes in delights;
And wasts in Luxury long Winter Nights:
280 Forgetful of her Fame, and Royal Trust;
Dissolv'd in Ease, abandon'd to her Lust.
The Goddess widely spreads the loud Report;
And flies at length to King *Hyarbas* Court.
When first possess'd with this unwelcome News,
Whom did he not of Men and Gods accuse?
This Prince, from ravish'd *Garamantis* born,
A hundred Temples did with Spoils adorn,
In *Ammon*'s Honour, his Cœlestial Sire;
A hundred Altars fed, with wakeful Fire:
290 And through his vast Dominions, Priests ordain'd,
Whose watchful Care these holy Rites maintain'd.
The Gates and Columns were with Garlands crown'd,
And Blood of Victim Beasts enrich the Ground.
He, when he heard a Fugitive cou'd move
The *Tyrian* Princess, who disdain'd his Love,
His Breast with Fury burn'd, his Eyes with Fire;
Mad with Despair, impatient with Desire.
Then on the Sacred Altars pouring Wine,
He thus with Pray'rs implor'd his Sire divine.
300 Great *Jove,* propitious to the *Moorish* Race,
Who feast on painted Beds, with Off'rings grace
Thy Temples, and adore thy Pow'r Divine
With Blood of Victims, and with sparkling Wine:
Seest thou not this? or do we fear in vain

---

279 Nights:] ~. F1–2.       283 *Hyarbas*] *Hyarba*'s F1–2.
285 accuse?] ~! F1–2.       303 Blood of] F2; offer'd F1.

Thy boasted Thunder, and thy thoughtless Reign?
Do thy broad Hands the forky Lightnings lance,
Are thine the Bolts, or the blind work of Chance?
A wandring Woman builds, within our State,
A little Town, bought at an easie Rate;
310 She pays me Homage, and my Grants allow
A narrow space of *Lybian* Lands to plough:
Yet scorning me, by Passion blindly led,
Admits a banish'd *Trojan* to her Bed:
And now this other *Paris,* with his Train
Of conquer'd Cowards, must in *Affrick* reign!
(Whom, what they are, their Looks and Garb confess;
Their Locks with Oil perfum'd, their *Lydian* dress:)
He takes the Spoil, enjoys the Princely Dame;
And I, rejected I, adore an empty Name.
320     His Vows, in haughty Terms, he thus preferr'd,
And held his Altar's Horns; the mighty Thund'rer heard,
Then cast his Eyes on *Carthage,* where he found
The lustful Pair, in lawless pleasure drown'd:
Lost in their Loves, insensible of Shame;
And both forgetful of their better Fame.
He calls *Cyllenius;* and the God attends;
By whom his menacing Command he sends.
Go, mount the Western Winds, and cleave the Skie;
Then, with a swift descent, to *Carthage* fly:
330 There find the *Trojan* Chief, who wastes his Days
In sloathful Riot, and inglorious Ease,
Nor minds the future City, giv'n by Fate;
To him this Message from my Mouth relate.
Not so, fair *Venus* hop'd, when twice she won
Thy Life with Pray'rs; nor promis'd such a Son.
Hers was a Heroe, destin'd to command
A Martial Race; and rule the *Latian* Land:
Who shou'd his ancient Line from *Teucer* draw;
And, on the conquer'd World, impose the Law.

307  Are thine] Thine are F1–2.      310  allow] ~, F1–2.
311  plough:] ~. F1–2.      323  drown'd:] ~. F1–2.
331  Ease,] ~. F1–2.      337  Land:] ~. F1–2.

340 If Glory cannot move a Mind so mean,
  Nor future Praise, from fading Pleasure wean,
  Yet why shou'd he defraud his Son of Fame;
  And grudge the *Romans* their Immortal Name?
  What are his vain Designs? what hopes he more,
  From his long ling'ring on a hostile Shore?
  Regardless to redeem his Honour lost,
  And for his Race to gain th' *Ausonian* Coast?
  Bid him with Speed the *Tyrian* Court forsake;
  With this Command the slumb'ring Warrior wake.
350   *Hermes* obeys; with Golden Pinions binds
  His flying Feet, and mounts the Western Winds:
  And whether o're the Seas or Earth he flies,
  With rapid Force, they bear him down the Skies.
  But first he grasps within his awful Hand,
  The mark of Sov'raign Pow'r, his Magick Wand:
  With this, he draws the Ghosts from hollow Graves,
  With this he drives them down the *Stygian* Waves;
  With this he seals in Sleep, the wakeful sight;
  And Eyes, though clos'd in Death restores to Light.
360 Thus arm'd, the God begins his Airy Race;
  And drives the racking Clouds along the liquid Space:
  Now sees the Tops of *Atlas,* as he flies;
  Whose brawny Back supports the starry Skies:
  *Atlas,* whose Head with Piny Forests crown'd,
  Is beaten by the Winds; with foggy Vapours bound.
  Snows hide his Shoulders; from beneath his Chin
  The Founts of rolling Streams their Race begin:
  A beard of Yce on his large Breast depends:
  Here pois'd upon his Wings, the God descends.
370 Then, rested thus, he from the tow'ring height
  Plung'd downward, with precipitated Flight:
  Lights on the Seas, and skims along the Flood:
  As Water-fowl, who seek their fishy Food,
  Less, and yet less, to distant Prospect show,
  By turns they dance aloft, and dive below:

---

343  Name?] ~! F1-2.      344  Designs?] ~! F1-2.
347  Coast?] ~! F1-2.      361  Space:] ~. F1-2.

P. Clero inv. W. Hollar fecit                                    Æ. 4. l. 380.

To John Walkeden of ỹ Inner Temple Esq:

NON EST MORTALE QUOD OPTO

Like these, the steerage of his Wings he plies;
And near the surface of the Water flies:
'Till having pass'd the Seas, and cross'd the Sands,
He clos'd his Wings, and stoop'd on *Lybian* Lands:
380 Where Shepherds once were hous'd in homely Sheds,
Now Tow'rs within the Clouds, advance their Heads.
Arriving there, he found the *Trojan* Prince,
New Ramparts raising for the Town's defence:
A Purple Scarf, with Gold embroider'd o're,
(Queen *Dido*'s Gift) about his Waste he wore;
A Sword with glitt'ring Gems diversify'd,
For Ornament, not use, hung idly by his side.
Then thus, with winged Words, the God began;
(Resuming his own Shape) Degenerate Man,
390 Thou Woman's Property, what mak'st thou here,
These foreign Walls, and *Tyrian* Tow'rs to rear,
Forgetful of thy own? All pow'rful *Jove,*
Who sways the World below, and Heav'n above,
Has sent me down, with this severe Command:
What means thy ling'ring in the *Lybian* Land?
If Glory cannot move a Mind so mean,
Nor future Praise, from flitting Pleasure wean,
Regard the Fortunes of thy rising Heir;
The promis'd Crown let young *Ascanius* wear:
400 To whom th' *Ausonian* Scepter, and the State
Of *Rome*'s Imperial Name, is ow'd by Fate.
So spoke the God; and speaking took his flight,
Involv'd in Clouds; and vanish'd out of sight.
    The Pious Prince was seiz'd with sudden Fear;
Mute was his Tongue, and upright stood his Hair:
Revolving in his Mind the stern Command,
He longs to fly, and loaths the charming Land.
What shou'd he say, or how shou'd he begin,  ⎫
What Course, alas! remains, to steer between  ⎬
410 Th' offended Lover, and the Pow'rful Queen?  ⎭
This way, and that, he turns his anxious Mind,

377  flies:] ∼. F1–2.          389  Degenerate] degenerate F1–2.
391  rear,] ∼? F1–2.           399  wear:] ∼. F1–2.
410  Queen?] ∼! F1–2.

And all Expedients tries, and none can find:
Fix'd on the Deed, but doubtful of the Means;
After long Thought to this Advice he leans.
Three Chiefs he calls, commands them to repair
The Fleet, and ship their Men with silent Care:
Some plausible Pretence he bids them find,
To colour what in secret he design'd.
Himself, mean time, the softest Hours wou'd chuse,
420 Before the Love-sick Lady heard the News;
And move her tender Mind, by slow degrees,
To suffer what the Sov'raign Pow'r decrees:
*Jove* will inspire him, when, and what to say:
They hear with Pleasure, and with haste obey.
    But soon the Queen perceives the thin Disguise;
(What Arts can blind a jealous Woman's Eyes?)
She was the first to find the secret Fraud,
Before the fatal News was blaz'd abroad.
Love, the first Motions of the Lover hears,
430 Quick to presage, and ev'n in Safety fears.
Nor impious Fame was wanting to report    ⎫
The Ships repair'd; the *Trojans* thick Resort, ⎬
And purpose to forsake the *Tyrian* Court.    ⎭
Frantick with Fear, impatient of the Wound,
And impotent of Mind, she roves the City round.
Less wild the Bacchanalian Dames appear,    ⎫
When, from afar, their nightly God they hear, ⎬
And houl about the Hills, and shake the wreathy Spear. ⎭
At length she finds the dear perfidious Man;
440 Prevents his form'd Excuse, and thus began.
Base and ungrateful, cou'd you hope to fly,
And undiscover'd scape a Lover's Eye?
Nor cou'd my Kindness your Compassion move,
Nor plighted Vows, nor dearer bands of Love?
Or is the Death of a despairing Queen

---

420  News;] ~. F1–2.                    426  Eyes?] ~! F1–2.
436  Bacchanalian] *Bacchanalian* F1–2.      442  undiscover'd] F2; undisover'd F1.
442  Eye?] ~! F1–2.                   444  Love?] ~! F1–2.

Not worth preventing, though too well foreseen?
Ev'n when the Wint'ry Winds command your stay,
You dare the Tempests, and defie the Sea.
False, as you are, suppose you were not bound
450 To Lands unknown, and foreign Coasts to sound;
Were *Troy* restor'd, and *Priam*'s happy Reign,
Now durst you tempt for *Troy*, the raging Main?
See, whom you fly; am I the Foe you shun?
Now by those holy Vows, so late begun,
By this right Hand, (since I have nothing more
To challenge, but the Faith you gave before;)
I beg you by these Tears too truly shed,
By the new Pleasures of our Nuptial Bed;
If ever *Dido*, when you most were kind,
460 Were pleasing in your Eyes, or touch'd your Mind;
By these my Pray'rs, if Pray'rs may yet have Place,
Pity the Fortunes of a falling Race.
For you I have provok'd a Tyrant's Hate,
Incens'd the *Lybian*, and the *Tyrian* State;
For you alone I suffer in my Fame;
Bereft of Honour, and expos'd to Shame:
Whom have I now to trust, ungrateful Guest,
(That only Name remains of all the rest!)
What have I left, or whither can I fly;
470 Must I attend *Pygmalion*'s Cruelty?
Or till *Hyarbas* shall in Triumph lead
A Queen, that proudly scorn'd his proffer'd Bed?
Had you deferr'd, at least, your hasty Flight, ⎫
And left behind some Pledge of our delight, ⎬
Some Babe to bless the Mother's mournful sight; ⎭
Some young *Æneas*, to supply your place;
Whose Features might express his Father's Face;
I should not then complain to live bereft
Of all my Husband, or be wholly left.

447  Ev'n] F2; Even F1.                     467  ungrateful Guest,] (∼ ∼,) F1–2.
468  (That . . . rest!)] ∧∼ . . . ∼!∧ F1–2.     470  Cruelty?] ∼! F1–2.
471  *Hyarbas*] *Hyarba* F1–2.                472  Bed?] ∼! F1–2.

480    Here paus'd the Queen; unmov'd he holds his Eyes, ⎞
By *Jove*'s Command; nor suffer'd Love to rise,            ⎟
Tho' heaving in his Heart; and thus at length, replies. ⎠
Fair Queen, you never can enough repeat
Your boundless Favours, or I own my Debt:
Nor can my Mind forget *Elisa*'s Name,
While vital Breath inspires this Mortal Frame.
This, only let me speak in my Defence,
I never hop'd a secret Flight from hence:
Much less pretended to the Lawful Claim
490 Of Sacred Nuptials, or, a Husband's Name.
For if indulgent Heav'n would leave me free,
And not submit my Life to Fate's Decree,
My Choice would lead me to the *Trojan* Shore, ⎞
Those Reliques to review, their Dust adore;       ⎟
And *Priam*'s ruin'd Palace to restore.               ⎠
But now the *Delphian* Oracle Commands,
And Fate invites me to the *Latian* Lands.
That is the promis'd Place to which I steer,
And all my Vows are terminated there.
500 If you, a *Tyrian,* and a Stranger born,
With Walls and Tow'rs a *Lybian* Town adorn;
Why may not we, like you, a Foreign Race,
Like you seek shelter in a Foreign Place?
As often as the Night obscures the Skies
With humid Shades, or twinkling Stars arise,
*Anchises* angry Ghost in Dreams appears;
Chides my delay, and fills my Soul with fears:
And young *Ascanius* justly may complain,
Of his defrauded Fate, and destin'd Reign.
510 Ev'n now the Herald of the Gods appear'd,
Waking I saw him, and his Message heard.
From *Jove* he came commission'd, Heav'nly bright
With Radiant Beams, and manifest to Sight.
The Sender and the Sent, I both attest,
These Walls he enter'd, and those Words express'd.
Fair Queen, oppose not what the Gods command;

---

485  *Elisa's*] *Eliza's* F1–2.                    496  Oracle] *Oracle* F1–2.

Forc'd by my Fate, I leave your happy Land.
   Thus, while he spoke, already She began,
With sparkling Eyes, to view the guilty Man:
520 From Head to Foot survey'd his Person o're,
Nor longer these outrageous Threats forbore.
False as thou art, and more than false, forsworn;
Not sprung from Noble Blood, nor Goddess-born,
But hewn from hardned Entrails of a Rock;
And rough *Hyrcanian* Tygers gave thee suck:
Why shou'd I fawn, what have I worse to fear? )
Did he once look, or lent a list'ning Ear; )
Sigh'd when I sob'd, or shed one kindly Tear? )
All Symptoms of a base Ungrateful Mind,
530 So foul, that which is worse, 'tis hard to find.
Of Man's Injustice, why shou'd I complain?
The Gods, and *Jove* himself behold in vain
Triumphant Treason, yet no Thunder flyes: )
Nor *Juno* views my Wrongs with equal Eyes; )
Faithless is Earth, and Faithless are the Skies! )
Justice is fled, and Truth is now no more;
I sav'd the Shipwrack'd Exile on my Shore:
With needful Food his hungry *Trojans* fed;
I took the Traytor to my Throne and Bed:
540 Fool that I was———'tis little to repeat
The rest, I stor'd and Rigg'd his ruin'd Fleet.
I rave, I rave: A God's Command he pleads,
And makes Heav'n accessary to his Deeds.
Now *Lycian* Lotts, and now the *Delian* God;
Now *Hermes* is employ'd from *Jove*'s abode,
To warn him hence; as if the peaceful State
Of Heav'nly Pow'rs were touch'd with Humane Fate!
But go; thy flight no longer I detain;
Go seek thy promis'd Kingdom through the Main:
550 Yet if the Heav'ns will hear my Pious Vow,
The faithless Waves, not half so false as thou,
Or secret Sands, shall Sepulchers afford
To thy proud Vessels, and their perjur'd Lord.

---

525  suck:] ~. F1–2.            551  thou,] F2; ~; F1.

Then shalt thou call on injur'd *Dido*'s Name;  
*Dido* shall come, in a black Sulph'ry flame;  
When death has once dissolv'd her Mortal frame:  
Shall smile to see the Traitor vainly weep;  
Her angry Ghost arising from the Deep,  
Shall haunt thee waking, and disturb thy Sleep.  
560 At least my Shade thy Punishment shall know;  
And Fame shall spread the pleasing News below.  

Abruptly here she stops: Then turns away  
Her loathing Eyes, and shuns the sight of Day.  
Amaz'd he stood, revolving in his Mind  
What Speech to frame, and what Excuse to find.  
Her fearful Maids their fainting Mistress led;  
And softly laid her on her Iv'ry Bed.  

But good *Æneas*, tho' he much desir'd  
To give that Pity, which her Grief requir'd,  
570 Tho' much he mourn'd, and labour'd with his **Love**,  
Resolv'd at length, obeys the Will of *Jove*:  
Reviews his Forces; they with early Care  
Unmoor their Vessels, and for Sea prepare.  
The Fleet is soon afloat, in all its Pride:  
And well calk'd Gallies in the Harbour ride.  
Then Oaks for Oars they fell'd; or as they stood,  
Of its green Arms despoil'd the growing Wood;  
Studious of Flight: The Beach is cover'd o're  
With *Trojan* Bands that blacken all the Shore:  
580 On ev'ry side are seen, descending down,  
Thick swarms of Souldiers loaden from the Town.  
Thus, in Battalia, march embody'd Ants,  
Fearful of Winter, and of future Wants,  
T' invade the Corn, and to their Cells convey  
The plunder'd Forrage of their yellow Prey.  
The sable Troops, along the narrow Tracks,  
Scarce bear the weighty Burthen on their Backs:  
Some set their Shoulders to the pond'rous Grain;  
Some guard the Spoil, some lash the lagging Train;  
590 All ply their sev'ral Tasks, and equal Toil sustain.  

---

556  frame:] ∼. F1–2.                557  weep;] ∼, F1–2.  
577  Wood;] ∼. F1–2.

What Pangs the tender Breast of *Dido* tore,
When, from the Tow'r, she saw the cover'd Shore,
And heard the Shouts of Sailors from afar,
Mix'd with the Murmurs of the wat'ry War!
All pow'rful Love, what Changes canst thou cause
In Human Hearts, subjected to thy Laws!
Once more her haughty Soul the Tyrant bends;
To Pray'rs and mean Submissions she descends.
No female Arts or Aids she left untry'd,
600 Nor Counsels unexplor'd, before she dy'd.
Look, *Anna*, look; the *Trojans* crowd to Sea,
They spread their Canvass, and their Anchors weigh.
The shouting Crew, their Ships with Garlands bind;
Invoke the Sea-Gods, and invite the Wind.
Cou'd I have thought this threatning Blow so near,
My tender Soul had been forewarn'd to bear.
But do not you my last Request deny,          ⎞
With yon perfidious Man your Int'rest try;    ⎬
And bring me News, if I must live or dye.     ⎠
610 You are his Fav'rite, you alone can find
The dark recesses of his inmost Mind:
In all his trusted Secrets you have part,
And know the soft Approaches to his Heart.
Haste then, and humbly seek my haughty Foe;
Tell him, I did not with the *Grecians* goe;
Nor did my Fleet against his Friends employ,
Nor swore the Ruin of unhappy *Troy*,
Nor mov'd with Hands prophane his Father's Dust;
Why shou'd he then reject a suit so just?
620 Whom does he shun, and whither would he fly;
Can he this last, this only Pray'r deny?
Let him at least his dang'rous Flight delay,
Wait better Winds, and hope a calmer Sea.
The Nuptials he disclaims I urge no more;
Let him pursue the promis'd *Latian* Shore.
A short delay is all I ask him now,

594  War!] ∼? F1–2.          603  bind] F2; binds F1.
604  Wind] F2; Winds F1.     617  *Troy*,] ∼. F1–2.
619  just?] ∼! F1–2.         621  deny?] ∼! F1–2.

A pause of Grief; an interval from Woe:
'Till my soft Soul be temper'd to sustain
Accustom'd Sorrows, and inur'd to Pain.
630 If you in Pity grant this one Request,
My Death shall glut the Hatred of his Brest.
This mournful message, Pious *Anna* bears,
And seconds, with her own, her Sister's Tears:
But all her Arts are still employ'd in vain;
Again she comes, and is refus'd again.
His harden'd Heart nor Pray'rs nor Threatnings move;
Fate, and the God, had stop'd his Ears to Love.
    As when the Winds their airy Quarrel try;
Justling from ev'ry quarter of the Sky;
640 This way and that, the Mountain Oak they bend,
His Boughs they shatter, and his Branches rend;
With Leaves, and falling Mast, they spread the Ground,
The hollow Vallies echo to the Sound:
Unmov'd, the Royal Plant their Fury mocks;
Or shaken, clings more closely to the Rocks:
Far as he shoots his tow'ring Head on high,
So deep in Earth his fix'd Foundations lye:
No less a Storm the *Trojan* Heroe bears;      ⎞
Thick Messages and loud Complaints he hears; ⎬
650 And bandy'd Words, still beating on his Ears. ⎠
Sighs, Groans and Tears, proclaim his inward Pains,
But the firm purpose of his Heart remains.
    The wretched Queen, pursu'd by cruel Fate,
Begins at length the light of Heav'n to hate:
And loaths to live: Then dire Portents she sees,
To hasten on the Death her Soul decrees:
Strange to relate: for when before the Shrine
She pours, in Sacrifice, the Purple Wine,
The Purple Wine is turn'd to putrid Blood:
660 And the white offer'd Milk, converts to Mud.
This dire Presage, to her alone reveal'd,
From all, and ev'n her Sister, she conceal'd.

---

631   glut the Hatred of his Brest] F2; leave you of my Crown possess'd F1.
647   lye:] ~. F1–2.                    656   decrees:] ~. F1–2.

A Marble Temple stood within the Grove,
Sacred to Death, and to her murther'd Love;
That honour'd Chappel she had hung around
With snowy Fleeces, and with Garlands crown'd:
Oft, when she visited this lonely Dome,
Strange Voices issu'd from her Husband's Tomb:
She thought she heard him summon her away;
670 Invite her to his Grave; and chide her stay.
Hourly 'tis heard, when with a bodeing Note
The solitary Screech-Owl strains her Throat:
And on a Chimney's top, or Turret's hight,
With Songs obscene, disturbs the Silence of the Night.
Besides, old Prophesies augment her Fears;
And stern *Æneas* in her Dreams appears,
Disdainful as by Day: She seems alone,
To wander in her Sleep, thro ways unknown,
Guidless and dark: or, in a Desart Plain,
680 To seek her Subjects, and to seek in vain:
Like *Pentheus,* when distracted with his Fear,
He saw two Suns, and double *Thebes* appear:
Or mad *Orestes,* when his Mother's Ghost
Full in his Face, infernal Torches tost;
And shook her snaky locks: He shuns the sight,
Flies o're the Stage, surpris'd with mortal fright;
The Furies guard the Door; and intercept his flight.
Now, sinking underneath a load of Grief,
From Death alone, she seeks her last Relief:
690 The Time and Means, resolv'd within her Breast,
She to her mournful Sister, thus address'd.
(Dissembling hope, her cloudy front she clears,
And a false Vigour in her Eyes appears.)
Rejoice she said, instructed from above,
My Lover I shall gain, or lose my Love.
Nigh rising *Atlas,* next the falling Sun,
Long tracts of *Ethiopian* Clymates run:

---

680 vain:] ~. F1–2.
697 *Ethiopian*] F1 (*corrected state*); *Ethiopyan* F1 (*uncorrected state*); *Æthiopian*
F2.

To Henry Tasburgh                    Esq. of Bodney in ẏ
        County of                         Norfolk.

There, a *Massylian* Priestess I have found,
Honour'd for Age; for Magick Arts renown'd:
700 Th' *Hesperian* Temple was her trusted Care;
'Twas she supply'd the wakeful Dragons Fare.
She Poppy-Seeds in Honey taught to steep;
Reclaim'd his Rage; and sooth'd him into sleep.
She watch'd the Golden Fruit; her Charms unbind
The Chains of Love; or fix them on the Mind.
She stops the Torrents, leaves the Channel dry;
Repels the Stars; and backward bears the Sky.
The yawning Earth rebellows to her Call;
Pale Ghosts ascend; and Mountain Ashes fall.
710 Witness, ye Gods, and thou my better part,
How loth I am to try this impious Art!
Within the secret Court, with silent Care,
Erect a lofty Pile, expos'd in Air:
Hang on the topmost part, the *Trojan* Vest;
Spoils, Arms, and Presents of my faithless Guest.
Next, under these, the bridal Bed be plac'd,
Where I my Ruin in his Arms embrac'd:
All Relicks of the Wretch are doom'd to Fire;
For so the Priestess, and her Charms require.
720 Thus far she said, and farther Speech forbears:
A Mortal Paleness in her Face appears:
Yet, the mistrustless *Anna,* could not find          )
The secret Fun'ral, in these Rites design'd;          }
Nor thought so dire a Rage possess'd her Mind.        )
Unknowing of a Train conceal'd so well,
She fear'd no worse than when *Sichæus* fell:
Therefore obeys. The fatal Pile they rear,
Within the secret Court, expos'd in Air.
The cloven Holms and Pines are heap'd on high;
730 And Garlands on the hollow Spaces lye.
Sad Cypress, Vervain, Eugh, compose the Wreath;
And ev'ry baleful green denoting Death.
The Queen, determin'd to the fatal Deed,               )
The Spoils and Sword he left, in order spread:         }
And the Man's Image on the Nuptial Bed.                )

And now (the sacred Altars plac'd around)  ⎫
The Priestess enters, with her Hair unbound,  ⎬
And thrice invokes the Pow'rs below the Ground.  ⎭
Night, *Erebus,* and Chaos she proclaims,
740 And threefold *Hecat,* with her hundred Names,
And three *Diana's:* next she sprinkles round,
With feign'd *Avernian* Drops, the hallow'd ground;
Culls hoary Simples, found by *Phœbe*'s Light,
With brazen Sickles reap'd at Noon of Night:
Then mixes baleful Juices in the Bowl:
And cuts the Forehead of a new-born Fole;
Robbing the Mother's love. The destin'd Queen
Observes, assisting at the Rites obscene:
A leaven'd Cake in her devoted Hands
750 She holds, and next the highest Altar stands:
One tender Foot was shod, her other bare;
Girt was her gather'd Gown, and loose her Hair.
Thus dress'd, she summon'd with her dying Breath,
The Heav'ns and Planets conscious of her Death:
And ev'ry Pow'r, if any rules above,
Who minds, or who revenges injur'd Love.
     'Twas dead of Night, when weary Bodies close
Their Eyes in balmy Sleep, and soft Repose:
The Winds no longer whisper through the Woods,
760 Nor murm'ring Tides disturb the gentle Floods.
The Stars in silent order mov'd around,
And Peace, with downy wings, was brooding on the ground.
The Flocks and Herds, and parti-colour'd Fowl,
Which haunt the Woods, or swim the weedy Pool;
Stretch'd on the quiet Earth securely lay,
Forgetting the past Labours of the day.
All else of Nature's common Gift partake;
Unhappy *Dido* was alone awake.
Nor Sleep nor Ease the Furious Queen can find,
770 Sleep fled her Eyes, as Quiet fled her mind.
Despair, and Rage, and Love, divide her heart;
Despair and Rage had some, but Love the greater part.

---

739  Chaos] *Chaos* F1–2.               744  Night:] ∼. F1–2.

Then thus she said within her secret Mind:
What shall I do, what Succour can I find?
Become a Supplyant to *Hyarbas* Pride,
And take my turn, to Court and be deny'd?
Shall I with this ungrateful *Trojan* go,
Forsake an Empire, and attend a Foe?
Himself I refug'd, and his Train reliev'd;
780 Tis true; but am I sure to be receiv'd?
Can Gratitude in *Trojan* Souls have place?
*Laomedon* still lives in all his Race!
Then, shall I seek alone the Churlish Crew,
Or with my Fleet their flying Sails pursue?
What force have I but those, whom scarce before
I drew reluctant from their Native Shore?
Will they again Embark at my desire,
Once more sustain the Seas, and quit their second *Tyre?*
Rather with Steel thy guilty Breast invade,
790 And take the Fortune thou thy self hast made.
Your pity, Sister, first seduc'd my Mind;
Or seconded too well, what I design'd.
These dear-bought Pleasures had I never known,
Had I continu'd free, and still my own;
Avoiding Love; I had not found Despair:
But shar'd with Salvage Beasts the Common Air.
Like them a lonely life I might have led,
Not mourn'd the Living, nor disturb'd the Dead.
These Thoughts she brooded in her anxious Breast;
800 On Boord, the *Trojan* found more easie rest.
Resolv'd to sail, in Sleep he pass'd the Night;
And order'd all things for his early flight.
    To whom once more the winged God appears; ⎫
His former Youthful Meen and Shape he wears, ⎬
And with this new alarm invades his Ears. ⎭

---

774  find?] ∼! F1–2.
775  *Hyarbas*] *Hyarba's* F1–2.
776  deny'd?] ∼! F1–2.
780  *after this line F1 (only) has another, making a triplet:* An Exile follows whom a Queen reliev'd!
781  place?] ∼! F1–2.

Sleep'st thou, O Goddess born! and can'st thou drown
Thy needful Cares, so near a Hostile Town?
Beset with Foes; nor hear'st the Western Gales
Invite thy passage, and Inspire thy sails?
810 She harbours in her Heart a furious hate;
And thou shalt find the dire Effects too late;
Fix'd on Revenge, and Obstinate to die:
Haste swiftly hence, while thou hast pow'r to fly.
The Sea with Ships will soon be cover'd o're,
And blazing Firebrands kindle all the Shore.
Prevent her rage, while Night obscures the Skies;
And sail before the purple Morn arise.
Who knows what Hazards thy Delay may bring?
Woman's a various and a changeful Thing.
820 Thus *Hermes* in the Dream; then took his flight,
Aloft in Air unseen; and mix'd with Night.

Twice warn'd by the Cœlestial Messenger,
The pious Prince arose with hasty fear:
Then rowz'd his drowsie Train without delay, ⎞
Haste to your banks; your crooked Anchors weigh; ⎬
And spread your flying Sails, and stand to Sea. ⎠
A God commands; he stood before my sight;
And urg'd us once again to speedy flight.
O sacred Pow'r, what Pow'r so e're thou art,
830 To thy bless'd Orders I resign my heart:
Lead thou the way; protect thy *Trojan* Bands;
And prosper the Design thy Will Commands.
He said, and drawing forth his flaming Sword,
His thund'ring Arm divides the many twisted Cord:
An emulating Zeal inspires his Train;
They run, they snatch; they rush into the main.
With headlong haste they leave the desert Shores,
And brush the liquid Seas with lab'ring Oars.
*Aurora* now had left her Saffron Bed,
840 And beams of early Light the Heav'ns o'respread,
When from a Tow'r the Queen, with wakeful Eyes,
Saw Day point upward from the rosie Skies:

823  Prince] F1 *errata*, F2; Pious F1.

She look'd to Seaward, but the Sea was void,
And scarce in ken the sailing Ships descry'd:
Stung with despight, and furious with despair,
She struck her trembling Breast, and tore her Hair.
And shall th' ungrateful Traytor go, she said,
My Land forsaken, and my Love betray'd?
Shall we not Arm, not rush from ev'ry Street,
850 To follow, sink, and burn his perjur'd Fleet?
Haste, haul my Gallies out, pursue the Foe:
Bring flaming Brands, set sail, and swiftly row.
What have I said? where am I? Fury turns
My Brain; and my distemper'd Bosom burns.
Then, when I gave my Person and my Throne,
This Hate, this Rage, had been more timely shown.
See now the promis'd Faith, the vaunted Name,
The Pious Man, who, rushing through the Flame,
Preserv'd his Gods; and to the *Phrygian* Shore
860 The Burthen of his feeble Father bore!
I shou'd have torn him piecemeal; strow'd in Floods
His scatter'd Limbs, or left expos'd in Woods:
Destroy'd his Friends and Son; and from the Fire
Have set the reeking Boy before the Sire.
Events are doubtful, which on Battels wait;
Yet where's the doubt, to Souls secure of Fate?
My *Tyrians,* at their injur'd Queen's Command,
Had toss'd their Fires amid the *Trojan* Band:
At once extinguish'd all the faithless Name;
870 And I my self, in vengeance of my Shame,
Had fall'n upon the Pile to mend the Fun'ral Flame.
Thou Sun, who view'st at once the World below,
Thou *Juno,* Guardian of the Nuptial Vow,
Thou *Hecat,* hearken from thy dark abodes;
Ye Furies, Fiends, and violated Gods,
All Pow'rs invok'd with *Dido*'s dying breath,
Attend her Curses, and avenge her death.
If so the Fates ordain, and *Jove* commands,
Th' ungrateful Wretch should find the *Latian* Lands,

866  Fate?] ~! F1–2.

880 Yet let a Race untam'd, and haughty Foes,
His peaceful Entrance with dire Arms oppose;
Oppress'd with Numbers in th' unequal Field,
His Men discourag'd, and himself expell'd,
Let him for Succour sue from place to place,
Torn from his Subjects, and his Son's embrace:
First let him see his Friends in Battel slain;
And their untimely Fate lament in vain:
And when, at length, the cruell War shall cease;
On hard Conditions may he buy his Peace.
890 Nor let him then enjoy supreme Command; ⎫
But fall untimely, by some hostile Hand:   ⎬
And lye unbury'd on the barren Sand.        ⎭
These are my Pray'rs, and this my dying Will:
And you my *Tyrians* ev'ry Curse fulfill.
Perpetual Hate, and mortal Wars proclaim,
Against the Prince, the People, and the Name.
These grateful Off'rings on my Grave bestow;
Nor League, nor Love, the hostile Nations know:
Now, and from hence in ev'ry future Age,
900 When Rage excites your Arms, and Strength supplies the Rage:
Rise some Avenger of our *Lybian* Blood,
With Fire and Sword pursue the perjur'd Brood:
Our Arms, our Seas, our Shores, oppos'd to theirs,
And the same hate descend on all our Heirs.
        This said, within her anxious Mind she weighs
The Means of cutting short her odious Days.
Then to *Sichæus* Nurse, she briefly said,
(For when she left her Country, hers was dead)
Go *Barcè,* call my Sister; let her Care
910 The solemn Rites of Sacrifice prepare:
The Sheep, and all th' attoneing Off'rings bring;
Sprinkling her Body from the Crystal Spring
With living Drops: then let her come, and thou
With sacred Fillets, bind thy hoary Brow.
Thus will I pay my Vows, to *Stygian Jove;*
And end the Cares of my disastrous Love.

---

898  hostile] F2 (Hostile); jarring F1.       907  *Sichæus*] *Sicheus*'s F1–2.

Then cast the *Trojan* Image on the Fire;
And as that burns, my Passion shall expire.
    The Nurse moves onward, with officious Care,
920 And all the speed her aged Limbs can bear.
But furious *Dido*, with dark Thoughts involv'd,
Shook at the mighty Mischief she resolv'd.
With livid Spots distinguish'd was her Face,
Red were her rowling Eyes, and discompos'd her Pace:
Ghastly she gaz'd, with Pain she drew her Breath,
And Nature shiver'd at approaching Death.
    Then swiftly to the fatal place she pass'd;
And mounts the Fun'ral Pile, with furious haste:
Unsheaths the Sword the *Trojan* left behind,
930 (Not for so dire an Enterprise design'd,)
But when she view'd the Garments loosely spred,
Which once he wore, and saw the conscious Bed,
She paus'd, and, with a Sigh, the Robes embrac'd;
Then on the Couch her trembling Body cast,
Repress'd the ready Tears, and spoke her last.
Dear Pledges of my Love, while Heav'n so pleas'd,
Receive a Soul, of Mortal Anguish eas'd:
My fatal Course is finish'd; and I go
A glorious Name, among the Ghosts below.
940 A lofty City by my Hands is rais'd;
*Pygmalion* punish'd, and my Lord appeas'd.
What cou'd my Fortune have afforded more,
Had the false *Trojan* never touch'd my Shore?
Then kiss'd the Couch; and must I die, she said;
And unreveng'd? 'tis doubly to be dead!
Yet ev'n this Death with Pleasure I receive;
On any Terms, 'tis better than to live.
These Flames, from far, may the false *Trojan* view;
These boding Omens his base flight pursue.
950 She said, and struck: Deep enter'd in her side
The piercing Steel, with reeking Purple dy'd:
Clog'd in the Wound the cruel Weapon stands;

---

928   haste:] ∼. F1–2.                    943   Shore?] ∼! F1–2.
945   unreveng'd?] ∼; F1–2.

To Dorothy Brownlowe Daughter &Coheiress of Sʳ Richard Mason
Kᵗ Clerk Comtroler of ye Greencloth to K.Charles ye 2ᵈ & K.Iames ye 2
Wife to William Brownlowe 2.Son to Sʳ Richard Brownlowe
Barᵗ of Humby in ye County of Lincolne

The spouting Blood came streaming on her Hands.
Her sad Attendants saw the deadly Stroke,
And with loud Cries the sounding Palace shook.
Distracted from the fatal sight they fled;
And thro the Town the dismal Rumor spread.
First from the frighted Court, the Yell began,
Redoubled thence from House to House it ran:
960 The groans of Men, with Shrieks, Laments, and Cries
Of mixing Women, mount the vaulted Skies:
Not less the Clamour, than if ancient *Tyre,*
Or the new *Carthage,* set by Foes on Fire,
The rowling Ruin, with their lov'd Abodes,
Involv'd the blazing Temples of their Gods.
Her Sister hears, and, furious with Despair,
She beats her Breast, and rends her yellow Hair:
And calling on *Elisa's* Name aloud,
Runs breathless to the Place, and breaks the Crowd.
970 Was all that Pomp of Woe for this prepar'd,
These Fires, this Fun'ral Pile, these Altars rear'd;
Was all this Train of Plots contriv'd, said she,
All only to deceive unhappy me?
Which is the worst, didst thou in Death pretend
To scorn thy Sister, or delude thy Friend?
Thy summon'd Sister, and thy Friend had come:
One Sword had serv'd us both, one common Tomb.
Was I to raise the Pile, the Pow'rs invoke,
Not to be present at the fatal Stroke?
980 At once thou hast destroy'd thy self and me;
Thy Town, thy Senate, and thy Colony!
Bring Water, bathe the Wound; while I in death
Lay close my Lips to hers; and catch the flying Breath.
This said, she mounts the Pile with eager haste;
And in her Arms the gasping Queen embrac'd:
Her Temples chaf'd; and her own Garments tore
To stanch the streaming Blood, and cleanse the Gore.
Thrice *Dido* try'd to raise her drooping Head,

---

961  Skies:] ∼. F1–2.                    968  *Elisa's*] *Eliza's* F1–2.
975  Friend?] ∼! F1–2.

And fainting thrice, fell grov'ling on the Bed:
990 Thrice op'd her heavy Eyes, and sought the Light, ⎞
But having found it, sicken'd at the sight; ⎟
And clos'd her Lids at last, in endless Night. ⎠
Then *Juno,* grieving that she shou'd sustain
A Death so ling'ring, and so full of Pain;
Sent *Iris* down, to free her from the Strife
Of lab'ring Nature, and dissolve her Life.
For since she dy'd, not doom'd by Heav'ns Decree,
Or her own Crime; but Human Casualty;
And rage of Love, that plung'd her in Despair;
1000 The Sisters had not cut the topmost Hair;
Which *Proserpine,* and they can only know;
Nor made her sacred to the Shades below.
Downward the various Goddess took her flight;
And drew a thousand Colours from the Light:
Then stood above the dying Lover's Head,
And said, I thus devote thee to the dead.
This Off'ring to th' Infernal Gods I bear: ⎞
Thus while she spoke, she cut the fatal Hair; ⎟
The strugling Soul was loos'd; and Life dissolv'd in Air. ⎠

---

989  Bed:] ~. F1–2.                 999  Despair;] ~, F1–2.
1007  th'] F2; the F1.

To the most Illustrious     Prince Charles Duke of
S.ᵗ Albans Master     Falconer to his Ma.ᵗʸ and
Captaine of ẙ Hon.ᵇˡᵉ     Band of Gen.ᵗ Pensioners

## *The Fifth Book of the Æneis*

### THE ARGUMENT.

*Æneas setting sail from* Africk, *is driven by a Storm on the Coasts of* Sicily: *Where he is hospitably receiv'd by his friend* Acestes, *King of part of the Island, and born of* Trojan *Parentage. He applies himself to celebrate the Memory of his Father with Divine Honours: And accordingly institutes Funeral Games, and appoints Prizes for those who shou'd conquer in them. While the Ceremonies were performing,* Juno *sends* Iris *to perswade the* Trojan *Women to burn the Ships, who upon her instigation set fire to them, which burnt four, and would have consum'd the rest, had not* Jupiter *by a miraculous Shower extinguish'd it. Upon this* Æneas *by the advice of one of his Generals, and a Vision of his Father, builds a City for the Women, Old Men, and others, who were either unfit for War, or weary of the Voyage, and sails for* Italy: Venus *procures of* Neptune *a safe Voyage for him and all his Men, excepting only his Pilot* Palinurus, *who is unfortunately lost.*

M EAN time the *Trojan* cuts his wat'ry way,
 Fix'd on his Voyage, thro the curling Sea:
 Then, casting back his Eyes, with dire Amaze,
Sees on the *Punic* Shore the mounting Blaze.
The Cause unknown; yet his presaging Mind, ⎫
The Fate of *Dido* from the Fire divin'd:  ⎬
He knew the stormy Souls of Woman-kind: ⎭
What secret Springs their eager Passions move,
How capable of Death for injur'd Love.
10 Dire Auguries from hence the *Trojans* draw;
'Till neither Fires, nor shining Shores they saw.
Now Seas and Skies, their Prospect only bound;
An empty space above, a floating Field around.
But soon the Heav'ns with shadows were o'respread;

16 *is*] F2; *was* F1.

A swelling Cloud hung hov'ring o're their Head:
Livid it look'd, (the threatning of a Storm;)
Then Night and Horror Ocean's Face deform.
The Pilot, *Palinurus,* cry'd aloud,
What Gusts of Weather from that gath'ring Cloud
20 My Thoughts presage; e're yet the Tempest roars,
Stand to your Tackle, Mates, and stretch your Oars;
Contract your swelling Sails, and luff to Wind:
The frighted Crew perform the Task assign'd.
Then, to his fearless Chief, Not Heav'n, said he, ⎱
Tho *Jove* himself shou'd promise *Italy,*        ⎰
Can stem the Torrent of this raging Sea.          ⎰
Mark how the shifting Winds from West arise,
And what collected Night involves the Skies!
Nor can our shaken Vessels live at Sea,         ⎱
30 Much less against the Tempest force their way;  ⎰
'Tis Fate diverts our Course; and Fate we must obey. ⎰
Not far from hence, if I observ'd aright
The southing of the Stars, and Polar Light,
*Sicilia* lies; whose hospitable Shores
In safety we may reach with strugling Oars.
*Æneas* then reply'd, Too sure I find,
We strive in vain against the Seas, and Wind:
Now shift your Sails: What place can please me more
Than what you promise, the *Sicilian* Shore;
40 Whose hallow'd Earth *Anchises* Bones contains,
And where a Prince of *Trojan* Lineage reigns?
The Course resolv'd, before the Western Wind
They scud amain; and make the Port assign'd.
     Mean time *Acestes,* from a lofty Stand,
Beheld the Fleet descending on the Land;
And not unmindful of his ancient Race,        ⎱
Down from the Cliff he ran with eager Pace;   ⎰
And held the Heroe in a strict Embrace.       ⎰
Of a rough *Lybian* Bear the Spoils he wore;
50 And either Hand a pointed Jav'lin bore.
His Mother was a Dame of *Dardan* Blood;

24  Not] not F1–2.                    36  Too] too F1–2.

His Sire *Crinisus,* a *Sicilian* Flood;
He welcomes his returning Friends ashore
With plenteous Country Cates; and homely Store.
   Now, when the following Morn had chas'd away
The flying Stars, and light restor'd the Day,
*Æneas* call'd the *Trojan* Troops around;
And thus bespoke them from a rising Ground.
Off-spring of Heav'n, Divine *Dardanian* Race,
60 The Sun revolving thro' th' Etherial Space,
The shining Circle of the Year has fill'd,
Since first this Isle my Father's Ashes held:
And now the rising Day renews the Year,
(A Day for ever sad, for ever dear,)
This wou'd I celebrate with Annual Games,
With Gifts on Altars pil'd, and holy Flames,
Tho banish'd to *Getulia*'s barren Sands,
Caught on the *Grecian* Seas, or hostile Lands:
But since this happy Storm our Fleet has driv'n,
70 (Not, as I deem, without the Will of Heav'n,)
Upon these friendly Shores, and flow'ry Plains,
Which hide *Anchises,* and his blest Remains;
Let us with Joy perform his Honours due;
And pray for prosp'rous Winds, our Voyage to renew.
Pray, that in Towns, and Temples of our own,   )
The Name of great *Anchises* may be known;   }
And yearly Games may spread the Gods renown. )
Our Sports, *Acestes* of the *Trojan* Race,
With royal Gifts, ordain'd, is pleas'd to grace:
80 Two Steers on ev'ry Ship the King bestows;
His Gods and ours, shall share your equal Vows.
Besides, if nine days hence, the rosy Morn
Shall with unclouded Light the Skies adorn,
That Day with solemn Sports I mean to grace;
Light Gallies on the Seas, shall run a wat'ry Race.
Some shall in Swiftness for the Goal contend,
And others try the twanging Bow to bend:
The strong with Iron Gauntlets arm'd shall stand,

---

88  Gauntlets] F1 *(corrected state),* F2; Gnntlets F1 *(uncorrected state).*

Oppos'd in Combat on the yellow Sand.
90 Let all be present at the Games prepar'd;
And joyful Victors wait the Just Reward.
But now assist the Rites, with Garlands crown'd;
He said, and first his Brows with Myrtle bound.
Then *Helymus,* by his Example led,
And old *Acestes,* each adorn'd his Head;
Thus, young *Ascanius,* with a sprightly Grace,
His Temples ty'd, and all the *Trojan* Race.
    *Æneas* then advanc'd amidst the Train,
By thousands follow'd thro' the flowry Plain,
100 To great *Anchises* Tomb: Which when he found,
He pour'd to *Bacchus,* on the hallow'd Ground,
Two Bowls of sparkling Wine, of Milk two more,
And two from offer'd Bulls of Purple Gore.
With Roses then the Sepulchre he strow'd;
And thus, his Father's Ghost bespoke aloud.
Hail, O ye Holy *Manes;* hail again
Paternal Ashes, now review'd in vain!
The Gods permitted not, that you, with me, ⎫
Shou'd reach the promis'd Shores of *Italy;* ⎬
110 Or *Tiber's* Flood, what Flood so e're it be. ⎭
Scarce had he finish'd, when, with speckled Pride,
A Serpent from the Tomb began to glide;
His hugy Bulk on sev'n high Volumes roll'd;
Blue was his breadth of Back, but streak'd with scaly Gold:
Thus riding on his Curls, he seem'd to pass
A rowling Fire along; and singe the Grass.
More various Colours thro' his Body run,
Than *Iris* when her Bow imbibes the Sun;
Betwixt the rising Altars, and around,
120 The sacred Monster shot along the Ground;
With harmless play amidst the Bowls he pass'd;
And with his lolling Tongue assay'd the Taste:
Thus fed with Holy Food, the wond'rous Guest
Within the hollow Tomb retir'd to rest.

---

96  *Ascanius,*] F1 (*corrected state*), F2; ~∧ F1 (*uncorrected state*).
99  flowry] F2; fruitful F1.          106  *Manes*] Manes F1–2.

The Pious Prince, surpris'd at what he view'd,
The Fun'ral Honours with more Zeal renew'd:
Doubtful if this the Place's Genius were,
Or Guardian of his Father's Sepulchre.
Five Sheep, according to the Rites, he slew;
130 As many Swine, and Steers of sable Hue;
New gen'rous Wine he from the Goblets pour'd,
And call'd his Fathers Ghost, from Hell restor'd.
The glad Attendants in long Order come,
Off'ring their Gifts at great *Anchises* Tomb:
Some add more Oxen, some divide the Spoil, )
Some place the Chargers on the grassy Soil; }
Some blow the Fires and offer'd Entrails broil. )
   Now came the Day desir'd; the Skies were bright
With rosy Lustre of the rising Light:
140 The bord'ring People, rowz'd by sounding Fame
Of *Trojan* Feasts, and great *Acestes* Name;
The crowded Shore with Acclamations fill,
Part to behold, and part to prove their Skill.
And first the Gifts in Publick view they place,
Green Lawrel Wreaths, and Palm, (the Victors grace:)
Within the Circle, Arms and Tripods lye; )
Ingotts of Gold, and Silver, heap'd on high; }
And Vests embroider'd of the *Tyrian* dye. )
The Trumpet's clangor then the Feast proclaims;
150 And all prepare for their appointed Games.
Four Gallies first which equal Rowers bear,
Advancing, in the wat'ry Lists appear.
The speedy *Dolphin,* that out-strips the Wind,
Bore *Mnestheus,* Author of the *Memmian* kind:
*Gyas,* the vast *Chymæra's* Bulk commands,
Which rising like a tow'ring City stands:
Three *Trojans* tug at ev'ry lab'ring Oar; )
Three Banks in three degrees the Sailors bore; }
Beneath their sturdy Stroaks the Billows roar. )
160 *Sergesthus,* who began the *Sergian* Race,
In the great *Centaur* took the leading Place:

---

153 *Dolphin*] Dolphin F1–2.      155 *Chymæra's*] Chymœra's F1–2.

To the Right Hon:ble                    Arthur Herbert
Earle of Torrington &              Baron of Torbay

*Cloanthus* on the Sea-green *Scylla* stood;
From whom *Cluentius* draws his *Trojan* Blood.
   Far in the Sea, against the foaming Shoar,
There stands a Rock; the raging Billows roar
Above his Head in Storms; but when 'tis clear,
Uncurl their ridgy Backs, and at his Foot appear.
In Peace below the gentle Waters run;
The Cormorants above, lye basking in the Sun.
170 On this the Heroe fix'd an Oak in sight,
The mark to guide the Mariners aright.
To bear with this, the Seamen stretch their Oars;
Then round the Rock they steer, and seek the former Shoars.
The Lots decide their place; above the rest,
Each Leader shining in his *Tyrian* Vest:
The common Crew, with Wreaths of Poplar Boughs,
Their Temples crown, and shade their sweaty Brows.
Besmear'd with Oil, their naked Shoulders shine;
All take their Seats, and wait the sounding sign.
180 They gripe their Oars, and ev'ry panting Breast
Is rais'd by turns with Hope, by turns with Fear depress'd.
The clangor of the Trumpet gives the Sign;
At once they start, advancing in a Line:
With shouts the Sailors rend the starry Skys, ⎫
Lash'd with their Oars, the smoaky Billows rise; ⎬
Sparkles the briny Main, and the vex'd Ocean fries. ⎭
Exact in time, with equal Strokes they row; ⎫
At once the brushing Oars, and brazen prow ⎬
Dash up the sandy Waves, and ope the Depths below. ⎭
190 Not fiery Coursers, in a Chariot Race,
Invade the Field with half so swift a Pace.
Not the fierce Driver with more Fury lends ⎫
The sounding Lash; and, e're the Stroke descends, ⎬
Low to the Wheels his pliant Body bends. ⎭
The partial Crowd their Hopes and Fears divide;
And aid, with eager shouts, the favour'd Side.
Cries, Murmurs, Clamours, with a mixing Sound,

---

188   prow] F1 *errata*, F2; ptow F1.

From Woods to Woods, from Hills to Hills rebound.
　Amidst the loud Applauses of the Shore,
200 *Gyas* outstrip'd the rest, and sprung before;
*Cloanthus,* better mann'd, pursu'd him fast;
But his o're-masted Gally check'd his Haste.
The *Centaur*, and the *Dolphin,* brush the brine
With equal Oars, advancing in a Line:
And now the mighty *Centaur* seems to lead,
And now the speedy *Dolphin* gets a head:
Now Board to Board the rival Vessels row;
The Billows lave the Skies, and Ocean groans below.
They reach'd the Mark; proud *Gyas* and his Train,
210 In Triumph rode the Victors of the Main:
But steering round, he charg'd his Pilot stand
More close to Shore, and skim along the Sand.
Let others bear to Sea. *Menœtes* heard,
But secret shelves too cautiously he fear'd:
And fearing, sought the Deep; and still aloof he steer'd.
With louder Cries the Captain call'd again;
Bear to the rocky Shore, and shun the Main.
He spoke, and speaking at his stern he saw
The bold *Cloanthus* near the Shelvings draw;
220 Betwixt the mark and him the *Scylla* stood,
And in a closer Compass plow'd the Flood,
He pass'd the Mark; and wheeling got before;
*Gyas* blasphem'd the Gods, devoutly swore,
Cry'd out for Anger, and his Hair he tore.
Mindless of others Lives, (so high was grown
His rising Rage,) and careless of his own:
The trembling Dotard to the Deck he drew,
Then hoisted up, and over-board he threw,
This done he seiz'd the Helm; his Fellows cheer'd;
230 Turn'd short upon the Shelfs, and madly steer'd.
　Hardly his Head, the plunging Pilot rears,
Clog'd with his Cloaths, and cumber'd with his Years:
Now dropping wet, he climbs the Cliff with Pain;

---

203, 206　*Dolphin*] Dolphin F1–2.　　　　213　*Menœtes*] Menætes F1–2.
226　Rage,] *comma printed as period or not at all in some copies of F1.*

The Crowd that saw him fall, and float again,
Shout from the distant Shore; and loudly laught,
To see his heaving Breast disgorge the briny Draught.
The following *Centaur,* and the *Dolphin*'s Crew,
Their vanish'd hopes of Victory renew:
While *Gyas* lags, they kindle in the Race,
240 To reach the Mark; *Sergesthus* takes the place:
*Mnestheus* pursues; and while around they wind,
Comes up, not half his Gally's length behind:
Then, on the Deck amidst his Mates appear'd,
And thus their drooping Courages he cheer'd.
My Friends, and *Hector*'s Followers heretofore;
Exert your Vigour, tug the lab'ring Oar;
Stretch to your Stroaks, my still unconquer'd Crew,
Whom from the flaming Walls of *Troy* I drew.
In this, our common Int'rest, let me find
250 That strength of Hand, that courage of the Mind,
As when you stem'd the strong *Malæan* Flood,
And o're the *Syrtes* broken Billows row'd.
I seek not now the foremost Palm to gain;                    ⎫
Tho yet———But ah, that haughty Wish is vain!  ⎬
Let those enjoy it whom the Gods ordain.                    ⎭
But to be last, the Lags of all the Race,
Redeem your selves and me from that Disgrace.
Now one and all, they tug amain; they row
At the full stretch, and shake the Brazen Prow.
260 The Sea beneath 'em sinks; their lab'ring sides
Are swell'd, and Sweat runs gutt'ring down in Tides.
Chance aids their daring with unhop'd Success;
*Sergesthus,* eager with his Beak, to press
Betwixt the Rival Gally and the Rock;
Shuts up th' unwieldy *Centaur* in the Lock.
The Vessel struck, and with the dreadful shock
Her Oars she shiver'd, and her Head she broke.
The trembling Rowers from their Banks arise,

---

237  *Centaur . . . Dolphin*'s) Centaur . . . Dolphin's F1–2.
242  behind:] ∼. F1–2.
251  *Malæan*] F1 (*corrected state*), F2; *Malœan* F1 (*uncorrected state*).
265  *Centaur*] Centaur F1–2.

And anxious for themselves renounce the Prize.
270 With Iron Poles they heave her off the Shores;
And gather, from the Sea, their floating Oars.
The Crew of *Mnestheus,* with elated Minds,
Urge their Success, and call the willing Winds:
Then ply their Oars, and cut their liquid way;
In larger Compass on the roomy Sea.
As when the Dove her Rocky Hold forsakes,
Rowz'd in a Fright, her sounding Wings she shakes;
The Cavern rings with clatt'ring; out she flies,
And leaves her Callow Care, and cleaves the Skies;
280 At first she flutters; but at length she springs,
To smoother flight, and shoots upon her Wings:
So *Mnestheus* in the *Dolphin* cuts the Sea,
And flying with a force, that force assists his Way.
*Sergesthus* in the *Centaur* soon he pass'd,
Wedg'd in the Rocky Sholes, and sticking fast.
In vain the Victor he with Cries implores,
And practices to row with shatter'd Oars.
Then *Mnestheus* bears with *Gyas,* and out-flies:
The Ship without a Pilot yields the Prize.
290 Unvanquish'd *Scylla* now alone remains;
Her he pursues; and all his vigour strains.
Shouts from the fav'ring Multitude arise,
Applauding *Echo* to the Shouts replies;
Shouts, Wishes, and Applause run ratling through the Skies.
These Clamours with disdain the *Scylla* heard;
Much grudg'd the Praise, but more the rob'd Reward:
Resolv'd to hold their own, they mend their pace;
All obstinate to dye, or gain the Race.
Rais'd with Success, the *Dolphin* swiftly ran,
300 (For they can Conquer who believe they can:)
Both urge their Oars, and Fortune both supplies;
And both, perhaps had shar'd an equal Prize;
When to the Seas *Cloanthus* holds his Hands,
And Succour from the Watry Pow'rs Demands:

277   shakes;] ∼∧ F1–2.                    293   *Echo*] Echo F1–2.

Gods of the liquid Realms, on which I row, )
If giv'n by you, the Lawrel bind my Brow, }
Assist to make me guilty of my Vow. )
A Snow-white Bull shall on your Shore be slain,
His offer'd Entrails cast into the Main;
310 And ruddy Wine from Golden Goblets thrown,
Your grateful Gift and my Return shall own.
The Quire of Nymphs, and *Phorcus* from below,
With Virgin *Panopea*, heard his Vow;
And old *Portunus,* with his breadth of Hand,
Push'd on, and sped the Gally to the Land.
Swift as a Shaft, or winged Wind, she flies;
And darting to the Port, obtains the Prize.
    The Herald summons all, and then proclaims
*Cloanthus* Conqu'ror of the Naval Games.
320 The Prince with Lawrel crowns the Victor's Head,
And three fat Steers are to his Vessel led;
The Ships Reward: with gen'rous Wine beside;
And Sums of Silver, which the Crew divide.
The Leaders are distinguish'd from the rest;
The Victor honour'd with a nobler Vest:
Where Gold and Purple strive in equal Rows;
And Needle-work its happy Cost bestows.
There, *Ganymede* is wrought with living Art,
Chasing thro' *Ida*'s Groves the trembling Hart:
330 Breathless he seems, yet eager to pursue;
When from aloft, descends in open view,
The Bird of *Jove;* and sowsing on his Prey,
With crooked Tallons bears the Boy away.
In vain, with lifted Hands, and gazing Eyes, )
His Guards behold him soaring thro' the Skies; }
And Dogs pursue his Flight, with imitated Cries. )
    *Mnestheus* the second Victor was declar'd;
And summon'd there, the second Prize he shar'd.
A Coat of Mail, which brave *Demoleus* bore; )
340 More brave *Æneas* from his Shoulders tore; }
In single Combat on the *Trojan* Shore. )
This was ordain'd for *Mnestheus* to possess;

In War for his Defence; for Ornament in Peace.
Rich was the Gift, and glorious to behold;
But yet so pond'rous with its Plates of Gold,
That scarce two Servants cou'd the Weight sustain;
Yet, loaded thus, *Demoleus* o're the Plain
Pursu'd, and lightly seiz'd the *Trojan* Train.
The Third succeeding to the last Reward,
350 Two goodly Bowls of Massy Silver shar'd;
With Figures prominent, and richly wrought:
And two Brass Caldrons from *Dodona* brought.
    Thus, all rewarded by the Heroe's hands,
Their conqu'ring Temples bound with Purple Bands.
And now *Sergesthus*, clearing from the Rock,
Brought back his Gally shatter'd with the shock.
Forlorn she look'd, without an aiding Oar;
And howted, by the Vulgar, made to Shoar.
As when a Snake, surpris'd upon the Road,
360 Is crush'd athwart her Body by the load
Of heavy Wheels; or with a Mortal Wound
Her Belly bruis'd, and trodden to the Ground:
In vain, with loosen'd curls, she crawls along,
Yet fierce above, she brandishes her Tongue:
Glares with her Eyes, and bristles with her Scales,
But groveling in the Dust, her parts unsound she trails:
So slowly to the Port the *Centaur* tends,
But what she wants in Oars, with Sails amends:
Yet, for his Gally sav'd, the grateful Prince,
370 Is pleas'd th' unhappy Chief to recompence.
*Pholoe*, the *Cretan* Slave, rewards his Care,
Beauteous her self, with lovely Twins, as fair.
    From thence his way the *Trojan* Heroe bent,
Into the neighb'ring Plain, with Mountains pent;
Whose sides were shaded with surrounding Wood:
Full in the midst of this fair Vally stood
A Native Theatre, which rising slow,
By just degrees, o're-look'd the Ground below.

---

366    trails:] ∼. F1–2.
377    slow] *appears as* flow *in some copies of F1 (dirty type).*

High on a Sylvan Throne the Leader sate;
380 A num'rous Train attend in Solemn State;
Here those, that in the rapid Course delight,
Desire of Honour, and the Prize invite.
The Rival Runners, without Order stand,
The *Trojans,* mix'd with the *Sicilian* Band.
First *Nisus,* with *Euryalus,* appears,
*Euryalus* a Boy of blooming Years;
With sprightly Grace, and equal Beauty crown'd:
*Nisus,* for Friendship to the Youth, renown'd.
*Diores,* next, of *Priam*'s Royal Race,
390 Then *Salius,* join'd with *Patron* took their Place:
But *Patron* in *Arcadia* had his Birth,
And *Salius* his, from *Acarnanian* Earth:
Then two *Sicilian* Youths, the Names of these
Swift *Helymus,* and lovely *Panopes:*
Both jolly Huntsmen, both in Forests bred,
And owning old *Acestes* for their Head:
With sev'ral others of Ignobler Name;
Whom Time has not deliver'd o're to Fame.
　　To these the Heroe thus his Thoughts explain'd,
400 In Words, which gen'ral Approbation gain'd.
One common Largess is for all design'd:
The Vanquish'd and the Victor shall be join'd:
Two Darts of polish'd Steel, and *Gnosian* Wood,
A Silver-studded Ax alike bestow'd.
The foremost three have Olive Wreaths decreed;
The first of these obtains a stately Steed
Adorn'd with Trappings; and the next in Fame,
The Quiver of an *Amazonian* Dame,
With feather'd *Thracian* Arrows well supply'd; ⎞
410 A Golden Belt shall gird his Manly side, ⎬
Which with a sparkling Diamond shall be ty'd: ⎠

---

392　Earth:] ~. O1–2, F1–2.
396　Head:] ~. O1–2, F1–2.
402　join'd:] ~. F1–2; *see collation for different text in* O1–2.
404　Silver-studded] Silver'd studded F1–2; *different text in* O1–2.
408　Dame,] O1–2; ~; F1–2.
409　supply'd;] ~∧ O1–2; ~, F1–2.
410　side,] ~; F1–2; *different text in* O1–2.

Æ.5.1:425.
Lombart sculpsit londini

To Anthony Ham-   -mond of Somersham
in the County   of Huntingdon Esqr.

The third this *Grecian* Helmet shall content.
He said; to their appointed Base they went:
With beating Hearts th' expected Sign receive,
And, starting all at once, the Barrier leave.
Spread out, as on the winged Winds, they flew,
And seiz'd the distant Goal with greedy view.
Shot from the Crowd, swift *Nisus* all o're-pass'd;
Nor Storms, nor Thunder, equal half his haste.
420 The next, but tho' the next, yet far dis-join'd,
Came *Salius,* and *Euryalus* behind;
Then *Helymus,* whom young *Diores* ply'd,
Step after step, and almost side by side:
His Shoulders pressing, and in longer Space,
Had won, or left at least a dubious Race.

Now spent, the Goal they almost reach at last;
When eager *Nisus,* hapless in his haste,
Slip'd first, and slipping, fell upon the Plain,
Soak'd with the Blood of Oxen, newly slain:
430 The careless Victor had not mark'd his way;
But treading where the treach'rous Puddle lay,
His Heels flew up; and on the grassy Floor,
He fell, besmear'd with Filth, and Holy Gore.
Not mindless then, *Euryalus,* of thee,
Nor of the Sacred Bonds of Amity;
He strove th' immediate Rival's hope to cross;
And caught the Foot of *Salius* as he rose:
So *Salius* lay extended on the Plain;
*Euryalus* springs out, the Prize to gain;
440 And leaves the Crowd; applauding Peals attend
The Victor to the Goal, who vanquish'd by his Friend.
Next *Helymus,* and then *Diores* came;
By two Misfortunes made the third in Fame.

But *Salius* enters; and, exclaiming loud
For Justice, deafens, and disturbs the Crowd:
Urges his Cause may in the Court be heard;
And pleads the Prize is wrongfully conferr'd.
But Favour for *Euryalus* appears;

His blooming Beauty, with his tender Tears,
450 Had brib'd the Judges for the promis'd Prize;
Besides *Diores* fills the Court with Cries,
Who vainly reaches at the last Reward,
If the first Palm on *Salius* be conferr'd.
Then thus the Prince; Let no Disputes arise:
Where Fortune plac'd it, I award the Prize.
But Fortune's Errors give me leave to mend,
At least to pity my deserving Friend.
He said, and from among the Spoils, he draws,
(Pond'rous with shaggy Main, and Golden Paws)
460 A Lyon's Hide; to *Salius* this he gives:
*Nisus,* with Envy sees the Gift, and grieves.
If such Rewards to vanquish'd Men are due,
He said, and Falling is to rise by you,
What Prize may *Nisus* from your Bounty claim,
Who merited the first Rewards and Fame?
In falling, both an equal Fortune try'd;
Wou'd Fortune for my Fall so well provide!
With this he pointed to his Face, and show'd
His Hands, and all his Habit smear'd with Blood.
470 Th' indulgent Father of the People smil'd;
And caus'd to be produc'd an ample Shield;
Of wond'rous Art by *Didymaon* wrought,
Long since from *Neptune*'s Bars in Triumph brought.
This giv'n to *Nisus;* he divides the rest;
And equal Justice, in his Gifts, express'd.
The Race thus ended, and Rewards bestow'd;
Once more the Prince bespeaks th' attentive Crowd.
If there be here, whose dauntless Courage dare
In Gauntlet fight, with Limbs and Body bare,
480 His Opposite sustain in open view,
Stand forth the Champion; and the Games renew.
Two Prizes I propose, and thus divide,

450   for the promis'd Prize] F2; to protect his Claim O1–2, F1.
451   fills the Court with Cries,] F2 (Cry's); does as loud exclaim: O1–2, F1.
454   Let] let O1–2, F1–2.
466   falling,] F1–2 *(some copies of F1 have a semicolon)*; ∼∧ O1–2.

A Bull with gilded Horns, and Fillets ty'd,
Shall be the Portion of the conqu'ring Chief:
A Sword and Helm shall chear the Loser's Grief.
　　Then haughty *Dares* in the Lists appears;
Stalking he strides, his Head erected bears:
His nervous Arms the weighty Gauntlet weild;
And loud Applauses echo thro' the Field.
490 *Dares* alone, in Combat us'd to stand
The match of mighty *Paris* hand to hand:
The same, at *Hector*'s Fun'rals undertook
Gygantick *Butes,* of th' *Amician* Stock;
And by the Stroak of his resistless Hand,
Stretch'd the vast Bulk upon the yellow Sand.
Such *Dares* was; and such he strode along,
And drew the Wonder of the gazing Throng.
His brawny Back, and ample Breast he shows; ⎫
His lifted Arms around his Head he throws; ⎬
500 And deals, in whistling Air, his empty Blows. ⎭
His Match is sought; but thro' the trembling Band,
Not one dares answer to the proud Demand.
Presuming of his Force, with sparkling Eyes,
Already he devours the promis'd Prize.
He claims the Bull with awless Insolence;
And having seiz'd his Horns, accosts the Prince.
If none my matchless Valour dares oppose,
How long shall *Dares* wait his dastard Foes?
Permit me, Chief, permit without Delay,
510 To lead this uncontended Gift away.
The Crowd assents; and, with redoubled Cries,
For the proud Challenger demands the Prize.
　　*Acestes,* fir'd with just Disdain, to see
The Palm usurp'd without a Victory;
Reproch'd *Entellus* thus, who sate beside,
And heard, and saw unmov'd, the *Trojan*'s Pride:
Once, but in vain, a Champion of Renown,
So tamely can you bear the ravish'd Crown?

496　strode] strod F1-2.

A Prize in triumph born before your sight,
520 And shun for fear the danger of the Fight?
Where is our *Eryx* now, the boasted Name,
The God who taught your thund'ring Arm the Game;
Where now your baffled Honour, where the Spoil
That fill'd your House, and Fame that fill'd our Isle?
*Entellus,* thus: My Soul is still the same,
Unmov'd with Fear, and mov'd with Martial Fame:
But my chill Blood is curdled in my Veins;
And scarce the Shadow of a Man remains.
Oh, cou'd I turn to that fair Prime again,
530 That Prime, of which this Boaster is so vain,
The Brave who this decrepid Age defies,
Shou'd feel my force, without the promis'd Prize.
He said, and rising at the word, he threw
Two pond'rous Gauntlets down, in open view:
Gauntlets, which *Eryx* wont in Fight to wield,
And sheath his hands with in the listed field.
With Fear and Wonder seiz'd, the Crowd beholds
The Gloves of Death, with sev'n distinguish'd folds,
Of tough Bull Hides; the space within is spread
540 With Iron, or with loads of heavy Lead.
*Dares* himself was daunted at the sight,
Renounc'd his Challenge, and refus'd to fight.
Astonish'd at their weight the Heroe stands,
And poiz'd the pond'rous Engins in his hands.
What had your wonder, said *Entellus,* been,        ⎫
Had you the Gauntlets of *Alcides* seen,        ⎬
Or view'd the stern debate on this unhappy Green!        ⎭
These which I bear, your Brother *Eryx* bore,
Still mark'd with batter'd Brains, and mingled Gore.
550 With these he long sustain'd th' *Herculean* Arm;
And these I weilded while my Blood was warm:
This languish'd Frame, while better Spirits fed,
E're Age unstrung my Nerves, or Time o'resnow'd my Head.
But if the Challenger these Arms refuse,
And cannot wield their weight, or dare not use;

If great *Æneas,* and *Acestes* joyn
In his Request, these Gauntlets I resign:
Let us with equal Arms perform the Fight,
And let him leave to Fear, since I resign my Right.
560 This said, *Entellus* for the Strife prepares;
Strip'd of his quilted Coat, his Body bares:
Compos'd of mighty Bones and Brawn, he stands,
A goodly tow'ring Object on the Sands.
Then just *Æneas* equal Arms supply'd,
Which round their Shoulders to their Wrists they ty'd.
Both on the tiptoe stand, at full extent,
Their Arms aloft, their Bodies inly bent;
Their Heads from aiming Blows they bear a far;
With clashing Gauntlets then provoke the War.
570 One on his Youth and pliant Limbs relies;
One on his Sinews, and his Gyant size.
The last is stiff with Age, his Motion slow,
He heaves for Breath, he staggers to and fro;
And Clouds of issuing Smoak his Nostrils loudly blow.
Yet equal in Success, they ward, they strike;
Their ways are diff'rent, but their Art alike.
Before, behind, the blows are dealt; around
Their hollow sides the ratling Thumps resound.
A Storm of Strokes, well meant, with fury flies,
580 And errs about their Temples, Ears, and Eyes:
Nor always errs; for oft the Gauntlet draws
A sweeping stroke, along the crackling Jaws.
Heavy with Age, *Entellus* stands his Ground,
But with his warping Body wards the Wound.
His Hand, and watchful Eye keep even pace;
While *Dares* traverses, and shifts his place,
And like a Captain, who beleaguers round,
Some strong built Castle, on a rising Ground,
Views all th' approaches with observing Eyes,
590 This, and that other part, in vain he tries;
And more on Industry, than Force relies.

___

580  Eyes:] ∼. F1–2.          586  place,] ∼. F1–2.

To Henry St John of     Lydiard Tregoz Esqr

With Hands on high, *Entellus* threats the Foe;
But *Dares* watch'd the Motion from below,
And slip'd aside, and shun'd the long descending Blow.
*Entellus* wasts his Forces on the Wind;
And thus deluded of the Stroke design'd,
Headlong, and heavy fell: his ample Breast,
And weighty Limbs, his ancient Mother press'd.
So falls a hollow Pine, that long had stood
600 On *Ida*'s height, or *Erymanthus* Wood,
Torn from the Roots: the diff'ring Nations rise,
And Shouts, and mingl'd Murmurs, rend the Skies.
*Acestes* runs, with eager haste, to raise
The fall'n Companion of his youthful Days:
Dauntless he rose, and to the Fight return'd:
With shame his glowing Cheeks, his Eyes with fury burn'd.
Disdain, and conscious Virtue fir'd his Breast;
And with redoubled Force his Foe he press'd.
He lays on load with either Hand, amain,
610 And headlong drives the *Trojan* o're the Plain:
Nor stops, nor stays; nor rest, nor Breath allows,
But Storms of Strokes descend about his Brows;
A ratling Tempest, and a Hail of Blows.
But now the Prince, who saw the wild Increase
Of Wounds, commands the Combatants to cease:
And bounds *Entellus* Wrath, and bids the Peace.
First to the *Trojan* spent with Toil he came,
And sooth'd his Sorrow for the suffer'd Shame.
What Fury seiz'd my Friend? the Gods, said he,
620 To him propitious, and averse to thee,
Have giv'n his Arm superior Force to thine;
'Tis Madness to contend with Strength Divine.
The Gauntlet Fight thus ended, from the Shore,
His faithful Friends unhappy *Dares* bore:
His Mouth and Nostrils, pour'd a Purple Flood;
And pounded Teeth, came rushing with his Blood.
Faintly he stagger'd thro the hissing Throng;
And hung his Head, and trail'd his Legs along.

610   Plain:] ∼. F1–2.                    619   Friend?] ∼, F1–2.

*To Stephen Waller,*          *D.ʳ of Laws*

The Sword and Casque, are carry'd by his Train;
630 But with his Foe the Palm and Ox remain.
    The Champion, then, before *Æneas* came,
Proud of his Prize; but prouder of his Fame;
O Goddess-born, and you *Dardanian* Host,
Mark with Attention, and forgive my Boast:
Learn what I was, by what remains; and know
From what impending Fate, you sav'd my Foe.
Sternly he spoke; and then confronts the Bull;  )
And, on his ample Forehead, aiming full,     }
The deadly Stroke descending, pierc'd the Skull. )
640 Down drops the Beast; nor needs a second Wound:
But sprawls in pangs of Death; and spurns the Ground.
Then, thus: In *Dares* stead I offer this;
*Eryx,* accept a nobler Sacrifice:
Take the last Gift my wither'd Arms can yield,
Thy Gauntlets I resign; and here renounce the Field.
    This done, *Æneas* orders, for the close,
The strife of Archers, with contending Bows.
The Mast, *Sergesthus* shatter'd Gally bore,
With his own Hands, he raises on the Shore.
650 A flutt'ring Dove upon the Top they tye,
The living Mark, at which their Arrows fly.
The rival Archers in a Line advance;
Their turn of Shooting to receive from Chance.
A Helmet holds their Names: The Lots are drawn,
On the first Scroll was read *Hippocoon:*
The People shout; upon the next was found
Young *Mnestheus,* late with Naval Honours crownd.
The third contain'd *Eurytion's* Noble Name,
Thy Brother, *Pandarus,* and next in Fame:
660 Whom *Pallas* urg'd the Treaty to confound,
And send among the *Greeks* a feather'd Wound.
*Acestes* in the bottom, last remain'd;
Whom not his Age from Youthful Sports restrain'd.
Soon, all with Vigour bend their trusty Bows,
And from the Quiver each his Arrow chose,
*Hippocoon's* was the first: with forceful sway

It flew, and, whizzing, cut the liquid way:
Fix'd in the Mast the feather'd Weapon stands,
The fearful Pidgeon flutters in her Bands;
670 And the Tree trembled: and the shouting Cries
Of the pleas'd People, rend the vaulted Skies.
Then *Mnestheus* to the head his Arrow drove, ⎞
With lifted Eyes; and took his Aim above; ⎬
But made a glancing Shot, and miss'd the Dove: ⎠
Yet miss'd so narrow, that he cut the Cord
Which fasten'd, by the Foot, the flitting Bird.
The Captive thus releas'd, away she flies,
And beats with clapping Wings, the yielding Skies.
His Bow already bent, *Eurytion* stood,
680 And having first invok'd his Brother God,
His winged Shaft with eager haste he sped;
The fatal Message reach'd her as she fled:
She leaves her Life aloft, she strikes the Ground;
And renders back the Weapon in the Wound.
*Acestes* grudging at his Lot, remains,
Without a Prize to gratifie his Pains:
Yet shooting upward, sends his Shaft, to show
An Archer's Art, and boast his twanging Bow.
The featherd Arrow gave a dire Portent;
690 And latter Augures judge from this Event.
Chaf'd by the speed, it fir'd; and as it flew,
A Trail of following Flames, ascending drew:
Kindling they mount; and mark the shiny Way: ⎞
Across the Skies as falling Meteors play, ⎬
And vanish into Wind; or in a Blaze decay. ⎠
The *Trojans* and *Sicilians* wildly stare:
And trembling, turn their Wonder into Pray'r.
The *Dardan* Prince put on a smiling Face,
And strain'd *Acestes* with a close Embrace:
700 Then hon'ring him with Gifts above the rest,
Turn'd the bad Omen, nor his Fears confess'd.
The Gods, said he, this Miracle have wrought;

---

674   Dove:] ∼. F1–2.                    686   Pains:] ∼. F1–2.
689   featherd] F2; pointed F1.

And order'd you the Prize without the Lot.
Accept this Goblet rough with figur'd Gold,
Which *Thracian Cisseus* gave my Sire of old:
This Pledge of ancient Amity receive,
Which to my second Sire I justly give.
He said, and with the Trumpets chearful sound,
Proclaim'd him Victor, and with Lawrel crown'd.
710  Nor good *Eurytion* envy'd him the Prize;
Tho' he transfix'd the Pidgeon in the Skies.
Who cut the Line, with second Gifts was grac'd;
The third was his, whose Arrow pierc'd the Mast.
The Chief, before the Games were wholly done,
Call'd *Periphantes*, Tutor to his Son;
And whisper'd thus; With speed *Ascanius* find,
And if his Childish Troop be ready join'd,
On Horse-back let him grace his Grandsire's Day,
And lead his Equals arm'd, in just Array.
720  He said, and calling out, the Cirque he clears;
The Crowd withdrawn, an open Plain appears.
And now the Noble Youths, of Form Divine,    )
Advance before their Fathers, in a Line:      }
The Riders grace the Steeds; the Steeds with Glory shine. )
   Thus marching on, in Military Pride,
Shouts of Applause resound from side to side.
Their Casques, adorn'd with Lawrel Wreaths, they wear:
Each brandishing aloft a Cornel Spear.
Some at their Backs their guilded Quivers bore;
730  Their Chains of burnish'd Gold hung down before.
Three graceful Troops they form'd upon the Green;  )
Three graceful Leaders at their Head were seen;    }
Twelve follow'd ev'ry Chief, and left a Space between. )
The first young *Priam* led; a lovely Boy,
Whose Grandsire was th' unhappy King of *Troy:*
His Race in after times was known to Fame,      )
New Honours adding to the *Latian* Name;        }
And well the Royal Boy his *Thracian* Steed became. )

716  With] with F1–2.          717  join'd,] ∼; F1–2.
727  wear:] ∼. F1–2.

To y.ᵉ most Illustrious Prince William Duke of Glocester &.ᶜᵗ

White were the Fetlocks of his Feet before;
740 And on his Front a snowy Star he bore:
Then beauteous *Atys*, with *Iulus* bred,
Of equal Age, the second Squadron led.
The last in Order, but the first in place,
First in the lovely Features of his Face;
Rode fair *Ascanius* on a fiery Steed,
Queen *Dido*'s Gift, and of the *Tyrian* breed.
Sure Coursers for the rest the King ordains;
With Golden Bitts adorn'd, and Purple Reins.
    The pleas'd Spectators peals of Shouts renew;
750 And all the Parents in the Children view:
Their Make, their Motions, and their sprightly Grace;
And Hopes and Fears alternate in their Face.
    Th' unfledg'd Commanders, and their Martial Train,
First make the Circuit of the sandy Plain,
Around their Sires: And at th' appointed Sign,
Drawn up in beauteous Order form a Line:
The second Signal sounds; the Troop divides,
In three distinguish'd parts, with three distinguish'd Guides.
Again they close, and once again dis-join,
760 In Troop to Troop oppos'd, and Line to Line.
They meet, they wheel, they throw their Darts afar
With harmless Rage, and well dissembled War.
Then in a round the mingl'd Bodies run;
Flying they follow, and pursuing shun.
Broken they break, and rallying, they renew
In other Forms the Military shew.
At last, in order, undiscern'd they join;
And march together, in a friendly Line.
And, as the *Cretan* Labyrinth of old,
770 With wand'ring Ways, and many a winding fold,
Involv'd the weary Feet, without redress,
In a round Error, which deny'd recess;
So fought the *Trojan* Boys in warlike Play,
Turn'd, and return'd, and still a diff'rent way.
Thus Dolphins, in the Deep, each other chase,
In Circles, when they swim around the wat'ry Race.

This Game, these Carousels *Ascanius* taught;
And, building *Alba,* to the *Latins* brought:
Shew'd what he learn'd: The *Latin* Sires impart,
780 To their succeeding Sons, the graceful Art:
From these Imperial *Rome* receiv'd the Game;
Which *Troy,* the Youths the *Trojan* Troop, they name.
Thus far the sacred Sports they celebrate:
But Fortune soon resum'd her ancient hate.
For while they pay the dead his Annual dues,
Those envy'd Rites *Saturnian Juno* views:
And sends the Goddess of the various bow,
To try new Methods of Revenge below:
Supplies the Winds to wing her Airy way;
790 Where in the Port secure the Navy lay.
Swiftly fair *Iris* down her Arch descends;
And undiscern'd her fatal Voyage ends.
She saw the gath'ring Crowd; and gliding thence,
The desart Shore, and Fleet without defence.
The *Trojan* Matrons on the Sands alone,
With Sighs and Tears, *Anchises* death bemoan.
Then, turning to the Sea their weeping Eyes,
Their pity to themselves, renews their Cries.
Alas! said one, what Oceans yet remain
800 For us to sail; what Labours to sustain!
All take the Word; and with a gen'ral groan,
Implore the Gods for Peace; and Places of their own.
The Goddess, great in Mischief, views their pains;
And in a Woman's Form her heav'nly Limbs restrains.
In Face and Shape, old *Beroe* she became, ⎞
*Doriclus* Wife, a venerable Dame; ⎟
Once bless'd with Riches, and a Mother's Name. ⎠
Thus chang'd, amidst the crying Crowd she ran,
Mix'd with the Matrons, and these words began.
810 O wretched we, whom not the *Grecian* Pow'r,
Nor Flames destroy'd, in *Troy*'s unhappy hour!
O wretched we, reserv'd by Cruel Fate,

---

778  brought:] ∼. F1–2.              786  views:] ∼. F1–2.
808  Crowd] F2; Crow'd F1.           810  we] F2; wc F1.

Beyond the Ruins of the sinking State!
Now sev'n revolving Years are wholly run,
Since this improsp'rous Voyage we begun:
Since toss'd from Shores to Shores, from Lands to Lands,
Inhospitable Rocks and barren Sands;
Wand'ring in Exile, through the stormy Sea,
We search in vain for flying *Italy*.
820 Now Cast by Fortune on this kindred Land,
What shou'd our Rest, and rising Walls withstand,
Or hinder here to fix our banish'd Band?
O, Country lost, and Gods redeem'd in vain,
If still in endless Exile we remain!
Shall we no more the *Trojan* Walls renew,
Or Streams of some dissembl'd *Simois* view?
Haste, joyn with me, th' unhappy Fleet consume:
*Cassandra* bids, and I declare her doom.
In sleep I saw her; she supply'd my hands,
830 (For this I more than dreamt) with flaming Brands:
With these, said she, these wand'ring Ships destroy;
These are your fatal Seats, and this your *Troy*.
Time calls you now, the precious Hour employ.
Slack not the good Presage, while Heav'n inspires
Our Minds to dare, and gives the ready Fires.
See *Neptune*'s Altars minister their Brands;
The God is pleas'd; the God supplies our hands.
Then, from the Pile, a flaming Fire she drew,
And, toss'd in Air, amidst the Gallies threw.
840 Wrap'd in amaze, the Matrons wildly stare:
Then *Pyrgo,* reverenc'd for her hoary Hair,
*Pyrgo,* the Nurse of *Priam*'s num'rous Race,
No *Beroe* this, tho she belies her Face:
What Terrours from her frowning Front arise;
Behold a Goddess in her ardent Eyes!
What Rays around her heav'nly Face are seen,
Mark her Majestick Voice, and more than mortal Meen!
*Beroe* but now I left; whom pin'd with pain,

---

826   view?] ∼! F1–2.          838   Fire] F2; Firr F1.
840   amaze] a maze F1–2.

Her Age and Anguish from these Rites detain.
850 She said; the Matrons, seiz'd with new Amaze,
Rowl their malignant Eyes, and on the Navy gaze.
They fear, and hope, and neither part obey:
They hope the fated Land, but fear the fatal Way.
The Goddess, having done her Task below,
Mounts up on equal Wings, and bends her painted Bow.
Struck with the sight, and seiz'd with Rage Divine;
The Matrons prosecute their mad Design:
They shriek aloud, they snatch, with Impious Hands,
The food of Altars, Fire, and flaming Brands.
860 Green Boughs, and Saplings, mingled in their haste;
And smoaking Torches on the Ships they cast.
The Flame, unstop'd at first, more Fury gains;
And *Vulcan* rides at large with loosen'd Reins:
Triumphant to the painted Sterns he soars,
And seizes in his way, the Banks, and crackling Oars.
*Eumelus* was the first, the News to bear,
While yet they crowd the Rural Theatre.
Then what they hear, is witness'd by their Eyes;
A storm of Sparkles, and of Flames arise.
870 *Ascanius* took th' Alarm, while yet he led
His early Warriors on his prancing Steed:
And spurring on, his Equals soon o'repass'd,
Nor cou'd his frighted Friends reclaim his haste.
Soon as the Royal Youth appear'd in view,
He sent his Voice before him as he flew;
What Madness moves you, Matrons, to destroy
The last Remainders of unhappy *Troy?*
Not hostile Fleets, but your own hopes you burn,
And on your Friends, your fatal Fury turn.
880 Behold your own *Ascanius:* while he said,  ⎫
He drew his glitt'ring Helmet from his Head; ⎬
In which the Youths to sportful Arms he led. ⎭
By this, *Æneas* and his Train appear;
And now the Women, seiz'd with Shame and Fear,

---

859   Fire] Firs F1; Fires F2.          860   Boughs] F2; Leaves F1.
871   Steed:] ~. F1–2.                  877   *Troy?*] ~! F1–2.

Dispers'd, to Woods and Caverns take their Flight;
Abhor their Actions, and avoid the Light:
Their Friends acknowledge, and their Error find;
And shake the Goddess from their alter'd Mind.
   Not so the raging Fires their Fury cease;
890 But lurking in the Seams, with seeming Peace,
Work on their way, amid the smouldring Tow,
Sure in Destruction, but in Motion slow.
The silent Plague, thro' the green Timber eats,
And vomits out a tardy Flame, by fits.
Down to the Keels, and upward to the Sails,
The Fire descends, or mounts; but still prevails:
Nor Buckets pour'd, nor strength of Human Hand,
Can the victorious Element withstand.
   The Pious Heroe rends his Robe, and throws
900 To Heav'n his Hands, and with his Hands his Vows.
O *Jove,* he cry'd, if Pray'rs can yet have place;
If thou abhorr'st not all the *Dardan* Race;
If any spark of Pity still remain;
If Gods are Gods, and not invok'd in vain;
Yet spare the Relicks of the *Trojan* Train.
Yet from the Flames our burning Vessels free:
Or let thy Fury fall alone on me.
At this devoted Head thy Thunder throw,
And send the willing Sacrifice below.
910    Scarce had he said, when Southern Storms arise;
From Pole to Pole, the forky Lightning flies;
Loud ratling shakes the Mountains, and the Plain:
Heav'n bellies downward, and descends in Rain.
Whole Sheets of Water from the Clouds are sent,
Which hissing thro' the Planks, the Flames prevent:
And stop the fiery Pest: Four Ships alone
Burn to the wast; and for the Fleet attone.
   But doubtful thoughts the Hero's Heart divide;
If he should still in *Sicily* reside,
920 Forgetful of his Fates; or tempt the Main,
In hope the promis'd *Italy* to gain.

---

910  arise;] ∼, F1–2.

Then *Nautes,* old, and wise, to whom alone
The Will of Heav'n, by *Pallas* was fore-shown;
Vers'd in Portents, experienc'd and inspir'd,
To tell Events, and what the Fates requir'd:
Thus while he stood, to neither part inclin'd,
With chearful Words reliev'd his lab'ring Mind.
O Goddess-born, resign'd in ev'ry state,
With Patience bear, with Prudence push your Fate.
930 By suff'ring well, our Fortune we subdue;
Fly when she frowns, and when she calls pursue.
Your Friend *Acestes* is of *Trojan* Kind,
To him disclose the Secrets of your Mind:
Trust in his Hands your old and useless Train,
Too num'rous for the Ships which yet remain:
The feeble, old, indulgent of their Ease,
The Dames who dread the Dangers of the Seas,
With all the dastard Crew, who dare not stand
The shock of Battel with your Foes by Land;
940 Here you may build a common Town for all;
And from *Acestes* name, *Acesta* call.
The Reasons, with his Friend's Experience join'd,
Encourag'd much, but more disturb'd his Mind.
'Twas dead of Night; when to his slumb'ring Eyes,
His Father's Shade descended from the Skies;
And thus he spoke: O more than vital Breath
Lov'd while I liv'd, and dear ev'n after Death;
O Son, in various Toils and Troubles tost,
The King of Heav'n employs my careful Ghost
950 On his Commands; the God who sav'd from Fire
Your flaming Fleet, and heard your just desire:
The Wholsom Counsel of your Friend receive;
And here, the Coward Train, and Women leave:
The chosen Youth, and those who nobly dare,
Transport; to tempt the Dangers of the War.
The stern *Italians* will their Courage try;
Rough are their Manners, and their Minds are high.
But first to *Pluto*'s Palace you shall go,
And seek my Shade among the blest below.

960 For not with impious Ghosts my Soul remains, ⎫
    Nor suffers, with the Damn'd, perpetual Pains; ⎬
    But breaths the living Air of soft *Elysian* Plains. ⎭
    The chast *Sibylla* shall your steps convey;
    And Blood of offer'd Victims free the way.
    There shall you know what Realms the Gods assign;
    And learn the Fates and Fortunes of your Line.
    But now, farewel; I vanish with the Night; ⎫
    And feel the blast of Heav'ns approaching Light: ⎬
    He said, and mix'd with Shades, and took his airy flight. ⎭
970 Whether so fast, the filial Duty cry'd,
    And why, ah why, the wish'd Embrace deny'd?
    He said, and rose: as holy Zeal inspires
    He rakes hot Embers, and renews the Fires:
    His Country Gods and *Vesta*, then adores
    With Cakes and Incense; and their Aid implores.
    Next, for his Friends, and Royal Host he sent,
    Reveal'd his Vision and the Gods intent,
    With his own Purpose: All, without delay,
    The Will of *Jove*, and his Desires obey.
980 They list with Women each degenerate Name,
    Who dares not hazard Life, for future Fame.
    These they cashier; the brave remaining few,
    Oars, Banks, and Cables half consum'd renew.
    The Prince designs a City with the Plough;
    The Lots their sev'ral Tenements allow.
    This part is nam'd from *Ilium,* that from *Troy;*
    And the new King ascends the Throne with Joy:
    A chosen Senate from the People draws;
    Appoints the Judges, and ordains the Laws.
990 Then on the top of *Eryx*, they begin
    A rising Temple to the *Paphian* Queen:
    *Anchises,* last, is honour'd as a God, ⎫
    A Priest is added, annual Gifts bestow'd; ⎬
    And Groves are planted round his blest Abode. ⎭

---

963  *Sibylla*] *Sybilla* F1–2.
973  Fires:] ~. F1–2.
991  A rising] F2; To raise a F1.

971  deny'd?] ~! F1–2.
987  Joy:] ~. F1–2.
994  Abode.] F2; ~, F1.

Nine days they pass in Feasts, their Temples crown'd;
And fumes of Incense in the Fanes abound.
Then, from the South arose a gentle Breeze,
That curl'd the smoothness of the glassy Seas:
The rising Winds, a ruffling Gale afford,
1000 And call the merry Marriners aboard.
    Now loud Laments along the Shores resound,
Of parting Friends in close Embraces bound.
The trembling Women, the degenerate Train,
Who shun'd the frightful dangers of the Main;
Ev'n those desire to sail, and take their share
Of the rough Passage, and the promis'd War:
Whom Good *Æneas* chears; and recommends
To their new Master's Care, his fearful Friends.
On *Eryx* Altars three fat Calves he lays;
1010 A Lamb new fallen to the stormy Seas;
Then slips his Haulsers, and his Anchors weighs.
High on the Deck, the Godlike Heroe stands;
With Olive crown'd; a Charger in his Hands;
Then cast the reeking Entrails in the brine,
And pour'd the Sacrifice of Purple Wine.
Fresh Gales arise, with equal Strokes they vye,
And brush the buxom Seas, and o're the Billows fly.
    Mean time the Mother-Goddess, full of Fears,
To *Neptune* thus address'd, with tender Tears.
1020 The Pride of *Jove*'s Imperious Queen, the Rage,
The malice which no Suff'rings can asswage,
Compel me to these Pray'rs: Since neither Fate,
Nor Time, nor Pity, can remove her hate.
Ev'n *Jove* is thwarted by his haughty Wife;
Still vanquish'd, yet she still renews the Strife.
As if 'twere little to consume the Town
Which aw'd the World; and wore th' Imperial Crown:
She prosecutes the Ghost of *Troy* with Pains;
And gnaws, ev'n to the Bones, the last Remains.
1030 Let her the Causes of her Hatred tell;
But you can witness its Effects too well.

---

1006  War:] ∼. F1–2.              1010  fallen] fall'n F1–2.

You saw the Storm she rais'd on *Lybian* Floods,
That mix'd the mounting Billows with the Clouds:
When, bribing *Æolus,* she shook the Main;
And mov'd Rebellion in your wat'ry Reign.
With Fury she possess'd the *Dardan* Dames;
To burn their Fleet with execrable Flames:
And forc'd *Æneas,* when his Ships were lost,
To leave his Foll'wers on a Foreign Coast.
1040 For what remains, your Godhead I implore;
And trust my Son to your protecting Pow'r.
If neither *Jove*'s, nor Fate's decree withstand,
Secure his Passage to the *Latian* Land.
    Then thus the mighty Ruler of the Main,
What may not *Venus* hope, from *Neptune*'s Reign?
My Kingdom claims your Birth: my late Defence
Of your indanger'd Fleet, may claim your Confidence.
Nor less by Land than Sea, my Deeds declare,
How much your lov'd *Æneas* is my Care.
1050 Thee *Xanthus,* and thee *Simois* I attest:
Your *Trojan* Troops, when proud *Achilles* press'd,
And drove before him headlong on the Plain,          )
And dash'd against the Walls the trembling Train,   }
When Floods were fill'd with bodies of the slain:     )
When Crimson *Xanthus,* doubtful of his way,        )
Stood up on ridges to behold the Sea;                 }
New heaps came tumbling in, and choak'd his way: )
When your *Æneas* fought, but fought with odds
Of Force unequal, and unequal Gods;
1060 I spread a Cloud before the Victor's sight,
Sustain'd the vanquish'd, and secur'd his flight:
Ev'n then secur'd him, when I sought with joy
The vow'd destruction of ungrateful *Troy.*
My Will's the same: Fair Goddess fear no more,
Your Fleet shall safely gain the *Latian* Shore:
Their lives are giv'n; one destin'd Head alone
Shall perish, and for Multitudes attone.

---

1033  Clouds:] ~. F1–2.                 1034  *Æolus*] *Eolus* F1–2.
1037  Flames:] ~. F1–2.                1061  flight:] ~. F1–2.

To Edmond Waller of Beaconsfield in the
County of Bucks Esq₃

Thus having arm'd with Hopes her anxious Mind,
His finny Team *Saturnian Neptune* join'd:
1070 Then, adds the foamy Bridle to their Jaws;
And to the loosen'd Reins permits the Laws.
High on the Waves his Azure Car he guides, ⎫
Its Axles thunder, and the Sea subsides; ⎬
And the smooth Ocean rowls her silent Tides. ⎭
The Tempests fly before their Father's face,
Trains of inferiour Gods his Triumph grace;
And Monster Whales before their Master play,
And Quires of Tritons crowd the wat'ry way.
The Martial'd Pow'rs, in equal Troops divide, ⎫
1080 To right and left: the Gods his better side ⎬
Inclose, and on the worse the Nymphs and Nereids ride. ⎭
    Now smiling Hope, with sweet Vicissitude,
Within the Hero's Mind, his Joys renew'd.
He calls to raise the Masts, the Sheats display; ⎫
The Chearful Crew with diligence obey; ⎬
They scud before the Wind, and sail in open Sea. ⎭
A Head of all the Master Pilot steers,
And as he leads, the following Navy veers.
The Steeds of Night had travell'd half the Sky,
1090 The drowzy Rowers on their Benches lye;
When the soft God of Sleep, with easie flight,
Descends, and draws behind a trail of Light.
Thou *Palinurus* art his destin'd Prey;
To thee alone he takes his fatal way.
Dire Dreams to thee, and Iron Sleep he bears;
And lighting on thy Prow, the Form of *Phorbas* wears.
Then thus the Traytor God began his Tale: ⎫
The Winds, my Friend, inspire a pleasing gale; ⎬
The Ships, without thy Care, securely sail. ⎭
1100 Now steal an hour of sweet Repose; and I
Will take the Rudder, and thy room supply.
To whom the yauning Pilot, half asleep;
Me dost thou bid to trust the treach'rous Deep?
The Harlot-smiles of her dissembling Face,

1069  join'd:] ~.  F1–2.                    1103  Deep?] ~!  F1–2.

And to her Faith commit the *Trojan* Race?
Shall I believe the Syren South again,
And, oft betray'd, not know the Monster Main?
He said, his fasten'd hands the Rudder keep,
And fix'd on Heav'n, his Eyes repel invading Sleep.
1110  The God was wroth, and at his Temples threw
A Branch in *Lethe* dip'd, and drunk with *Stygian* Dew:
The Pilot, vanquish'd by the Pow'r Divine,
Soon clos'd his swimming Eyes, and lay supine.
Scarce were his Limbs extended at their length,
The God, insulting with superiour Strength,
Fell heavy on him, plung'd him in the Sea,
And, with the Stern, the Rudder tore away.
Headlong he fell, and strugling in the Main,
Cry'd out for helping hands, but cry'd in vain:
1120  The Victor Dæmon mounts obscure in Air;
While the Ship sails without the Pilot's care.
On *Neptune*'s Faith the floating Fleet relies;       ⎫
But what the Man forsook, the God supplies;           ⎬
And o're the dang'rous Deep secure the Navy flies:    ⎭
Glides by the Syrens Cliffs, a shelfy Coast,
Long infamous for Ships, and Sailors lost;
And white with Bones: Th' impetuous Ocean roars;
And Rocks rebellow from the sounding Shores.
The watchful Heroe felt the knocks; and found
1130  The tossing Vessel sail'd on shoaly Ground.
Sure of his Pilot's loss, he takes himself
The Helm, and steers aloof, and shuns the Shelf.
Inly he griev'd; and groaning from the Breast,
Deplor'd his Death; and thus his Pain express'd:
For Faith repos'd on Seas, and on the flatt'ring Sky,
Thy naked Corps is doom'd, on Shores unknown to lye.

---

1106  Syren] *Syren* F1–2.                    1124  flies:] ~. F1–2.
1125  Syrens] Syren's F1–2.                   1133  the] F2; his F1.

## The Sixth Book of the Æneis

THE ARGUMENT.

*The Sibyl foretels Æneas the Adventures he should meet with in* Italy. *She attends him to Hell; describing to him the various Scenes of that Place, and conducting him to his Father* Anchises: *Who instructs him in those sublime Mysteries of the Soul of the World, and the Transmigration: And shews him that glorious Race of Heroes, which was to descend from him, and his Posterity.*

HE said, and wept: Then spread his Sails before
    The Winds, and reach'd at length the *Cuman* Shore:
    Their Anchors drop'd, his Crew the Vessels moor.
They turn their Heads to Sea; their Sterns to Land;
And greet with greedy Joy th' *Italian* Strand.
Some strike from clashing Flints their fiery Seed;
Some gather Sticks, the kindled Flames to feed:
Or search for hollow Trees, and fell the Woods,
Or trace thro Valleys the discover'd Floods.
10 Thus, while their sev'ral Charges they fulfil,
The Pious Prince ascends the sacred Hill
Where *Phœbus* is ador'd; and seeks the Shade,
Which hides from sight, his venerable Maid.
Deep in a Cave the Sibyl makes abode;
Thence full of Fate returns, and of the God.
Thro *Trivia's* Grove they walk; and now behold,
And enter now, the Temple roof'd with Gold.
When *Dedalus*, to fly the *Cretan* Shore,
His heavy Limbs on jointed Pinions bore,
20 (The first who sail'd in Air,) 'tis sung by Fame,
To the *Cumæan* Coast at length he came;
And, here alighting, built this costly Frame.
Inscrib'd to *Phœbus,* here he hung on high

---

3 Anchises:] ∼. F1–2.                  18 fly] F2; shun F1.

The steerage of his Wings, that cut the Sky:
Then o're the lofty Gate his Art emboss'd
*Androgeos* Death, and Off'rings to his Ghost:
Sev'n Youths from *Athens* yearly sent, to meet
The Fate appointed by revengeful *Creet.*
And next to those the dreadful Urn was plac'd,
30 In which the destin'd Names by Lots were cast:
The mournful Parents stand around in Tears;
And rising *Creet* against their Shore appears.
There too, in living Sculpture, might be seen
The mad Affection of the *Cretan* Queen:
Then how she cheats her bellowing Lover's Eye:
The rushing leap, the doubtful Progeny,
The lower part a Beast, a Man above,
The Monument of their polluted Love.
Nor far from thence he grav'd the wond'rous Maze;
40 A thousand Doors, a thousand winding Ways;
Here dwells the Monster, hid from Human View,
Not to be found, but by the faithful Clue:
'Till the kind Artist, mov'd with Pious Grief,
Lent to the loving Maid this last Relief:
And all those erring Paths describ'd so well,
That *Theseus* conquer'd, and the Monster fell.
Here hapless *Icarus* had found his part;
Had not the Father's Grief restrain'd his Art.
He twice essay'd to cast his Son in Gold;
50 Twice from his Hands he drop'd the forming Mould.
    All this with wond'ring Eyes *Æneas* view'd:
Each varying Object his Delight renew'd.
Eager to read the rest, *Achates* came,
And by his side the mad divining Dame;
The Priestess of the God, *Deiphobe* her Name.
Time suffers not, she said, to feed your Eyes
With empty Pleasures: haste the Sacrifice.
Sev'n Bullocks yet unyok'd, for *Phœbus* chuse,

26   Ghost:] ∼. F1-2.              29   those] F2; these F1.
30   Names] F2; Name F1.          44   Relief:] ∼. F1-2.
53   Eager] F2; Prepar'd F1.

And for *Diana* sev'n unspotted Ewes.
60 This said, the Servants urge the Sacred Rites;
While to the Temple she the Prince invites.
A spacious Cave, within its farmost part,
Was hew'd and fashion'd by laborious Art,
Thro' the Hills hollow sides: Before the place,
A hundred Doors a hundred Entries grace:
As many Voices issue; and the sound
Of Sibyl's Words as many times rebound.
Now to the Mouth they come: Aloud she cries,
This is the time, enquire your Destinies.
70 He comes, behold the God! Thus while she said,
(And shiv'ring at the sacred Entry staid)
Her Colour chang'd, her Face was not the same,
And hollow Groans from her deep Spirit came.
Her Hair stood up; convulsive Rage possess'd
Her trembling Limbs, and heav'd her lab'ring Breast.
Greater than Human Kind she seem'd to look:
And with an Accent, more than Mortal, spoke.
Her staring Eyes with sparkling Fury rowl;
When all the God came rushing on her Soul.
80 Swiftly she turn'd, and foaming as she spoke,
Why this Delay? she cry'd; the Pow'rs invoke.
Thy Pray'rs alone can open this abode,
Else vain are my Demands, and dumb the God.
She said no more: The trembling *Trojans* hear;
O're-spread with a damp Sweat, and holy Fear.
The Prince himself, with awful Dread possess'd,
His Vows to great *Apollo* thus address'd.
Indulgent God, propitious Pow'r to *Troy*,
Swift to relieve, unwilling to destroy;
90 Directed by whose Hand, the *Dardan* Dart
Pierc'd the proud *Grecian's* only Mortal part:
Thus far, by Fates Decrees, and thy Commands,
Through ambient Seas, and thro' devouring Sands,
Our exil'd Crew has sought th' *Ausonian* Ground:

63  Art,] ~. F1–2.          78  sparkling] F2; sparling F1.
81  Delay?] ~, F1–2.

And now, at length, the flying Coast is found.
Thus far the Fate of *Troy,* from place to place,
With Fury has pursu'd her wand'ring Race:
Here cease ye Pow'rs, and let your Vengeance end,
*Troy* is no more, and can no more offend.
100 And thou, O sacred Maid, inspir'd to see
Th' Event of things in dark Futurity;
Give me, what Heav'n has promis'd to my Fate,
To conquer and command the *Latian* State:
To fix my wand'ring Gods; and find a place
For the long Exiles of the *Trojan* Race.
Then shall my grateful Hands a Temple rear
To the twin Gods, with Vows and solemn Pray'r;
And Annual Rites, and Festivals, and Games,
Shall be perform'd to their auspicious Names.
110 Nor shalt thou want thy Honours in my Land,
For there thy faithful Oracles shall stand,
Preserv'd in Shrines: and ev'ry Sacred Lay,
Which, by thy Mouth, *Apollo* shall convey.
All shall be treasur'd, by a chosen Train
Of holy Priests, and ever shall remain.
But, oh! commit not thy prophetick Mind
To flitting Leaves, the sport of ev'ry Wind:
Lest they disperse in Air our empty Fate:
Write not, but, what the Pow'rs ordain, relate.
120     Strugling in vain, impatient of her Load,
And lab'ring underneath the pond'rous God,
The more she strove to shake him from her Breast,
With more, and far superior Force he press'd:
Commands his Entrance, and without Controul,
Usurps her Organs, and inspires her Soul.
Now, with a furious Blast, the hundred Doors )
Ope of themselves; a rushing Whirlwind roars }
Within the Cave; and Sibyl's Voice restores. )
    Escap'd the Dangers of the wat'ry Reign,
130 Yet more, and greater Ills, by Land remain.
———
127  Whirlwind] Wirlwind F1–2.

The Coast so long desir'd, (nor doubt th' Event)
Thy Troops shall reach, but having reach'd, repent.
Wars, horrid Wars I view; a field of Blood;
And *Tyber* rolling with a Purple Flood.
*Simois* nor *Xanthus* shall be wanting there;
A new *Achilles* shall in Arms appear:
And he, too, Goddess-born: fierce *Juno*'s Hate,
Added to hostile Force, shall urge thy Fate.
To what strange Nations shalt not thou resort,
140 Driv'n to sollicite Aid at ev'ry Court!
The Cause the same which *Ilium* once oppress'd,
A foreign Mistress, and a foreign Guest.
But thou, secure of Soul, unbent with Woes,
The more thy Fortune frowns, the more oppose.
The dawnings of thy Safety, shall be shown,
From whence thou least shalt hope, a *Grecian* Town.

    Thus, from the dark Recess, the Sibyl spoke, }
And the resisting Air the Thunder broke; }
The Cave rebellow'd; and the Temple shook. }
150 Th' ambiguous God, who rul'd her lab'ring Breast, }
In these mysterious Words his Mind exprest: }
Some Truths reveal'd, in Terms involv'd the rest. }
At length her Fury fell; her foaming ceas'd,
And, ebbing in her Soul, the God decreas'd.
Then thus the Chief: No Terror to my view,
No frightful Face of Danger can be new.
Inur'd to suffer, and resolv'd to dare,
The Fates, without my Pow'r, shall be without my Care.
This let me crave, since near your Grove the Road }
160 To Hell lies open, and the dark Abode, }
Which *Acheron* surrounds, th' innavigable Flood: }
Conduct me thro' the Regions void of Light,
And lead me longing to my Father's sight.
For him, a thousand Dangers I have sought; }
And, rushing where the thickest *Grecians* fought, }
Safe on my Back the sacred Burthen brought. }

155 No] no F1-2.

He, for my sake, the raging Ocean try'd,
And Wrath of Heav'n, my still auspicious Guide; ⎫
And bore beyond the strength decrepid Age supply'd. ⎭
170 Oft since he breath'd his last, in dead of Night,
His reverend Image stood before my sight;
Enjoin'd to seek below, his holy Shade;
Conducted there, by your unerring aid.
But you, if pious Minds by Pray'rs are won,
Oblige the Father, and protect the Son.
Yours is the Pow'r; nor *Proserpine* in vain
Has made you Priestess of her nightly Reign.
If *Orpheus,* arm'd with his enchanting Lyre,
The ruthless King with Pity could inspire;
180 And from the Shades below redeem his Wife:
If *Pollux,* off'ring his alternate Life,
Cou'd free his Brother; and can daily go
By turns aloft, by turns descend below:
Why name I *Theseus,* or his greater Friend,
Who trod the downward Path, and upward cou'd ascend?
Not less than theirs, from *Jove* my Lineage came:
My Mother greater, my Descent the same.
So pray'd the *Trojan* Prince; and while he pray'd
His Hand upon the holy Altar laid.
190 Then thus reply'd the Prophetess Divine:
O Goddess-born! of Great *Anchises* Line;
The Gates of Hell are open Night and day;
Smooth the Descent, and easie is the Way:
But, to return, and view the chearful Skies;
In this the Task, and mighty Labour lies.
To few great *Jupiter* imparts this Grace:
And those of shining Worth, and Heav'nly Race.
Betwixt those Regions, and our upper Light,
Deep Forrests, and impenetrable Night
200 Possess the middle space: Th' Infernal Bounds
*Cocytus,* with his sable Waves, surrounds.
But if so dire a Love your Soul invades,

---

168  Heav'n, . . . Guide;] ∼; . . . ∼, F1–2.    185  ascend?] ∼! F1–2.
191  Goddess-born] F2; Goddess born F1.    202  invades,] ∼; F1–2.

As twice below to view the trembling Shades;
If you so hard a Toil will undertake,
As twice to pass th' innavigable Lake;
Receive my Counsel. In the Neighb'ring Grove
There stands a Tree; the Queen of *Stygian Jove*
Claims it her own; thick Woods, and gloomy Night,
Conceal the happy Plant from Humane sight.
210 One Bough it bears; but, wond'rous to behold;
The ductile Rind, and Leaves, of Radiant Gold:
This, from the vulgar Branches must be torn,
And to fair *Proserpine,* the Present born:
E're leave be giv'n to tempt the neather Skies: )
The first thus rent, a second will arise; }
And the same Metal the same room supplies. )
Look round the Wood, with lifted Eyes, to see
The lurking Gold upon the fatal Tree:
Then rend it off, as holy Rites command:
220 The willing Metal will obey thy hand,
Following with ease, if, favour'd by thy Fate,
Thou art foredoom'd to view the *Stygian* State:
If not, no labour can the Tree constrain:
And strength of stubborn Arms, and Steel are vain.
Besides, you know not, while you here attend,
Th' unworthy Fate of your unhappy Friend:
Breathless he lies: And his unbury'd Ghost,
Depriv'd of Fun'ral Rites, pollutes your Host.
Pay first his Pious Dues: And for the dead,
230 Two sable Sheep around his Herse be led.
Then, living Turfs upon his Body lay; )
This done, securely take the destin'd Way, }
To find the Regions destitute of Day. )
She said: and held her Peace. *Æneas* went )
Sad from the Cave, and full of Discontent; }
Unknowing whom the sacred Sibyl meant. )
*Achates,* the Companion of his Breast,
Goes grieving by his side; with equal Cares oppress'd.
Walking, they talk'd, and fruitlesly divin'd

225 attend,] ~ₐ F1-2.

240  What Friend, the Priestess by those Words design'd.
But soon they found an Object to deplore;
*Misenus* lay extended on the Shore.
Son of the God of Winds; none so renown'd,
The Warrior Trumpet in the Field to sound:
With breathing Brass to kindle fierce Alarms;
And rouze to dare their Fate, in honourable Arms:
He serv'd great *Hector;* and was ever near;
Not with his Trumpet only, but his Spear.
But, by *Pelides* Arms when *Hector* fell,
250  He chose *Æneas,* and he chose as well.
Swoln with Applause, and aiming still at more,
He now provokes the Sea Gods from the Shore;
With Envy *Triton* heard the Martial sound,
And the bold Champion, for his Challenge, drown'd;
Then cast his mangled Carcass on the Strand:
The gazing Crowd around the Body stand.
All weep, but most *Æneas* mourns his Fate;
And hastens to perform the Funeral state.
In Altar-wise, a stately Pile they rear;
260  The Basis broad below, and top advanc'd in Air.
An ancient Wood, fit for the Work design'd,
(The shady Covert of the Salvage Kind)
The *Trojans* found: The sounding Axe is ply'd:
Firs, Pines, and Pitch-Trees, and the tow'ring Pride
Of Forest Ashes, feel the fatal Stroke:
And piercing Wedges cleave the stubborn Oak.
Huge Trunks of Trees, fell'd from the steepy Crown
Of the bare Mountains, rowl with Ruin down.
Arm'd like the rest the *Trojan* Prince appears:
270  And, by his pious Labour, urges theirs.
Thus while he wrought, revolving in his Mind,
The ways to compass what his Wish design'd,
He cast his Eyes upon the gloomy Grove;
And then with Vows implor'd the Queen of Love.
O may thy Pow'r, propitious still to me,

243  of the] F2; to the F1.        246  Arms:] ∼. F1–2.
249  Arms] ∼, F1–2.             254  drown'd;] ∼. F1–2.

Conduct my steps to find the fatal Tree,
In this deep Forest; since the Sibyl's Breath
Foretold, alas! too true, *Misenus* Death.
Scarce had he said, when full before his sight
280 Two Doves, descending from their Airy Flight,
Secure upon the grassy Plain alight.
He knew his Mother's Birds: and thus he pray'd:
Be you my Guides, with your auspicious Aid:
And lead my Footsteps, 'till the Branch be found,
Whose glitt'ring Shadow guilds the sacred Ground:
And thou, great Parent! with Cœlestial Care,
In this Distress, be present to my Pray'r.
Thus having said, he stop'd: With watchful sight,
Observing still the motions of their Flight:
290 What course they took, what happy Signs they shew.
They fed, and flutt'ring by degrees, withdrew
Still farther from the Place; but still in view.
Hopping, and flying, thus they led him on
To the slow Lake; whose baleful Stench to shun,
They wing'd their Flight aloft; then, stooping low,
Perch'd on the double Tree, that bears the golden Bough.
Thro' the green Leafs the glitt'ring Shadows glow;
As on the sacred Oak, the wintry Misleto:
Where the proud Mother views her precious Brood;
300 And happier Branches, which she never sow'd.
Such was the glitt'ring; such the ruddy Rind,
And dancing Leaves, that wanton'd in the Wind.
He seiz'd the shining Bough with griping hold;
And rent away, with ease, the ling'ring Gold:
Then, to the Sibyl's Palace bore the Prize.
Mean time, the *Trojan* Troops, with weeping Eyes,
To dead *Misenus* pay his Obsequies.
First, from the Ground, a lofty Pile they rear,
Of Pitch-trees, Oaks, and Pines, and unctuous Firr:
310 The Fabrick's Front with Cypress Twigs they strew;
And stick the sides with Boughs of baleful Yeugh.

---

285  glitt'ring] F2; glittering F1.          289  Flight:] ~. F1–2.
304  Gold:] ~. F1–2.

F. Cleyn inv.      W. Hollar fecit.      Æ.5.l. 280.

To Sⁱ Tho: Dyke                of Horeham in yͤ
County of                      Sussex. Barᵗ

The topmost part, his glitt'ring Arms adorn;
Warm Waters, then, in brazen Caldrons born,
Are pour'd to wash his Body, Joint by Joint:
And fragrant Oils the stiffen'd Limbs anoint.
With Groans and Cries *Misenus* they deplore:
Then on a Bier, with Purple cover'd o're,
The breathless Body, thus bewail'd, they lay: ⎞
And fire the Pile, their Faces turn'd away: ⎟
320 (Such reverend Rites their Fathers us'd to pay.) ⎠
Pure Oyl, and Incense, on the Fire they throw:
And Fat of Victims, which his Friends bestow.
These Gifts, the greedy Flames to Dust devour;
Then, on the living Coals, red Wine they pour:
And last, the Relicks by themselves dispose;
Which in a brazen Urn the Priests inclose.
Old *Chorineus* compass'd thrice the Crew;
And dip'd an Olive Branch in holy Dew;
Which thrice he sprinkl'd round; and thrice aloud
330 Invok'd the dead, and then dismiss'd the Crowd.
　　But good *Æneas* order'd on the Shore ⎞
A stately Tomb; whose top a Trumpet bore: ⎟
A Souldier's Fauchion, and a Sea-man's Oar. ⎠
Thus was his Friend interr'd: And deathless Fame
Still to the lofty Cape consigns his Name.
　　These Rites perform'd, the Prince, without delay,
Hastes to the neather World, his destin'd Way.
Deep was the Cave; and downward as it went
From the wide Mouth, a rocky rough Descent;
340 And here th' access a gloomy Grove defends;
And there th' unnavigable Lake extends:
O're whose unhappy Waters, void of Light,
No Bird presumes to steer his Airy Flight;
Such deadly Stenches from the depth arise,
And steaming Sulphur, that infects the Skies.
From hence the *Grecian* Bards their Legends make,
And give the name *Avernus* to the Lake.
Four sable Bullocks, in the Yoke untaught,

341　extends:] ∼. F1–2.

*S. Gribelin fecit. Lambert Sculpsit.*                                      Æ. 6. l. 310.

To Mrs. Anne Baynard, Daughter of Dr. Edwd.
Baynard of the Family of Leckham
in ye County of Wilts

VIVE UT VIVAS

For Sacrifice the pious Heroe brought.
350 The Priestess pours the Wine betwixt their Horns:
Then cuts the curling Hair; that first Oblation burns:
Invoking *Hecate* hither to repair;
(A pow'rful Name in Hell, and upper Air.)
The sacred Priests with ready Knives bereave
The Beasts of Life; and in full Bowls receive
The streaming Blood: A Lamb to Hell and Night,
(The sable Wool without a streak of white)
*Æneas* offers: And, by Fates decree,
A barren Heifar, *Proserpine* to thee.
360 With Holocausts he *Pluto*'s Altar fills:
Sev'n brawny Bulls with his own Hand he kills:
Then on the broiling Entrails Oyl he pours;
Which, ointed thus, the raging Flame devours.
Late, the Nocturnal Sacrifice begun;
Nor ended, 'till the next returning Sun.
Then Earth began to bellow, Trees to dance;
And howling Dogs in glimm'ring Light advance;
E're *Hecate* came. Far hence be Souls prophane,
The Sibyl cry'd, and from the Grove abstain.
370 Now, *Trojan*, take the way thy Fates afford:
Assume thy Courage, and unsheath thy Sword.
She said, and pass'd along the gloomy Space:
The Prince pursu'd her Steps with equal pace.

Ye Realms, yet unreveal'd to human sight,
Ye Gods, who rule the Regions of the Night,
Ye gliding Ghosts, permit me to relate
The mystick Wonders of your silent State.

Obscure they went thro dreery Shades, that led
Along the waste Dominions of the dead:
380 Thus wander Travellers in Woods by Night,
By the Moon's doubtful, and malignant Light:
When *Jove* in dusky Clouds involves the Skies;
And the faint Crescent shoots by fits before their Eyes.

Just in the Gate, and in the Jaws of Hell,
Revengeful Cares, and sullen Sorrows dwell;

---

351  burns:] ∼. F1–2.          368  came.] ∼: F1–2.

F. Cleyn inv.   Æ. 6. l. 290.

To John Lewknor Esq.ᵗ   of West Deane in the
County of   Sussex

And pale Diseases, and repining Age;
Want, Fear, and Famine's unresisted rage.
Here Toils, and Death, and Death's half-brother, Sleep,
Forms terrible to view, their Centry keep:
390 With anxious Pleasures of a guilty Mind,
Deep Frauds before, and open Force behind:
The Furies Iron Beds, and Strife that shakes
Her hissing Tresses, and unfolds her Snakes.
Full in the midst of this infernal Road,
An Elm displays her dusky Arms abroad;
The God of Sleep there hides his heavy Head:
And empty Dreams on ev'ry Leaf are spread.
Of various Forms unnumber'd Specters more;
*Centaurs,* and double Shapes, besiege the Door:
400 Before the Passage horrid *Hydra* stands,
And *Briareus* with all his hundred Hands:
*Gorgons, Geryon* with his triple Frame;
And vain *Chimæra* vomits empty Flame.
The Chief unsheath'd his shining Steel, prepar'd,
Tho seiz'd with sudden Fear, to force the Guard;
Off'ring his brandish'd Weapon at their Face;
Had not the Sibyl stop'd his eager Pace,
And told him what those empty Fantomes were;
Forms without Bodies, and impassive Air.
410 Hence to deep *Acheron* they take their way;
Whose troubled Eddies, thick with Ooze and Clay,
Are whirl'd aloft, and in *Cocytus* lost:
There *Charon* stands, who rules the dreary Coast:
A sordid God; down from his hoary Chin
A length of Beard descends; uncomb'd, unclean:
His Eyes, like hollow Furnaces on Fire:
A Girdle, foul with grease, binds his obscene Attire.
He spreads his Canvas, with his Pole he steers;
The Freights of flitting Ghosts in his thin Bottom bears.
420 He look'd in Years; yet in his Years were seen
A youthful Vigour, and Autumnal green.
An Airy Crowd came rushing where he stood;

405  Guard;] ~. F1–2.

Which fill'd the Margin of the fatal Flood.
Husbands and Wives, Boys and unmarry'd Maids;
And mighty Heroes more Majestick Shades;
And Youths, intomb'd before their Fathers Eyes,
With hollow Groans, and Shrieks, and feeble Cries:
Thick as the Leaves in Autumn strow the Woods:
Or Fowls, by Winter forc'd, forsake the Floods,
430 And wing their hasty flight to happier Lands: ⎫
Such, and so thick, the shiv'ring Army stands: ⎬
And press for passage with extended hands. ⎭
    Now these, now those, the surly Boatman bore:
The rest he drove to distance from the Shore.
The Heroe, who beheld with wond'ring Eyes,
The Tumult mix'd with Shrieks, Laments, and Cries;
Ask'd of his Guide, what the rude Concourse meant?
Why to the Shore the thronging People bent?
What Forms of Law, among the Ghosts were us'd?
440 Why some were ferry'd o're, and some refus'd?
    Son of *Anchises,* Offspring of the Gods,
The Sibyl said; you see the *Stygian* Floods,
The Sacred Stream, which Heav'n's Imperial State
Attests in Oaths, and fears to violate.
The Ghosts rejected, are th' unhappy Crew
Depriv'd of Sepulchers, and Fun'ral due;
The Boatman *Charon;* those, the bury'd host,
He Ferries over to the Farther Coast.
Nor dares his Transport Vessel cross the Waves,
450 With such whose Bones are not compos'd in Graves.
A hundred years they wander on the Shore,
At length, their Pennance done, are wafted o're.
The *Trojan* Chief his forward pace repress'd;
Revolving anxious Thoughts within his Breast.
He saw his Friends, who whelm'd beneath the Waves,
Their Fun'ral Honours claim'd, and ask'd their quiet Graves.
The lost *Leucaspis* in the Crowd he knew;
And the brave Leader of the *Lycian* Crew:

425  Shades;] ~. F1–2.               446  Sepulchers,] F2; ~. F1.
446  due;] ~. F1–2.

Whom, on the *Tyrrhene* Seas, the Tempests met;
460 The Sailors master'd, and the Ship o'reset.
Amidst the Spirits *Palinurus* press'd;
Yet fresh from life; a new admitted Guest:
Who, while he steering view'd the Stars, and bore
His Course from *Affrick,* to the *Latian* Shore,
Fell headlong down. The *Trojan* fix'd his view;
And scarcely through the gloom the sullen Shadow knew.
Then thus the Prince. What envious Pow'r, O Friend,
Brought your lov'd life to this disastrous end?
For *Phœbus,* ever true in all he said,
470 Has, in your fate alone, my Faith betray'd.
The God foretold you shou'd not die, before
You reach'd, secure from Seas, th' *Italian* Shore.
Is this th' unerring Pow'r? The Ghost reply'd,
Nor *Phœbus* flatter'd, nor his Answers ly'd;
Nor envious Gods have sent me to the Deep: ⎫
But while the Stars, and course of Heav'n I keep, ⎬
My weary'd Eyes were seiz'd with fatal sleep. ⎭
I fell; and with my weight, the Helm constrain'd,
Was drawn along, which yet my gripe retain'd.
480 Now by the Winds, and raging Waves, I swear,
Your Safety, more than mine, was then my Care:
Lest, of the Guide bereft, the Rudder lost,
Your Ship shou'd run against the rocky Coast.
Three blust'ring Nights, born by the Southern blast,
I floated; and discover'd Land at last:
High on a Mounting Wave, my head I bore:
Forcing my Strength, and gath'ring to the Shore:
Panting, but past the danger, now I seiz'd
The Craggy Cliffs, and my tyr'd Members eas'd:
490 While, cumber'd with my dropping Cloaths, I lay,
The cruel Nation, covetous of Prey,
Stain'd with my Blood th' unhospitable Coast:
And now, by Winds and Waves, my lifeless Limbs are tost:

---

462  Guest:] ∼. F1–2.
472  Shore.] ∼? F1–2.
488  but] F1 *errata,* F2; but but F1.

470  betray'd.] ∼? F1–2.
483  the] F2; the the F1.
493  tost:] ∼. F1–2.

Which O avert, by yon Etherial Light
Which I have lost, for this eternal Night:
Or if by dearer tyes you may be won,
By your dead Sire, and by your living Son,
Redeem from this Reproach, my wand'ring Ghost;
Or with your Navy seek the *Velin* Coast:
500 And in a peaceful Grave my Corps compose:
Or, if a nearer way your Mother shows,
Without whose Aid, you durst not undertake
This frightful Passage o're the *Stygian* Lake;
Lend to this Wretch your Hand, and waft him o're
To the sweet Banks of yon forbidden Shore.
Scarce had he said, the Prophetess began;
What Hopes delude thee, miserable Man?
Think'st thou thus unintomb'd to cross the Floods, ⎫
To view the Furies, and Infernal Gods;          ⎬
510 And visit, without leave, the dark abodes?     ⎭
Attend the term of long revolving Years:
Fate, and the dooming Gods, are deaf to Tears.
This Comfort of thy dire Misfortune take;
The Wrath of Heav'n, inflicted for thy sake,
With Vengeance shall pursue th' inhumane Coast:
Till they propitiate thy offended Ghost,
And raise a Tomb, with Vows, and solemn Pray'r;
And *Palinurus* name the Place shall bear.
This calm'd his Cares: sooth'd with his future Fame;
520 And pleas'd to hear his propagated Name.
    Now nearer to the *Stygian* Lake they draw:
Whom from the Shore, the surly Boatman saw:
Observ'd their Passage thro' the shady Wood;
And mark'd their near Approaches to the Flood:
Then thus he call'd aloud, inflam'd with Wrath;
Mortal, what e're, who this forbidden Path
In Arms presum'st to tread, I charge thee stand,
And tell thy Name, and Buis'ness in the Land.
Know this, the Realm of Night; the *Stygian* Shore:
530 My Boat conveys no living Bodies o're:

515   Coast:] ~. F1–2.

Nor was I pleas'd great *Theseus* once to bear;
Who forc'd a Passage with his pointed Spear;
Nor strong *Alcides,* Men of mighty Fame;
And from th' immortal Gods their Lineage came.
In Fetters one the barking Porter ty'd,
And took him trembling from his Sov'raign's side:
Two sought by Force to seize his beauteous Bride.
To whom the Sibyl thus, Compose thy Mind:
Nor Frauds are here contriv'd, nor Force design'd.
540 Still may the Dog the wand'ring Troops constrain
Of Airy Ghosts; and vex the guilty Train;
And with her grisly Lord his lovely Queen remain.
The *Trojan* Chief, whose Lineage is from *Jove,*
Much fam'd for Arms, and more for filial Love,
Is sent to seek his Sire, in your *Elysian* Grove.
If neither Piety, nor Heav'n's Command,
Can gain his Passage to the *Stygian* Strand,
This fatal Present shall prevail, at least;
Then shew'd the shining Bough, conceal'd within her Vest.
550 No more was needful: for the gloomy God
Stood mute with Awe, to see the Golden Rod:
Admir'd the destin'd Off'ring to his Queen;
(A venerable Gift so rarely seen.)
His Fury thus appeas'd, he puts to Land:
The Ghosts forsake their Seats, at his Command:
He clears the Deck, receives the mighty Freight,
The leaky Vessel groans beneath the weight.
Slowly he sails; and scarcely stems the Tides:
The pressing Water pours within her sides.
560 His Passengers at length are wafted o're;
Expos'd in muddy Weeds, upon the miry Shore.
No sooner landed, in his Den they found
The triple Porter of the *Stygian* Sound:
Grim *Cerberus;* who soon began to rear
His crested Snakes, and arm'd his bristling Hair.
The prudent Sibyl had before prepar'd

538  Compose] compose F1–2.
545  *Elysian*] *Elisian* F1–2.

Æ. 9. l: 158.

To S.ʳ Fleetwood                    Sheppard Knight,
Gent: Usher of y.ᵉ                    Black Rod.

A Sop, in Honey steep'd, to charm the Guard:
Which, mix'd with pow'rful Drugs, she cast before
His greedy grinning Jaws, just op'd to roar:
570 With three enormous Mouths he gapes; and streight,
With Hunger prest, devours the pleasing Bait.
Long draughts of Sleep his monstrous Limbs enslave;
He reels, and falling, fills the spacious Cave.
The Keeper charm'd, the Chief without Delay
Pass'd on, and took th' irremeable way.
Before the Gates, the Cries of Babes new born,
Whom Fate had from their tender Mothers torn,
Assault his Ears: Then those, whom Form of Laws
Condemn'd to die, when Traitors judg'd their Cause.
580 Nor want they Lots, nor Judges to review
The wrongful Sentence, and award a new.
*Minos*, the strict Inquisitor, appears;
And Lives and Crimes, with his Assessors, hears.
Round, in his Urn, the blended Balls he rowls;
Absolves the Just, and dooms the Guilty Souls.
The next in Place, and Punishment, are they
Who prodigally throw their Souls away:
Fools, who repining at their wretched State,
And loathing anxious life, suborn'd their Fate.
590 With late Repentance, now they wou'd retrieve
The Bodies they forsook, and wish to live:
Their Pains and Poverty desire to bear,
To view the Light of Heav'n, and breath the vital Air:
But Fate forbids; the *Stygian* Floods oppose;
And, with nine circling Streams, the captive Souls inclose.
    Not far from thence, the mournful Fields appear;
So call'd, from Lovers that inhabit there.
The Souls, whom that unhappy Flame invades,
In secret Solitude, and Myrtle Shades,
600 Make endless Moans, and pining with Desire,
Lament too late, their unextinguish'd Fire.
Here *Procris, Eryphile* here, he found

---

567  Guard:] ∼. F1–2.                587  away:] ∼. F1–2.
591  live:] ∼. F1–2.

Pet. Cleyn inv.    Hollar fecit    Æ 61. 515.

To John Pulteney         of the Parish
of St James's         Westminster Esqꝛ.

Baring her Breast, yet bleeding with the Wound
Made by her Son. He saw *Pasiphae* there,
With *Phædra*'s Ghost, a foul incestuous pair;
There *Laodamia*, with *Evadne*, moves:
Unhappy both; but loyal in their Loves:
*Cæneus*, a Woman once, and once a Man;
But ending in the Sex she first began.
610 Not far from these *Phœnician Dido* stood;
Fresh from her Wound, her Bosom bath'd in Blood:
Whom, when the *Trojan* Heroe hardly knew,
Obscure in Shades, and with a doubtful view,
(Doubtful as he who sees thro' dusky Night,
Or thinks he sees the Moon's uncertain Light:)
With Tears he first approach'd the sullen Shade;
And, as his Love inspir'd him, thus he said.
Unhappy Queen! then is the common breath
Of Rumour true, in your reported Death,
620 And I, alas, the Cause! by Heav'n, I vow,
And all the Pow'rs that rule the Realms below,
Unwilling I forsook your friendly State:
Commanded by the Gods, and forc'd by Fate:
Those Gods, that Fate, whose unresisted Might ⎞
Have sent me to these Regions, void of Light, ⎬
Thro' the vast Empire of eternal Night. ⎠
Nor dar'd I to presume, that, press'd with Grief,
My Flight should urge you to this dire Relief.
Stay, stay your Steps, and listen to my Vows:
630 'Tis the last Interview that Fate allows!
In vain he thus attempts her Mind to move,
With Tears, and Pray'rs, and late repenting Love.
Disdainfully she look'd; then turning round,
But fix'd her Eyes unmov'd upon the Ground:
And, what he says, and swears, regards no more
Than the deaf Rocks, when the loud Billows roar:

606  There] F2; Chast F1.          607  Loves:] ~. F1–2.
611  Blood:] ~. F1–2.          623  Fate:] ~. F1–2.
634  Ground:] ~. F1–2.          636  roar:] ~. F1–2.

But whirl'd away, to shun his hateful sight,
Hid in the Forest, and the Shades of Night:
Then sought *Sicheus,* thro' the shady Grove,
640 Who answer'd all her Cares, and equal'd all her Love.
Some pious Tears the pitying Heroe paid;
And follow'd with his Eyes the flitting Shade:
Then took the forward Way, by Fate ordain'd,
And, with his Guide, the farther Fields attain'd;
Where, sever'd from the rest, the Warrior Souls remain'd.
*Tideus* he met, with *Meleager*'s Race;
The Pride of Armies, and the Souldier's Grace;
And pale *Adrastus* with his ghastly Face.
Of *Trojan* Chiefs he view'd a num'rous Train:
650 All much lamented, all in Battel slain:
*Glaucus* and *Medon,* high above the rest,
*Antenor*'s Sons, and *Ceres* sacred Priest:
And proud *Ideus, Priam*'s Charioteer;
Who shakes his empty Reins, and aims his Airy Spear.
The gladsome Ghosts, in circling Troops, attend,
And with unweary'd Eyes behold their Friend:
Delight to hover near; and long to know
What buis'ness brought him to the Realms below.
    But *Argive* Chiefs, and *Agamemnon*'s Train,
660 When his refulgent Arms flash'd thro' the shady Plain,
Fled from his well known Face, with wonted Fear,
As when his thund'ring Sword, and pointed Spear,
Drove headlong to their Ships, and glean'd the routed Reer.
They rais'd a feeble Cry, with trembling Notes:
But the weak Voice deceiv'd their gasping Throats.
Here *Priam*'s Son, *Deiphobus,* he found:
Whose Face and Limbs were one continu'd Wound.
Dishonest, with lop'd Arms, the Youth appears:
Spoil'd of his Nose, and shorten'd of his Ears.
670 He scarcely knew him, striving to disown
His blotted Form, and blushing to be known:

---

638  Night:] ~. F1–2.                642  Shade:] ~. F1–2.
650  slain:] ~. F1–2.                656  Friend:] ~. F1–2.
671  known:] ~. F1–2.

And therefore first began. O *Teucer's* Race,
Who durst thy faultless Figure thus deface?
What heart cou'd wish, what hand inflict this dire Disgrace?
Twas fam'd, that in our last and fatal Night,
Your single Prowess long sustain'd the Fight:
Till tir'd, not forc'd, a glorious Fate you chose:
And fell upon a Heap of slaughter'd Foes.
But in remembrance of so brave a Deed,
680 A Tomb, and Fun'ral Honours I decreed:
Thrice call'd your *Manes,* on the *Trojan* Plains:
The place your Armour, and your Name retains.
Your Body too I sought; and had I found,
Design'd for Burial in your Native Ground.
    The Ghost reply'd, Your Piety has paid
All needful Rites, to rest my wand'ring Shade:
But cruel Fate, and my more cruel Wife,
To *Grecian* Swords betray'd my sleeping Life.
These are the Monuments of *Helen's* Love:
690 The Shame I bear below, the Marks I bore above.
You know in what deluding Joys we past
The Night, that was by Heav'n decreed our last.
For when the fatal Horse, descending down,
Pregnant with Arms, o'rewhelm'd th' unhappy Town;
She feign'd Nocturnal Orgyes: left my Bed,
And, mix'd with *Trojan* Dames, the Dances led:
Then, waving high her Torch, the Signal made,
Which rouz'd the *Grecians* from their Ambuscade.
With Watching overworn, with Cares opprest,
700 Unhappy I had laid me down to rest;
And heavy Sleep my weary Limbs possess'd.
Mean time my worthy Wife, our Arms mislay'd;
And from beneath my head my Sword convey'd:
The Door unlatch'd; and with repeated calls,
Invites her former Lord within my walls.
Thus in her Crime her confidence she plac'd:
And with new Treasons wou'd redeem the past.

---

685   Your] your F1–2.
696   led:] ∼. F1–2.

What need I more? into the Room they ran;
And meanly murther'd a defenceless Man.
710 *Ulysses,* basely born, first led the way: ⎞
Avenging Pow'rs! with Justice if I pray, ⎬
That Fortune be their own another day. ⎠
But answer you; and in your turn relate,
What brought you, living, to the *Stygian* State?
Driv'n by the Winds and Errors of the Sea, ⎞
Or did you Heav'ns Superior Doom obey? ⎬
Or tell what other Chance conducts your way? ⎠
To view, with Mortal Eyes, our dark Retreats,
Tumults and Torments of th' Infernal Seats?
720 While thus, in talk, the flying Hours they pass,
The Sun had finish'd more than half his Race:
And they, perhaps, in Words and Tears had spent
The little time of stay, which Heav'n had lent.
But thus the Sibyl chides their long delay;
Night rushes down, and headlong drives the Day:
Tis here, in different Paths, the way divides:
The right, to *Pluto*'s Golden Palace guides:
The left to that unhappy Region tends, ⎞
Which to the depth of *Tartarus* descends; ⎬
730 The Seat of Night profound, and punish'd Fiends. ⎠
Then thus *Deiphobus:* O Sacred Maid!
Forbear to chide; and be your Will Obey'd:
Lo to the secret Shadows I retire,
To pay my Penance 'till my Years expire.
Proceed Auspicious Prince, with Glory Crownd,
And born to better Fates than I have found.
He said; and while he said, his Steps he turn'd
To Secret Shadows; and in silence Mourn'd.
The Heroe, looking on the left, espy'd
740 A lofty Tow'r, and strong on ev'ry side
With treble Walls, which *Phlegethon* surrounds, ⎞
Whose fiery Flood the burning Empire bounds: ⎬
And press'd betwixt the Rocks, the bellowing noise resounds. ⎠
Wide is the fronting Gate, and rais'd on high

708   more?] ∼, F1–2.

With Adamantine Columns, threats the Sky.
Vain is the force of Man, and Heav'ns as vain,
To crush the Pillars which the Pile sustain.
Sublime on these a Tow'r of Steel is rear'd;
And dire *Tisiphone* there keeps the Ward:
750 Girt in her sanguine Gown, by Night and Day,
Observant of the Souls that pass the downward way:
From hence are heard the Groans of Ghosts, the pains
Of sounding Lashes, and of dragging Chains.
The *Trojan* stood astonish'd at their Cries;
And ask'd his Guide, from whence those Yells arise?
And what the Crimes and what the Tortures were,
And loud Laments that rent the liquid Air?
She thus reply'd: The chast and holy Race,
Are all forbidden this polluted Place.
760 But *Hecate,* when she gave to rule the Woods, ⎫
Then led me trembling thro' these dire Abodes: ⎬
And taught the Tortures of th' avenging Gods. ⎭
These are the Realms of unrelenting Fate:
And awful *Rhadamanthus* rules the State.
He hears and judges each committed Crime;
Enquires into the Manner, Place, and Time.
The conscious Wretch must all his Acts reveal:
Loath to confess, unable to conceal:
From the first Moment of his vital Breath,
770 To his last Hour of unrepenting Death.
Straight, o're the guilty Ghost, the Fury shakes ⎫
The sounding Whip, and brandishes her Snakes: ⎬
And the pale Sinner, with her Sisters, takes. ⎭
Then, of it self, unfolds th' Eternal Door:
With dreadful Sounds the brazen Hinges roar.
You see, before the Gate, what stalking Ghost
Commands the Guard, what Centries keep the Post:
More formidable *Hydra* stands within;
Whose Jaws with Iron Teeth severely grin.
780 The gaping Gulph, low to the Centre lies;

---

746  vain] F1 *errata*, F2; van F1.          749  Ward:] ∼. F1–2.
768  confess] F2; confefs F1.

And twice as deep as Earth is distant from the Skies.
The Rivals of the Gods, the *Titan* Race,
Here sing'd with Lightning, rowl within th' unfathom'd space.
Here lye th' *Alœan* Twins, (I saw them both)
Enormous Bodies, of Gigantick Growth;
Who dar'd in Fight the Thund'rer to defy;
Affect his Heav'n, and force him from the Sky.
*Salmoneus,* suff'ring cruel Pains, I found,
For emulating *Jove;* the ratling Sound
790 Of Mimick Thunder, and the glitt'ring Blaze
Of pointed Lightnings, and their forky Rays.
Through *Elis,* and the *Grecian* Towns he flew:
Th' audacious Wretch four fiery Coursers drew:
He wav'd a Torch aloft, and, madly vain,
Sought Godlike Worship from a Servile Train.
Ambitious Fool, with horny Hoofs to pass
O're hollow Arches, of resounding Brass;
To rival Thunder, in its rapid Course:
And imitate inimitable Force.
800 But he, the King of Heav'n, obscure on high,
Bar'd his red Arm, and launching from the Sky
His writhen Bolt, not shaking empty Smoak,
Down to the deep Abyss the flaming Felon strook.
There *Tityus* was to see; who took his Birth
From Heav'n, his Nursing from the foodful Earth.
Here his Gygantic Limbs, with large Embrace,
Infold nine Acres of Infernal Space.
A rav'nous Vulture in his open'd side,
Her crooked Beak and cruel Tallons try'd:
810 Still for the growing Liver dig'd his Breast;
The growing Liver still supply'd the Feast.
Still are his Entrails fruitful to their Pains:
Th' immortal Hunger lasts, th' immortal Food remains.
*Ixion* and *Perithous* I cou'd name;
And more *Thessalian* Chiefs of mighty Fame.
High o're their Heads a mould'ring Rock is plac'd,
That promises a fall; and shakes at ev'ry Blast.

784  *Alœan*] *Alœan* F1–2.

They lye below, on Golden Beds display'd,
And genial Feasts, with Regal Pomp, are made.
820 The Queen of Furies by their sides is set;
And snatches from their Mouths th' untasted Meat:
Which, if they touch, her hissing Snakes she rears:
Tossing her Torch, and thund'ring in their Ears.
Then they, who Brothers better Claim disown,
Expel their Parents, and usurp the Throne;
Defraud their Clients, and to Lucre sold,
Sit brooding on unprofitable Gold:
Who dare not give, and ev'n refuse to lend
To their poor Kindred, or a wanting Friend:
830 Vast is the Throng of these; nor less the Train
Of lustful Youths, for foul Adultry slain.
Hosts of Deserters, who their Honour sold,
And basely broke their Faith for Bribes of Gold:
All these within the Dungeon's depth remain:
Despairing Pardon, and expecting Pain.
Ask not what Pains; nor farther seek to know
Their Process, or the Forms of Law below.
Some rowl a weighty Stone; some laid along,
And bound with burning Wires, on Spokes of Wheels are hung.
840 Unhappy *Theseus*, doom'd for ever there,
Is fix'd by Fate on his Eternal Chair:
And wretched *Phlegias* warns the World with Cries; ⎫
(Cou'd Warning make the World more just or wise,) ⎬
Learn Righteousness, and dread th' avenging Deities. ⎭
To Tyrants others have their Country sold,
Imposing Foreign Lords, for Foreign Gold:
Some have old Laws repeal'd, new Statutes made;
Not as the People pleas'd, but as they paid.
With Incest some their Daughters Bed prophan'd,
850 All dar'd the worst of Ills, and what they dar'd, attain'd.
Had I a hundred Mouths, a hundred Tongues,
And Throats of Brass, inspir'd with Iron Lungs,
I could not half those horrid Crimes repeat:
Nor half the Punishments those Crimes have met.

821   Meat:] ∼. F1–2.

But let us haste our Voyage to pursue;
The Walls of *Pluto*'s Palace are in view.
The Gate, and Iron Arch above it, stands:
On Anvils labour'd by the *Cyclops* Hands.
Before our farther way the Fates allow,
860 Here must we fix on high the Golden Bough.
She said, and thro' the gloomy Shades they past,
And chose the middle Path: Arriv'd at last,
The Prince, with living Water, sprinkl'd o're
His Limbs, and Body; then approach'd the Door,
Possess'd the Porch, and on the Front above
He fix'd the fatal Bough, requir'd by *Pluto*'s Love.
These Holy Rites perform'd, they took their Way,
Where long extended Plains of Pleasure lay.
The verdant Fields with those of Heav'n may vye;
870 With Æther vested, and a Purple Sky:
The blissful Seats of Happy Souls below:
Stars of their own, and their own Suns they know.
Their Airy Limbs in Sports they exercise,
And, on the Green, contend the Wrestler's Prize.
Some, in Heroick Verse, divinely sing;
Others in artful Measures lead the ring.
The *Thracian* Bard, surrounded by the rest,
There stands conspicuous in his flowing Vest.
His flying Fingers, and harmonious Quill,
880 Strike sev'n distinguish'd Notes, and sev'n at once they fill.
Here found they *Teucer*'s old Heroick Race;
Born better times and happier Years to grace.
*Assaracus* and *Ilus* here enjoy
Perpetual Fame, with him who founded *Troy*.
The Chief beheld their Chariots from afar;
Their shining Arms, and Coursers train'd to War:
Their Lances fix'd in Earth, their Steeds around,
Free from their Harness, graze the flow'ry Ground.
The love of Horses which they had, alive,
890 And care of Chariots, after Death survive.
Some chearful Souls, were feasting on the Plain;

---

864  Door,] ∼. F1–2.                    870  Æther] Æther F1–2.

Some did the Song, and some the Choir maintain,
Beneath a Laurel Shade, where mighty *Po*
Mounts up to Woods above, and hides his Head below.
Here Patriots live, who, for their Countries good,
In fighting Fields, were prodigal of Blood:
Priests of unblemish'd Lives here make Abode;
And Poets worthy their inspiring God:
And searching Wits, of more Mechanick parts,
900 Who grac'd their Age with new invented Arts:
Those who, to worth, their Bounty did extend;
And those who knew that Bounty to commend.
The Heads of these with holy Fillets bound;
And all their Temples were with Garlands crown'd.

   To these the Sibyl thus her Speech address'd: }
And first, to him surrounded by the rest; }
Tow'ring his Height, and ample was his Breast; }
Say happy Souls, Divine *Musæus* say,
Where lives *Anchises,* and where lies our Way
910 To find the Heroe, for whose only sake
We sought the dark Abodes, and cross'd the bitter Lake?
To this the Sacred Poet thus reply'd;
In no fix'd place the Happy Souls reside.
In Groves we live; and lye on mossy Beds
By Crystal Streams, that murmur through the Meads:
But pass yon easie Hill, and thence descend,
The Path conducts you to your Journeys end.
This said, he led them up the Mountains brow, }
And shews them all the shining Fields below; }
920 They wind the Hill, and thro' the blissful Meadows go. }
But old *Anchises,* in a flow'ry Vale,
Review'd his muster'd Race; and took the Tale:
Those Happy Spirits, which ordain'd by Fate,
For future Beings, and new Bodies wait:
With studious Thought observ'd th' illustrious Throng;
In Nature's Order as they pass'd along:

---

892  maintain,] ∼. F1–2.         900  Arts:] ∼. F1–2.
922  Tale:] ∼. F1–2.             924  wait:] ∼. F1–2.
926  along:] ∼. F1–2.

Their Names, their Fates, their Conduct, and their Care,
In peaceful Senates, and successful War.
He, when *Æneas* on the Plain appears,
930 Meets him with open Arms, and falling Tears.
Welcome, he said, the Gods undoubted Race, ⎫
O long expected to my dear Embrace; ⎬
Once more 'tis giv'n me to behold your Face! ⎭
The Love, and Pious Duty which you pay,
Have pass'd the Perils of so hard a way.
'Tis true, computing times, I now believ'd
The happy Day approach'd; nor are my Hopes deceiv'd.
What length of Lands, what Oceans have you pass'd,
What Storms sustain'd, and on what Shores been cast?
940 How have I fear'd your Fate! But fear'd it most,
When Love assail'd you, on the *Lybian* Coast.
To this, the Filial Duty thus replies; ⎫
Your sacred Ghost, before my sleeping Eyes, ⎬
Appear'd; and often urg'd this painful Enterprise. ⎭
After long tossing on the *Tyrrhene* Sea,
My Navy rides at Anchor in the Bay.
But reach your Hand, oh Parent Shade, nor shun
The dear Embraces of your longing Son!
He said; and falling Tears his Face bedew:
950 Then thrice, around his Neck, his Arms he threw;
And thrice the flitting Shadow slip'd away;
Like Winds, or empty Dreams that fly the Day.
Now in a secret Vale, the *Trojan* sees ⎫
A sep'rate Grove, thro' which a gentle Breeze ⎬
Plays with a passing Breath, and whispers thro' the Trees. ⎭
And just before the Confines of the Wood,
The gliding *Lethe* leads her silent Flood.
About the Boughs an Airy Nation flew,
Thick as the humming Bees, that hunt the Golden Dew;
960 In Summer's heat, on tops of Lillies feed,
And creep within their Bells, to suck the balmy Seed.
The winged Army roams the Fields around;
The Rivers and the Rocks remurmur to the sound.
*Æneas* wond'ring stood: Then ask'd the Cause,

Which to the Stream the Crowding People draws.
Then thus the Sire. The Souls that throng the Flood
Are those, to Whom, by Fate, are other Bodies ow'd:
In *Lethe*'s Lake they long Oblivion tast;
Of future Life secure, forgetful of the Past.
970 Long has my Soul desir'd this time, and place,
To set before your sight your glorious Race:
That this presaging Joy may fire your Mind,
To seek the Shores by Destiny design'd.
O Father, can it be, that Souls sublime,
Return to visit our Terrestrial Clime?
And that the Gen'rous Mind, releas'd by Death,
Can Covet lazy Limbs, and Mortal Breath?
*Anchises* then, in order, thus begun
To clear those Wonders to his Godlike Son.
980 Know first, that Heav'n, and Earth's compacted Frame,
And flowing Waters, and the starry Flame,
And both the Radiant Lights, one Common Soul
Inspires, and feeds, and animates the whole.
This Active Mind infus'd through all the Space,
Unites and mingles with the mighty Mass.
Hence Men and Beasts the Breath of Life obtain;
And Birds of Air, and Monsters of the Main.
Th' Etherial Vigour is in all the same,
And every Soul is fill'd with equal Flame:
990 As much as Earthy Limbs, and gross allay    ⎫
Of Mortal Members, subject to decay,              ⎬
Blunt not the Beams of Heav'n and edge of Day. ⎭
From this course Mixture of Terrestial parts,
Desire, and Fear, by turns possess their Hearts:
And Grief, and Joy: Nor can the groveling Mind, ⎫
In the dark Dungeon of the Limbs confin'd,            ⎬
Assert the Native Skies; or own its heav'nly Kind. ⎭
Nor Death it self can wholly wash their Stains;
But long contracted Filth, ev'n in the Soul remains.
1000 The Reliques of inveterate Vice they wear;
And Spots of Sin obscene, in ev'ry Face appear.

971   Race:] ∼. F1–2.

For this are various Penances enjoyn'd;
And some are hung to bleach, upon the Wind;
Some plung'd in Waters, others purg'd in Fires,
Till all the Dregs are drain'd: and all the Rust expires:
All have their *Manes*, and those *Manes* bear: ⎫
The few, so cleans'd to these Abodes repair: ⎬
And breath, in ample Fields, the soft *Elysian* Air. ⎭
Then are they happy, when by length of time
1010 The Scurf is worn away, of each committed Crime.
No Speck is left, of their habitual Stains;
But the pure Æther of the Soul remains.
But, when a Thousand rowling Years are past,
(So long their Punishments and Penance last;)
Whole Droves of Minds are, by the driving God,
Compell'd to drink the deep *Lethæan* Flood:
In large forgetful draughts to steep the Cares
Of their past Labours, and their Irksom Years:
That, unrememb'ring of its former Pain,
1020 The Soul may suffer mortal Flesh again.
Thus having said; the Father Spirit, leads
The Priestess and his Son through Swarms of Shades:
And takes a rising Ground, from thence to see
The long Procession of his Progeny.
Survey (pursu'd the Sire) this airy Throng;
As, offer'd to thy view, they pass along.
These are th' *Italian* Names, which Fate will join
With ours, and graff upon the *Trojan* Line.
Observe the Youth who first appears in sight;
1030 And holds the nearest Station to the Light:
Already seems to snuff the vital Air;
And leans just forward, on a shining Spear,
*Silvius* is he: thy last begotten Race;
But first in order sent, to fill thy place,
An *Alban* Name; but mix'd with *Dardan* Blood;
Born in the Covert of a shady Wood:
Him fair *Lavinia*, thy surviving Wife,
Shall breed in Groves, to lead a solitary Life.

1018   Years:] ∼. F1–2.          1022   Shades:] ∼. F1–2.

Æ.S.L. 1685.    F. Clern in

To Robert Harley          of Bramton Castle
    in y.e County       of Hereford Esq.3

In *Alba* he shall fix his Royal Seat:
1040 And, born a King, a Race of Kings beget.
Then *Procas,* Honour of the *Trojan* Name,
*Capys,* and *Numitor,* of endless Fame.
A second *Silvius* after these appears;
*Silvius Æneas,* for thy Name he bears:
For Arms and Justice equally renown'd;
Who, late restor'd, in *Alba* shall be crown'd.
How great they look, how vig'rously they wield
Their weighty Lances, and sustain the Shield!
But they, who crown'd with Oaken Wreaths appear,
1050 Shall *Gabian* Walls, and strong *Fidena* rear:
*Nomentum, Bola,* with *Pometia,* found;
And raise *Colatian* Tow'rs on Rocky Ground.
All these shall then be Towns of mighty Fame;
Tho' now they lye obscure; and Lands without a Name.
See *Romulus* the great, born to restore
The Crown that once his injur'd Grandsire wore.
This Prince, a Priestess of your Blood shall bear;
And like his Sire in Arms he shall appear.
Two rising Crests his Royal Head adorn;
1060 Born from a God, himself to Godhead born.
His Sire already signs him for the Skies,
And marks his Seat amidst the Deities.
Auspicious Chief! thy Race in times to come
Shall spread the Conquests of Imperial *Rome:*
*Rome* whose ascending Tow'rs shall Heav'n invade;
Involving Earth and Ocean in her Shade:
High as the Mother of the Gods in place;
And proud, like her, of an Immortal Race.
Then when in Pomp she makes the *Phrygian* round;
1070 With Golden Turrets on her Temples crown'd:
A hundred Gods her sweeping Train supply;
Her Offspring all, and all command the Sky.
Now fix your Sight, and stand intent, to see

---

1044  bears:] ~. F1–2.  　　　　1057  your] F2; our F1.
1064  *Rome:*] ~. F1–2.  　　　　1066  Shade:] ~. F1–2.

Your *Roman* Race, and *Julian* Progeny.
The mighty *Cæsar* waits his vital Hour;
Impatient for the World, and grasps his promis'd Pow'r.
But next behold the Youth of Form Divine,
*Cæsar* himself, exalted in his Line;
*Augustus,* promis'd oft, and long foretold, ⎫
1080 Sent to the Realm that *Saturn* rul'd of old; ⎬
Born to restore a better Age of Gold. ⎭
*Affrick,* and *India,* shall his Pow'r obey, ⎫
He shall extend his propagated Sway, ⎬
Beyond the Solar Year; without the starry Way: ⎭
Where *Atlas* turns the rowling Heav'ns around;
And his broad Shoulders with their Lights are crown'd.
At his fore-seen Approach, already quake
The *Caspian* Kingdoms, and *Mæotian* Lake.
Their Seers behold the Tempest from afar;
1090 And threatning Oracles denounce the War.
*Nile* hears him knocking at his sev'nfold Gates;
And seeks his hidden Spring, and fears his Nephews Fates.
Nor *Hercules* more Lands or Labours knew,
Not tho' the brazen-footed Hind he slew;
Freed *Erymanthus* from the foaming Boar,
And dip'd his Arrows in *Lernæan* Gore:
Nor *Bacchus,* turning from his *Indian* War,
By Tygers drawn triumphant in his Car,
From *Nisa*'s top descending on the Plains;
1100 With curling Vines around his purple Reins.
And doubt we yet thro' Dangers to pursue
The Paths of Honour, and a Crown in view?
But what's the Man, who from afar appears,
His Head with Olive crown'd, his Hand a Censer bears?
His hoary Beard, and holy Vestments bring
His lost Idea back: I know the *Roman* King.
He shall to peaceful *Rome* new Laws ordain:
Call'd from his mean abode, a Scepter to sustain.
Him, *Tullus* next in Dignity succeeds;

1084  Way:] ∼. F1–2.                    1092  Nephews] Nephew's F1–2.
1096  Gore:] ∼. F1–2.                   1099  *Nisa*'s] *Nisus* F1–2.

1110 An active Prince, and prone to Martial Deeds.
He shall his Troops for fighting Fields prepare,
Disus'd to Toils, and Triumphs of the War.
By dint of Sword his Crown he shall increase;
And scour his Armour from the Rust of Peace:
Whom *Ancus* follows, with a fawning Air;
But vain within, and proudly popular.
Next view the *Tarquin* Kings: Th' avenging Sword
Of *Brutus,* justly drawn, and *Rome* restor'd.
He first renews the Rods, and Axe severe;
1120 And gives the Consuls Royal Robes to wear.
His Sons, who seek the Tyrant to sustain,
And long for Arbitrary Lords again,
With Ignominy scourg'd, in open sight,
He dooms to Death deserv'd; asserting Publick Right.
Unhappy Man, to break the Pious Laws
Of Nature, pleading in his Children's Cause!
Howe're the doubtful Fact is understood,        )
'Tis Love of Honour, and his Country's good:     }
The Consul, not the Father, sheds the Blood.    )
1130 Behold *Torquatus* the same Track pursue;
And next, the two devoted *Decij* view,
The *Drusian* Line, *Camillus* loaded home
With Standards well redeem'd, and foreign Foes o'recome.
The Pair you see in equal Armour shine;
Now, Friends below, in close Embraces join:
But when they leave the shady Realms of Night,
And, cloath'd in Bodies, breath your upper Light,
With mortal Hate each other shall pursue:
What Wars, what Wounds, what Slaughter shall ensue!
1140 From *Alpine* Heights the Father first descends;   )
His Daughter's Husband in the Plain attends:       }
His Daughter's Husband arms his Eastern Friends.  )
Embrace again, my Sons, be Foes no more:
Nor stain your Country with her Childrens Gore.

---

1111  He shall his Troops for fighting Fields] F2; For fighting Fields his Troops he shall F1.
1114  Peace:] ∼. F1–2.
1131  view,] ∼. F1–2.
1131  two] F1 *errata,* F2; three F1.
1135–1137  Now . . . Light,] (∼ . . . ∼,) F1–2.

And thou, the first, lay down thy lawless claim;
Thou, of my Blood, who bear'st the *Julian* Name.
Another comes, who shall in Triumph ride;
And to the Capitol his Chariot guide;
From conquer'd *Corinth*, rich with *Grecian* Spoils.
1150  And yet another, fam'd for Warlike Toils,
On *Argos* shall impose the *Roman* Laws:
And, on the *Greeks*, revenge the *Trojan* Cause:
Shall drag in Chains their *Achillæan* Race;  ⎫
Shall vindicate his Ancestors Disgrace:       ⎬
And *Pallas*, for her violated Place.          ⎭
Great *Cato* there, for Gravity renown'd,
And conqu'ring *Cossus* goes with Lawrels crown'd.
Who can omit the *Gracchi*, who declare
The *Scipios* Worth, those Thunderbolts of War,
1160  The double Bane of *Carthage?* Who can see,
Without esteem for virtuous Poverty,
Severe *Fabritius*, or can cease t' admire
The Ploughman Consul in his Course Attire?
Tir'd as I am, my Praise the *Fabij* claim;
And thou great Heroe, greatest of thy Name;
Ordain'd in War to save the sinking State,
And, by Delays, to put a stop to Fate!
Let others better mold the running Mass    ⎫
Of Mettals, and inform the breathing Brass;  ⎬
1170  And soften into Flesh a Marble Face:        ⎭
Plead better at the Bar; describe the Skies,
And when the Stars descend, and when they rise.
But, *Rome*, 'tis thine alone, with awful sway,  ⎫
To rule Mankind; and make the World obey;       ⎬
Disposing Peace, and War, thy own Majestick Way. ⎭
To tame the Proud, the fetter'd Slave to free;
These are Imperial Arts, and worthy thee.
He paus'd: And while with wond'ring Eyes they view'd
The passing Spirits, thus his Speech renew'd.
1180  See great *Marcellus!* how, untir'd in Toils,
He moves with Manly grace, how rich with Regal Spoils!

---

1159  *Scipios*] *Scipio's* F1–2.          1163  Attire?] ~! F1–2.

He, when his Country, (threaten'd with Alarms,)
Requires his Courage, and his Conqu'ring Arms,
Shall more than once the *Punic* Bands affright:
Shall kill the *Gaulish* King in single Fight:
Then, to the Capitol in Triumph move,
And the third Spoils shall grace *Feretrian Jove.*
*Æneas,* here, beheld of Form Divine
A Godlike Youth, in glitt'ring Armour shine:
1190 With great *Marcellus* keeping equal pace;
But gloomy were his Eyes, dejected was his Face:
He saw, and, wond'ring, ask'd his airy Guide,
What, and of whence was he, who press'd the Hero's side?
His Son, or one of his Illustrious Name,
How like the former, and almost the same?
Observe the Crowds that compass him around;
All gaze, and all admire, and raise a shouting sound:
But hov'ring Mists around his Brows are spread,
And Night, with sable Shades, involves his Head.
1200 Seek not to know (the Ghost reply'd with Tears)
The Sorrows of thy Sons, in future Years.
This Youth (the blissful Vision of a day)
Shall just be shown on Earth, and snatch'd away.
The Gods too high had rais'd the *Roman* State;
Were but their Gifts as permanent as great.
What groans of Men shall fill the *Martian* Field!
How fierce a Blaze his flaming Pile shall yield!
What Fun'ral Pomp shall floating *Tiber* see,
When, rising from his Bed, he views the sad Solemnity!
1210 No Youth shall equal hopes of Glory give:
No Youth afford so great a Cause to grieve:
The *Trojan* Honour, and the *Roman* Boast;
Admir'd when living, and Ador'd when lost!
Mirror of ancient Faith in early Youth!
Undaunted Worth, Inviolable Truth!
No Foe unpunish'd in the fighting Field,
Shall dare thee Foot to Foot, with Sword and Shield:

1195  same?] ~: F1–2.          1211  grieve:] ~. F1–2.
1217  Shield:] ~. F1–2.

Much less, in Arms oppose thy matchless Force,
When thy sharp Spurs shall urge thy foaming Horse.
1220 Ah, cou'dst thou break through Fates severe Decree,
A new *Marcellus* shall arise in thee!
Full Canisters of fragrant Lillies bring,
Mix'd with the Purple Roses of the Spring:
Let me with Fun'ral Flow'rs his Body strow; ⎞
This Gift which Parents to their Children owe, ⎬
This unavailing Gift, at least I may bestow! ⎠
Thus having said, He led the Heroe round
The confines of the blest *Elysian* Ground:
Which, when *Anchises* to his Son had shown,
1230 And fir'd his Mind to mount the promis'd Throne,
He tells the future Wars, ordain'd by Fate;
The Strength and Customs of the *Latian* State:
The Prince, and People: And fore-arms his Care
With Rules, to push his Fortune, or to bear.
Two Gates the silent House of Sleep adorn;
Of polish'd Iv'ry this, that of transparent Horn:
True Visions through transparent Horn arise,
Through polish'd Iv'ry pass deluding Lyes.
Of various things discoursing as he pass'd,
1240 *Anchises* hither bends his Steps at last.
Then, through the Gate of Iv'ry, he dismiss'd
His valiant Offspring, and Divining Guest.
Streight to the Ships *Æneas* took his way; ⎞
Embarqu'd his Men, and skim'd along the Sea: ⎬
Still Coasting, till he gain'd *Cajeta*'s Bay. ⎠
At length on Oozy ground his Gallies moor:
Their Heads are turn'd to Sea, their Sterns to Shoar.

---

1228   Ground:] ∼. F1–2.
1237–1238   *omitted from* F1, *but printed in the "Notes and Observations" at the end of the volume; printed by* F2, *which omits the entry in the "Notes and Observations."*